D1796736

Politics of Patronage and Protest

Politics of Patronage and Protest

The State, Society, and Artisans in Early Modern Rajasthan

Nandita Prasad Sahai

OXFORD
UNIVERSITY PRESS

OXFORD
UNIVERSITY PRESS

YMCA Library Building, Jai Singh Road, New Delhi 110 001
Oxford University Press is a department of the University of Oxford. It
further the University's objective of excellence in research, scholarship, and
education by publishing worldwide in

Oxford New York
Auckland Cape Town Dar es Salaam Hong Kong Karachi Kuala Lumpur
Madrid Melbourne Mexico City Nairobi New Delhi Shanghai Taipei Toronto

With office in
Argentina Austria Brazil Chile Czech Republic France Greece Guatemala
Hungary Italy Japan Poland Portugal Singapore South Korea Switzerland
Thailand Turkey Ukraine Vietnam

Oxford is a registered trade mark of Oxford University Press in the UK and in
certain other countries

Published in India
by Oxford University Press, New Delhi

ISBN-13: 978-0-19-567896-3
ISBN-10: 0-19-567896-6

Typeset in Calisto MT 9.5/11.5
By S.R. Enterprises, New Delhi 110 024
Printed in India Sai Printopack Pvt. Ltd, New Delhi 110 020
Published by Manzar Khan, Oxford University Press
YMCA Library Building, Jai Singh Road, New Delhi 110 001

Contents

Tables and Maps

Preface

Visits to my ancestral home in Varanasi for Diwali were an annual feature of my unmarried days. As an adolescent, something that always surprised me during these visits was the horde of servants who would descend to celebrate the festival with our family, and get gifts of clothes and money from my grandfather. They made themselves comfortable in his large mansion, gave all of us leisurely oil massages, and helped in preparing the Diwali delicacies. Many of them were no longer in *Baba*'s (grandfather's) employ, and I would feel rather intrigued as to why they felt obliged to help and participate in the festivities in an extraneous home and, more than that, why my grandfather, otherwise a person not known for extravagance, allowed himself to be fleeced by these people. Why on earth did he waste so much money on them, (perhaps it could be better utilized by getting me what I wanted!) and how could these presumptuous servants imagine that they had any such 'rights' over him. On asking about these strange manifestations of mutual obligations, the answer from both Baba—the 'elite'—and Mohan, Dulhaniya, Kedar, Hardeo, etc.—the subordinate— was that this was our culture, the tradition, and age-old custom that had been observed ever since either could remember.

These memories sat rather uncomfortably with the perceptions that I developed from my graduate days about elite–subaltern relations, about the nature of power, and about the relationship between the 'state' and the 'subjects'. Perhaps they were somewhat responsible for leading me to explore these questions. The choice of the early modern state of Rajasthan as the representative of 'elite' was guided by the desire to verify its stereotypical image of being an oppressive 'Oriental' despotism and that of artisans as representatives of the subaltern was governed by the fact that they appeared the most marginalized of the subordinate groups in historical literature, even in studies on subordinate groups. I have consciously written the names of all castes, including that of the rajputs, in the lower case. My mental resistance against spelling the name of an elite caste with a small letter while feeling comfortable using small letters for artisanal castes, shows how deep hierarchical consciousness has struck roots in our mindsets.

This book is based on my doctoral thesis, and its completion saw me amass intellectual debts that would defy accounting. During my student days at the Delhi University, my teachers at Hindu College, as well as late professor Nurul Hasan and Satish Chandra broadened my understanding of the discipline of history. H.C.Verma was an affectionate and supportive guide of an MPhil dissertation on the role of rajputs in the evolution of Mughal nobility, and I hope to rework the same some day.

In the initial stages of pursuing research, the most difficult barrier to cross was the decipherment of the documents by learning the medieval Marwari language and script. Poonam Chand Joiyya, the research officer at the Rajasthan State Archives, Bikaner, spent hours to help me learn the language. The late Komal Kothari, Vijay Dan Detha, Dilbagh Singh, Ghanshyam Lal Devra, Rajendra Joshi, and Chandramani Singh provided insights into Rajasthani culture and social behaviour, helping to clarify doubts that surfaced ever so often in the mind of an 'outsider'.

Sunil Kumar under whose generous supervision the thesis was written, taught me to go 'beyond' empirical facts, towards a more 'nuanced' history. Patient, often even indulgent, he taught me the 'craft of history-writing', trying to engender a rigour that I have found especially valuable.

The Indian Council of Historical Research and Training extended a leave-cum-travel grant that partially financed the numerous trips to Bikaner, Jodhpur, and Jaipur. I am grateful for this aid. I am also grateful to its library staff, as also the library staff at the National Archives of India, the Nehru Memorial Museum and Library, the Vidya Jyoti, and the Ratan Tata Library at the Delhi School of Economics. Of invaluable assistance was the staff at the Bikaner Archives, Mehrangarh Museum Trust, Jodhpur and at the Jodhpur Shodh Sansthan, Chaupasani.

A generous fellowship from the American Association of University Women enabled me to take a year off from teaching and enjoy the immense resources, intellectual and infrastructural, as a visiting faculty at the department of history, Princeton University, and as a visiting fellow at the Institute for Research on Women, Rutgers University. At Princeton, Gyan Prakash's interest and encouragement was reassuring, and the weekly seminars at the Davis Centre helped me think through many of the questions that had been confusing me. At Rutgers, stimulating discussions with Sue Cobbles, and support from Beth Hutchison were comforting. Indrani Chatterjee's warmth yet refusal to hold my hand in an alien environment went a long way in making me self-reliant, and I truly appreciate her for it. The libraries at these universities were a scholar's paradise, and helped me read hungrily more than I had ever before been able to.

Amongst friends, Nayanjot will always be special for the support she gave through every stage of this work, and egged me on each time my spirits flagged and enthusiasm dampened. Mahesh Rangarajan's helpful advice bailed me out on many occasions and I am extremely grateful to him for taking time out often at short notice. Other friends and relatives who encouraged and displayed a healthy concern for the early completion of this work include Tripta Wahi, Ravikant Sharma, Sanjay Subrahmanyam, Seema, Manika, Manjari, Tuk Tuk, Nini, Jyoti, Dabboo and Ruma.

At a personal level, my greatest debt is to Sanjiv, who supported me in every possible way. He made me computer literate, critiqued the arguments extensively and thus was an enormous help in tightening them. In fact, practically every aspect of writing this volume benefitted from his contribution and, without his willingness to share the burden of this enterprise, I would never have been able to complete it. Garima always wondered why I was giving 'so much' to something that would bring 'so little'. But once convinced that it meant a lot to me, she encouraged me wholeheartedly, and even helped in converting dates from the *Vikram Samvat* to the Gregorian calendar.

Encouragement and support from my parents and parents-in-law has always been a source of strength. On many occasions I was unable to perform my 'daughterly' duties to catch deadlines related to this study, but they understood and indulged me in every way. My father convinced me not to be over-ambitious and dream of writing a magnum opus, and instead pursue more humble goals of publishing the study in its current shape. My brothers, Alok and Ashu, felt anxious as the thesis took its time to transform into a manuscript, and then a book. Dubs, whose care and concern for my well-being has made her more of a mother than a sister, showed pride and appreciation for every little step I took in my professional life. Lata *bhabhi* personally introduced me to various people in Jaipur who could be of help, and arranged for government publications on local industries. My visits to her and *bare bhaiyya* in my student days were occasions that engendered a fascination for the rich and varigated culture of Rajasthan. I dedicate this work to bare bhaiyya, my eldest brother Anand, who is no more with us physically, but whose love for his little sister gave a self-esteem that stood steadfast through all the trials and tribulations of life. Ma, my mother-in-law who gradually became a mother, constantly urging me to have greater faith in my abilities, suddenly expired, but not before she had organized a *puja* to celebrate my getting a doctorate. I cannot see this work published without remembering and missing her acutely on this occasion, and wonder how much she would have rejoiced to see my efforts take the shape of this book.

1

Situating the State, Society, and Artisans in Early Modern Marwar

Akare ki jhompri phogan ki bar,
Huts of akara and fences of phog (poor quality shelters),

Bajri ka sogara mothan ki dar,
Bread made of bajra flour and *dal* of *mothan*, (the cheapest flour and lentil)

Dekhi ho raja teri Marwar!
Behold O king, your Marwar![1]

This pithy doggerel of unknown provenance has a multilayered message, interesting not merely because its authorial voices appear to belong to the plebeian, describing their harsh living conditions, but more because it tells us something about the nature of relationship the lower formations had with their rulers and other elites in an early, modern kingdom. The fact that many in Marwar (Jodhpur state), the arid 'Land of Death' in the western part of the modern state of Rajasthan, were poor and ill-provided is neither new nor surprising, and one more than expects the impoverished subordinate groups to be discontented with their lot. Embedded in this verse and worthy of notice and comment, however, is the 'agency' of the poor. Rather than submission or passive resignation to fate, the authors of the verse appear to be expressing resentment, indicting the state for its inability to provide better entitlements to its subjects. In that sense, it is a form of 'everyday resistance' against the rulers, evoking a critique of extant conditions. Couched in a sarcastic tone, their outcry clearly appears to demand a certain level of responsibility from the rulers in the performance of their duties.[2] It points, thereby, towards processes of state formation at grass roots level. These have remained unnoticed till now, and this book tries to highlight them.

Pushing this perception further, one might even say that the injustices endemic to the elite-subordinate dialogue, and the tensions in an inherently exploitative relationship notwithstanding, the verse is indicative of a personalized relationship between the Rathor king as the pater familias accountable to his family, a virtual patriarch morally bound to ensure the subsistence of his people. This explains why rather that fatalism, blaming God, nature, or destiny for their hardships, these humble folk looked to their rulers for relief and rehabilitation.[3] As is evident by the lament echoing through the verse, this was mere posturing on the part of the rulers, unable to erase the inherent contradictions in their relations. It was often a mere veneer that could neither create social equilibrium, nor order and harmony. 'Pressures from below' were recurrent in the routine political life of Rajasthan, and numerous archival records, folk tales, and proverbs from the region suggest that direct engagements between the rulers and the lower formations, not merely among the elites and the dominant sections of society but also with the plebeian ranks, were common.

Yet, from Orientalist studies that had assumed the presence of a schism between the South Asian 'state' and 'society', to recent scholarship such as that of M.N. Pearson, historians have asserted that the political system in medieval and early modern India reflects 'a paradigm of the negligible contact and lack of communication between social groups in general and the state', society organized and controlled by autonomous local units. The schism, or gap in this state-society juxtaposition appeared particularly wide in scholarly discussion of relationships between elites and subordinate classes. Constructing the Indian state as no more than a paper tiger that played a negligible role in the social, political, and economic lives of its subjects, this thesis of the absence of political connections between the state and society found support in the works of other doyens of South Asian history as well.[4] Subsequently, in a comparative perspective, Pearson contrasted West European nation states with the empires in Asia and, reiterating his earlier position, argued that   the different trajectories of their historical development may be explained by the fact that in the latter the relationship between state and society was marked by mutual aloofness and disengagement.[5]

Contrary to this 'paper tiger' Image, Imperialist writings, in building the contrast between the 'Self' and the 'Other' had also inscribed the Indian pre-colonial state and kingship with an all-powerful tyrannical image. Arguing that the State was prone to ruthless suppression of the subjects so that the voice of the people either never surfaced or was effectively silenced, they explained that state despotism rendered subordinate groups, in particular, completely docile and inert.[6] In perceiving the (Mughal) state as an all-pervasive, domineering Leviathan, its relationship with society uni-dimensional in terms of the flow of influences from the former to the latter, the 'Aligarh' school seemed to agree. In fact not merely Aligarh scholars but several generations of historical scholarship even outside have been exercised by extensive debates on Asiatic kingship and the early modern Indian polity. Even till a couple of decades ago, it was assumed that states in pre-colonial South Asia suffered no limits or checks on the scope of their authority, which they tended to exercise in a capricious and arbitrary manner.[7]

Historians saw craftsmen to be amongst the chief victims of despots, who allegedly abused and oppressed them mercilessly. Their sources, after all, led them to many of these conclusions. The French traveller, Bernier, for example, wrote about the artisans at the Mughal capitals of Delhi and Agra:

But these unhappy men are condemned, treated with harshness, and inadequately remunerated for their labour. The rich will have every article at a cheap rate. When an omrah or mansabdar requires the service of an artisan, he sends to the bazaar for him, employing force, if necessary, to make the poor man work; and after the task is finished, the unfeeling lord pays, not according to the value of the labour, but agreeably to his own standard of fair remuneration; the artisan having reason to congratulate himself if the korrah (whip) has not been given in part of payment. How then can it be expected that any spirit of emulation should animate the artist or manufacturer? Instead of contending for a superiority of reputation, his only anxiety is to finish his work and to earn the pittance that shall supply him with a piece of bread.[8]

And again, that:

...in the Indies the gold and silver disappear in consequence of the tyranny of Timariots, Governors, and Revenue contractors—a tyranny that even the monarch, if so disposed, has no means of controlling in provinces not contiguous to his capital—a tyranny often so excessive as to deprive the peasant and artisan of the necessaries of life, and leave them to die of misery and exhaustion—a tyranny owing to which those wretched people either have no children at all, or have them only to endure the agonies of starvation, and to die at a tender age...[9]

Francisco Pelsaert's view resonated the same perception when he wrote:

For the workman there are two scourges, the first of which is low wages....The second is (the oppression of) the Governor, the nobles, the Diwan, the Kotwal, the Bakhshi, and other royal officers. If any of these wants a workman, the man is not asked if he is willing to come, but is seized in the house or in the street, well beaten if he should dare to raise any objection, and in the evening paid half his wages, or nothing at all.[10]

Evidence of recurrent episodes of ritualized whipping and flogging, performed in public spaces as a deterrent, is available from British times rather than pre-colonial.[11] Yet reports of individuals like Bernier led the most discerning of historians such as Tapan Raychaudhuri to conclude, 'The whip and the cudgel were freely used not only by the nobles' minions but by the middlemen as well' presumably meeting with little or no resistance from those at the receiving end.[12]

How valid are these images? Did despotism and coercive disciplining alone constitute the contours of state-subordinate interactions? Were the 'social politics' of the pre-colonial Rathor regime of the kingdom of Marwar as simple as this single dimension of relentless suppression and class conflict reveal? While one cannot but agree with Sumit Guha's generalization that the state was 'hard with the soft and soft with the hard', it is still worth asking whether material and ideological constrains allowed the state to rule through brute force alone in its dealings with the lower formations.[13] That the maximization of material resources through tax and labour appropriations was fundamental to the logic of the state's survival is stating the obvious. In fact, for a majority of the subjects, the state primarily represented a revenue extracting body that constantly dipped into their meagre earnings. Suspecting, however, that the state's concerns were multi, rather than uni-dimensional, this work uses the case study of artisans in their relations with the eighteenth-century Jodhpur state to operate as an interlocutor in larger debates on state formation and popular protest in early modern South Asia. The focus of the study is to discern the multiple levels of social contestation in which a variety of agents participated to push their distinctive agendas in a dynamic, contentious society.

Acknowledging the in-built 'everyday' tensions over conflicting interests in the state-artisan concatenation in rural and urban scenarios, I suggest, however, that ideological underpinnings encapsulated in notions of 'legitimacy' were equally important players in this interface, constantly moderating and mediating engagements. Chitra Joshi and S.S. Sivakumar's recent work has noticed that '...the normative order was central to the social order. If appeal to tradition failed to restrain an individual in the exercise of power, divine retribution certainly would'.[14] In a structural functional mode, what they unfortunately fail to recognize is the relentless contestation that challenged the 'normative order'. As a result, they present a static, internally consistent picture of primordial harmony in the pre-colonial society, as though the existence of norms and adherence to 'ancient traditions' was successful in dissolving tensions by lubricating hierarchical relations into smooth exchanges. Rejecting the romanticization of the pre-colonial Indian past, this study demonstrates the continuous marginalization of the poor through the early modern period, and their condition worsening during the colonial era.[15] It questions the claim that cultural 'morality' succeeded in creating anything close to consensual politics.

I do ask, however, if states in eighteenth-century India could afford to practise exclusionary politics. In a recent study, Mridu Rai convincingly argues that it was British authorization and support of Hindu Dogra sovereignty over the Muslim subjects of the Kashmir valley that ensured the sustenance of the Dogra regime, despite its failure to employ incorporative strategies for wooing the Muslim populace.[16] Such exclusionary policies negligent towards substantial sections of subjects were perhaps possible where strong imperialist powers buttressed the authority of local rajas. But when circumstances caused such support to be withdrawn, as in the case of the Mughals in the 'dark century', would local rulers of Rajasthan, like the Rathors of Jodhpur, not experience an exaggerated sense of precariousness and feel constrained to build a more incorporative state?

The question then would have been limited to the choice regarding groups that might be wooed and incorporated for a broad-based stable state. In pre-industrial times, human labour was in high demand, and eighteenth-century kingdoms constantly competed not only for material but also manpower resources. Christopher Bayly and Sumit Guha have noticed in their studies that landed potentates recognized the potential value of commerce for their regimes, and that consequent eagerness to concentrate mercantile and artisanal forces in their territories saw them embroiled in an unceasing competition for productive forces.[17] Would these tendencies not be much more intense in Marwar, the 'Land of Death' whose arid, desert-like landscape incapable of supporting high agricultural yields, put an unusually high premium on artisanal labour engaged in commercial production? This study addresses the above questions in an effort to advance our perceptions about early modern state formation in South Asia.

Located in the western part of modern-day Rajasthan, Marwar, also called Marudhar, Marusthal, and Marudesh due to high mortality rates, especially among the poor, the region suffered frequent droughts, famines, and epidemics. Though the epithet Marwari is often mistakenly used for all Rajasthanis all over India, Marwar (or more specifically, the Jodhpur state), was only one, albeit the largest kingdom in Suba Ajmer under the Mughals. There were other substantial princely states with contiguous boundaries to that of Marwar, such as the chieftaincies of Dhundhar around Jaipur, Mewar with its capital at Udaipur, Mad—located around Jaisalmer, Jangal based at Bikaner, and Hadauti, centred around Bundi and Kota. Given the context of Jodhpur's intensely inhospitable environment and low man-to-land ratio, I examine how material realities affected the politics of the region. To what extent did shifting vicissitudes of the Marwari rulers and elites during the eighteenth century impact the social worlds of the artisans and, in turn, get impacted by flexible and fluctuating responses from the latter? Conscious of the meaninglessness of categorizing social phenomenon into the binaries of superior and inferior castes, domination and subordination, coercion and concessions, great tradition and little tradition, and passivity and resistance, this is an attempt to notice the sometimes fuzzy boundaries between them, especially in situations when the two tended to collaborate or work in tandem. In exploring the political culture in which authority and statecraft operated, this volume focuses on the varied implications of caste ordering in India, popularly recognized as the keystone of Indian society.

CASTE HIERARCHY AND CONSEQUENT DEBILITATION

Attributing to caste a deterministic, all-encompassing role, a wide spectrum of scholarship has suggested Hinduism and caste hierarchy as the fundamental factors that ensured the social dependence of the lower groups. Recognized widely as the chief signifier of asymmetrical relations, caste is universally perceived as the primary impediment that retarded the growth of a revolutionary mentalite among the underlings of Indian society. Hegel viewed caste as the defining institution of India, identifying it as a factor that truly shackled and chained the lower castes into their lowly position, and condemned them 'to the most degrading spiritual serfdom'.[18] Thereafter, from Weber to Dumont, numerous theorists have argued that caste inequities rendered groups low down on the social ladder devoid of agency. This basic fact is said to have circumscribed the Indian historical trajectory, leaving Indian society outmoded and uncivilized.[19] Indologists such as J.C. Heesterman agreed, and even studies such as those of Barrington Moore Jr. did not go beyond lending sophistication to the argument for the passivity of Indian lower formations. Emphasizing hegemonic functions of the caste system and the theory of reincarnation as responsible for their condition, he maintained that the Indian peasant was stasis-prone because the 'system emphasized the individual's duty to caste, not individual rights against society' and he was therefore willing in the 'acceptance of personal degradation'.[20] On a similar note, Claude Welch, argued that 'caste customs and regulations...maintained a compartmentalized and essentially homeostatic society and crippled any attempts at joint action'.[21]

Notions of social segmentation and hierarchy were recognized as so deeply embedded in Indian society that they not only determined rank, marital relations, commensality and village morphology, but also economic change. Economic historians like Gunnar Myrdal have argued that Indian poverty was due to its caste system and the 'soft state's' inability to impose societal change.[22] Wallerstein and other analysts of world systems distinguished the 'European miracle' from the Indian traditional, stagnant, economy that was easily overtaken and incorporated into European capitalism.[23] Holding caste as the most vital barrier to economic change, the Hindu value system was said to have despised the profit-motive, and thereby prevented 'traditional India' from modernizing, till the impact of colonial rule changed social correlates.

Challenging the above model that saw caste as symbolic of a 'traditional' scheme that had disabled any transformation to 'modernity', neo-classical economic historians such as Morris D. Morris have argued that the significance of Indian values as obstacles to economic change in South Asia had been vastly overestimated. Explicitly attacking Weber, Morris dismissed cultural hurdles as being relevant and argued instead that Indian entrepreneurs and labour—the agents of economic change—were 'rational actors' focused on maximizing pecuniary benefits as much as their European counterparts.[24] Unfortunately, however, Morris's teleological framework saw him assert that India was not peculiar—it was only four to five hundred years behind Western Europe![25]

Chris Bayly neither agreed with Weber's formulation that changes in pre-colonial India were frustrated due to caste fragmentation and passivity of Hinduism, nor with Morris's argument that the Indian subcontinent was like Western Europe, with a lag of several centuries. He rather argued that caste and religion in fact provided building blocks from which mercantile and urban solidarities emerged in pre-colonial India.[26] Conceding that though western practices such as corporate dining relations and marriage bonds were absent and could not build corporate solidarities, he emphasized that there were yet other means for the purpose. He thereby rejected the paradigm that attributed a negative, deterministic, all-encompassing role to caste in understanding the Indian society.

My reading of Marwari materials places me closer to Bayly, and I try to look closely at artisanal caste dialectics to unravel how caste structures animated artisanal life, both in the rural and urban environments. I assess the role of caste in defining the relationship of its members with others, especially dominant castes and the state. That a low position in the ritual hierarchy of caste regulated various aspects of the artisans' lives and resulted in myriad forms of exploitation is indeed well known. This book, instead, focuses on the political and civic overtones of caste to examine if caste merely oppressed, as of course it did, or was it, paradoxically enough, empowering and enabling too, offering possibilities for association and action to the underlings? In an effort to go beyond the colonial discourse in the production of knowledge on caste, and its role in the relationship of elites with subordinate groups, this study explores the multiple dimensions of caste politics.

ELITIST DISCOURSES ON STATE FORMATION

Under the influence of perceptions that have denied agency to Indian subordinate groups, an elitist colonization of history-writing has been the bane of conventional scholarship. 'History' and 'politics' have, as a result continued to be defined almost exclusively in terms of the ideas and activities of the elite, hugely peripheralizing the role of subordinate groups.[27] The last couple of decades have indeed witnessed several significant works build paradigms that have abandoned Orientalist and Marxist notions of a dichotomy and a hiatus between the Indian state and society, the rulers, and the ruled. Recent writings instead recognize the existence of a close nexus between ruling dynasties and dominant groups—the nobility, military, warrior elites, theological heads, and the mercantile cliques. Earlier, especially after the intervention of Chris Bayly, a host of works on different regions of the subcontinent have focused on the inclusion of 'middle classes', intermediate groups such as traders, townsmen, and a rural gentry as completely enmeshed in the processes of state formation.[28] Nevertheless, as I demonstrate in the following pages, these studies have continued to highlight upper and middle-level politics, refusing to recognize the possibility of grass root politics of groups lower in the social hierarchy.

'Rulers could only incorporate powerful groups in their realms by alienating resources and honours to them' and a state 'could only survive if it penetrated further beneath the level of the *pargana* administration and into the tight clan-like brotherhood of peasant farmers...' noted Bayly. He also pointed out that penetration 'required not only the coercive force of the state, but also an ideology which justified the appropriation of growing quantities of revenue'.[29] Deepening and extending perceptions on the ideological basis of authority, Tambiah's thesis conceived legitimate power as flowing from the imperial centre, partly derived from the ruler's claim to divine right to rule due to high descent from a superior lineage, and more importantly from royal claims of personal achievement in terms of righteousness and justice. Though highlighting Buddhist norms and virtues of kingship, Tambiah rightly noticed that being a *chakravartin* or universal monarch was not enough; legitimate rule would entail the image of a *dharmaraja* or righteous ruler too.[30] In this top-down analysis, however, there is no recognition of the fact that the claims of the ruler have to be counterposed against the evaluation of the rule by the subjects. It is they who, after all, scrutinize the claims to righteousness, justice, and thus legitimacy, and they who give their verdict ranging from acceptance and identification to rejection and rebellion.

Yet another major intervention in the cultural construction of authority suffers from a similar flaw. Leading the Chicago School Nicholas Dirks' model emphasized the king as the centre of social hierarchy, organized around the royal activity of prestations, whether in the shape of land, honours, or service tenures. This Dirksean emphasis on royal gift-giving in the south Indian 'little kingdom' of Pudukkottai as the ritual and symbolic dimension—the ideological basis—that secured political authority, is significant.[31] Seeing transactions and exchanges in 'coded substances' as constituting Hindu kingship and polity, critical to sustaining the political hierarchy, Dirks highlighted the incorporation of the receiver into the kingdom through these gifts. He further postulates that this ritual sovereignty provided order, equilibrium, and obedience—the unsaid assumption being that royal gifts could dispel dissent and protest. But is that true? Who were the recipients of these favours, and could generous gifts to some satisfy the aspirations of all? Surely, gifts represented simultaneously both incorporation as well as exclusion, the latter in the case of non-recipients who could not be similarly gratified. What strategies would the rulers devise for those excluded from the privilege of receiving land grants, or could they be totally peripheralized to the political process?

Ronald Inden expanded on the Chicago model by detailing how numerous performative rituals affirmed the centrality of the king. His study of the early medieval kingdom of the Rashtrakutas led him to note multiple rites and their role in regenerating kinghip in its constant struggle for sovereignty. He rightly saw the former as 'less of a fixed state than an unending process that granted a vital place to its nemesis'.[32]

Rejecting Dirks' structural model, Norbert Peabody's recent study agrees with Inden in arguing for a dynamic view of sovereignty. He rightly notes that since Dirks derived his data from late nineteenth-century land records by when Pudukkottai was the sole princely state in Tamil Nadu, colonial rule having eliminated all other rival claims to sovereignty within and without, Dirks did not locate the 'little kingdom' in a field of similarly constructed polities and political dependencies. He thereby failed to see how each of these centres advanced rival claims to kingship and sovereignty. In Rajputana, in contrast, such contestations among contiguous states and chiefships remained pervasive through pre-colonial to colonial times. In line with Andre Wink's analysis of *fitna* or sedition characterizing the Indian state as 'a form of institutionalized dissidence', Peabody charted how kings, warrior elites, sectarian hierarchs, and traders formulated their specific agendas to realize their individual aspirations in pre-colonial Kota in Rajasthan. Peabody wrote that for 'Dirks, the Hindu state was decisively centre-oriented and the pressures of unity far outweighed those of fragmentation. Contra Dirks, I argue that rebellion was not only common but it was a defining feature of the Hindu polity'.[33] He rightly argued that the polity in Kota could not be a morally cohesive system, as Dirks had suggested, because allegiances of clients and supporters still remained open to contestation and negotiation, 'inflected as they were by interests of rival third parties'.[34] Peabody extended Tambiah's 'galactic polity' model beyond South-East Asia to Rajputana, noticing the realms of *jagirdars* or tributary 'kings', who constantly strove to assert their own authority while the centre tried to undermine them.

Though Peabody critiques Dirks for his 'top down' view, unresponsive to the 'ground up' centrifugal tendencies in state formation that simultaneously tend to undermine it, he in fact is guilty of the same elitist perspective. His formulation of course allows for far greater contradictions and dissent within the polity than Dirks'; yet his work, too, is focused on the dynamics of 'high culture', limited to seeing rebellions within the ruling class alone. In that sense, he too does not go far enough. His explorations, and those of his predecessors, have contributed immensely to our understanding of high politics and the web of networks that interpenetrated elitist social and political domains of pre-colonial India. As such, they are helpful in providing a perspective 'from above' about the state's interactions with the superior segments of society. The critical silence in these studies, however, relates to a monochromatic construction of state and sovereignty that takes into account the aspirations, agendas, manipulations, and manoeuvres of dominant groups alone, marginalizing, in the process, the place and role of subaltern groups. Though Peabody rightly contests and qualifies Dirks' conclusions, by pointing out that dominant discourses could not be created without reference and accommodation with other discourses, he does not display any interest in probing but the elitist ones. He ignores subaltern negotiations and challenges to elite hegemony. Were subordinate groups incorporated into the polity or not? How did they perceive their rulers and the quality of governance provided by them? And how did the lower formation respond to perceived injustices and unrighteous conduct?

More recently, a strong argument for noticing the state and its power relations as an incorporative process has been made in an important study by Farhat Hasan. Noticing the politics of the lower strata of the bureaucracy— the *mutsaddis*, *faujdars*, *qazis*, and *kotwals*—and corporate bodies of *bania* mercantile interests in the ports of Surat and Cambay in Suba Gujarat during the Mughal period, Hasan rightly argues that 'imperial sovereignty entailed a politic incorporation of an ever-increasing number of local intermediaries, on the principle of shared sovereignty'. And again, that the 'center of political gravity, as it were, was shifting downward to the lower, more locally rooted, links in the system'.[35] More importantly, from my perspective, he rightly points out that 'the political sphere was quite inclusive and included even the *common subjects*. Their acquiescence was indeed crucial for the success of any political expedition or conquest'[36] (emphasis added.) Unfortunately, however, his study leaves undefined and undifferentiated terms like 'common subjects' and 'urban dwellers', and presenting negligible documentation on the state's power relations with peasants, artisans, and other 'common subjects', appears to define the lower and the subaltern primarily in terms of the banias!

SHIFTING THE GAZE TO SUBORDINATE CASTES AND EARLY MODERN EVERYDAY POLITICS

Though this elitist colonization of history-writing on pre-colonial politics has persisted, the colonial era has been rescued from this imbalance by the *Subaltern Studies* collective and their analysis of the anti-imperialist struggle 'from below'.[37] Highlighting numerous aspects of the struggles of peasants, tribals, and the working class, they successfully established that subaltern resistance, far from being creations of 'elite nationalism', were independent of it, and far more radical too.[38] Their aim to reconstruct peasant consciousness and demonstrate its autonomy from elite thought saw them seek new sources and re-read the traditional archives. Shail Mayaram, a recent entrant to this group, made methodological interventions in this regard by employing the 'alternative archive' of myths and memory juxtaposed against written state records to study the defiance of the Mewati Meo community over time. From the sultanate rulers to the Mughals, and then the British imperial power, Meos had been marginalized by successive states and 'histories' produced by them. But through repeated persecution, they sustained their identity over several centuries.[39] With narratives of the Meo oral genre, Mayaram engages in an alternative construction of historical encounter to offer a counter perspective that challenges official 'history'. Her experiments with this innovative and challenging approach enable an exploration of constructions and contestations of state and sovereignty 'from below' and of perceptions of power from a subject perspective.

This book too moves down the social hierarchy to attempt a more differentiated formulation on state formation, shifting away from the Dirksean raja-centric polity, Peabodian jagirdar-centric rebellions, and the Baylian focus on intermediate groups, to reach deeper to the lower echelons of society. Rather than focussing on the cultural orientations and agency of rajput kings and kshatriya elites alone, this study attempts to bring centre-stage the social worlds of the labouring artisans and their politics. How did subordinate groups assess the administration, how did their discourses tame the dominant ones, and how were the former harnessed by the latter, especially given the ecological constraints of a low-man-to-land ratio? In agreement with Peabody's 'multi-agentive' view of history, I draw attention to the accommodations that not just the dominant, but the downtrodden too forced upon those who exploited them.

Peasant rebellions have generally been the focus of countless explorations, detailing contests between peasant groups of different social strata or cultivators and the agents of the state.[40] Though it is widely recognized that artisans constituted a vast proportion of the popular masses, they have not been accorded their rightful place. This study has chosen artisans, the subaltern of the subalterns in pre-colonial studies, to analyse the political culture and agency of subordinate groups in pre-colonial times. But what do we understand by the term 'artisans', and who were these people that we seek to resurrect and bring to the centre-stage of history-writing? From the earliest times, Western literature had identified handicraftsmen, those endowed with constructive skill, as the 'class' of artisans. The ironsmiths, carpenters, weavers, dyers, potters, cobblers, etc., had a well-established common occupational identity, and a somewhat shared socio-economic status. Was there such a class of artisans with a distinct group-identity in early modern India? Or are we imposing a modern and alien social category on disparate and very different occupational groups?

The Mughal records use the terms *karigaran*, *peshawaran*, *sana'tgaran*, *ahl-i-hirfa*, and *kasib* while referring to these occupational castes. The repeated references I find in medieval Marwari literature, even when of different genres, of a group name for craft castes is *pavan jatiyan*. Both Nainsi's *Vigat*[41] and the *ghazals* of the Jain *yatis* refer to certain lowly occupational groups by this term.[42] Said to be a group of thirty-six occupational castes, the term includes a diverse range of people from artisans and professionals, service castes, performing artists, to even prostitutes and beggars. Including textile spinners (*pinjaras*), weavers (*julahas*), dyers (*rangrezs*, *rangaras*, *nilgars* or indigo-dyers), printers (*chhipas*), tailors (*darzis*), goldsmiths (*sunars*), gold in-lay workers (*chitaras*), blacksmiths (*luhar*), copper and bronze casters (*kansaras/thatharas*), carpenters (*khatis*), potters (*kumhars*), stone-workers (*silawats*), laquer bangle-makers (*lakharas*), washermen (*dhobis*), cobblers (*mochis*), barbers (*nais*), soap-makers (*sabangars*), beggars (*kunjarhas*), garderners (*malis*), oil-pressers (*telis*), liquor-brewers (*kallals*), prostitutes (*nagar nayikas*), they all belonged to the shudra varna at the lowest rungs of the caste ladder.

Etymologically, the epithet pavan jat is derived from the term pavan—'the recipient'—deployed for castes who received patronage from the superior castes.[43] Other local terms to refer to artisans are *pun jat* or *naunipauni*, drawn from *paun* or *pun*—'little less than one'—implying an 'incomplete' person. The implicit connotations in all these appellations indicate the low status of this section in the perception of the higher castes, further corroborated by the use of another term *kamin* for them. Clearly, artisans were not recognized as a distinct or separate 'class' in contemporary literature, but they were indeed identified as constituent castes of the shudra varna, and within the varna itself there were several hierarchical sub-divisions.

Rather than a homogeneous class, artisans represented a distinct caste following different occupational trades, enjoying differential ranking, social status, and economic resources.[44] Though a shared identity in terms of possession of skills and low status in the social hierarchy were common for all of them, they did not present a uniform profile. Despite being encompassed by the broad category of pavan jat, levels of income, relationship with land, and the purity/pollution factor attenuated their position within this hierarchy. Customary laws varied widely for different castes, and provided each with unique attributes and a separate identity. Practices pertaining to marriage, remarriage, adoption, inheritance and property rights, religious observances, funerary rites, and so on, differed from one caste to another, extending to each its own special individuality. Even within each caste, class differences on the basis of resources possessed by individual members were common.[45] There were, therefore, both economic and social differences within the artisanal communities, and they cannot be perceived as one undifferentiated mass.

The overall low social status was hardly commensurate with the skilled labour they provided, shortfalls in material and technology more than compensated by remarkable ingenuity. Perhaps the hereditary aspect of learning the trade, the experience accumulated over the centuries passed on from generation to generation, was an important factor that brought about relative excellence.[46] Documents, however, do not indicate that there was a formal structured master-apprentice system in operation.[47] This hereditary passing of skills ensured increasing specialization, and a continuous proliferation of artisanal castes by latter part of the eighteenth century saw each caste attending to increasingly minute processes of production. This specialization in manufacturing appeared in distribution as well, and larger communities bifurcated into those that crafted and those that marketed the products. Virtually every operation connected with the production of textiles, ornaments, leather, and metal ware developed into distinct occupations practised by exclusive jatis or caste categories. In the fabrication of the most coarse of textiles, for instance, carding was handled by pinjaras,[48] spinning and weaving by julahas and *balais*, dyeing in general by the rangrez—though indigo-dyeing was a specific skill that *nilgars* alone were proficient in—and the communities of *bandharas* and *charhawas* practised *bandhej*, or tie-and-dye printing. The largest community of printers, however, were the chhipas who employed a variety of printing techniques, the most popular being block-printing.[49] Similarly, amongst carpenters, potters, and metal, stone and leather workers, a high degree of specialization was evident.

Since scholars on pre-colonial history have tended to largely exclude artisans from their gaze, focussing on peasant-oriented research, this volume fills in the gap by turning the scope towards the world of artisans, their concerns and compulsions during the 'dark century'. A survey of historical literature on the pre-modern period clearly demonstrates that the few references that are there on artisans pertain to the Mughal economy, but scholars, even when they conceded the significance of artisans to the Mughal economy, failed to view craftsmen as entities to be studied on their own terms.[50] Whether proponents or detractors of the 'deindustrialization' thesis, a majority of them mentioned the condition of artisans in passing, as a template used to measure the 'health' and vibrancy of the Mughal economy in contrast to the colonial economy that followed.[51] The issue that dominated the historiography thereafter was to gauge the potentialities of capitalistic development in Mughal India, and to assess the degree of subordination of craft production to mercantile capital.[52] Yet other studies focused on the eighteenth century, mentioning artisans to prove the hypothesis of economic resurgence in certain pockets of the Mughal empire,[53] or to argue for economic deprivation and hence a dark century where the processes of 'deindustrialization' were manifest.[54] Even as recent as last year, Eugenia Vanina's monograph on urban crafts, for instance, started with the laudable objective, explicitly stated, of studying not only the technology and organization of craft production but also the people who crafted them, and the social relations they were embroiled in. The discussion that followed, however, failed to recognize them as anything more than economic units, and did not analyse the politics of their life worlds.[55] Historical scholarship is clearly not convinced yet about perceiving artisans as politically significant members of the state whose relevance to politics and statecraft can be a meaningful subject of study.

Instead of thus obliterating them within a seamless, undifferentiated 'subject population', of interest only as tax payers,[56] this study focusses on artisans and their organizations, and examines the nature and the dynamics of the relationship between the Marwar state and its craftsmen, especially arising out of the situation of eighteenth-century imperatives. Were artisans actually bereft of a political existence in the 'everyday' context, and did they not have any links with the power processes at work? In other words, do they appear untouched and exteriorized by the political system? The use of the term 'citizen' in a early modern context is indeed anachronistic, but employed in the most general sense, I ask whether artisans were not 'citizens' and as such a part of the political process, jostling for space, exerting pressures, struggling to protect and even maximize their self-interest?[57] The thrust of this book seeks to address the question: Were the superior and intermediate castes alone incorporated into the state and its polity, as appears from the studies of Dirks, Tambiah, Wink, Peabody, and even Bayly, to the exclusion of subordinate castes like artisans, or were those engaged in crafts also form an integral part of the early modern polity in India? Further, could artisans constitute a 'pressure group' that moulded grass root politics, or were they culturally and socially suppressed to the point of having lost the capacity for resistance to dominant pressures?

The study of questions pertaining to 'everyday resistance and protest' was popularized in the Western context more than half a century ago, emerging mostly from probing slave societies and enserfed labour.[58] Gradually, historical works as much as anthropological, began to emphasize the importance of studying routine manifestations of unequal contests rather than the spectacular ones alone.[59] Studies on African and Asian societies, however, have begun to research on alternatives to confrontational protest only recently, giving rise to two related but different configurations of responses. Anthropologists such as James Scott, since they studied contemporary societies, explored forms of 'everyday resistance'—from mockery and sarcasm to pilfering and arson—that subordinate groups employ to combat extortionist claims of political elites.[60] Historians, however, constrained by source materials on the subject that are at best meagre, could only acknowledge responses, that Michael Adas characterized as 'avoidance protest'.[61] His research on Burma and Indonesia found formal petitions, flight to sparsely settled frontier areas or the domains of rival patrons, banditry, sit-ins before the residence of state officials, and clandestine retributive acts involving destruction of crops and implements as the forms of resistance particularly characteristic of the period before European rule, when indigenous states existed with only a limited capacity for repression.

But in the case of India, modes of avoidance protest have received scant attention, despite similarities and shared attributes in the character of the respective states.[62] Recent pieces in *Subaltern Studies* have indeed explored the 'continuum of intermediate attitudes' between subordination and revolt in the colonial period, but while assessing the responses of those pitted opposite one another in this unequal relationship, they have explored the colonial and postcolonial eras and underplayed relations of power prior to the inception of British rule. The recent study by Chitra Joshi too narrates the story of Kanpur workers during the late colonial period, tracing how they acted and reacted in their daily lives 'resisting pressures as well as submitting to demands, conforming to rules as well as negotiating with them', reproducing and reaffirming just as much as they resisted dominant structures of power and authority.[63] Questioning frameworks within which workers are seen as mired in a primordial culture, or as passive objects of managerial strategies, her book is persuasive in arguing that cultural pasts were reconstituted through worker practices and social identities, work norms constantly re-negotiated by workers. A search for precedents of subaltern agency in the pre-colonial past, especially among non-peasant groups, continues to remain a 'dark area'.

Since critiques of Orientalist writings have ignored, and thereby effaced the experience of subordinate subjects under non-European states, it is imperative to trace these in the pre-colonial context.[64] Neglecting rigorous empirical research, scholarship, depending on its ideological predilections, has tended to idealize or denigrate what it has all to often lumped under the convenient and undifferentiated label of 'traditional India' or a pre-capitalist society. Lacking in genuine historical content, this inane and insipid term has helped to hide and cover more than it has recovered for epistemological progress in history. Indigenous monarchical rule was also after all exploitative for the lower castes, but other than studies like that of Mayaram that takes note of this neglect and traces the resistance of the Meos from the early medieval times, few studies have cared to probe the experience of the 'Other' in relation to the 'Self' in the case of pre-colonial polities. This book moves back in time to assess how active the subaltern agency appears in the early modern period, before the different kingdoms in Rajasthan came under British influence.

ON CULTURAL HEGEMONY, AUTONOMY, AND CONSCIOUSNESS

The issues that need to be addressed would be impossible to comprehend unless contextualized in the cultural universe of the subalterns from which their acts of acquiescence or resistance to the power of the elites grew. Marxist labour histories had, however, rejected culture as homogenizing, de-historicizing and reifying the boundaries of specific groups and communities. Making teleological and deterministic assumptions based on linear notions of class consciousness, their social histories valorize processes of economic transformation in the making of class and argue that culture did not touch lives in the sphere of production, nor did it mediate political spaces.

Scholars working on regions far removed from India had, however, begun to notice and write about discontinuities between politics and culture of the 'polite' and the 'plebeian', and to focus on the cultural world of the latter to understand their politics. E.P. Thompson, for instance, wrote, 'Whatever this hegemony may have been, it did not envelope the lives of the poor, and it did not prevent them from defending their own modes of work and leisure, and forming their own rituals, their own satisfactions and view of life'. Further, that hegemony did not constitute a rigid, automatic, and all-determining structure of domination. It merely 'offered the bare architecture of a structure of relations of domination and subordination' within which 'many different scenes could be set and different dramas enacted'.[65]

Over the last decade-and-a-half, writings in India too have seen the emergence of a new labour history that explores the dynamics of power relationships between labour and its employers as embedded in culture. Since the initiation of the *Subaltern Studies* in particular, Gramscian notions of subaltern subjectivities have come to the fore, and a great deal of re-thinking has occurred around the issues of culture, hegemony, and consciousness to capture the complexity of the subalternist perspective on these questions. To begin with, Ranajit Guha emphasized the structural dominance of elites that caused the creation of an autonomous consciousness among the subordinated, resulting in revolts by the latter. Subsequent writings then engaged further with defining subalternity, and asked whether it implied complete acceptance of dominance and hierarchy. They went on to explore the play of power, hegemony, and ideology of subordination in routine interactions.

At least three major perceptions emerged out of this research: The first, modelled by Ranajit Guha and supported by David Arnold, argued for 'domination without hegemony', and an autonomous consciousness of the subaltern operating independently of elite agendas.[66] Dipesh Chakrabarty disagreed with Guha and emphasized the subaltern domain as entrapped in a pre-bourgeois hierarchical culture, so totally confined by elite ideology of social stratification as to disable resistance.[67] The third is traceable to Douglas Haynes and Gyan Prakash who focussed on the 'everydayness' and 'everywhereness' of subaltern resistance.[68]

Reifying culture, Chakrabarty, in his study of Calcutta mill-workers, noticed that the elite and subordinated were immersed in a shared culture that believed in hierarchy, perceptions, and actions formulated within the limits defined by the dominant. Subaltern autonomy was thus seen to be integral to the level of hegemony and control exercised by the dominant. He argued, however, that hegemony did not render the workers completely servile because the logic of hierarchy imposed particular roles on the masters and the servants, the patrons and dependants. The latter frequently employed patriarchal elements within the dominant culture to their own benefit, appealing to the paternalistic values and postures of the elites.

Sumit Sarkar and Gautam Bhadra concurred, seeing a patron's role embedded in the patriarchal culture of dominance. Sarkar conceived the relationship between the dominated and the dominant culture as one of 'assertion-within-deference'.[69] In his demonstration of the ability of the powerless to understand and manipulate the elements of justification for resistance, Sarkar evoked notions of benevolent patriarchy that the subalterns exploited to their benefit. Recognizing that the idioms of domination, subordination, and revolt are inextricably linked, Gautam Bhadra too highlighted the contribution of a subaltern towards the definition of what constituted rajdharma—the duty of kings, and a patron's role by referring to a higher but 'just' authority.[70]

Arising out of Chakrabarty's work, one wonders if his subjects were eternally entrapped in culturally fixed relationships of power. Was there no scope of disjunctions between workers' belief in the legitimacy of asymmetrically stratified culture and praxis of trying to undo the disadvantages born out of that hierarchy? Were they prisoners of this cultural system, and did they show no capacity to reconstitute these relations? Does the recognition of hierarchy and rajdharma in a complex dominant ideology of rank and mutuality in Indian culture mean that no alternative interpretations of any situation were possible?

Another significant recent work on labour history, though not quite within the folds of the *Subaltern Studies* collective, is Raj Chandavarkar's study on the Bombay cotton textile workers. Though Chandavarkar rightly breaks away from totalizing narratives of class that have been dominant in labour history-writing in India, suggesting that fractures within the workers, their sectionalism and inner divisions endure all solidarities that may momentarily unite them, he shares with Chakrabarty the assumption that workers have no agency in their everyday relationships at the workplace.[71] His rich analysis of labour *muhallas* refuses to recognize the potential ability of workers' to shape their culture. How pervasive was the hegemony of the dominant culture, and did it completely disable the development of a subaltern consciousness and autonomy? And if there was a subaltern autonomous culture that resented and resisted elite dominance, what were its constituent forms and shifting manifestations? What constituted 'just behaviour', and did the ideal of dominance and subordination actually contain the notions of fairness and righteousness that the subalterns were able to leverage for protest? Was this culture fixed, rigid, and static, and if not, where did the impulse for change come from?

Abandoning the traditional Gramscian line of total hegemony of the dominant culture, Haynes and Prakash are more in agreement with recent re-readings of Gramsci that suggest conflict as a constant part of hegemony and posit 'contradictory consciousness' as co-existing with hegemony. They recognize domination as fractured and not complete, and the subaltern autonomy partial, deriving from engagements with specific relationships of power.[72] More importantly, they widen the scope of meanings associated with resistance by even identifying actions that seemed to maintain the ideology of dominance as resistance. Instead of grappling with locating subaltern autonomy within or without the confines of dominant culture, they focuss on its non-confrontationist, ever-present-everydayness, as hidden discourses playing out in the non-public realm. Born out of the shared experience of being dominated, they note, subaltern autonomous consciousness is inevitably linked to particular relationships and their contexts.

This construction of the counter-hegemonic scholarly discourse needs to expiate more on strategies subalterns deployed to enhance or reduce the power of the dominant, about their collaborations with those in power, and about the dynamics and ambiguities of the subaltern discourse. Was their autonomy and consciousness simply a reaction to domination, a dependant variable, and if so, how did ideological changes and alterations in people's perceptions of their own situation occur? Did the subalterns contribute to notions of legitimacy in power relationships? How far did elite and popular culture intersect and inter-penetrate? Rather than seeing a simple dichotomy of discourses of the dominant and the dependant that blurs more than it reveals, the symbiosis between these, and relationships of conscious action to reflexive action will help unravel the play of power between the Jodhpur state and its dominant sections, on the one hand, and the artisans on the other.

QUESTIONS OF DOMINATION, COLLABORATION, RESISTANCE, AND PROTEST

A series of theoretical studies surrounding the subject of resistance have been made, in large measure refining and qualifying the simple binary of domination versus resistance. Almost three decades ago Raymond Williams had recognized that a ' lived hegemony is always a process' and that it is not a rigid, all-encompassing, unchallenged structure, but 'has continually to be renewed, recreated, defended and modified'. There are always counter-hegemonic values at work to resist, restrict, and qualify the operations of the hegemonic order.[73] Foucauldian perspectives too attended to less institutionalized, more pervasive, and more 'everyday' forms of power, while James Scott's writings focussed on less organized but widespread everyday forms of resistance.[74] Scott argued that the presence of struggles in the quotidian lives of the unprivileged is proof that ruling groups in most societies are unable to exert any form of cultural domination over the subordinate. Critiquing a conventional reading of the Gramscian perspective, he questioned the view that dominant groups were able to impress upon the subordinate a hegemonic culture or ideology. Foucault and Scott have together also shifted away the erstwhile emphasis on dramatic confrontational protests and rebellions. In a relationship of power, the dominant often had something to offer, though of course at the price of continuing in power. The subordinate, thus, had many grounds for ambivalence about resisting the relationship. In fact, the ambiguities of resistance and the subjective ambivalence of the acts for those who engaged in them are among the issues this story focusses on. Also pertinent is understanding what constitutes resistance, and how it is different from survival strategies.

Moreover, as noted before, there was never a single, unitary subordinate—invariably differentiated as they were along numerous indices of income, status, gender, and age, etc. As such, they would obviously have different, even opposite and but still legitimate perspectives on the situation, and would engender contradictory strands in resistance to domination. In this context, Sherry Ortner's observations are relevant. She writes 'one can only appreciate the ways in which resistance can be more than mere opposition, can be truly creative or transformative, if one appreciates the multiplicity of projects in which social beings are always engaged, and the multiplicity of ways in which those projects feed as well as collide with one another'.[75] To then romanticize resistance by ignoring those who were accomplices collaborating in the perpetuation of power, or effacing those who were passive and acquiescing with the dominant would, as warns Lila Abu-Lughod, not only construct a partial but also a unhistorical account of state-subaltern relations.[76] Those continuously co-opted into collaborative roles within the polity were equally significant members of artisanal communities, and hence a parallel story of everyday modes of collaboration also needs to be traced.[77]

At the same time, since the subordinates did not merely react to their oppressors but also had their own mutual intra-caste frictions and tensions, it is imperative to analyse the internal politics of their endogenous world. Their diverse constructions of social identity and material rivalries have been noticed in recent studies such as that of Chandavarkar, who shows how business strategies at the workplace and the volatility of the labour market fractured and sectionalized the working class, their inner divisions causing tensions that were often more enduring than caste solidarities. More recently, Chitra Joshi's study and that by Nandini Gooptu analyse for the twentieth century the schisms within the working poor. Joshi, for instance, notices the ruptures between *mistris* and labour, trade union leaders and workers, and multiple identities of the toiling lot playing out in different contexts in colonial Kanpur.[78] But in studies on early modern Indian society, castes and groups continue to be perceived as unified, undifferentiated masses, often pursuing a singular agenda. Economic antagonisms were of, course omnipresent, and the category of class conflict cannot of course be negated, but without jettisoning the notion of community solidarity, this volume examines the internal divisions amongst producers of craft goods.

THE SOCIOLOGY OF POWER, STATE FORMATION, AND THE NOTION OF WAJABI

Thus moving away from elite-centred discourses, this book seeks to construct the distinctive contours of the politics of patronage and those of protest that artisans in Rajasthan routinely found themselves implicated in, arguing for the expansion of the constitutive scope of state formation to include lower strata like that of the crafts and their politics within its ambit. Chris Bayly had noted that 'The political elites maintained agrarian dependence and supplies of labour through the use of force and the 'sale' of protection. But force had to be seen to be legitimate, and here notions of patronage and distribution...become important'.[79] The relevant questions then are: what strategies did the dominant employ to display their power? If the power of the dominant was dependent on the support of the subordinate, how unilaterally rapacious could it afford to be? Could power then reside with the elites alone, and were caste status and economic standing the sole determinants of the strength of an individual in society? Did social relevance and the use society had of an individual or a community not have any bearings and also constitute significant criteria that shaped the parameters of power of individuals or groups in any society?

As members of the shudra varna, artisans were indeed at the lowest rung of the social ladder, ritually unclean and culturally inferior, universally recognized as 'weak' and vulnerable. The rulers, state administrators engaged in governance, landed elites, merchants and moneylenders, on the other hand, were of course 'powerful'. Historical scholarship has rightly emphasized that medieval states suppressed the 'weak' and the feeble and protected the 'powerful', habitually exploiting and oppressing those subordinate to them, whether in the shape of revenue and labour exactions, or by reducing them to the status of servile labour. This larger equation between the artisans and the state is the starting point of this study, a fact neither contested nor in need of further reiteration.

What does strike me as important, and this constitutes the foundation of this study, is that subordinate castes such as artisans occupied a far more ambiguous position in society than usually imagined. It cannot be reduced to the simplistic formula of exploitation/subordination without compromising much of the richly textured realities of their lifeworlds. The roots of the anomalies of their position, and the fuzziness of agendas the dominant pursued in their relationships with artisans is perplexing at first glance, but fairly simple to comprehend at closer scrutiny. It is well known that the caste system inscribed craft castes with a ritually unclean status and this constituted the source of their subordination. Paradoxically, artisanal manipulation of their polluting functions and status simultaneously lent them strength. With the clean castes' proscription from performing polluting functions, unwillingness to 'dirty' their hands, and consequent absence of skills needed to craft routine consumption items, the superior groups experienced an immense amount of dependence on subordinate labour. Though shunned for their unclean presence and functions, it was their ritually polluting status and the services they provided to a caste society, that made artisanal roles vital and their work indispensable. Susan Bayly, in her study of caste politics, emphasized that pre-colonial kings and other dominant groups did not treat caste status as unidimensional and absolute, but rather as a reference point to be negotiated, challenged and even reshaped to fit the needs of their times.[80] Documentary evidence from eighteenth-century Jodhpur too shows decisively that artisans, since they possessed skills and provided specialized labour, were in great demand and this enabled them to challenge exploitation, limit appropriations, and negotiate for better conditions. Artisans' impure status thus constituted the source of their 'power', however limited it may have been.

How did this ambiguous position relate to the unfolding of power? As mentioned earlier, different artisanal groups possessed specific skills for the manufacture of craft goods and the caste system prescribed that these be practised exclusively by the particular craft group. None but the *luhars* could craft ploughshares and iron tools; the khatis alone manufactured the Persian wheel for irrigation, the cots and stools that made homes comfortable, and different wooden implements. The presence of kumhars was essential for every household to procure cooking and storing vessels of clay. Equally indispensable to every settlement were *bhambhi*, *raigar*, and mochis for none other than one from their caste would remove dead carcasses, flay rotting animals, and manufacture commodities of routine use from the hides thus procured. As manufacturers of ornaments and skilled essayers of coins, sunars, churigars, and lakharas too were extremely critical, while the presence of julahas, rangrez, nilgar, charhawas, and chhipas facilitated local production and procurement of textiles. It was inconceivable for rulers to perpetuate their glory without erecting magnificent monuments that future generations could remember them by, and construction as well as repair activities made it imperative for the dominant to have access to silawats and *chejaras*. Extreme dependence for the fulfilment of these myriad needs rendered the elites vulnerable, both their functional needs as well as those for pomp and ceremony requiring large numbers of artisans.[81] The latter were basic 'passports to legitimate power' and the contenders for authority had to assert themselves not merely through brute force, but also through the display of piety and generous patronage towards craft groups.

The fact that early modern states did not possess adequate resources to exercise sustained coercion and ensure the submission of the subordinate over prolonged periods of time also implied that appeasement would have to be a basic tenet of the rulers' policies. In an arid kingdom, unable to raise its agricultural yields without substantial breakthroughs in irrigation, income from the non-agricultural commercial sector was vital to the state's stability. Records indicate that revenues from the latter far exceeded the former, and investments towards courting assiduously mercantile and artisanal talent seem to have been the thrust of state policies. The point I am therefore making is that new alliances were forged without dismantling old ones with dominant groups and lineages.

The possession of skills and their non-substitutibility due to caste rigidities strengthened the position of craftsmen and ensured that the elites did not take liberties with them in a thoughtless manner, without due consideration for the repercussions of their actions. A vast presence of political and mercantile elites resulted in a substantial demand for manufactured goods, and locally-based skilled artisans who were specialists in their trade, tended to meet them locally. Hence, retention of these productive castes in their respective territories was critical to the elites, and the ruling chiefs felt compelled to employ statecraft not only in their dealings with the elites but also with productive labour, spatially fixing them within their bounds.

This need for holding on to skilled labour in their territories was accentuated by the fact that Marwari craftsmen were habituated to recurrent emigrations. Harsh environmental conditions of extreme aridity and frequent droughts and famines had rendered craftsmen unusually mobile, their relocation from one to another *qasba* or village, a noticeable feature in Jodhpuri documents. Large tracts of land were still uninhabited, and this ensured that there was enough space where an aggrieved artisan could settle and find alternate patrons. Hence, artisans often deserted their ancestral homes for more conducive locales, and the state felt constrained to devise ways of retaining them. In situations where the local *khati* or kumhar had migrated, the agriculturists suffered immense inconveniences, and the village elites had few options but to try and coax or even cajole the aggrieved artisan to return. The artisans leveraged on this clout that they had due to their skills, and as will be evident from Chapters 4 and 5, dominant castes were forced to offer a range of concessions to enjoy uninterrupted services from the pavan jat without fears of disruption and shortage of labour. The imperative of self-preservation was paramount, and both the rulers and the ruled were locked in mutual dependence.

In this context, it appears necessary to explore the political dynamic and the sociology of power as it played out between the artisans and the Jodhpur state. What was the grammar, the basis, of state power and authority? Besides military might and coercive strength that were indeed essential to power, were there other more subtle ingredients that went into the crucible to produce power? Political theorists have repeatedly emphasized that the core problem of governance lies in the success of the efforts to incorporate people into a polity and economy in such a way that they accept the particular forms of political and legal authority that centre on the state. In the ultimate analysis, governance has always depended on the diverse ways in which various realms of civil society are made subject to the ultimate jurisdiction of the state and its judicial and administrative institutions. This process is said to have occurred through historically determined patterns of force and persuasion.

Weber, writing more than half a century ago, recognized that few regimes could sustain themselves on appeals to coercive power alone.[82] More recently, Foucauldian interpretations of power have elaborated that state power rests not only in the brute capacity to discipline or in the influence of dominant social groups, but also in political and ideological traditions of building consent. State formation and the construction of state authority is acknowledged as a deeply textured political and historical process where prospects of success rest on the establishment of a common ground of political dialogue and argument. Governments generally recognized the importance of containing social struggle and resistance within the ambit of state authority, and therefore sought non-coercive strategies to stabilize society and overcome centrifugal political forces. This entailed the problem of making people into 'citizens'. A proper historical understanding of the state requires that we reinterpret the term state to take account of 'the moral calculus of state power' that defined the nature of citizenship.[83] As argued in greater detail below, such a moral calculus required the grounding of a theory of government, a normative language of state power that secured

the state as the final arbiter of social order and public good. These processes appear to have been at work since long in the construction of kingship in
pre-colonial India, emphasizing an administrative strategy cast in a politi-
cal-incorporative idiom. With artisans performing significant functional roles
to sustain local economies, their integration into the body politic would not
only be desirable, but unavoidable. Without doubt, the power base of a
state tended to be too narrow unless it was able to achieve legitimation
through politico-ideological processes grounded in a broad consensus.[84]

Consensus or consent-building are indeed modern concepts, and I by
no means imagine the eighteenth-century Rathor state to be an *avatar* of a
modern polity. I would only like to argue that the processes leading to mod-
ernization were underway, and that these were far more developed than is
usually acknowledged. While recognizing that society was mired by caste
oppressions and class exploitation, wracked by state and landlord terror,
my point is that effective governance was not possible with elite support
alone, and that incorporative strategies extending to the lower formations
were fundamental to early-modern state authority. The eighteenth-century
states thereby came to construct a contradictory blend of coercive and legitimating political practices that tried to penetrate the lower strata of society.
As members of cohesive communities with their own organizational structures, performing roles critical to local economies, the artisans enjoyed power
much in excess of their lowly position in the social scale. Though the downtrodden underbelly of the region, they negotiated in their dealings with the
superior castes from a position of greater strength than is usually imagined.

The Jodhpur state did tend to generally give priority to elite concerns,
and was by no means immune to the pressures of the dominant. Its
sustenance, however, also depended on popular acceptance of its sovereignty. The interests of certain discrete rajput-mahajan groups often took
precedence over all others, and as discussed in Chapter 3, the rulers manipulated laws and traditions to accommodate their concerns. It must still
be emphasized that the ritually inferior castes could not altogether be ignored, for at the core of the politics of state formation lay efforts to achieve
a durable balance between control and consent. It was the dual and often
contradictory imperatives of domination and incorporation that were at
the heart of state-making politics.

Thus though it was an integral part of the elite psyche, and common for
the state and the elites to maximize their extraction of revenues in cash,
labour, and kind from the subordinate, it is equally true that this tendency
to enhance state appropriations indiscriminately was inhibited by a complex matrix of factors. For one, the means of coercion at the disposal of the
elites and the Rathor administration were limited, and it was prudent to
use troops and forces for subduing rival contenders for the throne and recal-

citrant lineage chiefs rather than one's own subjects. Sheer pragmatism suggested that a show of respect for the needs of the subordinate population would be beneficial.[85] Since land was abundant and labour scarce, subsistence insurance was virtually the only way to attach a labour force to their territory. Besides, in addition to the reasons cited above that made artisans indispensable to any settlement, there seem to have been two other major reasons that prompted the administration and local authorities to make every effort to induce the people who had left their villages to return home. The first lay in the systems of revenue appropriations, whether through formal collectors or revenue farmers. In the case of collectors, their remuneration often consisted of a certain proportion of the revenue, and desertion by the lower castes implied smaller amounts of collections and therefore reduced payments for them. Revenue farmers, too, stood to gain by ensuring continued residence of the local populace because when they were unable to collect the contracted amount of revenue due to the abscondence of the producers, they were obliged to fill up the deficiency from their own resources unless the government specifically exempted them from it. It was therefore crucial for both collectors and *ijaredar*s that as many people as possible should remain and work in their territory and enhance the total revenue that the collectors could pocket for themselves. Secondly, the vested interests of the indigenous privileged class of the *chaudhari*s and other hereditary village functionaries, who were entitled to receive a certain portion of the produce from the village-folk as their remuneration, also ensured that the administration maintain and promote the settlement of people in their villages, and prevent emigrations as best as possible.[86]

Finally, cognisance of the cultural mindset that tuned the interface and determined mutual roles of the elites and subordinate is required, for it constructed a discursive terrain on which state agencies and subordinate groups such as artisans negotiated definitions of duties, rights, traditions, and obligations. Statecraft necessitated the political mobilization of a popular base, and the cultural contours of kingship and rule, outlined in Chapter 1, defined the social responsibilities of the state as much as it stressed the obligations of the subjects. The rationale for this cultural ideal was, of course, embedded in the socio-economic and environmental setting in which elite-subordinate interactions operated, and these, too, were extremely significant dimensions in the matrix of factors that determined the dialogue of the 'weak' and the 'powerful'.

Records indicate that incorporation entailed adherence to certain normative standards that constituted 'appropriate' (*wajabi*) behaviour, and when the state acted, it felt pressured to do so according to patterns of conduct that were socially understood and recognized as 'legitimate'. Apart from material constrains, these cultural standards too defined the mutual exchanges between the dominant and the subordinate, and permeated the transfer of surplus from the producer to the consumer. Artisans were obligated to pay revenues, and the state obligated to guarantee them a minimum level of subsistence. A mutually acceptable level of demands and expectations—of 'give and take'—provided the rationale for innumerable state decisions that ordered *jo wajabi hoy so karay dena*, that is, 'have the "appropriate"done', in response to artisanal appeals for tax concessions. In that sense, the economy was not quite separable from morality.[87]

What is also inescapable in the records is that wajib or legitimate standards of conduct was a fluid category rather than being rigid, historically fixed norms. Gaps between the interests of different classes translated in variable readings and different interpretations of wajabi, and hence, though bolstered by cultural standards of kingship, it could not generate harmony. Whatever the rhetoric, they did not represent a shared culture of consensus. Neither were they ideal arrangements that can be romanticized as the basis that ensured popular consent and order. The rulers may have claimed them to be just, a reflection of their altruism, but in fact they were equally the result of material criteria of realpolitik. The 'legitimate' course of action was equally influenced by personality traits of dominant individuals and circumstantial pressures specific to each context. But that cultural underpinnings of morality too, played some part seems writ large over the documentation from Jodhpur. Under recurrent negotiation, norms were therefore constantly formulated and reformulated over time, as is evident in the following chapters that document tensions between 'legitimate standards' as perceived by the subordinate and as sought to be implemented by the state. Clearly witnessed here are Samuel Popkin's findings that 'norms are malleable, renegotiated and shifting in accord with considerations of power and strategic interaction among individuals'.[88]

Exchanges rooted in past precedents constituted primary ingredients that shaped the notion of wajib or legitimate practice, and turning to these to substantiate state authority was a fundamental strategy in securing legitimacy. Political uses of tradition and appeals invoking it played a major role in the formation of state authority. Age-old or time-honoured traditions got accepted as being judicious and whenever artisans cited past practice as the basis of their demand for withdrawal of new taxes or hikes in labour exactions, state intercession in their favour was likely if not guaranteed. Antiquity of practice was viewed as a strong source of legitimacy and prima facie evidence of its propriety, its wajabi-ness, and many petitioners began their plaint with an assertion of such antiquity. The 'old way was definition right, and innovation wrong'.[89]

The rhetoric and practice of norms, termed 'moral economy' by several theorists, have been noticed in several parts of the pre-industrial world from England in the West to Malaysia in the East, illuminating the culture and politics of social groups at the fringes of, and often against, the state.[90] In this body of literature, moral economy is said to have underwritten locally understood concepts of property rights, community membership, and the social good that made subordinate communities resilient in the face of environmental or political stress. Studies have seen a close intertwining of elite and subordinate perceptions that informed 'a panoply of relations of social obligation and reciprocity'.

In the eighteenth century Indian context too, the natural proclivity of the state and the elites to enhance exactions was constrained by this moral parameter, defining the band-width within which extractions could be stretched. While alternate interpretations of 'legitimate' conduct and contestations to enlarge individual domains were substantial, that concerns of morality were embedded in elite-subaltern interactions too seem indisputable. Provision of basic entitlements and a minimal standard of living were recognized as fundamental duties of the administration, and this cultural factor tuned their relationship to determine the specific roles of the dominant and the dependant in each other's contexts. Both the 'exploiter' and the 'exploited' were informed by this moral heritage of wajabi, and by an awareness about 'legitimate' and 'illegitimate' demands and practices in matters of revenue and *begar*. Since the right of the poor to subsistence was well recognized, even sacrosanct, it was outrage against the violation of this minimum standard of living (that the dominant were supposed to ensure for the dependant) that gets reflected in the verse that introduced this volume. Numerous documents suggest that the state considered it it's responsibility that those unable to support themselves economically must be provided for by the administration, with documents recording orders for rations and other necessities to be extended to the visually and mentally challenged, the indigent, and widows, to enable them to survive.[91]

What was within endurance levels, and when was the threshold level crossed to render a demand extortionate and objectionable was pegged by these standards. It was this cultural make-up of society that decided what was correct, righteous, and wajabi, and set codes of propriety, of befitting behaviour for different sections. Administrative orders were constantly screened, judged, and evaluated against such notions of wajabi. Expectations, obligations, demands and even complaints were culturally constituted, though this culture was more flexible than fixed, and left open enough scope for manipulation.

Usually, exactions that had precedents and were within the limits set by 'tradition', were submitted by subordinate communities to the state without a murmur. The violation of these standards in contravention of custom, provoked resentment and resistance, not only because needs were not met, but also because rights were transgressed. Thus custom and culture played a dual role: on the one hand they sanctified exploitation, but on the other they also constrained it within certain limits. In situations of violation, artisans used the sanctity of custom and culture as a weapon to challenge 'illegitimate' demands, and asserted their right over a certain amount of patronage that the 'powerful' were supposed to extend to them.[92] The control that men of power and money still exercised over the lives and expectations of those below them remained enormous, but the polarities of social and economic antagonism were to some extent eroded by these cultural norms.

PETITIONS AND OTHER SOURCES: VARIETY OF GENRES, MULTIPLE PERSPECTIVES

These formulations are derived from Marwari literature, which from the eighteenth century begins to offer sources of a greater variety of genres that help engage with a relatively larger range of issues.[93] Their authorial voices span from folk sources to those of early British travellers and administrators, in addition of course to bardic literature and court chronicles,[94] gazetteer compilations such as *Marwar ra Pargana ri Vigat* (from now onwards *Vigat*),[95] Jain *munis*' ghazals, as also a large compendium of archival literature. The last four categories were indeed state-sponsored and, to that extent, suffer from limitations associated with statist perceptions; but as is discussed below diverse agendas prompted the state to commission different forms of writing, and each is different in nature and reliabilty as a source on society.

Ghazals or metrical compositions penned by Jain yatis were quite distinct from the popularly known Urdu ghazals in both style and content. Though both are poetic verse-forms, the Marwari ghazals were written in the folk literature tradition, and were essentially descriptions of contemporary urban centres of Marwar. The tradition of ghazal writing by Jain saints appears to have been initiated in Marwari literature from about the seventeenth century, and was extremely popular in the eighteenth and nineteenth centuries.[96] As is well known, Jain yatis travelled uninterruptedly all through the year spreading the message of their faith, but during the four monsoon months called *Chaumasa*, religious prescriptions constrained them to rest and recuperate before they embarked on their next travel. The royalty often invited them to accept the hospitality and shelter in their city, and treated them as esteemed guests for the period.[97] The city that they based themselves in for these four months became the subject of their ghazals, and they reciprocated royal favours by writing narrative poems, using plenty of meter, metaphor, and rhyme to paint pictorial accounts, although exaggerated, of these urban centres. Often named after the city they described such as *Jodhpur ki Ghazal*, *Nagaur ki Ghazal*, and *Maroth ki Ghazal* these poems construct a visual image, albeit through words, of major urban centres of eighteenth-century Marwar.[98]

In an overstated, dramatized style, combining fact with fiction and reality with hyperbole, these ghazals praised liberally the invincibility of the Rathor forts, the beauty of their temples, the vigour of their bazaars, the range of commerce their cities supported, the numerous occupational groups residing there, the administrative and security arrangements supporting them, and everything noticeable that might establish the 'greatness' of the city and its ruler. Though the essentially eulogistic nature of the ghazals makes their reliability as sources of information somewhat questionable, they certainly suggest contemporary ideals, notions of 'greatness', 'grandness' and 'excellence', and the standards and indices that went into making a ruler and his region 'eminent'. Paintings commissioned by the Jodhpur Court too offer idealized rather than actual portrayals of Marwari lives, whether depicting the royalty, the palace in-mates, the merchants and the bazaar, or the common peasants and artisans. That cross-checking their portrayals with literary sources helps corroborate evidence, can also not be disputed.

More promising, from my point of view, however, were the numerous archival documents, the maintenance of which had become one of the important functions that the eighteenth-century Marwar state engaged in. Of the numerous bahi series I perused, the *Jodhpur Sanad Parwana Bahis* at the Rajasthan State Archives at Bikaner proved extremely rewarding and, supported by other archival material and ethnographic data, helped map dialogues between the state and the subalterns during the latter half of the century.[99] This bahi series records *arzees* from the subjects, regardless of their social provenance. State decisions in response to petitions are recorded too, and we have thereby details about the engagements of people, individually and collectively, with the Rathor state.

Petition records seem to be a global phenomenon, stretching back in time to almost as far as writing, in various cultures and political settings is witnessed. These were used by subjects including those from the humble strata, to voice their demands for justice or seek favours and largesse. In many languages and periods, different kinds of petition-like documents were distinguished by different terms, their ubiquity suggesting that popular representations to rulers stretch across cultural boundaries. To be effective, petitions had to include not merely a reference to the rulers whose intervention was sought, but also provide details about the supplicant and the defendant that would help identify them, and of course, state the grievance or the request of the petitioner. They also point towards the way the petitioners perceived the government. These data make petitions a powerful historical source, for all these formal elements in a petition lend themselves to historical analysis.

More interestingly, petitions are perhaps the only historical sources with provenance that allow scholars to begin an investigation into a history 'from below' for the eighteenth century. Since illiterate masses did not leave private letters, diaries, autobiographies, and testaments that would help construct them as subjects of historical agency, they have generally appeared in history as objects of economic exploitation. It is sources such as petitions and the qualitative as well as quantitative data that they offer that can be effectively harnessed to understand ordinary people as historical agents.[100] Often made collectively by a group or corporate body, petitions also articulate shared interests, and give insights into the social profile of the signatories. Composed in the most varied situations of life, the heterogeneous contexts for supplications document needs and interests, hopes and aspirations, attitudes and activities, and circumstances and concerns of people's everyday lives, their pleas providing snippets from the life experiences of historical personae. Whether requests for material help, mercy or aid, formal demands for licenses, permits or dispensations, complaints against government or law courts, or supplications for justice, the addressees' response is included in these records and provides useful insights into the state's attitudes towards its myriod petitioners. The use of petitions is also useful because they lend themselves to various approaches, such as close reading in the hermeneutic tradition, serial analysis of petitioners, contents and addresses, prosopographical or micro-historical reconstructions and linkings and so on. With respect to social conflicts, petitions are useful for analysing the spatial and social diffusion and mentalities of contending parties, their, motives and aims, the rhetoric, language and legitimation strategies employed by them the course of frictions, and the success and failure of conflicts at multiple levels. Autobiographical in nature, these representations enable us to hear the voices of the 'silent masses' , who would otherwise have remained mute and unheard. Almost all other sources are more elitist—demonstrative of state-centric concerns, or are from the non-indigenous genre, mostly European travel accounts written from an alien mentality and worldview. Folk sources are of course embedded in subaltern culture, and should be used for a counter discourse, but the inability to date makes findings based on them historically questionable.

Indeed, when reading a petition, the author of the petition is not always obvious. Illiterate petitioners from the lower formations gave verbal accounts of their complaints and state scribes transcribed them for the judicial authorities, making copies that included the verdicts passed by state authorities. These records were preserved by the Jodhpur administration, and today provide researchers with ready sources to construct social histories. Indeed, as part of the state archives, they cannot be expected to be ideologically neutral. Recent theoretical positions, particularly those arising out of Foucauldian perspectives, have highlighted the relation between power and its control of knowledge. Having been transcribed by state notaries, these petitions record to an extent constitute elite authored evidence, inextricable from the discourses of the state. Though they cannot be called doctored versions, for they were generated in the course of normal functioning of the state, and served essentially as its memory, they cannot claim 'objective reporting', either because the biases and agendas of professional scribes and notaries of the state would have percolated and partially coloured the contents of the narrative. Indeed, as Natalie Zemon Davis warns us, choices of language, detail and order would have been made by the scribes to present the complaint of the plaintiff.[101] State paternalism, for instance, comes across strongly in these records, and one cannot take it at face value. The 'selection' of facts that seemed significant to the recorder would obviously colour our vision and perception of the case. Predilections of the educated, higher castes against the poor would have insidiously found their way into the narrative, and consciously or not, tend to camouflage the exploitation and injustices of an inherently unequal society. We are thus forced to interpret artisanal responses to elite excesses indirectly, through a filter often provided by the very dominant groups to whom they were reacting. We also do not know whether they were recorded during the judicial proceedings and the pronouncement of the state's decision, or later.

That brings up the fundamental question: How far can we rely on these petition documents? Is there any possibility of truthful portrayals of the voice of subordinate 'Others' through the use of these documents? A deconstruction of petitions as sources for the production of knowledge is pertinent because the actions of craftsmen who petitioned their choices and assertions reach us through the language and grammar of elitist discourse embedded in their mindset, and meanings notaries gave when they recorded and narrated the cases. Sherry Ortner rightly notes that our times face a crisis of representation in human sciences. After all, Edward Said warned that the discourse of Orientalism renders it virtually impossible to know anything real about the Orient; James Clifford asserts that all ethnographies are 'fictions'; and Gayatri Spivak laments that 'the subaltern cannot speak'.[102] In her Derridean deconstruction of the individual subjects Spivak's immensely influential writings have engendered an increasing consciousness that the textual narratives of written records on illiterate subjects cannot provide accuracy about their lived worlds. Said, Spivak, and others have established that elite domination of the subalterns ensures that their voices become hard to retrieve and write about.[103]

Indeed, my decoding petitions from subaltern subjects suffers from a dual mediation—in the first instance at the hands of the Jodhpur state's notary who transcribed petitions and newsletters registered from different districts during an annual year. Besides, given my privileged social and educational location, I am deeply aware of the limits beyond which I cannot know about artisans from the sources I have studied. While cognisant of these limits of historically understanding and interpreting subaltern communities' ability to resist and contest elite exploitation, I see this attempt as resulting from a desire to 'know' them through their choices, if not their voices. It is an exercise in deciphering and speaking by 'proxy' about artisans' concerns, embedded as they are in a selective production of the archive. The task of representation is not only tricky, but one that promises limited hope of success. Even so, one must remember that the subalterns do not merely resist political domination, but textual domination as well. Dominant agendas of course shape these texts, and we need to unfold those rather than accepting what is written at face value, but those being written about also fashion the content, substance, and texture of the text. Of course, there are variations in the degree to which different authors and different forms of writing allow this process to show, and it is absolutely critical to reflect on ways to enhance their reliability as sources of subaltern history. Court chronicles or state-commissioned ghazals, for instance, were written with the specific aim of celebrating the mighty, and would be able to offer much less as opposed to archival documents, especially petition records that document people's problems and appeals for justice. Archives, as is well known, are produced during the course of administrative processes and suffer much less from defined agendas of the rulers. As such, it seems absurd to insist that the text is not reflective of the lived reality of the people whom it claims to represent, and therefore not write ethnographical histories of the subordinate at all. The solution perhaps resides in refusing to be limited by any single text and by any existing definition of what should count as the corpus, and to play the texts off against one another 'in an endless process of coaxing up images of the real'.[104]

Instead of refusing to know and write about the worlds inhabited by the lowly artisans because such 'representations' run the risk of being inaccurate and even far removed from their actual desires, aspirations, and subjectivities, this book tries to delve into the subject and read their however oblique or indirect these voices may be. Rather than abandon the project for its possible inadequacies and weaknesses and thereby continue to leave the artisanal social worlds historically invisible, it seems worthwhile to attempt a scrutiny and critical analysis of these petitions, a reading against the grain, between the lines, and often deductions and inferences from the latent suggestions, hints, and implications in the petitions. In 'examining the intricacies of the written record, focussing on the phenomenological space of the historiographical construction'[105] lies the clue to better interpretation of state archives. To Spivak's key question 'Can the Subaltern speak?' the answer seems to be that they did speak and we should try to hear their voices, however imperfectly and unclearly they may reach us.

What then is the format of arzees in the *Jodhpur Sanad Parwana Bahis*, and how should a researcher propose to read them to represent the life worlds of its subjects? A sanad was a royal order and a parwana a letter of authorization that enunciated state directives to officials who had to implement state decisions. As a collation of judicial records that summarized disputes brought by people to the different levels of conflict-resolution authorities of the state, these arzees provided an important space for the articulation of identities and their engagements and contestations with other identities. As a medium for engaging with the state administration, these petitions are reflective of the fact that the subalterns were increasingly participating in the state's structures of judicial rule. Clearly, by making available these institutional devices to its subjects, and thereby opening up for them a channel of communication with the administration, the Jodhpur state comes across as susceptible to the exchange of ideas that flowed through these petitions. The purpose of the maintenance of these records seems to be referral in nature, so that the state could check the 'facts' of the case and the previous judicial pronouncement in case the litigants returned with the dispute.[106] The 'referral' purpose would also stand good in situations where different cases of the same category or nature came up for resolution.

As bureaucratically available vehicles of expression, the 'public' nature of the arzee, compelled the petition's language to be highly deferential, 'utterly embedded in forms of civility that operated within the logos of what it was to be a subject of' a princely Hindu kingdom in early modern Rajputana. It had a highly formalized narrative, completely lacking in candour that privacy might bring. Many of these arzees, constitute petitions against the state and its functionaries, while others are inter-caste or intra-caste dispute cases brought for resolution to the judicial agencies of the state. They often reveal differences between the state's ideas of governance when juxtaposed against those of the people. Their suitability for the different parties involved—the plaintiff, the defendant, and the government—was predicated on what a petition as a genre had to offer to the petitioners, and how it located the petitioner in relation to the extant structures of power in society and in the government. They even outline visions and models of the social order, in some senses.

What relevance could the problems and frictions in the lives of single individuals have for this study? How 'typical' and 'representative' of the lives of artisans in general can these petitions and the dispute cases detailed in them be taken to be? In an age of quantitative history, when many historians maintain that the reintegration of the subordinate classes into general history can only be accomplished through statistical series, how significant can some stray dispute records be? Many would argue, with good reason, that an acceptance of these would give a lopsided picture since they do not describe the 'normal', but rather the 'abnormal'; hence the conflict or dispute, and the need for state intervention to resolve the problem. A discerning reading, however, makes the 'normal' come alive, even if not spelt out because, in the first instance, the complaint was made only because something 'out of the ordinary' had happened. The basis or root of the resentment of the complainant becomes apparent when one reads between the lines, and precisely there lies the key to the 'normal', 'typical', or 'acceptable' mode of behaviour. Anything other than the customary, traditional, or conventional got mentioned as an 'objectionable' form of conduct in these records, and the state inevitably ordered for 'legitimate' practices to be restored.

Also, we must bear in mind that in Marwar, as in any social system, for every dispute case that was reported for resolution, there were many more of the kind that did not reach the judicial authorities. These tended to be resolved privately on the basis of precedents and existing verdicts in similar situations. This overwhelming amount of private dispute-resolution was caused by the uncertainty and cost of securing a formal settlement through courts. Decisions taken by Shri Huzur influenced the outcome of local unreported disputes due to the 'long shadow of the law'.[107] The 'abnormal' and the 'atypical' also, therefore, generally had many parallels, and were representatives of aberrant trends rather than solitary cases.[108]

The inadequacies of these archival documents can be somewhat mitigated through the search for an 'alternative archive' to illuminate the past. Excellent studies by Dube, Skaria, and Mayaram encourage the use of myths and the oral genre for the study of popular culture.[109] In fact, the latter can best be understood by examining how written and oral texts intersect and interpenetrate. An 'awareness of the role of the state in the constitution of marginality as also the resistance of the margins'.[110] Will be possible if, rather than limiting the study to written records due to the traditional valorization of them as the repositories of objective rationality and ultimate reality, they are interfaced in a dialectical relationship with sources of the oral genre. In the indigenous local vernacular, myths, folk tales (*lok gatha*), and proverbs (*lokoktiyan*), permeated by images and metaphors popular among artisans, enable a counter discourse of a popular perspective as against the statist biases embedded in petitions transcribed by notaries. As representations of collective memory, they constitute contestatory sites when counterposed against the official memory of the state, and provide 'alternative ontological perspectives...to reconstruct social and cultural textures of the past, although not necessarily precise representations of "fact" or "event" in a conventional sense'.[111] Said to be *kadim*, though lacking in provenance, I use them to understand the collective psychology of a preliterate society, and reconstruct the value systems and inter-personal tensions among different castes and communities. This study attempts to use these imaginatively for 'humanizing' history and bringing alive the artisans of a bygone era.[112]

In this context, a recent study by Demirci on the traditional Near Eastern concept of state justice—the Ottoman judicial system and its resolution of popular complaints about taxes by examining court cases and imperial orders documented in Sijill Records—is disappointing.[113] Demirci fails to appreciate and acknowledge the problems in using state archives alone to understand state behaviour. This makes his conclusions rather simplistic overstating his thesis. Totally negating the presence of maladministration or corruption, he sees the state as amazingly just and unexploitative, ever keen to uphold 'social justice' and undo any wrongs that tax officials may have committed towards the common people. He writes: 'Not a single case could be found in the sicils used in this study, in which the central government itself had acted unjustly or tolerated injustices to its subjects'.[114] Those at the receiving end of the revenue administration may have had different assessments, and while benevolent impulses of the Ottoman state, stimulated in large measure by concerns of pragmatism and expediency, seem perfectly plausible, the study would have most definitely gained by portraying counter-perspectives through an exploration of sources of other genres instead of the state archive alone.

Harnessing, therefore, sources of a variety of genres, juxtaposing perspectives from the official archives with folk sources, this book tries to offer a flavour of the ongoing tensions in early modern society of Rajasthan. Counter-posing multiple perspectives and diverse interpretations, corroborated by a range of ethnographic literature, census reports, gazetteers, medico-topographical reports, administrative and famine relief reports, it focusses on placing artisans in the grid or web of pressures and counter-pressures to see how the realities of complementarity and contestation manifested on the ground.

Chapter 2 maps the historical trajectory of the state during the period of its reconfiguration from a Mughal ancestral patrimony (*watan jagir*) to an autonomous kingdom. Eighteenth century pressures on the rulers translated in the evolution of new strategies of survival both for the 'exploiter' as well as the 'exploited'. These are discussed, as are 'investments' by the state, both capital and institutional, to promote the economic well-being of the region. It also presents an overview of the ecological conditions and associated economic patterns in eighteenth-century Marwar that constituted the contextual framework within which the elite-subordinate dialogue unfolded.

Chapter 3 describes the endogenous world of the artisans, beginning with a general discussion on asymmetrically gendered relationships in craft societies despite craftswomen's critical roles in their household economies.

It goes on to probe questions of law and the place of customary traditions in judicial dispensations by the state whenever there were intra-family, intra-caste, or even inter-caste disputes among artisans. Juxtaposing state governance against local governance through caste councils, the chapter discusses administrative regulation, disciplining, and organization of artisanal society enforced by these agencies. The chapter notices varied circumstances that prompted competing, yet collaborative interactions, between them.

This leads me to a discussion on material and ideological factors, cultural mindsets and forms of consciousness that together shaped the Jodhpur state's exchanges with artisanal communities residing in the villages of Jodhpur. Chapter 4 explores the unfolding of the above mentioned factors in the rural scenario, detailing artisanal strategies of survival in a harsh desert landscape. It examines the nature of subordinate-superordinate interactions in a sharply defined ethos of caste hierarchy, commenting on the validity of the 'predatory state' versus 'prey-like society' juxtaposition, popular in extant historiography. Based on documents from the latter half of the eighteenth century, it analyses trends in the early decades of Jodhpur's maharaja Vijai Singh's reign, and maps 'everyday relations' between the rulers, local landed elements, and village artisans' seeing these as mediated by the culturally recognized, yet constantly negotiated norms of 'legitimacy'. It notices that when the latter were transgressed by the dominant, the subordinate did not hesitate to challenge their violators, even if mostly within the dominant discourse.

Chapter 5 constructs the morphology and settlement pattern in urban Marwar to understand how close living aided the emergence of caste brotherhoods or *biradari*s, and a collective solidarity that helped artisans tackle pressures and tensions in their dealings with the urban elite, the state administration, and its *ohdadar*s. Still focussing on the early decades of Vijai Singh's reign, it outlines the contours of the Jodhpur state's paternalist discourse of legitimation in these years.

And finally, in Chapter 6, the book focusses on the last two decades of the eighteenth century when an all-round escalation in stresses, coinciding with increased Maratha presence and demands for tribute, saw a gradual transformation in the political context of the kingdom. Did the Rathor state adhere to its old standards of 'moral order' that had been part of the Rathor paternalist discourse in the previous three decades? Or was it compelled to redefine its principles of wajabi? And did the artisans turn revolutionary in the face of enhanced stresses and demands on their labour and resources? Expiating on state-society relations through the prism of artisanal experience, I conclude that during the eighteenth century, a qualitatively different idiom and vocabulary of politics had emerged. The fundamental instinct of the dominant continued to attempt the maximization of revenues and

from the subordinate, and since the latter resisted exploitation be-
.. 'traditional' limits, there were, as always, conflicting interests at play.
What was new, however, was increased political instability and rivalries
among the royalty in the absence of Mughal protection, and the acute competition for skilled labour among the numerous princely kingdoms.
Incorporative strategies of 'legitimate' conduct had, therefore, to be combined with appropriations since the weak and inadequate coercive power
of pre-modern states could not expect to discipline skilled labour and crush
dissent on a prolonged basis. Investments towards appeasement and accommodation became imperative for attracting and spatially fixing artisans
within the territories of the kingdom, and thereby chug along with all the
asymmetries and contentions intrinsic to an intensely hierarchical society.
By noticing artisanal resistance whenever their 'legitimate' expectations were
violated, the study questions stereotypes of passive, voiceless, complacence
attributed to the Indian subordinate groups in the early modern period of
Indian history, and highlights the agency of artisans even before the British
encounter.

NOTES

1. The verse was quoted by Lieutenant Colonel James Tod, the first political agent
to the western Rajput states in his *Annals and Antiquities of Rajasthan*, vol. 1, (1st
edn, Calcutta, 1829), p. 737; and again by Lieutenant A.H.E. Boileau in his
*Personal Narrative of a Tour Through the Western States of Rajwara, in 1835, Compris-
ing Beekaner, Jesulmer, and Jodhpoor* (Calcutta, 1837), p. 274.

2. Ann Grodzins Gold and Bhoju Ram Gujar note in their work *In the Time of
Trees and Sorrows: Nature, Power and Memory in Rajasthan* (Durham, 2002), popular memory even today relates closely to the idea of kings, the name Rajasthan
(the Land of Kings) suggesting a region where one 'would have to reckon with
kingship'; see Preface, p. xii.

3. That the lower formations perceived their rulers as the *mai-baap*, a paternalistic
authority, or atleast used this rhetoric in their appeals, seems to have been common
all over the subcontinent. P. Swarnalatha, for instance, cites petitions by weavers to the colonial authorities in late eighteenth-century Andhra, one of which
reads, 'We are like your children, you are like our parents. If you will not have
our petition, who then will? Remove our hunger and, support us'. See Swarnalatha's
article 'Revolt, Testimony, Petition: Artisanal Protests in Colonial Andhra', *International Review of Social History*, vol. 46, 2001, Supplement, p. 114.

4. See Ashin Das Gupta, *Indian Merchants and the Decline of Surat 1700–1740*
(Wiesbaden, 1979); and his 'Indian Merchants and the Trade in the Indian Ocean'
in Tapan Raychaudhuri and Irfan Habib (eds), *The Cambridge Economic History
of India*, vol. 1 (Cambridge, 1982), pp. 407– 33.

5. See M.N. Pearson, *Merchants and Rulers in Gujarat: The Response to the Portuguese in the Sixteenth Century* (New Delhi, 1976), pp. 2 and 92–154 and his

'Merchants and States' in James D. Tracey (ed.), *The Political Economy of Merchant Empires* (Cambridge, 1991), pp. 41–116, respectively.

6. Kate Teltscher discussed at length Orientalist depictions of the brutality and barbarism of the Mysore sultans Haider Ali and Tipu. See her study *India Inscribed*, (Delhi, 1995), pp. 229–58. Alexander Dow, a classic example of Orientalist writing, wrote, 'India presents us with a striking picture of the deplorable condition of a people subject to arbitrary sway.... The Emperor is absolute, and sole arbiter in everything and is controlled by no law'. See Alexander Dow's *History of Hindostan*, 2 vols (London, 1770), Preface, pp. xi–xviii. Sir Verney Lovett, an ICS officer, too echoed the same perception for eighteenth century India; see his *A History of the Indian Nationalist Movement* (London, 1920), p. 3. Even W.H. Moreland wrote, 'The Indian governments with which we are concerned were in all cases despotic...apart from religious obligations, the Ruler was untrammelled...'. See Moreland, *From Akbar to Aurangzeb*, (New Delhi, 1923) pp. 233–4.

7. See, for instance, John R. McLane, *Land and Local Kingship in Eighteenth Century Bengal* (Cambridge, 1993), pp. 69–75, where he describes the zamindari processes of revenue collection '...the agents used detentions and beatings simultaneously to discover the veracity of tenant pleas of poverty and to punish them for their delinquency' p. 70.

8. Francois Bernier, *Travels in the Mogul Empire, AD 656–1668* (London, 1934), p. 256.

9. Ibid., p. 226.

10. Francisco Pelsaert, *Jahangir's India, 1626*, trans. W.H. Moreland and P. Geyl, (Cambridge, 1925), p. 60.

11. Ravi Ahuja's 'Labour Relations in an Early Colonial Context: Madras, c.1750–1800', *Modern Asian Studies*, vol. 36, no. 4, 2002, offers ample evidence of such occurrences under Company rule; see p. 808. Also see Ahuja's 'The Origins of Colonial Labour Policy in Late Eighteenth Century Madras', *International Review of Social History*, vol. 44, 1999, pp. 159–95.

12. Tapan Raychaudhuri and Irfan Habib (eds) *The Cambridge Economic History of India*, vol. 1 (Cambridge, 1982), p. 284.

13. Sumit Guha's 'An Indian Penal Regime: Maharashtra in the Eighteenth Century', *Past and Present*, no. 147, 1995, pp. 101–26. Critical to remember, however, is the fact that Guha's discussion focussed on the Peshwa state's dispensation of criminal justice and its treatment of offenders and dissidents. How do we understand relations with common, law-abiding subjects?

14. Sivakumars', 'The Meaning of Social Order in the Tamil Country' in Peter Robb (ed.) *Meanings of Agriculture, Essays in South Asian History and Economics* (Delhi, 1996), p. 354.

15. Some recent studies have unequivocally argued in favour of better conditions for labour during pre-colonial times deteriorating during British times. These include Prasannan Parthasarathi's *The Transition to a Colonial Economy: Weavers, Merchants and Kings in South India, 1720–1800* (Cambridge, 2001);

Sivakumars', 'The Meaning of Social Order in the Tamil Country'; and to a much less degree, Basil A. Saju's 'Labour Relations in an Early Colonial Context Madras, c.1750–1800', *Modern Asian Studies*, vol. 36, no. 4, 2002, pp. 793–826. The latter takes a balanced position, marginally inclined to the indigenist one.

16. See Mridu Rai, *Hindu Kings, Muslim Subjects: Islam, Rights, and the History of Kashmir* (Delhi, 2004).

17. See Christopher Bayly, *Rulers, Townsmen and Bazaars: North Indian Society in the Age of British Expansion, 1770–1870* (Cambridge, 1983); and Sumit Guha's 'Potentates, Traders and Peasants: Western India, c.1700–1870', in Burton Stein and Sanjay Subrahmanyam (eds), *Institutions and Economic Change in South Asia* (Delhi, 1996), pp. 71–84.

18. G.W.F. Hegel, *The Philosophy of History*, trans. J. Sibree, (New York: 1899), p. 144. However, Ronald Inden in *Imagining India* (Oxford, 1990), casts doubts on the role of caste as merely petrifying, and sees it rather as an enabling and empowering structure that helped the formation of coherent communities and brotherhoods that together pushed their demands and interests vis-à-vis others.

19. See the classical works of Max Weber, *The Hindu Social System*, ed. and trans. H.H. Gerth and D. Martindale, (Minneapolis, 1950); and Louis Dumont, *Homo Hierarchicus: The Caste System and its Implications*, trans. Mark Sainsbury (London, 1970).

20. J.C. Heesterman, 'Caste, Village and Indian Society', *The Inner Conflict of Tradition: Essays in Indian Ritual, Kingship and Society* (Chicago, 1985); and Moore's *Social Origins of Dictatorship and Democracy: Lord and Peasant in the Making of the Modern World* (Boston, 1966), p. 340.

21. C. Welch, *Anatomy of a Rebellion* (New York, 1980), p. 56.

22. See Gunnar Myrdal, *Asian Drama: An Inquiry into the Poverty of Nations*, 3 vols (New York, 1968).

23. For the debate around Wallerstein's interpretation, see Sugata Bose (ed.) *South Asia and World Capitalism* (Delhi, 1990), and Sanjay Subrahmanyam, 'World Economies and South Asia, 1600–1750: A Sceptical note', *Review* (Fernand Braudel Center), vol. XII, no. 1, 1989, pp. 141–8.

24. Morris D. Morris, 'Values as an Obstacle to Economic Growth in South Asia: An Historical Survey', *Journal of Economic History*, vol. XXVII, no. 4, 1967.

25 For an explanation of this point, see Morris, 'The Growth of Large Scale Industry', in Dharma Kumar (ed.) *The Cambridge Economic History of India*, vol. I, (Cambridge, 1983).

26. Bayly's, *Rulers, Townsmen, and Bazaars*, p. 174.

27. Inadequate source materials and scholarly indifference have been mutually reinforcing the exclusion of the study of issues pertaining to subordinate groups like artisans.

28. For early works see Richard B. Barnett's *North India Between Empires* (Berkeley, 1980); M.N. Pearson's, *Merchants and Rulers in Gujarat*; or Frank Perlin's, 'Of

White Whale and Countrymen in the Eighteenth Century Maratha Deccan'
Journal of Peasant Studies (1978), pp. 172–237. After Bayly's *Rulers, Townsmen
and Bazaars*, Muzaffar Alam's *The Crisis of it Empire in Mughal North* India (Delhi,
1986) explored political dynamics in Awadh and Punjab; Andre Wink's *Land
and Sovereignty in India* (Cambridge, 1986) focussed on Maratha Deccan; and
Sushil Chaudhary's *From Prosperity to Decline* (New Delhi 1995) examined conditions in Bengal, to cite a few. In his subsequent work Perlin studied the great
'households' of Maratha revenue collectors and the processes by which they
used their positions as village headmen to weave their webs of kinship in the
countryside, thus sustaining the Maratha regional polity; see Perlin, 'Proto-In-
dustrialization and Pre-colonial South Asia', *Past and Present*, no. 89, 1983, pp.
30–95.

29. Bayly, *Rulers, Townsmen and Bazaars*, pp. 5 and 11 respectively.

30. Stanley Tambiah, 'The Galactic Polity in Southeast Asia' in *Culture, Thought
and Social Action: An Anthropological Perspective* (Cambridge, 1985), pp. 252–86.

31. Nicholas Dirks, *The Hollow Crown: Ethnohistory of an Indian Kingdom* (Cambridge, 1987).

32. Ronald Inden, 'Ritual, Authority, and Cyclic Time in Hindu Kingship', in
J.F. Richards (ed.), *Kingship and Authority in South Asia* (Madison-Wisconsin,
1978), pp. 41–91.

33. Norbert Peabody, *Kota Mahajagat*, p. 39.

34. Norbert Peabody emphasizes tensions and disjunctions in political relations; see Peabody, *Hindu Kingship and Polity in Precolonial India* (Cambridge,
2003). His work is substantially influenced by Wink's *Land and Sovereignty in
India: Agrarian Society and Politics under the Eighteenth Century Maratha Svarajya*
(Cambridge, 1986).

35. Farhat Hasan, *State and Locality in Mughal India: Power Relations in Western
India, c. 1572–1730* (Cambridge, 2004).

36. Ibid., p. 30.

37. Before them the nationalists had assumed the voiceless quiescence of the
lower orders by claiming that it was the harmony due to the jajmani or patron–
client relationships that made resistance from below redundant. According to
them, all was well authority resided with the indigenous elite, and that it was
the inception of foreign rule that generated antagonisms and hostility in the
socio-political fabric.

38. Nationalist Marxists appear suspicious about the possibility of independent
action on the part of subalterns, as argued in Mridula Mukherjee's two articles
'Peasant Resistance and Peasant Consciousness in Colonial India: Subalterns
and Beyond', part 1 and 2, *Economic and Political Weekly* (8 and 15 October,
1988), pp. 2109–20 and 2174–86, respectively.

39. See Shail Mayaram, *Against History, Against State: Counterperspectives from the
Margins* (Delhi, 2003).

40. Irfan Habib, *The Agrarian System of Mughal India, 1556–1707* (Bombay, 1963); the essays by R.P. Rana and Muzaffar Alam on agararian revolts in northern India during the late seventeenth and early eighteenth century discuss at length the participation/non-participation of different categories of zamindars and peasants in these revolts; see Rana 'Agrarian Revolts in Northern Indian During the Late 17th and Early 18th Centuries', *Indian Economic and Social History Review (IESHR)* and 'Aspects of Agrarian Uprising in North India in the Early Eighteenth Century', *IESHR*, vol. 17, nos 3 and 4 (1981) pp. 287–326 and Alam in Sabyasachi Bhattacharya and Romila Thapar (eds), *Situating Indian History for Sarvepalli Gopal* (Delhi, 1986), pp. 146–66.

41. Muhnot Nainsi's *Marwar ra Parganan ri Vigat* (ed.) Narain Singh Bhati, (Jodhpur, 1968–9), vol. I, pp. 390–1, and p. 497; and vol. II, p. 10, pp. 85–6, and p. 310. A gazetteer like compendium that enumerates the major castes residing in the different parganas and major qasbas of the Jodhpur kingdom, the *Vigat* includes the first crude census for the region.

42. Yati Shri Manrup's 'Nagaur ki Ghazal' in *Parampara, Rajasthani Ghazal Sangrah*, Jodhpur, 1964, pp. 48–9. I describe this genre in the section on sources.

43. I derive the etymological origin of the term pavan (recipient) from Sitaram Lalas, *Rajasthani Sabad Kosh, Tritiya Khand, Pratham Jild*, p. 2410. Norbert Peabody however, in his essay 'Cents, Sense, Census: Human Inventories in Late Precolonial and Early Colonial India', *Comparative Study in Society and History* (2001), pp. 827–8 translates the term as 'purifying castes', though he does not offer any explanation for his somewhat different rendering of the meaning.

44. Convinced by Margaret R. Somers' argument in 'Deconstructing and Reconstructing Class Formation Theory: Narrativity, Relational Analysis, and Social Theory,' in John R. Hall. (ed.) *Reworking Class* (Cornell, 1997), I move away from conceiving homogenized and unified notions of class interest to notice fragmentations and disunity among artisans.

45. For example, there are numerous instances of khatis in debt who had to mortgage their land or house; at the same time there were others like Khati Nurme who had a *patta* (an ownership certificate that outlined the rights and obligations of the holder) for an entire village. See *Jodhpur Sanad Parwana Bahis (JSPB)* 48, 1853/1796, f. 7A. There were still others who owned vast resources, like Khati Mehmat Ali who had a patta for the two wells of Baisar and Sekhsar in qasba Tausar, and was entitled to collect *malba* and *jhunki* taxes for the same. The state considered taking over the collection of these taxes from the khati, but on the latter's insistence against such a move, the decision went in favour of allowing him to continue collecting the same. *JSPB* 44, 1849/1792, f. 70B; *JSPB*, 183B; *JSPB* 47, 1853/1796, f. 95A.

46. In the midst of all the harsh blandness of the environment, the artisans displayed an imaginative usage of natural resources. For instance, dyers almost invented their colours and from every conceivable natural pigment pollinated their hues: red from terracotta, yellow from cow urine coagulated and boiled, blue from indigo, white from lime, green from terrs verte, and so on. See Col. Thomas Holbein Hendley, 'The Arts and Manufactures of Ajmere-Merwarra', *Journal of Indian Art*, vol. 3, (1890) part 25, pp. 5–8,

47. The length of apprenticeship, the relationship with the master and his family, the process and stages of training, and the final consecration as a master craftsman are all known in the case of eighteenth-century Iran. See Mehdi Keyvani's *Artisans and Guild Life in the Later Safavid Period* (Berlin, 1982), pp. 87–9. But sources from contemporary Marwar do not afford these interesting details.

48. The case of Pinjara Ladu of Didwana, who was not allowed to make pillows with the cotton he carded, and compelled to limit himself to his original occupation of carding alone, seems to suggest this; see *JSPB* 24, 1837/1780, f. 208B.

49. *Hand-Printed Textiles in Rajasthan: A Study*. Documentation and Survey, National Craft Institute for Hand-Printed Textiles, Jaipur 1986), p. 46.

50. See W.H. Moreland, *India at the Death of Akbar* (London, 1920), and its sequel, *From Akbar to Aurangzeb* (London, 1923); Habib's *The Agrarian System of Mughal India*; and Hamida Khatoon Naqvi, *Urban Centres and Industries in Upper India, 1556–1803* (Bombay, 1968). Naqvi's empirical data are mute indices to the prosperity of the Mughal empire; the craftsmen who worked in these industries are glossed over. Also see Stephen P. Blake, *Shahjahanabad: The Sovereign City in Mughal India, 1639–1739* (Cambridge, 1991), pp. 104–12.

51. While artisans mostly remained at the periphery of studies on north Indian economy, in the south, significant artisanal issues got picked up for study, atleast for the weaver community; see, for instance, Vijaya Ramaswamy's *Textiles and Weavers in Medieval South India* (Delhi, 1985). Her discussion of the history of textile manufacture and trade, and of weaving communities of the Coromandel region from the tenth to the seventeenth centuries represents the first attempt to treat this theme in a systematic manner at a regional or supra-regional level. Besides, she has harnessed a great variety of sources, supplementing the usual literary works, travellers' accounts and·Company records with published inscriptions, caste histories, and weaver community journals. Also see S. Arasaratnam, 'Weavers, Merchants, and the Company: The Handloom Industry in South-eastern India, 1750–1790', *IESHR*, vol. 17, no. 3, 1980, pp. 257–78, and Joseph Brennig, 'Textile Producers and Production in Late-seventeenth Century Coromandel', *IESHR*, vol. 23, no. 4, 1986 for contrasting views on the nature of production and marketing. Extremely interesting on related issues is Prasannan Parthasarathi's *The Transition to a Colonial Economy: Weavers, Merchants and Kings in South India, 1720–1800* (Cambridge, 2001). This anomaly can be explained partly by the difference in the nature of sources, the south having seen the establishment of European companies and the expansion of their trading network much before the north. The maintenance of abundant records by these companies detailed transactions of European merchants with their Indian counterparts and local artisans. However, for the north, sources on artisans are few and far between, and the data totally scattered. Consequently, the immense formidability of writing the history of north Indian artisans has perhaps deterred historians from making a serious attempt in this direction.

52. See Irfan Habib, 'Potentialities of Capitalistic Development in the Economy of Mughal India', *Journal of Economic History*, vol. XXIX, no. 1, March 1969;

the work of two Soviet scholars V. Pavlov, *Historical Premises for India's Transition to Capitalism* (Moscow, 1978) and A.I. Tchicherov, *India: Economic Development in the Sixteenth to Eighteenth Centuries, Outline History of Crafts and Trade* (Moscow, 1971) grappled with the same question, as did Tapan Raychaudhuri; see Raychaudhuri, *The Cambridge Economic History of India*, vol. 1 (Cambridge, 1982), chapter on Non-Agricultural Production.

53. Christopher Bayly, *Rulers, Townsmen, and Bazaars;* Meena Bhargava's *State, Society, and Ecology: Gorakhpur in Transition, 1750–1830* (Delhi, 1999) also studies artisans in this context.

54. B.L. Bhadani, *Peasants, Artisans and Entrepreneurs: Economy of Marwar in the Seventeenth Century* (Jaipur, 1999), pp. 360–73.

55. Eugenia Vanina, *Urban Crafts and Craftsmen in Medieval India* (Delhi, 2004).

56. Dilbagh Singh, in his *The State, Landlords, and Peasants: Rajasthan in the 18th Century* (New Delhi, 1990), p. 17, refers to artisans as *riyayatis*, taxed at concessional rates, as opposed to other low-caste cultivators, who paid taxes at the high raiyati rates. G.S.L. Devra, however, seems to disagree; see his *Rajasthan ki Prashasnik Vyavastha, 1574–1818* (Bikaner, 1991). I am aware of only two studies on artisanal struggles during the pre-colonial period: the first is Irfan Habib's 'Forms of Class Struggle in Mughal India: Peasant and Artisan Resistance', in his collection of articles titled *Essays in Indian History: Towards a Marxist Perception* (New Delhi, 1995). The second is Gautam Bhadra's essay entitled 'Two Frontier Uprisings', Ranajit Guha (ed.) *Subaltern Studies*, vol. 2 (Delhi,1983), pp. 43–59. The essay describes two revolts from the Bengal and Assam region, provoked by a major change in the Mughal policy towards particular occupational groups.

57. Gyan Pandey, 'Economic Dislocation in Nineteenth-century Eastern Uttar Pradesh: Some Implications of the Decline of Artisanal Industry in Colonial India', in Peter Robb (ed.) *Rural South Asia: Linkages, Change and Development* (London,1983) notices this neglected aspect of artisanal studies, their organization and consciousness, their periodic if shortlived demonstrations of solidarity, and their resistance and struggles against various developments of the colonial period. However, we have no full-length study, and certainly not for the pre-colonial period, which centres on artisanal concerns instead of treating them as mere units of production in a state-centric perspective.

58. Herbert Aptheker's study on *American Negro Slave Revolts* (New York, 1943) had insisted on violent outbursts as typical of slave resistance. In the early 1970s, revisionist studies of Eugene Genovese and Gerald Mullin provided critical correctives to the rebellious slave myth by stressing a whole range of non-confrontational slave responses as predominant modes of dealing with harsh systems of labour control; see Genovese, *Roll, Jordan, Roll* (New York, 1972) and Mullin's *Flight and Rebellion: Slave Resistance in Eighteenth Century Virginia* (Oxford, 1972). An excellent work along the same lines is Michael Craton's *Testing the Chains: Resistance to Slavery in the British West Indies* (New York, 1982). Jerome Blum's *Lord and Peasant in Russia* (Princeton, 1961) and Rodney Hilton's *Bond Men Made Free* (New York, 1973) corroborated these findings to show that in times of crisis, serfs, like slaves, preferred flight to violent confrontations, which they knew would be futile in the face of brutal repression.

59. A host of studies by Charles Tilly expand on this approach; see his work *From Mobilization to Revolution* (Reading, 1978) for a highly theoretical statement. See also his application to specific French examples in 'Routine Conflicts and Peasant Rebellions in Seventeenth Century France', in Scott Guggenheim and Robert P. Weller (eds), *Power and Protest in the Countryside* (Durham, N.C.,1982) and *The Contentious French* (Illinois, 1988). E.J. Hobsbawm's *Social Bandits and Primitive Rebels* (London, 1959) and *Bandits* (New York, 1969) explained millenarian movements of withdrawal and banditry as a form of rural protest.

60. See James Scott's *Weapons of the Weak* (Connecticut, 1985). For other examples on contemporary South-East Asia, see the contributions by Turton, White, Fegan, and Kerkvliet in Scott and Kerkvliet (eds), *Everyday Forms of Peasant Resistance in South-east Asia* (London, 1986). African examples on many of these patterns may be understood from Allen Isaacman, Stephen Michael, *et al.* 'Cotton is the Mother of Poverty', *International Journal of African Studies*, vol. 13, no. 4, 1980.

61. For historical examples on Asia, see Michael Adas, 'From Avoidance to Confrontation: Peasant Protest in Precolonial and Colonial Southeast Asia', *Comparative Studies in Society and History*, vol. 23, no. 2, 1981; and 'From Foot-dragging to Flight: The Evasive History of Peasant Avoidance Protest in South and Southeast Asia', in Scott and Kerkvliet (eds), *Everyday Forms of Peasant Resistance*, pp. 64–86. For case studies from Africa, see Allen Isaacman, *The Tradition of Resistance in Mozambique* (Berkeley, 1976) and Donald Crummey (ed.) *Banditry, Rebellion and Social Protest in Africa* (London, 1986).

62. One of the reasons for this lies in the paucity of sources for the study of avoidance protest, for, as Sumit Sarkar argues in 'The Conditions and Nature of Subaltern Militancy: Bengal from Swadeshi to Non-cooperation, c.1905–1922', *Subaltern Studies III*, pp. 273–4, 'Subaltern groups normally enter the world of conventional historical sources at moments of explosion, consequently breeding an assumption of total passivity or an opposite stereotype of heroic revolt'. An interesting collection of essays in this regard, though again located in the colonial era, is Douglas Haynes and Gyan Prakash (eds) *Contesting Power: Resistance and Everyday Social Relations in South Asia* (Delhi, 1991).

63. Chitra Joshi, *Lost Worlds: Indian Labour and Its Forgotten Histories* (Delhi, 2003).

64. The only exception to the chronological spread of the *Subaltern Studies* over the colonial and postcolonial era is Gautam Bhadra's article titled 'Two Frontier Uprisings', in Ranajit Guha (ed.) *Subaltern Studies* , vol. 2, (Delhi, 1983), pp. 43–59 that explores protest by subordinate groups in late-Mughal pre-colonial times.

65. Thompson, 'Eighteenth-Century English Society: Class Struggle Without Class?', *Social History*, vol. III, no. 2, 1978, pp. 133–66.

66. Ranajit Guha, *Elementary Aspects of Peasant Insurgency* (Delhi, 1983); Guha's essay 'Domination without Hegemony', *Subaltern Studies VI* (1989); also David Arnold, 'Gramsci and Peasant Subalternity in India', *Journal of Peasant Studies*, vol. 11, no. 4, (1984), pp. 155–77.

67. His readings of Gramsci influenced his pradigm, as defined in his seminal work *Rethinking Working Class History: Bengal 1890–1940* (Delhi, 1989).

68. This significant intervention came in Douglas Haynes and Gyan Prakash (eds) *Contesting Power: Resistance and Everyday Social Relations in South Asia* (Delhi, 1991).

69. Sumit Sarkar, 'The Kalki-Avatar of Bikrampur: A Village Scandal in Early Twentieth Century Bengal', in R.Guha (ed.) *Subaltern Studies VI* (Delhi, 1989), pp. 1–53.

70. Gautam Bhadra, 'The Mentality of Subaternity: *Kantanama* or *Rajdharma*', in R.Guha (ed.), *Subaltern Studies VI*, (Delhi, 1989), pp. 54–91.

71. Rajnarayan Chandavarkar, *The Origins of Industrial Capitalism in India: Business Strategies and Working Classes in Bombay, 1900–1940* (Cambridge, 1994).

72. They did not quite accept James Scott's paradigm of an autonomous consciousness of the subaltern that R. Guha seemed to support.

73. Williams, *Marxism and Literature* (Oxford, 1977), pp. 112–13.

74. See Michael Foucault, *The History of Sexuality* (New York, 1978); and James Scott, *Weapons of the Weak: Everyday Forms of Peasant Resistance* (New Haven, Yale, 1985), respectively.

75. In learning to appreciate some of the complexities involved in probing 'resistance' issues, I have been inspired by the work of Sherry Ortner; see her essay 'Resistance and the Problem of Ethnographic Refusal' in *Comparative Studies in Society and History*, vol. 37, no. 1, 1995, pp. 173–193.

76. See Abu-Lughod's 'The Romance of Resistance: Tracing Transformations of Power through Bedouin Women', *American Anthropologist*, vol. 17, no. 1, pp. 41–55.

77. See Saurabh Dube, *Untouchable Pasts: Religion, Identity and Power among a Central Indian Community* (New York, 1998) on collaboration of subalterns; also Christine Pelzer White 'Everyday Resistance, Socialist Revolution and Rural Development: The Vietnamese Case', *Journal of Peasant Studies*, vol. 13, no. 2, (1986), pp. 49–63.

78. See Rajnarayan Chandavarkar's *The Origins of Industrial Capitalism in India: Business Strategies and Working Classes in Bombay, 1900–1940* (Cambridge, 1994); Joshi's *Lost Worlds: Indian Labour and Its Forgotten Histories* (Delhi, 2003), especially pp. 143–176; and Nandini Gooptu's *The Politics of the Urban Poor in Early Twentieth Century India* (Cambridge, 2001).

79. Bayly, *Rulers, Townsmen and Bazaars*, p. 48.

80. See her study *Caste, Society, and Politics in India from the Eighteenth Century to the Modern Age: The New Cambridge History of India*, vol. 4, no. 3, (Cambridge, 1999).

81. Jan Brouwer, in his *Makers of the World: Caste, Crafts and Mind of South Indian Artisans* (Delhi, 1995) also emphasized the significant, yet historiographically neglected role of artisans; see his introductory chapter.

82. Max Weber 'Politics as a Vocation' in *From Max Weber: Essays in Sociology*, translated and edited by H.H. Gerth and C. Wright Mills (New York, 1946), p. 78

83. For an elaboration of this analysis, though cast in a relatively modern context, see William A. Munro, *The Moral Economy of the State: Conservation, Community Development, and State-Making in Zimbabwe* (Athens, 1998), p. 14.

84. For a detailed discussion on these issues see J. Habermas, *Legitimation Crisis*, tr. T. McCarthy, 1976, part 1.

85. In fact, as discussed later, norms did not *always* define a subsistence ethic; they also determined the repertoire of accepted forms of protest in response to violations of norms and customary practices.

86. Padmaja Sharma, *Maharaja Man Singh of Jodhpur and his Times* (Agra, 1972), pp. 225–6.

87. Though the contexts were different, and the responses of the subalterns too varied as per circumstances, E.P. Thompson, and following him, James Scott saw similar obligations imposed by the poor on their rich patrons. See E.P. Thompson's article 'The Moral Economy of the English Crowd in the Eighteenth Century', *Past and Present*, 50, February 1971, where he discusses this concept and its implications. James C. Scott adapted the concept to discuss the *Moral Economy of the Peasant: Rebellion and Subsistence in Southeast Asia* (New Haven, 1976).

88. See Popkin's *The Rational Peasant: The Political Economy of Rural Society in Vietnam* (Berkeley and Los Angeles, 1979), p. 22.

89. See Sumit Guha, 'Wrongs and Rights in the Maratha Country: Antiquity, Custom and Power in Eighteenth Century India', in M.R. Anderson and Sumit Guha (eds), *Changing Concepts of Rights and Justice in South Asia*, (Delhi, 1998), p. 17 for an elaboration of this idea.

90. See Eric Hobsbawm's *Primitive Rebels* (New York, Norton, 1959) and E.P. Thompson's 'The Moral Economy of the English Crowd in the Eighteenth Century', *Past and Present*, 50, February 1971, for the former and James C. Scott's *The Moral Economy of the Peasant Rebellion* for the latter. Though the contexts were different, and the responses of the plebeians too varied as per circumstances, E.P. Thompson, and following him, James Scott saw similar obligations imposed by the poor on their rich patrons.

91. *JSPB* 9, 1826/1769, f. 70A; *JSPB* 40, 1846/1789, f. 18A.

92. The Jodhpur state extended a small daily allowance, for subsistence, to Darzi Rupo, who had been a *gajdhar* (those carrying out measurements on land etc.) with the state. Though no longer in a position to serve the state due to eye injuries, the ruler felt obliged to shoulder the responsibility of providing for him; see *JSPB* 9, 1826/1769, f. 70A.

93. Marwar had a long and developed tradition of history-writing from the early medieval time from *bat sahitya* or bardic literature to clan histories, genealogies, and historical chronicles called the *pidhiavali, vamsavali,* and *khyat*. These are written predominantly in *Dimgal bhasa* or 'Old Western Rajasthani ' as designated by L.P. Tessitori; see L.P. Tessitori, 'Notes on the Grammar of the Old Western Rajasthani with Special Reference to Apabhramsa and to Gujarati and Marwari', *Indian Antiquary*, (Jan.–Feb., 1914), p. 21; and Sitaram Lalas,

'Rajasthani Bhasa ka Vivechan', *Rajasthani Sabd Kos* (Jodhpur, vol. 1, 1962), pp. 1–10. Also see N.S. Bhati (ed.) *Parampara*, part 11, 1961, pp. 9–13, part 12, 1961, and part 15–16, 1963, (Jodhpur) for a discussion of these and other forms of Rajasthani literature. This genre of history was preserved and transmitted in Rajasthan by charan, bhat, rao, motisar, and other specialist bardic castes; see Motilal Menariya, *Rajasthani Bhasa aur Sahitya* (Prayaga, vs 2017), pp. 31–40, for an introductory discussion on these castes.

94. Bardic literature has no insights to offer on the artisans since its basic concern was with celebrating the 'mighty'. Tod described this work as involving a 'barter of solid pudding against empty praise'; see Tod, vol. 2, p. 30. Tessitori too remarked 'there is probably no bardic literature in any part of the world, in which truth is so marked by fiction, or disfigured by hyperbole, as in the bardic literature of Rajputana'; see L.P. Tessitori, 'Progress Report from the Work Done during the Year 1916 in Connection with the Bardic and Historical Survey of Rajputana', *Journal of Asiatic Society of Bengal*, N.S.13, (1917), pp. 195–252, These views discount the value of bardic literature excessively and fail to recognize its importance in comprehending the political ethos of the age.

95. Compiled by Muhnot Nainsi, the diwan in Maharaja Jaswant Singh's reign, (AD1638–78), the author enjoyed considerable access to revenue and other records of the seventeenth century Jodhpur state, and, as such, the details furnished by him on the political economy of the region constitute a fairly reliable source.

96. Since those who wrote them were constantly travelling, words of different languages, including contemporary Urdu, Persian, and Khari boli freely and uninhibitedly found their way in these poems, and often led people to misunderstand them to be part of the Hindi poetry-literature tradition. But in fact Rajasthani is at the root of these poems.

97. Such letters of invitation were called *Vijnaptipatras*, the work *Ancient Vijnaptipatras* having collated several of these; see for instance, the letter dated 1791 (p. 48) to Sripujya Vijayajinendra, who was staying at Dabohi in Gujarat, and the one sent, again from Jodhpur, in 1835 to Vijayadevsuri residing at Surat. Also see the *Aitihasik Rukke Parwane*, published in *Parampara*, nos 39–40, which includes a letter sent by Maharaja Ajit Singh in the first quarter of the eighteenth century inviting the Jain muni Hir Chandra Suri to the city of Sojhat.

98. The credit for pioneering the collation and publication of some of these ghazals goes to Muni Kantisagar, whose efforts brought out the *Shri Nagar Varhnatmak Hindi-Padya Sangrah* a little before the mid-twentieth century. I have used another recent publication titled *Rajasthani Ghazal Sangrah* edited by Vikram Singh Rathor.

99. Composed in 'Old Western Rajasthani' or 'medieval Marwari' language and written in the Devanagari script, the *JSPB* have been systematically arranged chronologically, 102 volumes covering vs 1821–1995 Jodhpur Records at Rajasthan State Archives of Bikaner (RSAB). Records have been arranged pargana-wise, with documented provenance starting from the Vikram Samvat

month of *Chait Sudi* 1 upto *Falgun*, and ending on Chait Badi 15. Each folio is numbered, the sides conventionally identified as 'A' and 'B', and bears the name of the pargana and the name of the kachedi, chauntara or sayar at which the dispute was registered. I have used the first 60 bahis covering the period upto 1818 when contact with the British government and their intervention in the affairs of Jodhpur began.

100. For a detailed contextualization of petitions as sources, see Andreas Wurgler's 'Voices from Among the "Silent Masses": Humble Petitions and Social Conflicts in Early Modern Central Europe', *International Review of Social History*, vol. 46, 2001, Supplement, pp. 11–34. Also see Wayne te Brake, *Shaping History: Ordinary People in European Politics, 1500–1700* (Berkeley, CA 1998).

101. See her work *Fiction in the Archives: Pardon Tales and their Tellers in Sixteenth Century France* (Stanford, California, 1987), pp. 1–7, especially p. 3.

102. See Said's *Orientalism* (New York, 1979); James Clifford's, 'Introduction: Partial Truths', in Clifford and George Marcus (eds) *Writing Culture: The Poetics and Politics of Ethnography* (Berkeley, 1986); and Spivak's 'Can the Subaltern Speak?' in C. Nelson and L. Grossberg (eds) *Marxism and the Interpretation of Cultures* (Urbana, 1988), pp. 271–316, respectively.

103. In her subsequent study Spivak clarifies that she had not intended to refute the existence of subaltern agency but only alluded to the immense difficulties in accurately uncovering the same; see her essay 'History' in her work *A Critique of Postcolonial Reason: Toward A History of Vanishing Present* (Cambridge, 1999), pp. 198–311. One can hardly quarrel with her point that often they speak but do not get heard.

104. Ortner, 'Resistance and the Problem of Ethnographic Refusal', p. 190.

105. Mayaram, *Against History*, p. 86.

106. Some disputes persisted over long periods, and repeatedly came back to the state for resolution. For instance, the mochis' demand for closer access to deities in temples had to be referred to previous orders in this regard; see *JSPB* 34, 1843/1786, f. 140B and *JSPB* 39, 1845/1788, f. 169B. Many other examples abound in the records.

107. M. Galanter, in his article 'Justice in Many Rooms: Courts, Private Ordering, and Indigenous Law', *Journal of Legal Pluralism*, 19, (1981), pp. 1–47 discusses at length the manner in which the 'long shadow of law' operated on the ground, and unreported judicial conflicts tended to get resolved privately along the lines prescribed by the authorities.

108. See the 'Preface to the Italian Edition' of Carlo Ginzburg's *The Cheese and the Worms: The Cosmos of a Sixteenth Century Miller*, trans. by John and Anne Tedeschi (London, first published in 1980), for an elaboration of this point.

109. See Saurabh Dube, *Untouchable Pasts: Religion, Identity and Power among a Central Indian Community* (Albany, 1998); Ajay Skaria, *Hybrid Histories: Forests, Frontiers and Wild:ness in Western India* (Delhi, 1999) and Shail Mayaram's *Against History, Against State: Counterperspectives from the Margins* (Delhi, 2004).

110. For more on this, see Mayaram, *Against History*, p. 13

111. Ibid, p. 8.

112. The folk tales have been collected by Padmashri Komal Kothari and Sahitya Akademi award winner Vijay Dan Detha during the course of their fieldwork in villages around the city of Jodhpur. These folk tales have been published in a thirteen-volume set titled *Batan ri Phulwari*, authored by Detha and edited by Kothari. Proverbs have been listed and annotated through a joint collaboration of Detha and Bhagirath Kanorhiya in a monumental effort of several volumes, titled the *Rajasthani Hindi Kahavat Kosh*. Another work of the same nature by Kanorhiya and Govind Aggarwal, *Rajasthani Kahavat Kosh* (Jaipur, 1995) has also been consulted.

113. See Suleyman Demirci, 'Complaints about *Avariz* Assessment and Payment in the *Avariz*-Tax System: An Aspect of the Relationship between Centre and Periphery. A Case Study of Kayseri, 1618–1700', *Journal of the Economic and Social History of the Orient*, vol. 46, no. 4, 2003, pp. 437–74.

114. Demirci, p. 473.

2

The Rathors and the Marwar *Desh*

Marudhar desh hai motak, Annadhan ka ju nahin totak;
Marudhar is a vast expanse, where there is no dearth of food and wealth;

Jismen seher kete jor, Nipat hi adhik hai Nagaur,
It can boast of many mighty cities, though Nagaur is by far the best of them;

Mahipati Mansingh Maharaj, Sabahi bhup ka sirtaj;
Mansingh, the ruler, is the crown jewel among all other kings of the region;

Khagbal prabal ariyarhn khes, Dand hi bhare das hi des.[1]
The strength of his sword can destroy all enemies, several countries having
paid for their indiscretions!

A Jain yati Shri Manrup wrote the above verse in 1805 in his *Nagaur ki
Ghazal*, highlighting the material wealth, opulence, and accomplishments
of the Marwar state in the eighteenth century. The ghazal celebrates the
state as one that could boast of a vibrant political economy, generating
a plenitude of resources. Other travellers to the region too, even when
writing centuries apart, commended the area's thriving trade and commerce. Hsieun Tsang, a Chinese traveller who crossed the Thar desert
of Marwar in the seventh century, noticed the prosperity of the area[2]
and Col. Tod, who described late eighteenth-century Marwar, wrote eloquently about the buoyant urban centres of the kingdom.[3] Heber, another English contemporary of Tod, commented on the fertile soil, the
excellent state of cultivation, the fine cotton, and the maharaja's magnificent castle in Jodhpur, which was 'as large as Windsor', and 'in many
respects fully equal to its riva!'.[4]

As noted in Chapter 1, however, the region has been traditionally styled as Marubhumi, Marusthal, etc., and the earliest gazetteer on Marwar too emphasized the high mortality rate of the region. It bemoaned the abysmally miserable conditions of the people here and painted an obverse picture that justifies the epithet of 'Land of Death' attached to this region.[5] This image finds corroboration in the creation myth of this region, described in the twenty-second *sarg* of the Yudh Kand of Valmiki's Ramayana. The story runs that when Maharaja Ramchandra embarked upon a mission of devastating Lanka to rescue Sita, he needed to cross the ocean. Infuriated that the sea god refused to make way for him, he prepared to fire a special arrow that would cause the ocean to dry up. Realizing his folly, the sea god came and apologized and Ram's temper cooled down. Since the arrow, however, was already in motion, its direction was changed to point to the north, towards the ocean called Dumkulya. The ocean where the arrow fell dried up and, according to the epic, left behind a barren desert. The Ramkund in the neighbourhood of Jaisalmer is believed to be the spot, the *wran-kup* where the arrow fell, and the entire region is supposed to have transformed into an arid desert from that time.[6] Thus, folk memory of the great tradition, as well as modern archaeological findings ascribed to Marwar an ocean-turned-desert landscape.[7]

Two fundamental questions arise from these contrasting descriptions of eighteenth-century Marwar, used here to paint the conditions in which Marwari artisans lived and worked: First, the eighteenth century had traditionally been projected as the proverbial 'Dark Age', its hallmarks being political chaos and economic decline. Then how did this century of darkness, distress, and doom support a vibrant political economy and flourishing markets as described in the Jain yatis's ghazal? Recent regional studies, especially those on Awadh, Punjab, Doab, Maharashtra, Hyderabad, and Bengal, have taken 'revisionist' positions that suggest regional growth, and explore the crystallization of political power around new groups. What was the nature of political transformation occurring in Marwar, and precisely which way did the historical trajectory of the Jodhpur desh move during the century of its transition from a Mughal watan jagir to an autonomous kingdom? Shifting the spotlight from the Mughal centre to that of the Marwari experience, the focus is on regional reconfigurations, alignments, and politico-economic imperatives that governed Marwari statecraft during the eighteenth century.

Second, how do we reconcile these diametrically opposite assessments of the region, one that emphasizes Marwar as a vibrant political economy, and the other that conjures an image of harsh environmental conditions? Is it possible to think in terms of a uniform profile for the province, a stretch of about thirty thousand square miles that together constituted the province? Was it actually possible for the state to support the roughly two million people whose home Marwar was, or was life a struggle for survival for a large majority of them?[8] Most fundamentally, if the economy was indeed buoyant as depicted in the ghazal, were the benefits of this vibrant economy available to all the segments of society?

THE DESH AND THE RAJA

The Marwar region was originally inhabited by tribes, particularly the Mers, Bhils, and Minas, with the dominant position in society enjoyed by the Parihar, Gohel, Chauhan, and Parmar clans of rajputs.[9] The Rathor rajputs migrated to this area from Kanauj in the thirteenth century, conquered the local inhabitants, and planted their banner at Mandor. Under Rao Jodha, they shifted their capital to the strategically stronger location of Jodhpur in the mid-fifteenth century.[10] In the early phase of extension of Rathor rule, all the territories conquered by the Rathor raja were parcelled out among his *sardars*, the leaders of sub-clans (*khamps*), and their offshoots, as per the system of coparcenership (*bhai-bandh*) (Fig. 2.1). This made for a fairly decentralized political structure since land was divided among the sardars of the ruling clan and their right was hereditary.[11] In these large estates held by hereditary heads of branch sects, the sardars enjoyed considerable authority, and exercised a vast degree of jurisdiction, subject to the obligation of military service to the raja.[12] Though the raja was the chief of the clan, the

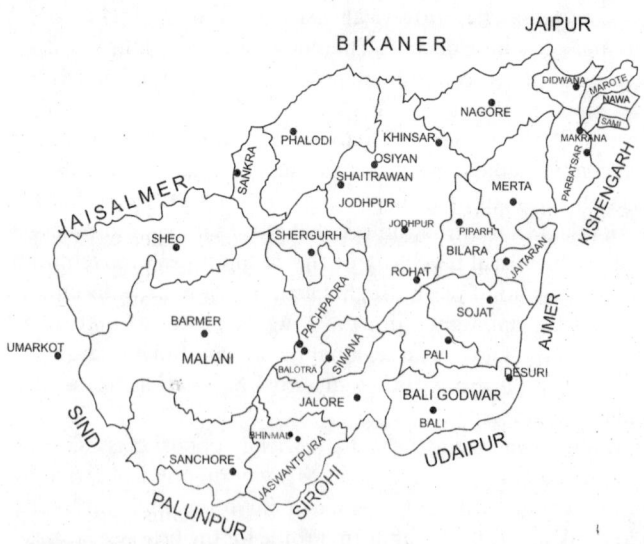

Not to Scale

Fig. 2.1. Parganas and Some Important Thikanas in Eighteenth-century Marwar
Courtesy: Author

semi-autonomous position of the sardars in terms of power and resources rendered him no more than a primus interpares. Despite being morally obliged to support the king, the sardars often assumed and asserted independence whenever there was a crisis in the court.[13]

As a result, when Rao Maldeo (1531–62) ascended the throne, he could assert his claim over only two parganas—Jodhpur and Sojhat. Finding his position vis-à-vis other powerful sardars far from enviable, he discarded the concept of bhai-bandh in an attempt to stabilize his precarious hold over the throne (*gaddi*). Instead, he pushed forward the alternative concept of *bhai-bandh-chakar* that implied the subordination of the Rathor clan leaders to the ruler. The sardars were handed letters of service (*chakari ke patte*), whereby the grant of land to these clan leaders became a royal prerogative rather than a hereditary right enjoyed by them.[14] In pursuance of his objective Maldeo began to dislodge those leaders who were reluctant to yield. These political reforms led to stiff resistance from those adversely affected.[15]

In the third quarter of the sixteenth century, the Mughals annexed Marwar and constituted it into the Jodhpur circle (*sarkar*) in Suba Ajmer.[16] They enrolled the Rathor sardars as imperial *mansabdar*s, and in an effort to forge a special alliance with these powerful rajput potentates, extended a special concession to them by improvising the mechanism of watan jagir for the self-administration of their hereditary ancestral domains. As long as the Rathor vassals served loyally, implemented imperial regulations in matters of military organization and land-revenue administration, and circulated imperial currency in their realm instead of minting their own, they were allowed self-governance over their patrimonial homelands. The rajput rulers thus continued to enjoy considerable autonomy in their ancestral homes.

Paradoxically, it was annexation by the Mughals and protection and patronage from them that helped the Rathors strengthen their position over the kingdom, especially vis-à-vis rival contenders for power. It was only then that the politico-administrative organization of the state of Marwar was successful in negotiating a transition from a decentralized to a relatively centralized one. The chakari ke patte were successfully extended, and relations of subordination enforced on much the same pattern as the Mughal jagirdari system. The alliance between the Mughals and their junior partners worked with amazing success because the ideological principles governing rajput society were not only honoured but fully supported and consolidated by the Mughals.[17] This vassalage brought the Jodhpur Rathors several advantages vis-à-vis rival clan leaders, both non-Rathor as well as collateral Rathor lineages. Imperial recognition strengthened the legitimacy of the raja against his nobles, and the vast resources put at his disposal by the Mughal masters enhanced his status. With the backing of the mighty Mughals, the threat of internal revolts diminished, and refractory nobles succumbed before a superior force. The ability of successive Rathor rajas to regulate both access to land in their dominions and deployment of military forces contributed significantly to the growth in the stature of these regional rulers. It enabled a degree of centralization within their dominions that had been a long-standing ambition. As a result, the state of Marwar gradually made the transition from a loose confederation of Rathor sardars, presided over by the Rathor raja, to a cohesive entity and an imperial formation in its own right, the centre of political gravity in Rajputana. With the relationship between the ruler and the clan leaders redefined, the concept of monarchical absolutism that was a characteristic feature of Mughal imperial authority now infiltrated rajput notions of kingship, making for a stricter subordination of the clan leaders to Rathor monarchical authority.

After Marwar was subsumed in Suba Ajmer, important tenets of governance were transposed from the Mughal centre to Marwar, and different aspects of Marwari administration came to be impressed by Mughal traditions over time. Even so, the *marwariyat* of the region, a self-identification that withstood Mughal incorporation, persisted as a continuing facet of the Jodhpur state. This Marwari identity asserted itself in the last decades of the seventeenth century when the Mughal emperor Aurangzeb estranged the Rathors by intervening in what they considered their internal watan matters. From this point, the relationship between the region and the empire altered fundamentally, and during the eighteenth century, even before imperial decline became apparent, Marwar's links with the imperial masters became strained. Increased political instability at the core of the imperial centre encouraged the Rathors to further distance themselves from the imperial hold.[18] In negotiating this path of growing selfhood, however, it became necessary for the local rulers of Marwar to consolidate their autonomous hold over their watan, and develop as well as widen the scope of their own administrative policies. As the Mughal state began to stagger on its last legs by the latter half of the century, the regional kingdom of Jodhpur was negotiating with myriad forces to emerge as an independent entity with its distinct identity. Though still paying formal allegiance to the Mughals, Marwar had in fact become substantially autonomous during the course of the eighteenth century.[19]

The territorial limits of Marwar altered repeatedly according to the changing fortunes of its kings, sometimes due to Mughal dictates, at others due to attacks by neighbouring kingdoms, and later due to Maratha interventions. The border parganas of Pokharan, Phalodi, Nagaur, and Merta in particular, changed hands frequently.[20] Apart from the disputed territories of twenty-two villages on the Ajmer–Merwara (so-called after the region passed under British dominance) border and that of Umarkot in Sind, which repeatedly came in and went out of the Rathor grip during the chequered vicissitudes of the eighteenth century, the chieftaincy roughly occupied about thirty-five thousand square miles. Of this, only about fifteen per cent of the area was directly under the crown (*khalisa*), while the remaining was under the control of Rathor kinsmen, prebendal chiefs, and local feudal jagirdars in the eighteenth century.[21]

KINGSHIP IN THE EIGHTEENTH-CENTURY CONTEXT

The collapse of the Mughal umbrella facilitated the Marathas to gain leverage in the power politics of Marwar. Their rapid advances under the Holkars and the Scindias towards the north, and the incursions they were making into Rathor territory, ushered in the era of Mughal control and supervision being replaced by that of the Scindias. The reigns of Abhay Singh (1724–49) saw early Maratha forays into the Marwari countryside, extracting movable wealth from villages and retreating quickly due to superior mobility. Soon they were able to co-ordinate larger raids that financed payments to their largely mercenary troops, and the opening of negotiations with some large zamindars succeeded in establishing safe bases for Maratha commanders.[22] Gradually, the Marathas began to attack garrisoned forts and towns, and cut off communications, with an adverse impact on the trade of the affected regions.

By the time Vijai Singh ascended the throne in 1752, control of the Mughal authority over the rulers of different kingdoms such as that of Jodhpur had been diluted to such an extent that other than maintaining the symbols of empire for legitimacy, contacts had practically been snapped. Five years of Scindia depredations from 1752–6 brought the economy of Jodhpur to a ruinous state. The treasury was depleted and the crownlands uncultivated. The peasantry dispersed, commerce diminished owing to the pillage at the behest of Pindari troops in the employ of Marathas, and generally insecure conditions prevailed.[23] The instability in the Rathor territories during the long Maratha campaign had divided the Marwar region into two parts, the eastern fertile one in the hands of Ram Singh, and the capital and arid desert parts of western Marwar under Vijai Singh. Under increasing Maratha pressure, Vijai Singh bought peace in 1756 and agreed to cede Ajmer to them. Besides, he had to surrender huge sums of money as war indemnity and agree to pay tributes.[24] The Jodhpur chieftaincy was thus reduced to the staus of a tribute-paying vassal of the *Dakhaniya*s, the local term used by the Marwaris for the Marathas. The latter placed their representatives at the courts of Jodhpur and other lineage centres to protect Maratha interests in the region. Maratha defeat in the battle of Panipat against Ahmad Shah Abdali provided temporary relief to Vijai Singh and helped him capture the entire kingdom by annihilating Ram Singh. Thereafter, he began to put his house in order, consolidate his position, and strengthen his army. Demands from the Marathas remained a constant irritant, however, and the resultant financial burden caused a heavy pressure on the empty exchequer of Jodhpur.[25] Payments to the Marathas often fell into arrears, and became the pretext for further Maratha inroads into Jodhpur territories.

Need for cash rose astronomically due to wider changes as well, particularly in the field of military technology and organization. Faced with European use of firearms, eighteenth-century patrimonial regimes, especially those in the east and the south of the Subcontinent, moved towards the inclusion of artillery formations in their defense structures. Jodhpur was slower to respond to this challenge, but the need for investments towards the recruitment of standing armies manned by mercenary soldiers, preferably adept in the use of firearms, was certainly felt—as was the requirement to import large numbers of war-horses. All these entailed a critical dependence on a considerably larger supply of cash, and military fiscalism made the regularity of revenue collections an even more pressing necessity.[26]

Despite these pressures, classical cultural prescriptions on royal obligations (rajdharma), believed to be the foundation of relations between the ruler and the ruled in 'traditional' India, could not be given short shrift. Descent from an eminent lineage, a commanding personal presence, competence at courtly etiquette, and bravery in the battlefield, were important indices that determined the legitimacy of royalty, though one requisite that stands out as being basic was that the king be a defender of his people, capable of preserving internal order, and preventing external aggression. From the ancient *Dharmasastra*[27], the *Arthasastra*[28], the *Manusmriti*,[29] to the eighteenth-century *Ajnapatra*[30], classical texts on kingship displayed a striking continuity with regard to the duties and obligations advised for a righteous ruler. Differences in emphasis may be discerned, but the king's right to govern the realm was invariably predicated on his protection of the subjects (*praja*).

The people, in turn, had to obey him, pay taxes, and perform labour, defined in some treatises as the king's salary or *vetana*. Protection of the subjects also meant attempts to improve their economic well-being and, in fact, most treatises on rajdharma and statecraft (*rajniti*) emphasized the upliftment of the people as fundamental to the enrichment of the treasury, for the two were intimately linked and fundamental to each other.[31] The relationship thus projected comes across as some kind of loosely-defined contract, treaty or accord, evocative of Rousseau's concept of a 'Social Contract'.

In the Kali age in particular, marked as it was by fatal diseases, hunger and fear, and the dread of drought and revolution, the highest virtue for the king was gift-giving and charity.[32] Several texts emphasized munificence as a religious duty of rulers, especially in times of crises. Though chronicles that cite these obligations on the part of kings and notables may be panegyric works or legends built around the generosity of the politically powerful, the significance of these sources lies in pointing to the expectations from 'good rulers' and the attributes of just and benevolent kings.[33] The rulers' role as a magnanimous donor, bestowing alms upon religious mendicants, supporting eleemosynary for religious establishments, feeding the subjects when crop failures occurred, extending *taccavi* advances to finance cultivation and construction of wells, sponsoring the construction of water reservoirs, and rescuing dependents through relief and rehabilitation, finds mention in numerous early modern textual narratives.

In this ethico-political terrain of state building, the 'Great Tradition' and the 'Little Tradition' converged, in some sense, around the ideological principles defining rulership that bound the king and his people to certain normative standards.[34] At least in rhetoric if not in reality, reciprocity vis-à-vis each other was acknowledged, a proverb popular in the Jodhpur region confirms this by claiming: *Raja rau daan are paraja rau samman*, that is 'It is befitting for a king to be generous with charity and the subjects to be deferential towards him'.[35] Even if derived from classical religious texts, this equation remained the guiding light for kings and subjects in early modern times as well, though how far rulers adhered to these principles varied from case to case. Whether of Hindu or Muslim faiths, patronage and charity were incumbent upon persons with means, considered 'duties' integral to the concept of rajdharma, irrespective of the religion of the recipient/dependent.[36]

The eighteenth century saw states struggling to survive and ambitious individuals struggling to rule. Even in this milieu, however, kingship remained the universal and appropriate form of government. The legitimacy of kingship interestingly emerges as one of the most pervasive threads in Indian classical literature that maintained that a society without a king (*a-rajaka*) was not viable for it would imply 'the logic of the fish' (i.e., the law of the jungle).[37] A fixed set of expectations about kingship amidst the political instability of the eighteenth century, meant that a 'fit' between the office of the king and the actual ruler was critical to his popular acceptance as legitimate. And this legitimacy was never decided once and for all—rather, repeated judgments of 'fit' between king and office and repeated decisions to give or withhold loyalty necessitated ceaseless exertions on the part of kings.[38]

Kingly power could, therefore, not be exercised through military might and coercive strength alone. Instead, a variety of subtle strategies to discipline and control, combining appeasement of the people—especially the productive assets of the state—needed to be employed for the purpose, and this was done through multiple initiatives. That Vijai Singh actively opted for the devotional (*bhakti*) tradition of worship that emphasized egalitarian values and had a positive appreciation of a householder's concerns, perhaps had something to do with his anxiety for legitimating his kingship in the perception of the widest possible numbers of his subjects. As opposed to adopting Brahmanical Hinduism that was associated with caste hierarchy and a belief in liberation from the cycle of rebirths (*moksa*) through renunciation (*sanyas*), adherence to bhakti forms of worship were perhaps geared to a larger agenda that was not merely religious in nature. The maharaja became a devotee of the Vaishnava sect and extended lavish patronage to the Vallabh *sampradaya* that believed in the worship of Krishna. More than simply representing Krishna, notes Peabody, 'Vallabha idols were believed to contain the deity's immanent presence and to possess (and emanate) his mystical powers'.[39] Rather than worshipping images of Krishna in dalliance with his beloved Radha, the Vallabha sect that Vijai Singh chose to adopt and popularize belief in the maternal or familial love that Krishna's foster-mother Yashoda felt for her 'divine charge when he was an infant'. Was Vijai Singh suggesting the replication of the mother–child bond between himself and his subjects, or perhaps that if people would worship him as they did Lord Krishna, he too had the divine power to shower benedictions on them? One can only conjecture on these issues, and suspect that he attempted the accumulation of 'symbolic capital', to quote Pierre Bourdieu, by binding the supernatural powers of Krishna's deity to the service of his rule, and thereby buttressing the legitimacy of his kingly authority.[40] The sect's distinctive non-ascetic position, the musical and congregational styles of worship, offerings of food, and the observation of daily routines of the Lord that closely resembled those of the domestic lives of ordinary people, helped the development of intimacy between the disciples and their Lord. The deities were renowned for satisfying various pleas of their devotees, which further aided the process of bonding between the ruler and his subjects.

His active patronage and grants of land to the sect helped Vijai Singh earn personal merit, and the propitious effect of lavish benefactions, it was hoped, would protect dynastic stability. Devotees from all over the kingdom congregated at Jodhpur for special occasions, and festivals such as the *Annakut* and the *Mahotsav* witnessed the distribution of lavish gifts by the state. Under the influence of this sect, Vijai Singh banned cow slaughter, the consumption of meat and alcohol, and instead ordered those engaged in the professions of slaughtering animals and brewing liquor to take up masonry and construction work. Royal and sectarian authority was thus sought to be linked to restore the political fortunes of the regime. Nobles and rich merchants became enthusiastic devotees, particularly drawn to this sampradaya, and many of them sponsored the costly rituals (*seva*) of the deity. The sect remained limited, however, to those with substantial resources, for its elaborate rituals entailed huge expenditure, and could not attract the common masses in substantial numbers.[41] Even so, by closely identifying polity with religion, Vijai Singh achieved greater alignment between his interests and those of Jodhpur's wealthy mercantile community, forging a king-merchant alliance through which income from religion-driven trade sustained and strengthened royal power. With the Mughal decline, its ability to bolster tributary rulers and their regimes diminished too, and in this scenario, access to greater amounts of merchant capital to finance professional standing armies became profitable.

Several other initiatives had also to be undertaken to meet the problem of an acute resource crunch. The first of these was the recruitment of merchants and financiers at the top levels of the bureaucracy, both for getting their financial support for the Crown, and also for counterpoising the rival factions of the nobility. This was also significant because it gave them a stake in the preservation of the state. It did not necessarily mean a decline in the power of the state, but an increase in the number of its participants and investors.[42] The dominance of the bhandari or oswal mahajans in the administration seems pervasive from the second quarter of the century. The latter gradually found their way to the top echelons of state administration.[43] Huge sums of money were taken as tokens from those who aspired to senior posts in the administration, and big financiers invariably bought the office of finance minister (*diwan*), minister in-charge of military affairs, (*fauj bakshi*), pay-master for non-army officials (*pyad bakshi*), etc.

Singhvi Bhimraj was bakshi under Vijai Singh, and Singhvi Vanraj under Maharaja Bhim Singh.[44] Singhvi Daulat Ram, Thanavi Shimbhudan, and Bhaya Shivdan worked as pyad bakshis under Vijai Singh.[45] During the latter's reign, Fatehchand Singhvi, Surat Ram Muhnot, Shobharam Bhandari, Khubchand Singhvi, and many other mahajans had emerged as alternate foci of power in addition to the rajput hereditary aristocrats. The purchasers of these top bureaucratic positions willingly paid money to get power, prestige, and pelf, and these developments ensured the emergence of new social groups.[46] Clearly, the bhandari, singhvi, and muhnot sub-castes of the mahajans had gained unprecedented power in eighteenth-century Jodhpur state and society.[47]

This dependence on financiers often translated into loans that the maharajas negotiated with the wealthy mahajans and bohras.[48] At critical moments, financial shortfalls were often covered by *peshkash* forcefully extracted from the local *sahukars*, merchant bankers, or the small feudal magnates magnets (*thikanedars*).[49] For instance, the financial pressures faced by Vijai Singh in the early years of his reign, especially during the initial phase of the Maratha inroads, prompted him to extract from Bhandari Daulatram, Suratram, Himmatram, Jodhmal, and Sawantmal a sum of two lakh rupees.[50] New taxes had also to be imposed to increase revenue collections.[51] The creation of revenue bureaucracies with scribes, records, standardized measures and accounts, and the serious attention paid to currency and money management—including minting operations—were undertaken in response to these new challenges, and are an indication of the fiscality of the royal polity.[52] Important scribes during the reign of Vijai Singh were again mostly from the merchant class, with a few brahmins and charans as well.[53] This new class of senior officers, locally called mutsaddis, controlled important positions due to their wealth and the possession of necessary skills. The emergence of these new social groups and their straining to elbow out the older foci of power based on kinship and military prowess generated new tensions and contradictions in an already difficult situation of poor resources.[54]

Intense battles among different groups for political domination and economic resources were pervasive, and so were the rulers' needs to secure and maintain political and material stability. In the absence of adequate capacity for surveillance, and institutions for monitoring and containing popular contention, investments towards appeasement and accommodation of a large cross-section of society became enormously important.

INFORMATION ORDER

To reiterate, the unstable environment of the century once Mughal imperial authority had weakened, and their protection was no longer available to the Marwar rulers, implied that military threats from within and without had to be faced by them through their own internal resources. Rathor rulers now often found their hold over the gaddi fragile and precarious since Mughal imperial sanction or recognition of a specific contender for the throne was earlier a strong stamp of legitimacy. Loss of Mughal endorsement of Rathor incumbents to the throne led to perennial internal feuds between rival claimants.[55] Through the century, internal strife, Maratha pressures, and their combined repercussions had exposed them to stresses. An already hard-pressed local economy was now tottering, and with Vijai Singh's authority over his realm having become tenuous, frequent succession rifts encouraged subordinate rajput lineages to get restive.[56] Leading nobles such as the thakurs of Pokharan, Aua, Nimaj, Rian, Asop, Kuchaman, Ras, Khairwa, Bhadrajun, and Raipur, and the heads of the Champawats, Udawats, Mertia, Kumpawats, Karnot, and Karamsot clans had always wielded considerable power by virtue of their claiming coparcenership with the Rathor ruling dynasty.[57] With their land holdings becoming practically hereditary again, these local aristocrats regained their earlier power in Marwar.[58] Independence from Mughal suzerainty could paradoxically not result in enhancement of authority for the rulers and they had to again contend with internal dissentions that had diminished during the previous century of Mughal patronage.

Pressures such as these caused a tremendous hunger for both material and manpower resources. The acutely adverse ecological conditions meant that physical resources were inflexible, and not much wealth could be generated by more efficient exploitation. In a pre-machine age, human labour was crucial to production, but nature repeatedly depleted the human resource. Efforts therefore needed to be concentrated towards developing and harnessing skilled manpower effectively. The Rathors appear to have fully appreciated the need to invest in their productive forces in particular, those in possession of special skills so that they remained within, rather than abandon the harsh environs of Marwar. In this intense competition for assets among the newly emergent successor regimes, the Rathors did not merely need to provide for lucre and labour, but in fact compete with others for this. The Rathor elite came to grips with these myriad problems by evolving a range of strategies to gradually infiltrate deeper into their realm, devising newer techniques to tackle their exacerbated pressures.

But the forms of appeasement and pacification could be decided only when the rulers had a certain pre-knowledge about the needs, problems, behavioural patterns, and the general mindset of different groups that mattered to the state. Intelligence gathering and surveillance therefore became a vital dimension of kingship in this century, for strategies of propitiation and governance could be formulated only if the rulers 'knew' the realm, the people they had conquered and wished to rule. While commanding men and money, the Rathors had to assemble stores of information,[59] for political allegiance could be monitored and control over resources tightened if the state could secure practical information about the peasants, artisans, and merchants. These customs enhanced the importance of what Christopher Bayly termed, though in a different context, an 'Information Order'. Intelligence gathering, political reporting, and written documentation became imperative in these conditions. This was true for not just Marwar but other regional states as well, for it was well recognized that the exercise of power was not just a matter of assembling tangible resources.

In the eighteenth and nineteenth centuries, therefore, the Jodhpur maharajas began to expand the scope of their archives, encouraging the documentation of the smallest episodes in the lives of their people. Their diwans were instructed to record grievances brought in by the people, and asked to provide immediate redressal. State *kasid*s or news-runners regularly fed the centre and pargana headquarters with intelligence to keep the rulers informed. Collation of records in an organized manner, such as in the *Sanad Parwana Bahi*, was advocated and endorsed by the Rathor rulers, and actively taken up towards the mid-century. The Rathors were clearly engaged in assembling centralized knowledge about the subjects through their espionage system and news-runners, and documenting people's petitions helped them comprehend popular 'voices'. Indeed, the fact that their intelligence system was dependent on the collaboration of local elites to keep runners running and newsletters flowing limited the success of their surveillance. Meagre resources meant that they could not communicate with their subjects easily, and entertaining petitions was one of the few mechanisms for the purpose. The effectiveness of their project is of course debatable, but that 'knowing' and monitoring the populace was part of the royal agenda of 'dominating and mastering' does not appear to be in question.[60]

Not having looked at sources for the period when there was de facto control of the Mughals over the Rathor kingdom, this study cannot comment on the nature of the relationship between the Marwar state and the subalterns during the seventeenth century. It appears, however that the protection extended by the imperial masters secured the position of the chieftains both internally, vis-à-vis other contenders for the gaddi, as well as externally, against invasions of rival states. Consequently, the need to consciously reach out to the 'people' may not have been felt as acutely earlier as it was during the eighteenth century. Once Mughal protection withered away, regional states could not depend on their military might and coercive strength alone but rather, had to depend on a variety of subtle ways. The use of brute force would have neither been efficient nor effective; hence, multiple initiatives of a vast variety were employed for the purpose.

Yet, the model of the pre-colonial Indian political system constructed by Orientalist historiography was of absolute and arbitrary state power, unchecked by any institution or agency, resting in the person of the despotic emperor—the fountainhead of all power. Writing in the early nineteenth century, James Mill, for instance, pointed to a wide schism between the Indian state and the subjects, and justified colonial takeover because of its democratic nature. Adherents of this view held that 'negotiation' and 'consensus-building' were strategies of governance that 'modern' states such as theirs ushered in; and that the pre-modern polities, the 'Oriental' states employed 'traditional' methods of despotism and repression to govern. The subjects were believed to have been defenceless and mute, when in fact it were the historians, even when writing from different ideological positions, who had left them silent in their meta-narratives of the past.

This sharp contrast between colonial perception and domestic practice is noteworthy. In exploring the question of relations between artisanal social formations and the Marwar state's meticulous recording of 'petty' matters relating to the most lowly of its subjects in the *Jodhpur Sanad Parwana*

Bahis, one finds a reflection of the state's efforts to collect, centralize, and store information, and thus penetrate deeper levels of Marwar society. Documents recorded their petitions and representations, and grievances vis-à-vis the intermediary ruling class and local magnates were also drawn up by state officials when issues of oppression were in question. They often spelt out artisanal inter-personal problems concerning customs, property rights, inheritance, and these, collated in the *Jodhpur Sanad Parwana Bahis*, may in fact be perceived as constituting primitive census information, to be accessed as referral records whenever necessary.[61]

This form of compilation was not without precedent; the empirical gazetteer-like compilation of Nainsi's *Vigat* represents the Jodhpur state's early endeavours to map details on revenue and military statistics, and physical assets like cultivable lands, water bodies, forests, pastures, etc.[62] It also endeavoured to map human resources, listing caste-wise the elite residents—the brahmins, rajputs, and banias of the major qasbas. At this stage, however, common subjects remained nameless anonymous units since no specific information on particular individuals was considered worthy of note. The lower castes, in particular, remained a monolithic undifferentiated mass of pavan jat, with minimal effort invested in deconstructing the term and comprehending numbers of different castes that together constituted this generic category. Empirical details on these subordinate groups, their economic engagements, resources, distribution, organization, etc., were not deemed necessary of cognisance.

Instead of the erstwhile bardic literature and chronicles that celebrated the gallantry of its rulers, the emergence of this new genre of sources was more than a mere academic exercise.[63] Coming up in the mid-seventeenth century, it was linked directly to an effort at making a deeper entry into the realm, cataloguing information on the significant assets of the region to achieve a more firm control over them. This empirical knowledge on the different elements, dimensions, and factors of the state's power constituted 'statistics', that is the science of the state, that formed the major components of a newly emerging political rationality.[64]

This trend was carried forward in the eighteenth century by the emergence of another form of collating information on the state, heralding in the era of the 'record culture'. Starting with *Rukka Parwana Bahis, Ohada Bahis, Hath Bahis*, and *Patta Bahis* that documented details on the political and economic affairs of the state, the Rathors went on to record matters of popular concern. A deeper archive was built where centralized knowledge about resources and society was created. Instead of the erstwhile clubbing together of the subalterns as the pavan jat, we now have records that documented each complainant's name, the place he hailed from, and the nature of his grievance. Clothing it in a discourse of patriarchal benevolence and paternal concern, the state now appears to be exerting to forge links and thereby establish a firmer control over its people, particularly those who possessed specialized skills. This was a political strategy that signalled a programme of political incorporation and constitutes the rationale for the Rathor rulers to extend the instrument of petitions as mechanisms of protest to the people in an effort to contain their struggle within the hegemonic superstructure. They entertained petitions from their subjects and the artisans, in the hope of resolving their grievances, resorted to the legal procedure of the Jodhpur court system on a regular basis. In their engagement, therefore, the dominant adapted tools of control to be able to tackle subaltern pressures more effectively, and the subalterns, too, reshaped their resistance in response to the principles of justice espoused by the ruling elite.

Thus, a different idiom of politics had emerged that was sensitive to the need to carry the 'people' along. This is not to say that in the earlier periods repression was the only form of exercising power; in fact this study is based on the premise that the exercise of power generally entails a combination of the 'carrot and the stick'. But in view of the aggravated competition for resources, there seems to have been a more intense need to be solicitous, particularly towards those who tilled and toiled. This trend was possibly a wider one, where regional states by and large grew closer to their 'people' than ever before, and the political institutions became more democratic, in some senses. Being far smaller in size, their reach appears to be deeper, and they seem far more closely integrated and responsive towards their realm than the erstwhile larger imperial government with its wider concerns. But before any discussion on the implications of these multiple developments that created spaces wherein competitive politics played out, and where rival agendas were advanced and negotiated with varying degrees of success, it would be useful to delineate the ecological background and economic context that provided the larger environment for elite initiatives.

THE ECOLOGICAL ENVIRONMENT

Situated outside the regular course of both north-east and south-west monsoons, aridity, as noticed earlier, was a universal fact all over Marwar, with low annual rainfalls causing droughts and famine to be the 'grand natural diseases' of this region.[65] Water supplies, crops and fodder frequently suffered destruction, though nature was more generous with eastern Marwar than western and offered considerable regional diversities. The river Luni marked the boundary between the western portion that was arid, sterile, sandy, and desolate, and the eastern relatively fertile, well-watered, green, and hilly zone (Fig. 2.2).[66] These western portions were largely infertile, with a minimum potential for productive endeavour to succeed, and generally inhospitable for human habitation.[67] Lt. Colonel Archibald Adams, a British administrator posted in this region, noticed that there were 'ever

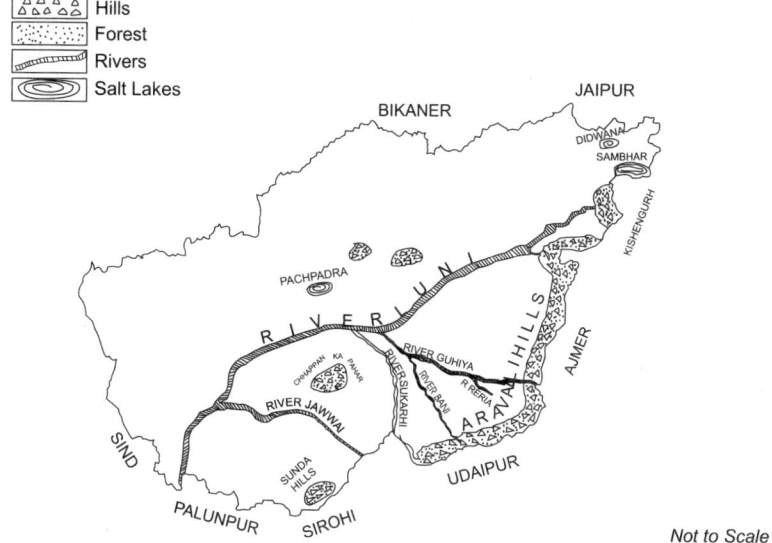

Fig. 2.2 Physical Features of Marwar
Courtesy: Author

recurring bad seasons, and many of the poor people, during years of scarcity, managed to subsist almost altogether on roots and seeds of grass found in the desert. Failure of crops and grass is so frequent in the western desert that the people are semi-nomadic in their habits. When the monsoon fails, they leave their homes with their herds and flocks, to find pasture before the animals become too impoverished to make the long journeys into Malwa, Kotah, and Sindh, which they have to do frequently on account of the capriciousness of the rainfall'.[68] A popular local proverb confirms rainfall scarcities as one of the primary reasons for migrations out of this region: *Bhadarve bhali kari din baisan jatan, hath gala ro bech ne karam phoriyan hathan.* Literally translated, it means 'O monsoons, you are late by twenty-two days! What use are you now when I have already sold my armlets and necklaces and am moving out of here?'[69]

Though the mainstay of the economy was agriculture,[70] the infertility of the dry soil and the acute dearth of cultivable lands resulted in pastoralism gradually becoming critical to the region. The four main sources of income for the state were *mal* or land revenue, tribute and succession fees paid by fief-holders, income accruing out of salt lakes, and the *sayar* or non-agricultural revenue, collected from a large number of commercial imposts and taxes.[71] Prone to suffer long dry spells (Fig. 2.3), residents of western Marwar cultivated only the most drought-resistant varieties of crops that could tolerate high levels of moisture stress. They had to make-do with the monsoon kharif crop alone, usually cultivating bajra and jawar (cereals), *moth*, and *til* (sesame seeds). Agriculture was a highly risky affair here, and every cultivator vied for a low-lying field so that he could catch the maximum rainfall. Local proverbs indicate some of the anxieties of the people: *Uncha jyaran baithawan, jyaran khet niwarhn* suggests that a field that was not low-lying was as good as not being there at all.[72] *Nichalo to khet dije,bich mein dije narhi; ghar hali ne chhoro dije, bhains lyave parhi*, expressed the most fundamental concerns of cultivators from this desert region.[73] In fact, the foremost dream of every cultivator was to have a perfect combination of winds that might facilitate agricultural production. Agriculturists pleaded that *Sawan mein to suriyo chale, bhadirhe purwai; asoja mein pichhwa chale, bhar-bhar garha lyai* that is 'if the north-westerlies blew in the month of July, and the easterlies in August, the month of September would see the winds blowing in a westerly direction and allow the harvest of a good crop'. Clearly, only a fortuitous combination of circumstances could make possible a successful harvest! Inadequate agricultural output was unable to sustain the local economy, and made livestock rearing as important as growing crops. Heber, the traveller who crossed this region in the early nineteenth century, commented on the local oxen and sheep that gave evidence 'of the goodness of their pasture, being the largest and most highly prized in all this part of India'.[74] Sheo, Sankara, Phalodi, Pokharan, and Malani had large pastures and grazing grounds with scattered herders' villages. Gujars and Raibaris/Raikas—pastoralist castes—reared cattle, buffaloes, and goats for milk, camels and bullocks as draft animals, and raised sheep for wool.[75] Owners of cows and buffaloes had to pay the tax (*ghasmari*) while those who possessed camels and goats paid *pancharai*.[76] Linked to the pastoral sector was the production of leather, which came mainly from skins of domesticated pastoral animals.

Under these conditions, settlements were generally small and scattered in the western parts of the kingdom, located near the few natural water bodies of the region. Vast expanses of sandy plains separated Barmer from Pokharan, Shergarh, and Sheo, with few routes criss-crossing the area. This maze, however, got denser eastwards. The numbers of villages, qasbas, and towns increased, and the size of settlements were also often larger. Jalor, Pali, Sojhat, Jaitaran, Bilara, Merta, Jodhpur, Nagaur, Parbatsar, Didwana, Maroth, etc., were flourishing towns, linked to one another with a network of roads, with numerous villages dotting the entire landscape. Proximity to water remained the one determining factor that dominated all others in deciding the location of a settlement, and people tended to migrate with their livestock once local resources of water got depleted. Emigration on a large scale, mostly to fertile Malwa with its rich black soil and its traditional

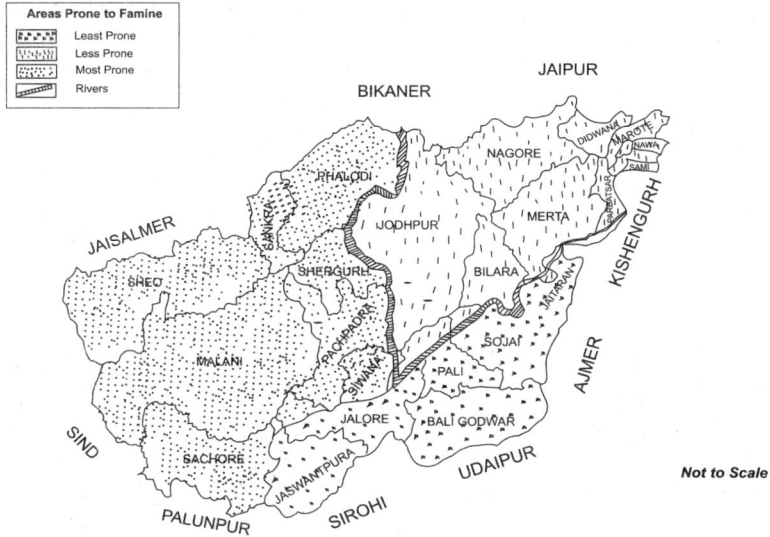

Fig. 2.3 Famine Susceptibile Regions of Marwar. *Source: Report on Relief Operations Undertaken in the Native States of Marwar during the Scarcity of 1891–2*

links with Marwar, was popular—although Kathiawar, Bhiwani, Delhi, and Sind were also attractive destinations. With negligble winter rains and minimal irrigation facilities, a winter crop was generally not possible in Marwar. Hence, many peasants emigrated seasonally in time for sowing the rabi crop, thereby temporarily depopulating the territories of Marwar, to return only after the harvest.[77]

In sharp contrast to the west, south-eastern Marwar presented a far brighter picture, bounded as it was on the east by the Aravalli ranges with a thick forest belt that staggered down to the fertile plains of the river Luni and its numerous tributaries.[78] The river arose in the Aravallis and cut across the landscape in a south-westerly direction till it disappeared into the Rann of Kutchh. It was the lifeline, ensuring the emergence of substantial settlements in the region. This south-eastern portion was responsible for much of the power and prosperity that the Nagaur ghazal, that introduced this chapter, attributed to Marwar. Though neither the Luni nor any of its tributaries was a perennial stream, it did irrigate the area during the monsoons.[79] Often overflowing its banks during the monsoons, the floods (*rel*) inundated the surrounding areas, and deposited rich alluvium all along.[80] The soil was thus regenerated, making possible the cultivation of bajra, jawar, moth, and til during the monsoonal kharif crop (*siyalu*) as well as wheat, barley, gram, and mustard seeds for the spring rabi crop (*unalu*). A higher watertable here made possible a profusion of wells, tanks, *nallah*s, and *bahlas* .[81]

Cash crops such as cotton, opium, and sugarcane were cultivated over a wide expanse, and several villages of Phalodi, Pokharan, Sojhat, Siwana, Jaitaran, and Merta were home to the production of raw cotton.[82]

TRADE, COMMERCE, AND THE ECONOMIC SCENARIO

The geographical location that, to some extent, impeded agricultural productivity of the region, also helped it develop alternate sectors of the economy. With inadequate monsoonal rains and complete reliance on agriculture or pastoralism impractical, the focus of the economy turned to trade from the earliest times, relying on the in-built advantages of a relatively arid environment. Trade routes passing through Marwar remained traversable throughout the year, even during the monsoons, facilitating the movement of merchandize laden on bullockcarts from the hinterland to the Gujarat ports of Surat, Cambay, etc. (Fig. 2.4). [83] This crucial placement of Marwar in the transit trade of the region saw many cities such as Bhinmal, Jalore, Mandor, Nagaur, and Pali become renowned for their commercial wealth.[84] Marwar, thus emerged as the only viable commercial channel in western India, crucial to the economy of not only Rajputana, but also the entire north India.[85]

That trade had become very important to this kingdom is evident from the immense concentration of mercantile groups in the urban centres of Marwar. The mahajans, banias, bohras, and sarrafs—the trading, transporting, and moneylending castes of the region—resided in large numbers here, as indicated in Table 2.1.[86]

Table 2.1
Merchant Households in Pargana Headquarters
by Late Seventeenth Century

Cities	Total Houses	Mahajan/Bania occupied houses	Percentage (%)
Sojhat	2254	738	32.7
Jaitaran	1839	720	39.2
Phalodi	659	242	36.7
Merta	5860	2158	36.8
Siwana	283	81	28.6
Pokharan	557	310	55.6

With the state help in the shape of free land to build shops and houses, and tax exemptions in initial stages, many established their business houses in the region.[87] The Rathor maharajas gave them robes of honour (*sirapaos*) as well, in addition to jagirs and numerous expensive gifts of elephants, horses,

Fig. 2.4 Important Trade Routes in Eighteenth-century Marwar
Courtesy:Author

Not to Scale

jewels, palanquins, etc.[88] The state often stood guarantee for the loans taken by traders, and went to the extent of mediating when they ran into trouble with moneylending sahukars.[89] State patronage helped many to develop into big financiers, bankers, money-changers, exporters, wholesalers, and retailers. The Rathor rulers clearly saw in this sphere an opportunity to raise finances through trade-related levies, and made vigorous attempts to create infrastructural facilities for the smooth transaction of trade. With transit duties, customs tariffs, and commercial taxes crucial to the income of the state, the rulers carefully nurtured and enhanced the transport, credit, and market mechanisms, transforming the arid uninviting landscape into one of the most vibrant commercial economies of contemporary India.[90]

Given the context of competing state formations in the eighteenth century, particularly all over Rajputana, it became imperative to offer lucrative terms to productive forces, especially skilled manpower, to settle in their territory.[91] The state extended incentives to attract skilled labour to migrate and add to its material wealth, and their active patronage and protection encouraged artisans and craftsmen to gravitate to their kingdom.[92] Chapters 4, 5, and 6 discuss the different dimensions of their interactions; suffice it to say here that their critical role ensured extensive patronage for them.[93]

Realizing the importance of trade as a source of income, the state made efforts to protect and promote the smooth and unhindered transportation of merchandize. Armed escorts were provided on the request of traders if they apprehended danger.[94] In the event of an accident, the government made efforts to recover the looted goods from the miscreants.[95] Extremely significant was the fact that the government took responsibility and compensated merchants in case of loss incurred in dacoity.[96] The administration posted its officials at check-posts and instructed them to ensure that unnecessary harassment of traders did not occur due to unreasonable demands. Such measures were executed to meet a dual purpose; the trader would of course benefit from royal magnanimity, but more importantly, the increased sales from within Marwar would bring income to the state.[97]

The export-import trade of Marwar was essentially in non-luxury items, and the most common merchandize exported out were tie-and-dye turbans and scarves for women, wooden furniture, iron implements, woollen goods, unwashed fabric, salt, bullocks, horses and camels, chilly, lead, *kasumba* dye, zinc, borax, incense (*asgandhi*), a powder used to anoint deities and worshippers (*roli*), ivory, coconuts (*catechu*), and silk.[98] Given Marwar's ecological constraints, export of some of the items such as ivory, coconuts, and silk are hard to explain. But Tod's remark that they were imported in large quantities from neighbouring Gujarat at low costs, and then exported to areas of high demand indicates the circuit that commodities often took before reaching their destination.[99] In turn, Marwar imported dry fruit, camels, woollen fabric, alum, lac, paper, aniseed, nutmeg, asafoetida, and dry ginger from Bikaner,[100] paper, gold borders used to embellish expensive costumes (*gota kinari*), rice, and diamonds from Jaipur,[101] and sugar, jaggery, wheat, gram, and opium from Kota.

Dacoity and loot of merchandize that moved along these routes was rampant despite measures taken by the state, and impoverished groups often attacked vulnerable targets. Hence, apart from protection from the state in the shape of armed escorts, merchants also took precautions for the safety of their wares and travelled in groups, sometimes with armed guards. More interestingly, however, they adopted a unique practice of hiring the services of charans and bhat to act as guardians of their merchandize. The sacred character of the charans, who were held in high regard by both the rajput chiefs and the tribals (Kolis, Bhils, and the Sahariyas) of the desert, was a sure way of avoiding mishaps. Foreign travellers who visited Rajputana in or about this period took particular notice of a strangely-touching custom called *chandani* or self-immolation, and vividly described it at length in their accounts. Heber wrote about the manner in which the robbers dreaded the anathema of chandani: 'If robbers appeared, the charan stepped forward waving his long white garments, and denouncing, in verse, infamy and disgrace on all who should injure travellers under the protection of the holy minstrel of Shiva. If this failed, he stabbed himself with his dagger, declaring that his blood was on their heads and if all failed, he was bound in honour to stab himself to the heart, a catastrophe of which there was little danger since the violent death of such a person was enough to devote the whole land to barrenness'.[102] Tod also corroborates that proceeding 'by degrees from a gash in the flesh to a death-wound or, if one victim was insufficient, a whole body of women and children was sacrificed, for whose blood the marauder is declared responsible hereafter'.[103] In the safety of charans or state guards, thus, commodities were transported from one region to another, often through long uninhabited stretches.

On arrival at a settlement, depending on its location and population density, a hierarchy of markets were available as sites for exchange. Large businessmen, importers and exporters called *kothiwals*, and regional and local wholesalers handled inter-provincial and inter-regional trade.[104] Extremely wealthy, they controlled the entire wholesale trade by virtue of their heavy investments, and had branches in different cities of the Subcontinent.[105] Regional wholesalers stood second in the hierarchy, and dealt in intra-provincial trade through branches in important commercial marts within Rajasthan, *gumastas* or *munims* looking after their business in various centres.[106] Small shopkeepers, pavement sellers, and peddlers controlled the retail trade, though the marketing system included brokers (*dalals*), weighers (*kayals*), and porters (*hammals* or *paledars*) as well. Standard weights and measures were in use in the markets all over Marwar, using the *kutchha* maund and the *pukka* maund, the latter a standard equivalent of forty *seers* where one seer was equal to *chhataks*. But the weight of a kutchha maund differed from one locality to another, equal to seers in Jodhpur[107] but only in Nohar.[108]

There were special markets or *mandis* in all big towns where edible commodities such as grains, pulses, sugar, jaggery, spices, oilseeds, salt, ghee, etc., were available. The administration, in alliance with the large merchants, carefully developed and fostered the mechanisms for procurement of grains and the organization of their disposal. The mahajans and the bohras, merchants who purchased a sizeable part of the peasants' crop in the village, controlled the marketing of agricultural surplus. Being poor, the peasants were often in debt, and in pursuance of the agreement made at the time of borrowing money, they handed over their produce to the mahajan. He, in turn, sent the grain for sale to the mandi of the nearby town, as did the zamindars and large farmers. Urban merchants also moved from village to village to purchase agricultural produce from peasants and mahajans, paying them the market rates after deducting their commission for the service rendered.[109]

Those who resided in qasbas and villages procured their needs more often from weekly *haat*s and periodical fairs.[110] Fairs, held annually on specific dates in specific towns, were extremely popular and fairly crucial for the economy of Marwar. They often lasted several weeks, and unlike *haats*, the focus of exchange in most of these fairs was more on the sale and purchase of cattle and draft animals, though the usual transaction in edible commodities, textiles, and other consumer goods was part of the fair attraction. Huge crowds thronged to these fairs, and they were significant in promoting not only local but long-distance trade too. They served to familiarize merchants from distant places with the specialities, expertise, and commercial potential of one another. Rathor rulers therefore took active interest in the organization of these fairs, and made security arrangements for merchants and their merchandize. The season of fairs (*mela*) began after the rainy months, when many centres in Marwar came alive in a spirit of bustling commerce and exchange. The more important cattle fairs were those at Tilwara, Parbatsar, Pushkar, Balotra, Gogameri, and Mundawa. Most of these were organized in the month of August, starting with the Tilwara Mela held in honour of Lord Mallinath at Malani. The most famous and largely attended cattle fair was the one at Pushkar near Ajmer.[111] Both the Pushkar fair and the one at Balotra were essentially horse fairs, where horses from Kutchh, Kathiawar, and Multan were brought for sale in huge numbers, and multitudes of merchants from Rajasthan as well as neighbouring provinces gathered. The Gogameri fair near Nohar, held in honour of Gogaji, was another annual event in the month of August and September, where people from adjacent areas attended in large numbers and actively engaged in the sale and purchase of bullocks.[112] Also extremely famous were the biannual religious fairs held in the months of August and later in January, at Ram Deora near Pokharan, in honour of the immensely respected and popular saint Ramdeoji. It was primarily attended by the lower castes of Marwar and the neighbouring regions of Mewar, Bikaner, and Jaisalmer, who crowded there to select from a wide range of merchandize sold in profusion.[113] Another fair at Mundawa, during December–January in honour of Girdhari, that is, Lord Krishna, lasted for six weeks and witnessed brisk business in horses, camels, and oxen.[114]

Commercial transactions during the eighteenth century were mostly monetized. Marwar, as other kingdoms of Rajputana that recognized imperial suzerainty, was prohibited from striking its own coins during the sixteenth and seventeenth centuries of Mughal ascendancy. Instead, they had the Mughal *rupiya* and *dam* in circulation.[115] In 1761, Maharaja Vijai Singh of Marwar received formal permission from the emperor to set up his own mints in Jodhpur, Nagaur, and Pali. Market exchanges and a rapid monetization of the economy ensued thereafter. The maharaja began to strike coins in his own name from 1780, and facilitated the growing trend of monetization in Marwar. These coins were struck in gold, silver, and copper, and bore on one side the name of the Mughal emperor Shah Alam, and on the other that of Vijai Singh, after whom they were eponymously named *Vijaishahi*. Gold coins, or *mohur*s were struck at the Jodhpur mint only; gradually, minting of silver and copper coins ensued in Merta and Pali, while the mint at Nagaur minted coins in all three metals, including gold.[116] By the end of Vijai Singh's reign, seven mints were in operation in the state, located at Jodhpur, Pali, Nagaur, Sojhat, Jalor, Merta, and Kuchawan, facilitating a larger circulation of money.[117]

In addition, there was a tremendous proliferation of common specie and base coinage in this period, indicating the profusion and penetration of the cash nexus to the lower levels of the Marwari economy. *Taka, paisa, adhela,* and *dhingala* were commonly used for small transactions, an adhela equal to half a paisa. Along with the Dhabbushahi paisa, *phadiya*s, *chhadami*s, *damari*s, *cowrie*s were the lowest mediums of exchange for ordinary transactions. The rapid establishment of mints over the latter half of the century, from none at the beginning of Vijai Singh's reign to a dozen by the end of the century, indicates burgeoning money-use and supply in the economy, and its percolation to all levels of economic activity in Marwar. The large-scale circulation of low-value, small denomination coins implied that the common people, engaged in low-level transactions, were also using metallic currency rather than depending on barter exchanges alone. The rural haats and countryside marts had come to be monetized, as is evident from the fact that all taxes, gunegari fines, patta contracts, and ijaredari transactions were expressed in monetary terms.[118]

Increased use of metallic currency meant that large transactions of sale or purchase were not feasible by personally carrying coins for the purpose; the mode of payment was therefore often through bills of exchange (*hundis*), the *darshani* payable on demand, and the *muddati* payable on the expiry of the stipulated period.[119] Almost every affluent sahukar issued and discounted hundis, and for this service they realized commission (*hundawan*), the rates varied according to distance or the agency arrangements of the bankers.[120] Hundis were rarely dishonoured because, among the mercantile community, non-payment by a drawer was taken to mean his insolvency. The presence of hundis on the one hand, and base coinage on the other, indicates a sophisticated market and credit system. A natural corollary of these developments was the existence of a primitive banking system, finance and banking in the hands of certain banking houses or kothiwals, and small bankers locally called bohras.[121]

With most states in Rajputana and outside striking their own coins that differed in weight and value, commercial transactions among them necessitated exchange of currencies at a discount. Hence sarrafs enjoyed a lucrative business, the rate of discount (*batta*) offered by them varying from coin to coin, as per its weight and metallic content.[122] A high volume of inter-regional trade made big money-changers indispensable for the smooth conduct of such business transactions. Bohras possessed much less capital to invest and handled small transactions, advancing moderate finance to petty traders, artisans, and peasants in the cities and in the countryside.[123]

Loans could be both unsecured or secured, the former involving reliance on the personal credibility of a respectable person. Secured loans required mortgage of land, house or shop, or pawning ornaments of gold and silver at fifty per cent to seventy-five per cent of the value of articles pawned. The sahukar generally did not secure possession of the property mortgaged, but at the same time, the debtor too could not sell it until he had repaid the loan. If the loan was not repaid within the stipulated period, the mortgagee had the right to obtain possession and offer the property on rent in lieu of interest, or sell the property to recover his capital. Innumerable documents record usurious transactions, and the attempts of the creditors to take firm possession of the mortgaged property.[124] The list of monetary disputes recorded in the latter half of the eighteenth century is unending; clearly, the volume and velocity of monetary exchanges was higher in nature than ever before.

Widespread money-use, loan contracts, banking, and financing necessitated the maintenance of ledgers and the evolution of sophisticated accounting to record monetary transactions. The fact that elaborate contracts were drawn was itself reflective of a fairly developed market economy where people depended on the written rather than the oral word. Old-world values of trust and an individual's verbal testimony were slowly giving way to an increasing preference for written records and documents for all transactions. As monetary exchanges became the norm, they made significant inroads into the subsistence-oriented system of rural manufacture, and many areas of revenue-payment shifted towards cash payments. Rapid increase in revenue farming established and extended the trend for paying land-revenue lump-sum in cash, though payments in kind persisted in some areas, grazing taxes, etc., began to be submitted in cash according to the number of cattle.[125] This required the cultivators to sell a certain portion of their crop, which took them to rural markets that had connections with larger urban markets.[126]

Based on archival sources from Maharashtra, Frank Perlin has noticed similar developments. He views with suspicion the conventional notion that monetary economy and commerce in pre-colonial India were dependant on and developed as a consequence of state taxation and emphasizes that 'taxation regimes' operated in a wider economic context that included formal and informal networks of credit and administration that often transcended political frontiers.[127] His perception seems highly plausible, though limited explorations of this issue do not allow the formulation of any categorical opinion on the matter. What records do allow is an unambiguous statement that foodgrains were not the only village products sold in the markets—cash crops such as indigo, opium, other foodstuffs, and animals, as well as manufactured goods such as textiles, metalware, and clayware, were also important.[128] It is difficult, however, to support the conventional logic that parasitical towns and cities drained their hinterlands of resources and exploited monadic villages, giving nothing in return.[129] Growth was certainly not confined to the supra-village level; in fact, evidence from the region strongly supports the view that commodity circulation and credit flows significantly affected village production and consumption.

While the overwhelming flow may have been from the countryside to the towns since the collection of revenue in cash generated a pressure to sell, and was a factor that served to integrate villages into a wider monetized economy, there were strong symbiotic relations between qasbas and the countryside. Interestingly, an overwhelming number of village sunars appear to have essayed coins, and the availability of a considerable amount of specie in the villages of eighteenth-century Marwar, though mostly of small denominations, facilitated the process of commercialization. Evaluation of coins was a lucrative business for them, and the sunars got a commission for the job. Growing commercialization resulted in some villages, for instance, getting renowned for a particular category of dyed textiles, or for making camel seats (*palarhn*).

Bolstered by wide-ranging initiatives of the state, commodity production and distribution picked momentum over time. As discussed, the surpluses and deficits in production due to diverse ecological conditions necessitated a multi-tiered and multifaceted structure of distribution and exchange of commodities. The presence of an elaborate network of trade routes and facilities available for the safe transportation of merchandize, a nexus of large and small settlements, the presence of fairly sophisticated credit and financial institutions equipped to handle complex monetary trans-actions, developed markets, and mints scattered all over the important urban centres of the region, all go to prove that the structural configurations for an economy to thrive had come up and was encouraged and patronized. In response to commercial demands, the indices that would normally go to construct the picture of a prosperous region were present in early modern Marwar—though class, caste, amd spatial differentiation of course resulted in differential experiences for different individuals. The next chapter looks at artisanal castes, their internal organization, and the intersection of the same with the Jodhpur state.

NOTES

1. See Vikram Singh Rathor (ed.), *Rajasthani Ghazal Sangrah*, p. 42. As noted earlier, Marudhar is another name for Marwar.

2. See Hsieun Tsang's, *Hsi-yu-chi* or *Si-yu-ki*, trans. S. Beal, under the title *Buddhist Records of the Western World*, 2 vols (London, 1869, photo-offset reprint, Delhi, 1969). Abridged trans. and commentary by T. Watters, *On Yuan Chwang's Travels in India*, AD *629–45*, T.W. Rhys Davids and S.W. Bushell (eds) 2 vols (London, 1904-5; photo-offset edn, Delhi, 1961).

3. Tod described the largest *shahar* Jodhpur, and claimed it contained more than 80,000 people inhabiting 20,000 houses; see Col. James Tod, *Annals and Antiquities of Rajasthan, or the Central and Western Rajput States of India* William Crook (ed.), 3 vols (Reprinted, Delhi, 1990), vol. 2, p. 821. Phiroz R. Kothawalla's *The Census of Marwar*, 1911, also placed the population of Jodhpur at a similar figure of 79,756.

4. Rev. Reginald Heber, *Narrative of a Journey Through the Upper Provinces of India: From Calcutta to Bombay, 1824–25*, vol. 2, p. 36 (London, 1828).

5. Political Agent, Marwar, Major C.K.M. Walter's *Gazetteers of Marwar, Mallani, and Jeysulmere* (Calcutta, 1877), p. 1.

6. Jagdish Singh Gehlot, *Marwar Rajya ka Itihas* (Jodhpur, Reprint 1991), p. 3.

7. This popular perception about the mythological origins of the desert land-scape in Marwar coincides with scientific and archaeological work done in this area. The discovery of seashell fossils and other remains indicates that the desert was indeed an ocean way back in history. See V.N. Misra and S.N. Rajaguru, 'Palaeoenvironment and Prehistory of the Thar Desert, Rajasthan, India', in Karen Frifelt and Per Sorensten (eds) *South Asian Archaeology*, 1985 (London, Reprint, 1989), pp. 296–320.

8. This estimate, based on data provided by Nainsi in his *Vigat* and the *Khyat*, assessed the size of the rural population of Marwar with reference to the number of ploughs in several villages of the different parganas, while the urban population was determined on the basis of the total number of houses listed for almost all pargana headquarters; see B.L. Bhadani, 'Population of Marwar in the Middle of the Seventeenth Century', *IESHR*, vol. 16, no. 4, 1979, and Sushila Kothari's two articles 'Estimated Rural Population of 17th Century Marwar' and 'The Urban Population of 17th Century Marwar', in *Shodhak*, vol. 23, part B, (1994), and vol. 24, part B, (1995), respectively.

9. B.D. Chattopadhyaya, *The Making of Early Modern India* (Delhi, 1994), chapter titled 'Origin of the Rajputs: The Political, Economic and Social Processes in Early Medieval Rajasthan', pp. 57–88.

10. In AD 1459, to be precise; see Norman P. Ziegler, 'Evolution of the Rathor state of Marvar: Horses, Structural Change and Warfare' in Karine Schomer, Joan L. Erdman, Deryck O. Lodrick, and Lloyd I. Rudolph (eds) *The Idea of Rajasthan, Explorations in Regional Identity*, vol. 2 (New Delhi, 1994), pp. 192–216.

11. Dasharatha Sharma (ed.), *Rajasthan Through the Ages*, 2 vols (Bikaner, 1966).

12. Though of a later period, the mutual relations between the maharaja and these senior nobles have been described quite accurately in the letter from Alves to Macnaughten, dated 10 January 1838, Cons. no. 11, Foreign Political.

13. See Ram Karn Asopa's *Marwar ka Sankshipt Itihas* (Jodhpur, 1934); the author traces at length the history of some of the prominent tribute-paying subordinate houses of Marwar such as those of *Nimbaj, Asop, and Pokharan*. The internecine conflicts and power play between them and the Rathors has been highlighted by the author.

14. G.D. Sharma, *Rajput Polity: A Study of Politics and Administration of the State of Marwar, 1638–1749* (New Delhi, 1977).

15. V.S. Bhargava, *Marwar and the Mughal Emperors, 1526–1748* (Delhi 1966).

16. Jodhpur was annexed by the Mughal emperor Akbar in 1565 and in 1583 he conferred the kingdom as a watan jagir on the Rathor chieftain Udai Singh. The Rathors were assured of their ancestral possessions in return for tribute and military service when demanded. Udai Singh accepted Mughal sovereignty and received a mansab commensurate with his status. See G.H. Ojha, *Jodhpur Rajya ka Itihas* (Ajmer, 1941), vol. I, pp. 335–7. G.H. Ojha, *Jodhpur Rajya ka Itihas*, vol. I, (Jodhpur, 1934), pp. 335–7.

17. Norman P. Ziegler's 'Some Notes on Rajput Loyalties during the Mughal Period', in J.F. Richards (ed.) *Kingship and Authority in South Asia* (Madison, 1978), pp. 215–51, adopts a structural functional approach to suggest a rajput code of conduct during Akbar and Jehangir's reign. And D. Kolff shows in *Naukar, Rajput, and Sepoy: The Ethnohistory of the Military Labour Market in Hindustan, 1450–1850* (Cambridge, 1990) that the rajput identity and political formation did not represent 'long cherished' ideals as often believed, but in fact began to take shape from late fifteenth century.

18. Bhargava, *Marwar and the Mughal Emperors*, pp. 115–76.

19. The only apparent indication of allegiance to their imperial masters could be seen in the Vijaishahi coins struck by the maharaja, which had the image of the Mughal emperor on one side and that of the maharaja on the other. This too was a clear change from the obsequious subservience observed earlier.

20. Jagdish Singh Gehlot, *Marwar Rajya ka Itihas* (2nd edn, Jodhpur, 1991), pp. 105–46.

21. Ibid., pp. 1–2.

22. See Stewart Gordon, 'The Slow Conquest: Administrative Integration of Malwa into the Maratha Empire, 1720–60', in his *Marathas, Marauders, and State Formation in Eighteenth Century India* (Oxford, 1994), pp. 23–63.

23. For details, see G.R. Parihar, *Marwar and the Marathas* (Jodhpur, 1968), pp. 90–1.

24. A letter from Mahad ji Scindia to Vijai Singh dated 8 June 1769, outlines the terms and conditions for these payments; also see G.R. Parihar, *Marwar and the Marathas* (Jodhpur, 1968), pp. 85–9. A whopping sum to the tune of 50 lacs was demanded by the Marathas as war indemnity, and a regular annual tribute of 150,000 rupees too.

25. The Marathas demanded three lacs of rupees in 1761 and another ten lacs in 1765. See *Marwar Khyat*, vol. 111, pp. 34–7.

26. Burton Stein, 'State Formation and Economy Reconsidered', in *Modern Asian Studies*, vol. 19, no. 3, 1985, pp. 387–413

27. P. V. Kane, *History of Dharmashastras*, 3 vols (Poona, 1946), pp. 210 and 223.

28. R.P. Kangle, *The Kautiliya Arthashastra: An English Translation* (Bombay, 1963), no. 2, part II, pp. 364–5.

29. *Manusmriti* with the *Manubhasya of Medhatithi*, Ganganath Jha (ed.), 2 vols.

30. Strikingly reminiscent of the *Arthasastra*, the *Ajnapatra* was written between AD 1700–16 by Ramchandra Nilkant, one of the senior ministers of the Marathas. See S.V. Puntambekar, 'The Ajnapatra or Royal Edict', *Journal of Indian History*, vol. VIII, no. 1 April 1929, p. 104.

31. For an elaboration of these ideas, see Eugenia Vanina, *Ideas and Society in India: From the Sixteenth to the Eighteenth Centuries* (Delhi, 1996), pp. 16–51.

32. See 'The Kali Age' cited from the *Visnu Purana* in Cornelia Dimmit and J.A.B. van Buitenen (eds and trans.) *Classical Hindu Mythology: A Reader in the Sanskrit Puranas* (Philadelphia, 1978), p. 41.

33. For an elaboration of these ideas, see Sanjay Sharma's *Famine, Philanthropy and the Colonial State: North India in the Early Nineteenth Century* (Delhi, 2001), pp. 171–181.

34. Prasannnan Parthasarathi's recent study *The Transition to a Colonial Economy: Weavers, Merchants and Kings in South India, 1720–1800* (Cambridge, 2002) pp. 121–48 elaborates at length the cultural context of 'moral polity' that character-ized the pre-colonial south Indian state. He traces the transformation in the nature of the state with the inception of British colonialism, and emphasizes

that they experienced no such constrains of legitimacy that would check and limit their power. Though relatively less direct on pre-colonial polity, Radhika Singha's conclusions about the colonial state also suggest similar distinctions between the pre-colonial and colonial polities; see Singha, *A Despotism of Law: Crime and Justice in Early Colonial India* (Delhi, 1998).

35. Vijay Dan Detha, *Rajasthani-Hindi Kahavat Kosh* (new series) vol. 5, Borunda, 2002), p. 3053.

36. For more on this, see Hiroyuki Kotani's essay 'Kingship, State and Local Society in the Seventeenth to Nineteenth Century Deccan with Special Reference to Ritual Functions', in Noboru Karashima (ed.), *Kingship in Indian History: Japanese Studies in South Asia*, no. 2 (Delhi, 1999), pp. 237–71.

37. Robert Lingat, *The Classical Law of India* (Berkeley, 1973), p. 207.

38. Stewart Gordon, 'Legitimacy and Loyalty in Some Successor States of the Eighteenth Century' in J.F. Richards (ed.) *Kingship and Authority in South Asia.*

39. Peabody, *Hindu Kingship and Polity*, p. 51.

40. Pierre Bourdieu, *Outline of a Theory of Practice*, trans. R. Nice, (Cambridge, 1977). I owe this line of argument to Peabody's case study of Kota, where he has meticulously traced somewhat similar trends.

41. Vikram Singh Rathor, *Marwar ka Sanskritik Itihas* (Jodhpur, 1996), pp. 27–30.

42. Richard B. Barnett's *North India Between Empires: Awadh, the Mughals and the British, 1720-1801* (Berkeley, 1980) and C.A. Bayly's *Rulers, Townsmen and Bazaars: North Indian Society in the Age of British Expansion, 1770-1870* (Cambridge, 1983) argue for similar developments in eighteenth-century north India.

43. Bhandari Suratram enjoyed a great degree of royal favour under Abhay Singh, even commanding important military operations, as the one against Ajmer in Oct. 1743; see Jagdish Singh Gehlot, *Marwar Rajya ka Itihas*, p. 132.

44. *Maharaja Vijai Singh ri Tawarikh*, p. 140, and *Jodhpur Khyat* part 3, p. 107, respectively.

45. See *Ohada Bahi* no. 1, p. 117, Jodhpur Records, RSAB.

46. These developments were akin to trends in eighteenth-century Maratha polity; see Andre Wink, *Land and Sovereignty in India: Agrarian Society and Politics under the Eighteenth Century Maratha Svarajya* (Cambridge, 1986). Also see Stewart Gordon, *The New Cambridge History of India: The Marathas, 1600–1818* (New Delhi, 1993).

47. By the turn of the century, even the post of Diwan was with merchants, Bhandari Gangaram annointed as such in 1803 Singhvi Indraraj was made the *musahib*, and the *hakimi* of Jalor and Sojhat, two of the most important parganas, went to Singhvi Kushalraj and Sukhraj. See *Khyat Mutsaddiyan* (Diary of Dayaldas), f. 82.

48. For instance, in 1754 Vijai Singh, in an effort to fight his cousin Ram Singh's attempt to wrest the throne from him with Maratha help, had to write to the bohras of Nandwana asking for a loan of Rs 15, 000 at an interest rate of 6 per

cent. Since the maharaja's position was still acutely unstable, he had to mort-gage the village Rataka in pargana Nagaur for this loan; see letter dated 1754, *Haqiqat Bahi* no. 4, f. 421, Jodhpur Records, and also in *Arzi Bahi* no. 4, f. 286. Again, Seth Daya Ram Roop Chand, a famous banker of Jodhpur, lent out Rs 1,00,000 to the Durbar for a period of two and a half months to clear off the debt to Tukoji Holkar. This loan was repayable from the income of *sair* or trea-sury of *daribas* of Nawa, Didwana, Parbatsar, and Maroth; see *Khas Rukka Parwana Bahi* no. 1, Chaitra vadi 13, 1847/1790, Jodhpur Records.

49. *Jama Kharach File* no. 44, *Dholion ka Kothar Records*, Jodhpur.

50. *Maharaja Bijai Singh ri Tawarikh*, p. 61.

51. A faction of the nobles shut the gates of Jodhpur on Vijai Singh, and placed Bhim Singh on the throne. To recapture power, Vijai Singh appealed to his sub-jects to aid his struggle in regaining the throne by imposing a fresh levy *Kiwadi*, charged per family; see Tod, vol. II, p. 163; *JSPB* 1, 1821/1764, f. 26B..

52. In 1781 Maharaja Vijai Singh established the first mint issuing silver cur-rency, to be followed in quick succession by the setting up of almost a dozen mints; see V.N. Reu, *Coins of Marwar* (Jodhpur, 1946), p. 4. The Daftar Shri Huzur under the diwan was established in the Jodhpur fort for maintaining revenue records, copies of state sanads and parwanas, and income and expen-diture returns. See Shivdutt Dan Barhat's *Jodhpur Rajya ka Itihas, 1753–1800* (Jaipur, 2nd edn, 1991).

53. Documents in the *JSPB*, from 1764–74 have been signed largely by those from the merchant and the brahmin castes; prominent among these are those of Bania Aaidan, Singhvi Fatehchand, Singhvi Jorawarmal, Singhvi Dhirajmal, Singhvi Bhinvraj, Muhnot Suratram, Singhvi Tejmal, Singhvi Tilokmal, Purohit Jayaram, Purohit Kesodas, Joshi Bramhadutt, Pandit Jivanram, Pandit Parsadiram. See *JSPB* 1–10. The trend remained the same through the century.

54. Similar trends have been outlined by Susan Bayly in the region of Maharashtra during the period of Peshwa rule; see her *Caste, Society and Politics in India from the Eighteenth Century to the Modern Age: The New Cambridge History of India*, vol. 4, no. 3 (Cambridge, 1999), pp. 64–96..

55. For instance, in the middle of the century a bitter conflict ensued after Maharaja Abhay Singh died; his son Ram Singh and brother Bakhat Singh vied for the throne, could enjoy extremely short-lived reigns of less than a year each, with the conflict persisting thereafter between Ram Singh and Bakhat's son Vijai Singh. Similarly, the last decade of the century saw cousins Bhim Singh and Man Singh simultaneously claim the throne of the state; see Jagdish Singh Gehlot's *Marwar Rajya ka Itihas*, pp. 132–46.

56. See Richard Fox *Kin, Clan, Raja and Rule: State-Hinterland Relations in Pre-Industrial India* (Berkeley, 1971). Also, Visheshwarnath Reu's 'Marwar ki Samant Pratha', in *Parampara*, no. 95–6, in which he analyses the pressures that these subordinate rajput sardars constantly exerted on the Rathor rulers.

57. Shivdutt Dan Barhat's *Jodhpur Rajya ka Itihas*, pp. 41–65.

58. Rosemary Crill, in her recently published work notes that during the early decades of the eighteenth century several thikanas had become powerful enough to develop their own ateliers where patronage to renowned artists was extended on a scale parallel to that of the Jodhpur Durbar; see Crill's *Marwar Paintings: A History of the Jodhpur Style* (Jodhpur, 2000), pp. 54–115.

59. I derive this argument from Christopher A. Bayly's *Empire and Information: Intelligence Gathering and Social Communication in India, 1780–1870* (Cambridge, 1996).

60. For more on this, see Chris Bayly, *Empire and Information*, pp. 365–70.

61. The English East India Company also collected a great deal of raw 'data' on the structure and production of textiles, through the representations or petitions of Indian weavers, dyers, printers, bleachers who had an acute understanding of the economic conditions which bore on their own livelihoods; see K.N. Chaudhari, *The Trading World of Asia and the English East India Company, 1600–1760* (Cambridge, 1978), p. 243.

62. Attempts to accumulate knowledge on geography, resources, and statistics were common to other late medieval states as well. For instance, the *Chahar Gulshan* of 1760 contains massive details on distances, marches and local resources; see Rai Chaturman Kayasth's *Chahar Gulshan*, trans. in Jadunath Sarkar (ed.), *The India of Aurangzeb: Topography, Statistics and Roads Compared with the India of Akbar* (Calcutta, 1901). The seventeenth-century courtier Inayat Khan included details on the distances, position of routeways, rivers and sources of fresh water, other descriptions of the economy and statistics of Tibet, in his work *Shahjahan Nama*, W. Begley and Z. Desai, trans and (eds), (Delhi, 1990), pp. 218–33.

63. N.P. Ziegler, 'Marwari Historical Chronicles: Sources for the Social and Cultural History of Rajasthan', *IESHR*, vol. 13, no. 2, 1976, pp. 219–50.

64. H. Maheswari, *A History of Rajasthani Literature* (Delhi, 1980), pp. 68–9, 71–6.

65. Col. James Tod, *Annals and Antiquities of Rajasthan, or the Central and Western rajput States of India* (Delhi,1990 reprint), vol. 2, p. 786.

66. Information in Nainsi's *Vigat* broadly corresponds with that in modern maps. Nainsi wrote that out of a total of 20 *tappa*s of Marwar, 13 located in the east, north-east and south-east did not contain any sand dunes or desert tracts. These 13 tappas in which sand dunes are not placed in modern maps too are Jodhpur (except a small portion in the north-west), Bilara, Asop, Pali, Piparh, Bahela, Kherwa, Gundoch, Rohat, Bhadrajan, Levera Kalan, Khinwsar, and Dunara. The remaining 7 tappas, namely Osiyan, Bahelwa, Ketu, Shetrawa, Dechhu, and Mahewah lay partly or mainly in the desert.cf. Quarter inch Map no. 450 and Census Map of Jodhpur state (Marwar),1931.

67. Political Agent, Marwar, Major C.K.M. Walter's *Gazetteers of Marwar, Mallani, and Jeysulmere* (Calcutta, 1877), pp. 5–6.

68. Lt.Colonel Archibald Adams, *The Western Rajputana States: A Medico-Topographical and General Account of Marwar, Sirohi, and Jaisalmer* (London, 1900), p. 153.

69. Jagdish Singh Gehlot, *Marwar Rajya ka Itihas* (Jodhpur, 1991), p. 15. The destination has not been spelt out, but in a vast majority of cases it was Malwa.

70. The *Vigat* records the number of wells and *baoris*, tanks, *nallahs* and *bahlas* in the different villages. Dispersed all over Marwar, those in the eastern portion were shallow wells called *kosita* and *dhabra*. However, in western Marwar, the wells had to be dug deep since the water-table was extremely low; hence the *kohar* or deep wells, the *chanch* or *dhenkli* which had a lever device with a bucket hung on a weighted wooden beam, and *arhat* or a geared Persian-wheel made entirely of wood and rope were constructed.These wells were either kuchcha-earthen, or pucca-brick-lined, depending on the resources available to its owners.

71. See the letter from Cavendish to Secretary, Political Department, 10 Oct., 1831, R.A. File no. 3 National Archives of India (NAI), New Delhi.

72. Vijay Dan Detha and Bhagirath Kanorhiya (ed.), *Rajasthani Hindi Kahavat Kosh*, vol. 1, (Jodhpur, 1977), p. 87.

73. This proverb indicates the typical requirements of a cultivator, and reads: 'May I have a low-lying field with a water channel running through it, and a son who will look after my buffaloes'.

74. Rev. Reginald Heber, *Narrative of a Journey through the Upper Provinces of India: From Calcutta to Bombay, 1824–25*, vol. 2, (London, 1828) p. 35.

75. Innumerable disputes over cattle were serious enough to reach the conflict-resolution agencies of the state. See *JSPB* 22, 1836/1779, f. 104B; *JSPB* 26, 1841/1784, f. 149B, and many others.

76. See B.L. Bhadani, 'The Pastoral Sector in the Economy of Seventeenth Century Marwar', paper presented at the Second International Seminar on Rajasthan, Udaipur, 17–21 December 1991.

77. See the *Report on the Relief Operations undertaken in the Native States of Marwar, Jaisalmer, Bikaner and Kishangarh in Rajputana during the Scarcity of 1891–92* at NAI.

78. Indicating villages of pargana Sojhat and Jaitaran that stood on the fringe of the forest belt, Nainsi noted that timber was procured in large quantities by the Rathors from here. See *Vigat* I, pp. 454–65; II, 517–19; 526–7and 536.

79. Nainsi describes at length the areas through which Luni and its tributaries flew. See *Vigat* II, pp. 281–2.

80. Apart from the beneficial consequences of the floods, considerable damage also resulted, washing away the crops along the river bank. The destruction of a Nilgar's nil crop due to the floods is described in *JSPB* 11, 1828/1771, f. 34A.

81. Nainsi lists 34 bahlas in Jaitaran and 37 in Sojhat; references are strewn all over the *Vigat*, especially p. 510.

82. Cotton could grow well in relatively less rain too. Salbanck noticed 'stores of cotton' in Merta in AD1609; see Hakluytus Posthumus *Purchas His Pilgrims*, (ed.) Mc Lahose, III, p. 84. Nainsi records the plantation of sugarcane in Siwana; see *Vigat*, II, p. 275. Another contemporary text mentions sugarcane cultiva-

tion in Sojhat. See *Sojhat-re-Mandal-ri-Vat*, published in *Parampara*, vol. 11, (ed.) Narain Singh Bhati, (Jodhpur, 1966) pp. 101–2.

83. See V.K. Jain, *Trade and Traders in Western India*, AD *1000–1300* (New Delhi, 1990).

84. See B.D. Chattopadhyaya, *The Making of Early Medieval India*, chapter 4, 'Markets and Merchants in Early Medieval Rajasthan', pp. 89–119. The author has noticed the emergence of two clusters of commercial settlements in the region during the pre-twelfth century period. Inscriptional evidence points to Ghatiyal, Mandor, and Ratanpur as substantial exchange centres around Jodhpur, and another cluster around Nadol, at Narlai, Dhalop, Sevadi and Badari. Chattopadhyaya postulates that despite being local centres of exchange, they were nevertheless points of intersection for traffic of varying origins, and it is perhaps the nature of interaction with traffic from the outside that gave rise to a certain measure of hierarchy among exchange centres.

85. Though the seventeenth-century commentator Nainsi described merely nine cities in his *des*, listing Jodhpur, Merta, Sojhat, Jaitaran, Siwana, Jalor, Sanchor, Pokharan, and Phalodi, the nineteenth-century *Mardum Shumari* mentions about two-dozen cities, and many more qasbas.

86. By the mid-seventeenth century the mahajans owned over one-third of the inhabited dwellings in five out of the six cities whose census Nainsi has offered in his *Vigat*. See Nainsi's *Vigat*, vol. I, pp. 391 and 497; and vol. II, pp. 9, 83, 224, 310. The city of Jodhpur had 616 shops owned by mahajans according to the same source; see *Vigat*, vol. I, pp. 186–7.

87. For instance, Heera Nand Manak Chand jewellers were given a haveli to live in and five bighas of land free of cost in Merta. See *JSPB* 2, 1822/1765, f. 42A. Moneylenders Sada Ram and Shri Ram were given in gratis one bigha of land in Jodhpur. See *Khas Rukka Parwana, Bahi* no. 1, document dated *Asoj vadi 13*, 1842/1785, Jodhpur Records. Ibid., document dated *Posh Sudi 2*, 1824/1767. Records mention Shah Bhola Nath of Agra, who set up shop in Jodhpur, as having received 50 per cent exemption from the payment of *dan, mapa, rahdari,* and other taxes. Similar concessions were extended to Bal Kishandas Gangadas Khandelwal of Bharatpur, whose business straddled the chieftaincies of Jodhpur and Bharatpur; ibid., document dated *Shrawan vadi 12*, 1847/1790.

88. *JSPB* 9, document dated *Kartik vadi 13* (folio number is not clear) 1826/1769, Jodhpur Records, RSAB.

89. *JSPB* 14, 1831/1774, ff. 44–5. When Jivandas Lohiya of Nagaur, for instance, incurred tremendous losses in his business, and the moneylenders were pressurizing him for an early repayment of the loan, he sought the maharaja's (Durbar's) intervention. On his request the Durbar persuaded the creditors to accept that Jivandas would pay 50 per cent of the loan immediately and the rest through instalments. Jivandas was indeed relieved and the claims of the sahukars settled amicably.

90. From the late seventeenth century, a rapid rise in the proportion of non-agrarian to agrarian taxes is evident, and the percentage of the former, called

*Bija Rakama (*other amounts*)* or *sair*, went upto 44 per cent of the total revenue collected in the year AD 1682; see *Vigat* I, pp. 167–8.

91. The Kachhwahas of Amber, Ranas of Udaipur, rulers of Kota and Bundi, of Sirohi, Alwar, as also Malwa, and the Peshwas in the Deccan, were all engaged in enticing skilled manpower to make their home in their respective states, extending patronage in different forms; see, for instance, *Dastur Komwar*, Jaipur Records, RSAB.

92. Gulam Muhammad, a well-known calico-printer of Nagaur, hailed from Multan; see *JSPB* 25, 1838/1781, f. 216. Outstanding workmanship was often rewarded with inam in the shape of cash, land, or an honour like the presentation of a turban (*pag*) from the maharaja, and artisanal petitions for clemency and relief from tax burdens often indicate state generosity.

93. The Jodhpur Durbar gave Rs 100 as inam to Darzi Asa, a tailor from Nagaur; see *JSPB* 4, 1831/1774. *Kotwali-Chabutara-Jamabandi Bahi* no. 754 of pargana Jalor records that *Sorgar* (gunpowder maker) Lala was given a turban as inam by the Durbar; see f. 25.

94. In 1778, when the traders of Nagaur were transporting goods from Kota to Nagaur for the Mundwa fair, they expressed apprehensions that they might be looted near Bundi. Hence about 400 gunmen were sent by the Durbar of Jodhpur to escort them till the boundary of Marwar; *JSPB* 21, 1835/1778, f. 239. Officers attached to the court in Parbatsar were ordered by the Jodhpur Durbar to escort safely the bullocks of Moti Ram Vyas, carrying salt from Nava to Ajmer; see *JSPB* 21, 1835/1778, f. 239.

95. In 1777, when the traders of Pali were carrying 32 camels loaded with cotton, lead, and grocery goods from Pali to Rajgarh (Bikaner) they were looted near Nawalgarh. The Jodhpur Durbar wrote a strong letter to Nawal Singh Shekhawat, thakur of Nawalgarh, to recover the goods from the robbers. See *JSPB* 19, 1834/1777, f. 280.

96. Maharaja Vijai Singh gave the huge sum of over Rs 5,000 from the customs treasury of Nagaur to Seth Manakchand Anopchand and Chokh Chand of Bikaner as compensation for their merchandize. Dalel Singh, the son of a big landed magnate Akhay Singh, had looted their goods near qasba Mandana, in 1765. See *JSPB* 2, 1822/1765, document dated *Posh vadi 14*, (folio number is unclear). In 1776 Malum Singh Ladkhani looted Jodhpur's merchant Heera Chand Vishnoi's gold coins (*asharfis*), expensive textiles, bullion and horses. The dacoity took place near Bundi when Heera Chand was returning from the Deccan to Jodhpur after selling his camels. On his request the Jodhpur Durbar sent a personal letter to the Bundi ruler to help the merchant recover his goods; see *JSPB* 17, 1833/1776, f. 299.

97. V.K. Jain, *Trade and Traders in Western India*, AD *1000–1300* (New Delhi, 1990). Similar concessions were granted to Seth Balkishan Das of Bharatpur who traded between Jodhpur and Bharatpur and Shah Radhakishan Roopchand of Dig who operated between Dig and Jodhpur; see *JSPB* 9, 1826/1769, (folio number unclear, document dated *Marghashirsha vadi 3*. Also see *Khas Rukka Parwana Bahi*

no. 1, doc. dated *Shrawan vadi 12*, 1847/1790; ibid., dated *Baisakh vadi 6*, 1824/1767.

98. *JSPB* 2, 1822/1765, f. 45B; *JSPB* 9, 1826/1769, document dated *Bhadrapad sudi 3*, and no. 25, 1838/1781, f. 236.

99. Tod, vol. 2, pp. 812–13.

100. See *Khas Rukka Parwana Bahi*, no. 1, 1822–88/1764–1831, Jodhpur Records.

101. *JSPB* 2, 1822/1765, f. 22; *JSPB* 6,1826/1769, f. 48; *JSPB* 21, 1835/1778, f. 292.

102. Bishop Reginald Heber, *Narrative of a Journey through the Upper Provinces of India*, AD *1824–25*, 2 vols (London, 1844), p. 454.

103. Tod, vol. II, pp. 1109–10.

104. B.D. Chattopadhyaya in his *The Making of Early Medieval India*, traces their growth to the eleventh and twelfth centuries which had witnessed the resurgence of local merchant lineages already in operation, such as the Dharkatas and the Sonis, both of whom represented the later day Oswals; p. 111. The period also saw the emergence of hitherto unfamiliar merchant lineages which established wide intra-regional and inter-regional networks. Shah Dwarkadas Jagjivandas Gujarati was a renowned merchant of Jodhpur who carried on trade on a large-scale between Jodhpur and Gujarat and Bohra Daudyar Khan of Surat brought merchandize from Surat and Gujarat for sale to Jodhpur; see *JSPB* 10, 1827/1770, document dated Chaira vadi *10* and *Khas Rukka Parwana Bahi* no. 1, 1824/1767 dated Shrawan vadi 11.

105. Seth Mohanlal Khatri of Multan had his branches in Nagaur and Pali, Bhoj Raj Ganga Raj Agrawal, kothiwal of Jaipur and Shah Bhola Nath, kothiwal of Jodhpur, had branches in Agra; see *Khas Rukka Parwana Bahi* no. 1, Posh Sud 9, 1846/1789; Parwana from Maharaja Prithvi Singh to Bhoj Raj Gang Raj Agrawal dated *Kartik Sud 15*, 1828/1771, *Draft Kharita and Parwana*, Jaipur Records, and *Khas Rukka Parwana Bahi* no. 1, Posh Sud 2, 1824/1767, Jodhpur Records, respectively.

106. Seth Khushal Chand Lohiya was a renowned merchant of Nagaur, who traded extensively between Jodhpur, Nagaur, and Harauti, in particular Kota and Bundi; *JSPB* 21, 1835/1778, f. 239. Two of Bikaner's kothiwals, Vinay Chand Santokh Chand, and Akhai Chand Keshri Chand, had branches in Jodhpur, Jalor, Pali, and Nagaur while Shah Jaskaran Mandas of Jaipur also had a branch in Pali. See *Khas Rukka Parwana Bahi* no. 1,1838/1781, *Baisakh Sud 5*; *Khas Rukka Parwana Bahi*, vs 1848, AD 1791, Kartik vadi 8, ibid.,1825/1768, *Bhadrapad Sudi 2*, Jodhpur Records.

107. *Jodhpur Bahiyat* no. 9, 1823/1766, Jodhpur Records.

108. The small weights used by goldsmiths (sunars), money-changers (sarrafs), moneylenders (sahukars) and makers of herbal medicines (*vaids*) were the *tola*, masha, and *ratti*, one tola being equal to 12 mashas, and one masha equal to eight rattis. Cloth was measured in yards, termed *gaz*, which in Jodhpur, measured 32 fingers. The length of a scroll of cloth was generally 24 gaz. Nainsi's

Vigat vol. II, p. 456 notes that a scroll of muslin of 24 gaz cost Rs 4, annas 4, and takas 3.

109. See B.L.Gupta, *Trade and Commerce in Rajasthan during the Eighteenth Century* (Jaipur,1987), p. 103.

110. From the Kota Records we know that in the qasbas of Manoharthana, Dhulat and Arand-Khera, the weekly markets were held on Sundays, Tuesdays and Fridays respectively. See *Bhandar* no. 4, *Basta* no. 3, *Zakat Bahi*, qasba Manoharthana, 1873/1816, Jaipur Records. In the haat on Jyeshtha vadi 11, 1884/1827, in Manoharthana 15 cobblers, 6 lac banglemakers, 9 weavers, 22 calicoprinters, 7 money-changers, 4 confectioners, 7 each of blacksmiths and goldsmiths, and 20 vegetable-sellers brought their goods for sale. *Bhandar* no. 8, *Basta* no. 3, *Zakat Bahi*, Qasba Manoharthana, Jaipur Records, cited by B.L. Gupta, *Trade and Commerce in Rajasthan* (Jaipur, 1987), p. 80.

111. Tod , vol. II, p. 125; A letter in the Jaipur Records from Madho Rao Scindia to Maharaja Sawai Pratap Singh dated *Asoj Sud* 11, 1848/1791, published by RSAB under the title *Kharita-Gwalior-Jaipur* documents that merchants came to this fair from even as far as Gwalior.

112. *Rajputana Gazetteer*, vol. III-A, p. 346.

113. *Vigat*, vol. II, p. 424.

114. Tod, vol. II, p. 29; *Rajputana Gazetteer*, vol. II, p. 258; *Khas Rukka Parwana Bahi* no. 1, *Asoj Sud* 5, 1824/1765; and *JSPB* 13, 1830/1773, f. 65, Jodhpur Records mention that camels were purchased from the Mundawa fair for Nawab Shuja-ud-Daulah of Awadh by his agent Hayat Khan.

115. Forty dams made a rupiya, and the rate remained constant from Akbar's time; see Abul Fazl's *Ain-i-Akbari*, trans. by Blochman, vol. I, (Calcutta, 1873), p. 41.

116. V.N. Reu, *Coins of Marwar* (Jodhpur, 1946), p. 5.

117. The weight of the *Bijaishahi rupiya* was 176.4 grains and it contained 169.9 grains of pure silver and 6.5 grains of alloy. The dyes used for coining rupees were also used for coining half, quarter and one-eighth pieces of the rupee.The Bijaishahi copper coins, the *Dhabbushahis*, varied between 310 to 320 grains, though during Maharaja Bhim Singh's reign (1793–1803 AD) their weight increased by 2 mashas; see Reu, *Coins of Marwar*, p. 10.

118. See Frank Perlin's 'Changes in the Production and Circulation of Money in Seventeenth and Eighteenth Century India: An Essay on Monetisation Before Colonial Occupation', in Sanjay Subrahmanyam (ed.) *Money and the Market in India,1100–1700* (Delhi, 1994), pp. 276–307; and 'Money-Use in Late Pre-Colonial India and the International Trade in Currency Media', in J.F. Richards (ed.) *Imperial Monetary System of Mughal India* (Delhi, 1987), pp. 232–373.

119. *JSPB* 13, 1830/1773, ff.14–15, and *JSPB* 1,1821/1764, f. 181 respectively.

120. Irfan Habib in 'The System of Bills of Exchange (*Hundis*) in the Mughal Empire', in Satish Chandra (ed.) *Essays in Medieval Indian Economic History* (New Delhi, 1987), pp. 207–21 traces the operative mechanisms of hundis at length.

121. For example, Seth Daya Ram Roop Chand, a famous banker of Jodhpur, lent out rupees one lakh to the Durbar for a period of two and a half months to clear off the debt to Tukoji Holkar. This loan was repayable from the income of *sair* or customs' treasury of Dariba Nawa, Didwana, Parbatsar and Maroth. *Khas Rukka Parwana Bahi* no. 1, *Chaitra vadi* 13, 1847/1790, Jodhpur Records.

122. Jeth Mal Sarraf was a money-changer in Didwana, as documented in *JSPB* 14, 1831/1774, f. 21A.

123. Brindavan Vyas, moneylender of Merta, advanced a loan of Rs 61 and annas 8 to Beni Kalani of the same town, at 15 per cent interest per annum on the surety of Ganeshji Kalani. See *Lokmani Sangrah Bahi* no. 5, *Magha Vadi 12*, 1830 1773, RSAB.

124. Chapters 3 and 4 cite several instances from eighteenth-century records.

125. See Nainsi's *Vigat*, part II, p. 88.

126. G.D. Sharma, 'State Land Revenue Demand in Marwar during the Seventeenth Century', *Proceedings of Rajasthan History Congress*, 1974, Pali session, pp. 69–73.

127. See Perlin's 'State Formation Reconsidered', in *Modern Asian Studies*, vol. 19, (3), 1985, pp. 415–80.

128. See Nainsi, *Vigat*, part II, p. 89.

129. This was not true for Marwar alone; Sumit Guha has noticed similar trends in eighteenth-century Maharashtra, and C.A. Bayly and Muzaffar Alam in North India. See Guha's 'Potentates, Traders and Peasants: Western India, c.1700–1870' in Burton Stein and Sanjay Subrahmanyam (eds) *Institutions and Economic Change in South Asia* (Delhi, 1996), pp. 71–84.

3

Artisanal Jatis, Jati Panchayats, and the State

Of their laws little or nothing is maintained, for the rulers are absolute, even though they have law books preserved by their jurists, the *cazis* (....) For who shall prescribe or demand of the governor, why do you judge us so, when our law commands otherwise? Such a thing will never happen, though every city has its court (*ketschari*) or hall of justice, where, in the king's name, the governor meets daily, or four times a week for the settling of disputes, albeit that nothing is decided, in which official greed does not play a role.[1]

Having mapped the contextual background in which artisans—the dramatis personae of this study—struggled to eke out a living, this chapter seeks to understand the social world of the artisans in terms of legally valid conventions. It begins by looking at gendered production processes in artisanal households, discussing broad patterns in the interactions between women of craft castes, and their families, communities, and the state. It notices the collusion amongst the three to domesticate and discipline women through a variety of customs and traditions.[2] It goes on to probe the consolidation of caste identities around shared norms, and examines the relative position of scriptures and customary laws in the early modern state's dispensation of justice, especially in the context of lower formations such as artisans. This chapter also looks at the internal organization and regulation of artisanal societies, and the institution of caste councils that monitored their everyday lives. Positing these artisanal caste assemblies in relation to the state, it attempts to comprehend the rationale that governed the interlocking of the two, and thereby comments on the nature of power play between the 'community' and the 'state' in the period.

GENDERED PRODUCTION RELATIONS
AND THE ARTISANAL WORLD

It is well known that since the bulk of manufactured goods in the pre-industrial era was meant for the qasba and rural markets, small units of production
were able to meet the demand. Hence, the characteristic form of artisanal
production involved the use of family labour, using very little capital. He-
redity was the chief determinant of an artisan's choice of trade in the country
as in the town, and an artisan's home became a typical workshop, with
capital provided from the surplus over the craftsmen's consumption needs.
Even in areas which specialized as metallurgy, knowledge about correct
temperatures and timing for melting metals was gained by observation,
experience, and oral guidance imparted by elders to youngsters. Male adults
of a family of weavers, for instance, worked under the guidance of the
head of the family, with adolescent boys permitted to help with the job,
observe closely the co-ordination of eyes, hands, and feet, and gradually
learn the trade.[3]

Marwar Mardum Shumari is emphatic in its acknowledgment that
craftswomen routinely participated in the production process of their husbands' trade. The julahi spun the yarn before her husband could work on
the loom, the chhipi worked both at printing tie-and-dye patterns and dyeing the fabrics, the kumharin helped in sifting, kneading and preparing the
clay, as her husband as shaped vessels on the wheel and later embellishing
the pots with intricate patterns, and the chamarin embroidered with cotton
and silk threads on the shoes, saddles, scabbards, and belts that her husband
crafted.[4] They did not live behind purdah or within the confines of their
homes since work took them out to the fields, to their patrons' houses, and
sometimes to the markets too. Cooking and rearing children were, of course,
women's responsibility, but the sharp public/private dichotomy so marked
in elite households, keeping feminine labour away from the professional
realm, was not true for artisanal families.[5] Men's and women's labours were
less spatially distinct, and internal differentiation within the family with
women's management of domestic chores alone and men's exclusive shoul-
dering of occupational burdens, was less marked than what has been
documented for families of superior castes.[6]

The gendered world of artisanal castes however displays a certain ambivalence and constant tension between the need to allow women autonomy
to conduct work in public spaces, and patriarchal imperatives of policing
their sexuality and tightly disciplining their lives. In addition to women's
critical contribution to craft production, agricultural work, and livestock-
rearing, their reproductive potential and ability to provide labouring hands
made them precious members of society. High mortality rates put immense
premium on fertility and their families, communities, as well as the state,

needed to exploit their reproductive potential to the fullest to maximize the production of working members. Both family economies and those of the region they inhabited could not be stable otherwise. The fear of loosing control over them was correspondingly acute, and misogynic anxieties dictated that they be placed under strict control and supervision.[7] Suspicions regarding the fidelity of women and their subjection to physical abuse by family and caste members were common.[8] Physical injuries and penalization that men inflicted on female relatives for the exaction of services or for the violation of behavioural norms included defacement and cutting off their ears and nose to make them physically unattractive and, thereby, neutered.

Women past their reproductive age were, however, of relatively minimal utility, especially if their ability to perform laborious work was also impaired. Viewed as burdens who would drain family resources without contributing in any way, they were readily labelled as witches (*dakans*) by the villagers, and often abused to force them to flee from their homes. For others younger in age, functional indispensability somewhat mitigated the asymmetry in the cultural constructions of the dominant and subordinate sex in the artisanal world, but women's critical role in the family economy did not translate into extending equality with their husbands. The patriarchal imprint of the larger culture ensured that artisanal women did not receive any training in the skilled aspects of the craft or develop any great expertise in commodity production. Left at the peripheries of the production process, gendered boundaries were strictly laid out regarding the processes the two sexes would handle. They were not trained to weave or work the potter's wheel under the pretext that the special skill and monopoly developed in the woman's natal family would otherwise disseminate to another family through her marriage. Thus, left lacking in professional expertise, they were not allowed to own the tools of production, did not earn wages as men could, and could not claim as their own the income from the sale of commodities they hugely participated in producing.[9]

The androcentric nature of craft society comes forth in the fact that the contribution women made to the production process was deliberately and invariably structured in a manner that assigned them the performance of tedious but non-mechanical, supposedly easy tasks. The organization of production, mostly in the seclusion of individual homes as part of an extension of their house-wifely chores, supposedly performed during leisure hours, rendered women's work relatively invisible.[10] Their work was thus simultaneously valued and devalued, and while the need to obtain a wife to perform certain laborious tasks requiring patience was intensely felt and painstakingly negotiated—this did not result in eradicating the asymmetry in gendered relations of artisanal society.

Demographic factors caused a much lower ratio of women-to-men among craft communities, women's numbers gradually dwindling over the centuries due to deaths caused by poverty and its attendant symptoms— malnutrition, frequent pregnancies, deaths during childbirth resulting from primitive obstetric interventions, and inadequate medical care. The resultant shortage of 'wives' in a society acutely dependent on its female labour, in response, led to the emergence of social customs. Marriages in craft society required the payment of bride-price rather than dowry; remarriage (*nata*) was considered legitimate both for divorced and widowed women, and when the latter remarried, the prospective groom had to pay widow-price despite the importance attached to the virginity of brides. Also interesting are the contrasting repercussions that wifely adultery invited in elite and artisanal households. The former held dishonour as the ultimate injury and did not even stop at physically liquidating an adulterous woman. But in artisanal families a woman's lover paid monetary compensation to the husband (*bair ke paise*) to claim the woman, and with the transaction turning legally valid, the woman and her lover were free to live 'happily ever after'!

These social customs and many others appear incongruous in view of the deep roots of patriarchy embedded across different arenas of Indian culture. Deeper analysis, however, clearly establishes that these customs were not a recognition of women's dominant position or of sexual needs of widows, but an arrangement to maximize the utilization of their labour and their fertility, which in turn would ensure the constant replenishment of the labouring and servicing castes.[11] In fact, the stability of the hierarchically stratified pre-industrial Indian society was predicated upon the lower manufacturing and service castes maximizing reproduction. Distinctive patriarchal arrangements and cultural codes, apparently polar opposite as far as the elite and subordinate castes are concerned, reflected ideological imperatives resulting from material constraints of a hierarchically ordered society.[12] Chastity of wives was, therefore, of relatively little concern to the lower castes, with husbands more interested in having their wives (labour) restored or material compensations earned if they eloped with their lovers.

The patriarchal culture of the Rathor state was complicit in the subjugation of craftswomen, the administration generally recognizing the identity of women through their male relatives. Documents record men alone in their manufacturing capacity, usually leaving women nameless, identifiable only with reference to their male guardians, be they husbands, fathers, or brothers. Even in situations where a woman from a craft group approached the administration with a petition, her name was in most cases excluded from the record, and she was merely referred to as the mother, sister, or wife of the male head of the household.[13] The phallogocentric lens of the male notaries and scribes who recorded the petitions could discern a world of males alone, ensuring that that they viewed women as no more than mere appendages of their male relatives.

As much as artisanal societies come across as ambiguous in their treatment of women, state interventions on gendered disputes also suggest anomalous and multiple responses, dependent on the specificities of the case. On the one hand, numerous petitions where craftswomen or their male guardians complained against sexual exploitation by men of superior castes, state reactions corroborate Guha's thesis about the pre-colonial state being 'soft with the hard and hard with the soft'. In the case of Khati Bakhtiya's wife, for instance, the woman's complaint about being repeatedly raped by four rajput brothers residing in her village was not able to stand in the face of the power and status of the alleged culprits. The immensely superior social status of the bhati rajputs, a power centre that the state could ill-afford to annoy, ensured that the state submitted to their pressures and denied the victim justice.[14] Caste-based discriminations on the part of the state, and arbitrary dispensations were neither unusual nor always a site of contestation.

The case of a lakhara's daughter lends further credence to the fact that often men of means, either by virtue of their social status or material strength, oppressed women of suppressed castes, and the latter had no recourse if the state failed them, as it often tended to do. A lakhara of village Nimbaj had given his daughter in marriage to another lakhara from Bikaner, but her husband, perhaps due to extreme poverty, sold her to a purohit. The latter, clearly a man of substantial means, sent away the hapless girl as a slave/maid (goli) with his daughter to her marital home. The lakhara then brought back his daughter and arranged for her remarriage. Annoyed at the loss of the girl's services, and keen to retrieve them, the purohit promptly levelled charges of theft of ornaments on the girl.[15] Such false allegations by the elites against those of the lower castes were common, and the state, though aware of these exploitative tendencies of superior castes, often tended to ignore the injustice committed.

However, when collective solidarity of an entire caste supported the cause of a woman, the state felt compelled to relent. This is evident in the case where the Kumhars of Desuri got together and came to the Durbar to complain that a petty official misbehaved with the daughter-in-law of their caste-fellow Kumhar Rupla. They claimed that the official, Ahmad Khan, had insulted another woman on an earlier occasion, and the hakim had desisted from taking Ahmad to task. Despite the hakim's best efforts to save the official, the combined pressure exerted by the kumhar community ultimately led to the dismissal of Ahmad Khan.[16] It were the concerns of statecraft and expediency which guided state action, and we should not be misled into perceiving in this action any genuine concern for protecting women's honour.

Yet another case is reflective of craftswomen's experiences vis-à-vis the state and this also points to the fact that, rather than a monolith, the state comprised of a complex structured hierarchy with several layers of authority, the multiple levels of command often at loggerheads pursuing rival agendas. A luhar's ten-years-old daughter was charged of theft by the wife of a landed jat. The latter called in a *bhopi* and she confirmed the jat woman's allegation as correct. The state officer posted in the village, Pandit Gopal, decreed that the luhar must pay him hundred and twenty rupees and another twenty to the bhopi. The young girl continually denied the charges, and her father complained at the *kachedi* against Gopal's high-handedness. Since Gopal's verdict was based on the bhopi's version, the kachedi asked her to predict the identity of other culprits of thefts that had or would be committed elsewhere in the state. She failed to do so, and now convinced that the whole affair was a conspiracy against the luhar, the kachedi ordered that Gopal must limit his role to collecting land revenue or hasil and not meddle in other affairs of the village. He was directed to report matters to the kachedi and not pass judgments himself, and was asked to return the luhar's money.[17] The state's motivation in this case was clipping the wings of Pandit Gopal, cutting him to size, and thereby gesturing that state officials must not over-step their brief. It was an occasion that the state utilized to assert its supremacy over petty officials who, unless checked, were prone to expand their local bases by extending patronage to some at the cost of others. Though the young luharan's innocence was established through state intervention, she was of course inconsequential to everyone concerned with the case.

Women from the craft castes were not merely subject to upper-caste exploitation, but also suffered inequities within the domestic domain of their own households. Often, there appears a tacit understanding between state magistrates, community heads as well as male adults of households that the latter had a certain right to chastise their women for discipline, and that the state need not restrain them in performing their patriarchal prerogatives. When Khati Sukha of Jaitaran cut off the nose and hands of Khati Khiwa's wife, the woman received no compensation. The Jaitaran kachedi instead deemed her husband as the injured party, and thought it appropriate to enquire from him whether Sukha had been instigated, or that Khiwa believed that his wife's (bad) character had invited this assault on her. The woman was denied justice and men, apparently oblivious of the grave physical and mental injury to her, deliberated on her propensities and moral disposition.[18] Defamation and character assassination of women was a long-standing prerogative of men, the simplest tactic for controlling and taming them.

A countervailing set of principles, however, came into play in some cases where the petitioner was a woman and 'good' governance demanded domestication of communal and familial patriarchy. The latter, after all, unlike powerful landed notables, could be tackled relatively easily and need not intrude to disrupt the rajdharma of the state. Rulers' paternalist postures and commitment to help the weakest subjects led them, in several cases, to treat women's petitions as an appeal to the *mai-baap* (paternal) element of their patriarchal disposition. Such pleas encouraged them to extend their magisterial authority in favour of the helpless 'weaker' sex, resonating with the state's charities towards the blind, the handicapped, and the mentally challenged in their territories. Nai Jhunga's wife in Parbatsar complained that a local sunar had raped her and run away when the state soldiers went to arrest him. She informed that he had returned to the qasba and pleaded that he must be punished. Immediate orders for imposing a fine (gunegari) on the sunar were passed.[19] This, of course, was a rather lenient penalty, but a barber's wife clearly deserved no compensation.

Gendered attitudes influenced the dispensation of justice in many more ways. For instance, even when women committed the severest of crimes, the state did not usually order death penalty for them. More commonly, serious offences by women caused them to be banished from the region.[20] Making a home in an alien environment away from one's community could indeed be extremely trying, and in ordering 'social death' rather than physical liquidation, the state's male chauvinism and perhaps the material concern to keep alive her womb had a role to play.

Though polygamy was tolerated, wilful neglect of wife and children was not. State intervention in the domestic domain was mostly geared towards ensuring the provision of maintenance for wives and children. Adultery and sexual misdemeanour were discouraged but often left unpunished, as opposed to abortion, which was punished severely through fines. Curbing public traffic in young girls without the consent of her guardians was also a concern and prostitution was discouraged, as evident from the following case:

Goldsmith (Sunar) Ramchandra of Merta petitioned to Shri Huzur (the King) that his grand-daughter had been married into (a family of) Nagaur. Her husband died. The wife of Sunar Mayaram of Jodhpur had gone for a holy dip (pilgrimage) to Sri Pokarji and on her way back, met and misled (*bhakaei*) his grand-daughter. The lady offered to arrange the young girl's remarriage with a man who would present her a three-string necklace. Thus tempting the young girl, she took her to Jodhpur and kept her in a *Nathi ka barha* (prostitution house). Thereafter she took the girl to *Anar ri beri* and was getting her remarried when the community leaders (*Panch*) learnt of this episode and informed the state. The lady and the young widow were detained at the city magistrate's office that (informed the girl's kin and her) brother Sunar Bhola came from Merta to Jodh-pur to take his sister back. The Durbar warned the lady of dire consequences if she repeated her ill-conceived attempts at enticement, and admonished the widow's family for negligence.[21]

Clearly, some regulation controlling the buying and selling of women was seen as necessary for otherwise, the crime of kidnapping infant girls and the inveigling of women from their families would become uncomfort-ably pervasive. It would encourage husbands to treat their wives as disposable property, and even encourage those unable to repay their debts to sell their children. The sale of women not merely for their labour as household menials but also as concubines and prostitutes was common because they possessed in their bodies a vendible commodity. The selling and buying of human beings and traffic in female slaves, therefore, seems to have been rampant, and the state's disapproval did not translate into banning this form of commerce. Women, in particular, were sold, bought, and resold into marriage or concubinage, and these transactions were insulated from mag-isterial penalties. Both in law and in custom, slavery was recognized without reprehension, akin to polygamous liaisons common all over.

Masculine authority over the domestic sphere, its women, and children in particular, was fully endorsed both by craft communities and the state. The extreme vulnerability of women from the craft castes, especially those belonging to exceptionally poor families, is revealed from a case where Luhar Panche was compelled to sell his daughter to Luhar Bhopa for twenty ru-pees. After getting the sale duly registered, Bhopa gave her in marriage to Luhar Jivarhinye in exchange for a bride price. Bhopa then decided to re-trieve her as her rightful master, and complained at the kachedi, which in its (unfathomable) wisdom, detained Jivarhinye. A whole year passed with the girl's fate unknown till finally her husband appealed to the state to re-consider their decision. The state then tried to resolve the dispute on the basis of the legalities of the case.[22] That it did not care to undo the injus-tices to the woman, or find out her preference on the issue, is only to be expected from an early modern androcentric state when sensitivity to women's rights would be anachronistic to expect.

Shorn of all rights of selfhood, such women and children were owned, inherited, sold or gifted like property, and as is evident from the cases cited below, the state viewed their sale as voluntary contracts that their guardians had wilfully entered into. The Mers abdicated the daughter-in-law of Kumhar Hire of village Thaneraw in Pali, and then sold her to Zorawar Mal, a rich bania of the area. The kumhar pleaded with the state, but it ordered that if the buyer had purchased the girl through proper procedure, the transaction supported by a registry, he alone could release her. If Zorawar agreed, the kumhar could compensate him monetarily and retrieve the girl, or else the kumhar would have to reconcile with some money.[23] In another case Kumhari Virki was sold off in her childhood to Mahajan Raje of Kuchaman. Some years later she was abandoned by her owner and got married to Kumhar Laliye. After the passage of considerable time, during which she bore Laliye four children, the mahajan began asserting his rights over her all over again. A dispute arose as to who she would live with now, and the authorities decided that if the mahajan had documents proving his purchase of the woman, he may have her; but if otherwise, she was to live with her husband.[24] In these cases, the rescue of the girls and their restoration to their families was considered inappropriate because the sale had already become legally valid. But in the case of the children of a kumhar from village Kailwari, who were kidnapped by a *jogi* in an attempt to sell them, sale could be prevented due to timely intervention. The infant boy died, but the girl survived, perhaps looked after better in the hope of getting a higher price for her. The aggrieved mother complained to the local authorities who managed to pre-empt the sale by rescuing the young girl in time.[25] Similarly, Khati Jesa of village Akhawas in Sojhat was fortunate to have located his daughter with the Mers in time, and was able to bring her back home.[26] The crux of the issue for the state was not that 'freedom' is a legally defensible status, but rather that contracts must be honoured—even if they do not take into account the will of the enslaved. The state therefore did not recognize or protect the status of individuals 'born free'.

Female slaves, commonly known by the terms goli, *bandaran*, and *bandi*, were far greater in number than male ones, and their possession was not confined to private use among aristocratic families alone, but in fact recognized, supported, and utilized by the government as well.[27] Interestingly, female slaves were owned and kept not just by people belonging to the higher echelons but also by those among the lower strata such as tailors, weavers, gardeners, etc. It was hard for any slave to get rid of her bondage, except in cases where her owner was willing and gave his consent to emancipate her. Such forms of servility were of course resented and challenged, and efforts made to break out of the chains of bondage. The alleged slave generally claimed that s/he was a servant and not a slave, while the master insisted to the contrary. In the face of petitions and counter-petitions, the authorities repeatedly took recourse to examining documents in the possession of affected parties. They ascertained whether the litigants' papers were authentic or not, determined whether the monetary transaction confirming the transformation of a free individual into a slave had actually been fully completed through a registry or not, and gave the verdict accordingly. The administration preferred to adopt the legally correct position, and supported the authority of the dominant purchaser/owner rather than the subordinated woman.

Guha notes that 'wifehood and slavery were not distinct states but rather two continua of experience; and that the lower end of the first came sufficiently close to the upper end of the second for one accustomed to the former to be able to resign herself to the latter.'[28] Indeed, indifference towards the concerns of the 'subordinate sex' seems ubiquitous. Khati Udiya of village Nibola in Parbatsar, for instance, complained at the kachedi that though he had not divorced his wife and no paperwork relinquishing his claims over her had been recorded, a caste-fellow Puriya had married his wife when she had gone to Malwa to attend her parents' funerary rites.[29] The least Udiya expected was monetary compensation for losing rights over his wife's labour. As was to be expected in a male-centric ethos, rather than seeking to know the preference and consent of the woman, the state decided to refer to the customs of the khati community to decide the appropriate custodian for the woman. How do we understand these customary traditions, how did they relate to classical Hindu laws, and what was the state's position regarding the enforcement of the two in the case of craft castes?

SCRIPTURES, CUSTOMARY LAWS, AND JUSTICE

The assumption that Hinduism was a unitary, monolithic tradition that prescribed a singular body of laws for everyone over centuries stands exposed today. No longer is the centrality of scriptures alone as the source of Hindu traditions, or the key to understanding them, a perception that is subscribed to.[30] In fact, the huge gap between customary traditions and Brahmanical prescriptions has been long recognized. The juridical prescriptions of classical texts are known to have been more germane to the lives of suvarna or high castes, providing no more than guidelines for the lower formations.

As for the 'lived practices' of the lower formations, the proliferation of jatis and the crystallization of caste identities over time saw society being increasingly governed by customary laws distinct to each community. Parallel to this process ran the inception of Muslims into the subcontinent and, under the Delhi sultans and the Mughals, the picture got more complex with numerous groups adopting the Islamic faith governed by the *Sharia* law, interpreted and implemented by qazis and *muftis*. These Arabic and Sanskrit classical laws were familiar to no more than an infinitesimally small segment of the population, and it was the vast array of local customs that had evolved in response to the exigencies of local environments that the rulers enforced. Pre-colonial legal discourses thus come across as a collage of chaotic diversity—and discerning from this mass of confusing and often contradictory evidence the principles and patterns of legal governance seems no easy task. The fact that as opposed to colonial legal developments, the study of pre-colonial jurisprudence is a hugely neglected area despite its criticality to an understanding of the nature of pre-colonial rule, would still warrant the attempt.

A clear demarcation between civil and penal jurisprudence does not seem to have evolved in pre-colonial times, though what is more than clear is the state's proactive intervention in cases of a political nature and those involving criminal offences. Also, as Jorg Fische notes, large robberies and dacoities drew direct intervention of the state and this, of course, is understandable in light of the fact that the enforcement of law and order constituted a core function of the state.[31] The sanction to rule was intimately linked to an individual's/dynasty's ability to provide safety and security of life and limb to its subjects, and reining those who caused any breakdown or disruption demanded penal action against the offender both to restore order and to serve as a deterrent for others. This was a fundamental concern of the state due to the rhetoric of rajdharma that the state constantly claimed to abide by. Dispensation of justice had, indeed, the symbolic significance of representing the ruler and his rule as a manifestation of judicious and righteous rule, the display of his ability to punish and the demonstration of his will and power to do so integral to the administration of criminal justice.

The characterization of the pre-colonial legal system and justice has therefore ranged from being labelled as an enlightened and paternal despotism to an arbitrary and discriminatory authoritarianism practising and enforcing a disorderly jumble of anarchical and confusing laws that varied—not only from region to region—but also from one community to another.[32] Was this then the law of the jungle, unregulated by any notion of universal principles, enforcing the survival of the fittest? Were there no cultural codes of rule, rank, status, and gender, or ideological principles that the state had to struggle with, for legitimizing its authority? In the state-subaltern encounter, in particular, this section seeks to identify strands that governed administrative concerns.

For one, upholding the jati order by ensuring the fixation, in time and space, of the rights and obligations of every member of society, was a fundamental concern of the state. Susan Bayly noticed that if kings did not issue and confirm jati titles, and order their retainers and subjects in the idiom of caste, they would not be perceived as embodiments of kingliness.[33] This maintenance of the caste order was a major component in the assertion of political supremacy, and therefore an essential ingredient in state-formation.[34] In the case of eighteenth-century Maharashtra, Fukazawa pointed out that the Peshwai and its central bureaucracy sought to preserve the caste hierarchy in the areas under its control through the legal apparatus of the state.[35] Uma Chakravarti and Sumit Guha emphasized that the Peshwas, brahmins by caste, sought to recreate the brahmanical Hindu kingdom that strictly upheld the brahmanical social order after capturing power. In this situation, writes Chakravarty, privileging brahmins and suppressing other lower castes were complementary trends. Functioning self-consciously as a dharmarajya, the Peshwa state privileged Shastric law over customary law, and ensured that brahmins retained the highest status by expressly forbidding lower castes from imitating customs practised by the former.[36]

Marwar, in the same period, reveals significant differences from this pattern. Being a rajput-ruled state, affiliation to ritualistic brahmanism seems much less rigid in the case of the Rathors. The state's attempt was restricted to broadly adhering to the caste system and its hierarchy—but rather than brahmins alone, the system privileged a larger spectrum of castes that were important and useful to society. Rajput landed potentates, wealthy mercantile castes, and religious functionaries were of course favoured groups who could manipulate the system, but even subordinate groups like artisans wielded power not always commensurate with their ritual status. Elite behaviour was assessed according to the prescriptions of Shastric laws but customary laws of different communities lower down the social scale enjoyed immense importance too, and the state made a deliberate attempt to enforce these and thus preserve distinct identities of specific groups. In eighteenth-century Marwar, therefore, the situation warrants greater care while labelling different social groups as 'powerful' or 'weak'.

Without doubt, due regard for the superiority of the upper echelons of society, and discretionary punishments in the administration of criminal justice was common in Marwar for the latter was not merely a judicial process but also a political one. In Guha's words, 'The penal regime is, after all an aspect of the political regime'.[37] The institutional core of the Rathor rulers' authority was rather fragile and, given the distributive component of kingship where the right to wield force, administer justice, and award punishment was a layered phenomenon, power and authority was dispersed rather than exclusively concentrated in a singular sovereign. Monarchial interventions had to therefore devise extraordinary justice for extraordinary subjects, assessing the weight of competing interests at play in each case. Such judgments were in many cases flagrant violations of wajabi, and a source of tension.

This broad principle appears to have been a pan-Indian phenomenon in pre-colonial times for, as quoted by Radhika Singha, the Mughal emperor Akbar—in stating the ideal for determining appropriate forms of punishment—prescribed that they should vary according to rank and status of the offender. 'In short, punishment is the most important affair of sovereignty... punishment of everyone should be befitting his condition... a severe glance at a man of lofty nature is equivalent to killing him, while a kick is of no avail to a man of low nature'.[38] Whatever justification the rulers may have believed in for the unequal justice they often meted out, the fact was that the state was far from being omnipotent, and in fact had to constantly reckon with the relative power and resources of multiple foci of power, many of whom were often the offenders and the accused. They posed threats of retaliation against any penal action curbing their unjust ways, and the state had few options but to reconcile to their status and accommodate their excesses. A news report of 1781 cites that Kumhar Narano of village Dudhorh in Sojhat was killed by the jagirdar's men, allegedly on the ground that the kumhar had made an attempt to steal from the fortress. They claimed that on seeing him prowl around in the night, they had presumed him to be a thief and stabbed him to death. Though the kumhar's family brought the facts to light that the kumhar was involved in a love affair with the jagirdar's goli, and that this indiscretion had cost him his life, the state merely ordered for verification of the allegation of theft and penalties to be decided accordingly.[39] The fact that even on suspicion of theft, the guards should have done no more than arrest the kumhar, and that killing him was clearly an abuse of their power, was neither noticed nor commented upon by the state authorities.[40] Clearly, the jagirdar's influential position made it undesirable to invite his ire and his men, as a consequence, were let off leniently. Rather than causing public humiliation or awarding incarceration, mutilation or capital punishment to men of means, the state dared go no further than mildly chastizing them, combined with the imposition of some fines in the name of justice.

As a mere primus interpares in a continuum of power centres whose fortunes constantly waxed and waned, the state was incapable of exercising sustained coercion against rival foci of authority. Their unceasing challenges to royal will and unremitting competitive struggles compelled the rulers to be acutely aware of constrains on their capacities, and left them with little choice but to capitulate. Exigencies of statecraft dictated that the support of rural and urban notables for the regime be obtained at all costs. Over a period, repeated surrenders before their pressures and adjustments made in view of their coercive might created precedents of royal authority succumbing to them, and compromises with them in view of their power and resources became the 'custom of the country'. Mahajan Fata of Bhinmal murdered Silawat Bahadur's wife, and for this crime, he was fined twenty-five rupees, a negligible amount for a man of substantial means as most mahajans were.[41] Corporal forms of pain were usually reserved for the lower castes, and the state order merely stated that the aggrieved had demanded this amount (and no more). In other cases of homicide, the state extorted a huge fine from the culprits apart from the 'blood money' that constituted compensation, the guilty were liable to pay to the victim's family. But in this case there is no mention of any other payment due from the mahajan, a clear evidence of his clout and the state's unwillingness to annoy those of means. The state had to, after all, ensure that powerful men did not turn refractory and rebellious, and had to assess the material and manpower resources that Fata could marshall if punished. Every time the state gave in to elite pressure, it began to seem natural and grew to enjoy sanction as custom and tradition. Thus, political expediency and customs derived from it dictated state judgements, invariably geared towards being agreeable to the rank of the offender. State orders therefore appear arbitrary and variable, depending on the relative degree and extent of clout enjoyed by the litigants. An unequal application of law was combined with abbreviated and summary judicial procedures that 'may give the stamp of due process to crude devices of policing and prosecution'.[42]

The judicial process was an arena of negotiation and contest and what is interesting is that politics did not merely shape the outcome of the judicial process, but also fashioned the nature of documentation preserved by the rulers. Without recording any details about the cause of the crime and the relationship between it and the punishment ordered, judicial documents are extremely sketchy accounts of events. Those transcribing petitions stated very briefly the offence and punishment announced, the narration of events devoid of any details, and the decision taken by the judicial authorities lacking in the record of explanation or rationale for state orders. The fact that scriptural enactments on criminal law were familiar to no more than a section of the minority community freed the judicial authorities to pursue their own agenda, as expedient in different cases. They did not cite laws that could become binding precedents and thereby potentially disrupt faith in their righteousness. Transparency in their rulings would after all expose them and their discretionary space.

As long as judicial decisions were acceptable to the people and did not generate a level of tension that was disruptive of peace and order, the administration was prone to practising partiality. That it did not always succeed in quelling stresses and resentments generated by unfair dispensations is obvious from the numerous petitions that questioned state orders and appealed for reconsideration by reiterating the injustice embedded in them. People also challenged state inaction in the face of pressures from the dominant groups, or from their employees. Rangrez Rahman complained that though the guard (*chopdar*) at the royal artillery (*top khana*) had been involved in illicit relationship with his wife for a year, and this had been brought to the notice of the kotwal, no action had been taken. Unable to ignore the matter any longer, the administration ordered that the chopdar's version be recorded, and the kotwal was ordered to do the needful.[43]

Co-existent with this need to protect the prestige of landed magnates was the necessity to check indiscreet expansion in their power. Rulers care-

fully gauged their vulnerability vis-à-vis a power centre. A sense of solidarity with one from superior echelons of society was balanced against the
need to erode the power of a competitor and, in the process, enhance the
legitimacy of their rule. It is in this context that we need to nuance Guha's
formula because the exigencies of politics itself dictated the state to not
merely be 'soft' with the 'hard' but also to soften the hard with a firm hand.
The extension of the instrument of petitions to the subjects served the purpose of legitimation, and as the final, superior-most locus of authority, the
state sought to be perceived as one that could intercede to provide justice to
the softest. The penal regime was, of course, an aspect of the political regime, but politics did not merely necessitate an alliance with those in
possession of material resources. Equally, statecraft demanded popular cog-
nizance of the state as the repository of just and legitimate authority.

In numerous instances, therefore, subjects from the lower formations
sought and obtained justice, their petitions to the state finding favourable
responses without undue discrimination. Sunar Chutare of village Idawa,
for instance, was to get money from the jagirdar for essaying coins, but the
latter had him thrown out of the village without any provocation. The sunar
made a representation against the jagirdar and was able to win justice.[44]
When there was a theft at Sunar Dahe's house at village Khairadi in Merta,
the *hawaldar* remained indifferent, and did not even bother to send the *pagi*
(footprints' reader) to search for the stolen gold. Dahe complained to the
state authorities who ordered the hawaldar to take necessary action.[45]

Judgments in criminal cases were, of course, subject to intercession,
and powerful individuals negotiated with judicial authorities—not merely
to protect themselves, but also to intercede on behalf of their clients. Patronal
commitments towards clients saw powerful magnates consider it their responsibility to bargain for their dependents, for their own power emanated
from the base that these dependent servants constituted. Their intercession
pushed for the reduction of punishments meted out to 'favoured' clients, as
reported by the wife of Lakhara Ali. She complained that Rangrez Bhikhiya
of her qasba had raped her, and though the gunegari imposed in the first
instance was rupees two hundred, it had later been reduced to a mere twenty-
three rupees due to pressures from some lower-level state functionaries.
She informed that Bhikhiya worked free of charge for these petty officials;
hence, despite being well-to-do and in a position to afford much more, his
patrons had interceded to reduce the fine imposed on him. On her appeal,
the Durbar raised the fine to the original amount and sought investigation
of her claims regarding favours shown by petty officials towards the offender.[46] Clearly, the infliction of discretionary penalties was the prerogative
of the state, and it exercised its power in a discriminatory manner to favour
those in the higher rungs of the chain of social authority. It did not, however, encourage or even allow petty officials to appropriate such powers.

Justice was dispensed not merely by the Durbar and the kachedis or the kotwalis located in important cities and qasbas, but by a multiplicity of power centres who felt empowered enough to exercise magisterial authority. Jagirdars, thakurs, village headmen, and a wide array of local magnates, prebends, and patrons asserted independent jurisdiction in matters of awarding punishments, and this led to great abuse and oppression. Ambitious forays of the notables and the bureaucracy into the realms of power were checked by the state, and overlapping judicial agencies served the purpose of counterposing indiscriminate aggression of administrative functionaries. The aggrieved complained to the state, which enjoyed final appellate authority. The maharajas practised the ritual of personally awarding punishments as part of their daily routine, the latter acting as a symbol of assurance for the weak against the injustices of the strong. Appeals to the maharaja against elite abuse of power brought into play a set of principles guided by the state's patriarchal rhetoric. The state asserted its monopoly as the inflictor of legitimate punishment and central adjudicatory authorities strove to curb subordinate officials from attempts to appropriate such powers. In the case where a rangrez of Pali complained of physical abuse by administrative officials, for instance, the Durbar felt compelled to react and punish. The plaintiff informed that he was using the expensive opium dye called *kasumba* to dye fabrics when the hakim and *silepos* who passed from the area in the midst of Holi celebrations, used six buckets of his dye in playing Holi without a thought about the heavy financial loss this would imply for the poor dyer. When he objected, they thrashed him till he bled. On the dyer's appeal, the state admonished the silepos and ordered him to compensate the dyer by paying rupees two (a significant amount in the eighteenth century).[47] The hakim of course was too big to be touched, his power base placing him above ordinary subjects, and qualifying him to be a recipient of 'extraordinary' justice!

In their role as providers of justice, the state was entitled to revenues that it earned primarily in the shape of fines (gunegari). Magisterial authority was in fact embedded within a social and moral order of 'legitimate conduct' through the extensive use of fines, employed as a form of mild chastisement. These were an added source of income for the state, the quantum fixed according to the nature of the crime and the caste of the culprit. What is striking is a third criterion that emerges in the documents, and that is one that states that the convict may pay 'as per resources' (*ghar mafak*). Numerous records indicate that the defendant cited poverty and pleaded for concessions in the amount of fine levied, and the state conceded by reducing the quantum of levy. For instance, the son of Kumhar Fula of village Lunwaro in Parbatsar had killed the donkey of Kumhar Suladiyo. A gunegari of twenty-one rupees was imposed on him. On his petition citing indigence, he was asked to deposit rupees eleven only.[48] This case and many

others of the kind may suggest royal magnanimity and appear hard to jus-
tify given the fact that the logic of survival of an early modern state rested
on maximization of appropriations. Effective administration was indeed
inconceivable without enhancement of revenue exactions and labour surplus from the subjects. The scaling of the magnitude of a fine to the income
of the offender, however, had its own rationale, both because any fine beyond a poor man's means would remain unrealized, and also because what
the lower classes would find crippling would scarcely be felt by the rich. It
was therefore a reasoned approach rather than venality that sometimes
caused huge gunegaris to be demanded from certain wealthy culprits.

As opposed to variable and arbitrary arbitrations in the case of criminal
justice, judicial dispensations in civil cases linked to conflicts over marriage, monetary transactions, inheritance or property, etc., are reflective of
relative consistency on the part of the state. Though state decisions in such
disputes appear a confusing collage of varying images, the underlying principle was to enforce strict adherence to customary laws of different
communities. Caste identities were entrenched, and though their customary traditions were generally not codified, we do have stray compilations
from different regions of the subcontinent, known variously as jati puranas,
kaifiyats, and rawayats. Notionally, every artisan's caste provided him with a
permanent body of associations that controlled his behaviour and contacts.
It was supposed to determine his occupation, dictate customs to be observed in the matter of diet, determine his choice in marriage, act as his
trade union, provide health insurance and, if need be, provide for his funeral.[49] It was expected to prescribe the rituals to be observed at birth,
marriage, and death, and state, for instance, whether his ears shall be pierced,
whether he may wear silver ornaments or not, and what headgear was proper
for him to adorn.

In Marwar, however, a more effective tie than his caste was an artisan's
sense of belonging to his sub-caste or nyat. Much more than the caste, it
was the sub-caste that spelt out his choice of occupation and regulated his
behaviour regarding commensality, social intercourse, and endogamy. Sub-
caste members generally tended to settle in close proximity, and thus a nyat
was a community of households of a sub-caste enjoying the same ritual
rank. They were spread over a village to over several score neighbouring
settlements in the region, depending on the density of the sub-caste concentration in the area. Thus, an artisanal nyat constituted those residing in
contiguous villages, qasbas or cities, in close association and interaction
with each other. The fundamental form of interaction among nyat members was in the community feasts organized on occasions of marriage, death,
and other lifecycle junctures in a family's existence. Invitation to these social gatherings indicated an individual's standing in the community, and
exclusion from the list of invitees was a form of social boycott. The feeling

of rejection borne out of exclusion from these social interactions was often acutely intense. The response of the nyat to invitations of a community member was the fundamental yardstick to assess one's equation with the community. That is why a chhipa of qasba Pali took the extreme step of committing suicide when his community refused to come for a feast he intended to host.[50]

Traditions and customary practices structured a range of interactions, whether within the community or sub-caste brotherhood, with other sub-castes of the same caste, or even with other occupational groups higher or lower in the hierarchy. Practices relating to commensality, endogamy, suitable marital partners, marriage rites, rules pertaining to widow remarriage, funerary rituals, questions of adoption, property rights of widows and sons-in-law, inheritance, and a myriad other issues differed widely, and provided each group with its special and exclusive mark of recognition. Differences among caste identities were of a wide and varied range, and different artisanal sub-castes followed distinct customary laws often at variance with aspects of traditional Hindu law. Some marital practices mentioned below show how every community was unique in its customary traditions, and even resorted to legal resolution of disputes in matters pertaining to community observances. Many sub-castes of an occupational caste, for instance, inter-married freely, but others, such as the bamaniya sunars, observed strict endogamy. Hence, a marriage alliance between a merh sunar and a bamaniya sunar snowballed into a major controversy, and the bamaniyas complained at the kotwali chauntara in an attempt to have the marriage stalled. They took the extreme step of ensuring that the erring individuals were not only excommunicated, but also banished from the state.[51]

Marriage (*byav*) and remarriage (nata) entailed the payment of bride price to the bride's kin, but the customary amounts exchanged were different for different communities. These ranged from rupees twenty-four for byav and sixteen for nata among Hindu luhars to forty to hundred rupees for byav, and an even higher amount for nata in the case of khatis.[52] Also, among khatis a betrothal was considered valid only if it had been attended by four community members who agreed to stand witness to it; Khati Nanag's betrothal was challenged on this ground though he was able to prove that he had not defaulted in this regard.[53] The practice of riding horses during a wedding indicated a high social status and practically all craft castes were forbidden from its observance. But sunars claimed a twice-born status, and therefore a traditional right to this practice.[54] Patri-virilocal residence after marriage was the norm in the case of all craft castes, but among banda and purabiya kumhars the unique custom of uxorilocal residence of sons-in-law at their wife's parental home was observed. The son-in-law lived and worked either for life or for a fixed probation period, at his parents-in-law's house. In case of the latter, if he abandoned his stay and left before the due date, the prospective bride's family went back on its commitment of giving the girl in marriage to him. Instead, they merely compensated him by giving wages as per the jati panchayat's directions for the labour he expended at their household.

Issues such as these necessitated a deep insight into the finer nuances of appropriate customary behaviour, and senior community members alone possessed the requisite knowledge. Those arbitrating disputes arising out of such issues needed an ability to contextualize a conflict correctly and comprehensive knowledge on matters of individual practice, to be able to interpret the relevant aspects of customary law before awarding appropriate retribution. Local caste bodies called jati panchayats, with their leaders (*panch*) drawn from within the community, were clearly the best suited to handle this complex task of enforcing customary laws.

JATI PANCHAYATS AND SELF-GOVERNANCE

As mechanisms for internal governance, jati panchayats were self-disciplinary organs that regulated the social conduct of community members through close supervision of their social and professional lives, and thereby preserved caste identities. Competition with the state for the expansion of their jurisdiction was common, and their domain could extend to practically all issues that concerned their members, from individual domestic problems to tax collection and the tackling of elite pressures. Due to the scattered nature of population settlements in the Jodhpur region, caste members often resided in too wide a territory to have shared corporate activities. Also, it was sub-caste affiliations that prescribed and proscribed forms of conduct for every artisan.[55] Hence adjudication structures and roles were at the sub-caste or jati rather than the caste level and each sub-caste had its individual jati panchayat.[56] Jodhpur records, however, identified the litigants in dispute cases by their castes rather than their sub-castes. This may be explained by the fact that for purposes of administration, an individual's name, caste, and place of residence were sufficient parameters for identification. It appears that the settlement pattern ensured that sub-caste members lived in close proximity and it was indeed unlikely for two blacksmiths or potters with the same name but different sub-castes to reside in the same village or qasba. In line with the documents, therefore, I use the term caste councils or jati panchayats when in fact I mean sub-caste/community panchayats.

While the territorial boundaries and jurisdictional areas of each panchayat is not indicated in the sources, what is indeed clear is that the kumhars of Nagaur constituted a different unit from those of Merta or Jodhpur, or the luhars of Phalodi from those of Sojhat and Jalor. The following case explicitly points to the fact that different areas, often districts or parganas, had their own separate branches of a caste council. Mochi Gomale of Merta performed his son's remarriage or nata with the daughter of Mochi Devala of Jodhpur. But some of their community members objected because the bride's first husband was from the same clan as Gomale. Since the norm among mochis was to desist from matrimonial liaisons between kinsmen or bhai-bandh, there was general disapproval of this marriage. The Jodhpur branch of the mochi caste council imposed a gunegari of twenty-one rupees on Gomale and disallowed him from bringing home his daughter-in-law. The mochi community at Merta, however, decided to accept the marriage since they considered it improper for a husband to abandon his wife once the marriage had been solemnized, and on Gomale's petition, they ordered that the Jodhpur panch must lift their ban and allow the woman to come to her new marital home. The logic given was that since a fine had already been taken for the impropriety committed by Gomale, and his community had accepted the woman, it would be appropriate for her to join her husband.[57] The control of a branch of a (sub)caste council could spread over a village, city, to over several score neighbouring settlements, depending on the density of the sub-caste concentration in the area. The size of the circle constituting the jati and its council therefore varied greatly.

Theoretically speaking, the jurisdictional domains of judicial organs were well defined: inter-caste disputes over land, debt, succession to office, ritual precedence, theft and assault, ritual norms that might cause village-wide pollution, and all those that pertained to matters of common concern in the settlement, would be referred to village councils (*ganv* panchayats) composed of village leaders who arbitrated to resolve conflicts. Intra-caste cases relating to breach of norms set for commensality, marriage, codes of customary conduct, property rights, inheritance, and monetary transactions, were addressed to the caste councils if these could not be settled internally within the household.[58] On occasions, the panch took the initiative of intervening when they got information through their own channels about wayward conduct of some caste member.[59] If the decision of the panch failed to satisfy the litigants and the conflict persisted, the aggrieved parties could confer with other neighbouring branches of their jati panchayat. In most cases, state intervention in such cases was to be sought only when friction between the contesting parties could not be contained by their local caste bodies. In fact, however, there was constant negotiation regarding these respective domains since each of these constituted foci of power that pursued variable agendas and often pulled in different directions.

After the litigants communicated their versions, jati panchayats relied on the testimony of a witness, under oath. In the absence of a dependable source to testify, the panch often sought divine sanction by means of *ghij pani*, an ancient practice of making the defendant go through tortuous ordeals to prove his innocence.[60] The alleged culprit had to go without water or have boiling oil poured over him, the assumption being that if he remained unscathed and unscalded, he was innocent. Implicit faith in this practice was so common that Sunar Karamchand of village Gandharhin was thrown out of his village when the ghij pani test he underwent showed him guilty. His wife pleaded that the money he was alleged to have stolen actually came from the sale of their bullocks but the panchayat reposed greater confidence in the verdict of the divine test.[61]

The functioning and maintenance of the jati panchayat, whether for Hindu or Muslim communities, was funded by contributions each member of the community made to a general pool, though the amounts and the occasions when these were paid, varied from one community to another.[62] The panch did not charge a fee when they arbitrated in a conflict, drawing their income from gunegari fines that erring members of the community were subjected to. Each member was also stipulated to contribute towards the upkeep of widows and abandoned women.[63] Disobedience against the directives of the jati panchayat invited the imposition of fines that ranged from one to one hundred rupees, depending on the severity of the offence. Sometimes they ordered the parties at dispute to make charities according to their resources.[64] As punishment it was also common for the panch to order that the culprit feast the community, or feast both community members and local brahmins.[65] Other penalties included a pilgrimage to expiate one's sins.[66]

Caste councils tended to act in an advisory capacity, mostly employing persuasion rather than coercion. Serious offences were sought to be checked through banishment and ex-communication, referred to in local parlance as *nyat bahar kadh devo*. An order of boycott or ex-communication by the jati panch deprived a caste-fellow of the right to share water or the tobacco pipe with his caste-fellows, to join their community feasts, and also deprived him from services of priests, barbers, and washermen, etc. This would be catastrophic in the worldview of individuals of early modern society, and as I discuss later, this power to ex-communicate was the site of tension and severe contestation between caste councils and the state.

Clearly, in any event, artisanal caste councils were operating as powerful internal mechanisms of control and supervision, and as bodies that enforced order and regulated the social conduct of different communities. Even if they did not possess administrative authority comparable to that of the state, the societal sanction they traditionally enjoyed was the premise underlying their enormous power. As such, they were centres of power and authority resident in society rather than created by the state. By implication, the Rathor state and elitist structures of power that historical scholarship tended to recognize as the sole repositories of governance, were in fact not so; rather, they faced competition and pressures from communal and other dispersed foci of power, each of which might have been constituted differently, but was, nevertheless, an effective agency of control and 'discipline'. Authority resided in the jati panchayats by virtue of their roots in indigenous local environments, and popular acceptance of their role as supervisors of community conduct. This authority was 'recognized' by the state in its efforts at legitimation and consolidation of state power, and as will be evident in the next section, expedience dictated that the state take care not to tread too far in offending the sensibilities of these community organizations.

COLLABORATIVE CO-EXISTENCE OF THE STATE AND ARTISANAL JATI PANCHAYATS

Despite their acceptance as dispute-resolution instruments, the stranglehold of jati panchayats was not so complete as to rule out the possibility of litigants accessing the judicial organs of the state. As noticed before, in a variety of circumstances a dissatisfied artisan unhappy with the verdict of the panch or unsure of their impartiality, appealed to the state for redressal of his grievance. This appeal could be addressed to the pargana kachedi, the kotwali chauntara, or the Durbar, since all three constituted and represented the state's formal apparatus of judicial dispensation.

The state, in its capacity as the appellate court of appeal, intervened to discharge its responsibility of judicial dispensation. A dispute involved Suthar Bira's wife, whose husband was alive, yet she was remarried to another suthar by her parents when she visited her natal home. Extreme poverty and a desire to earn additional bride price perhaps explains her parents' action. Both her first and second husbands asserted their claims on the woman and the dispute remained unresolved at the jati panchayat level. The litigants therefore approached the Merta kachedi for justice.[67] In yet another case, the state authorities had to take direct initiative to resolve a dispute over a betrothal between two groups of khatis, one of which hailed from village Kasari and the other from village Dhahari. The khatis in question refused to repose faith in their jati panchayat and petitioned the state to intervene.[68] Monetary disputes too were often referred directly to the state, which resolved them on the basis of available documents that detailed the transaction. In one such dispute between chhipas Ahmad and Fazal of Sojhat, the jati panch decreed that Fazal pay rupees seventy-five to Ahmad. Fazal felt wronged and took the dispute to the state. An examination of the papers in the possession of the litigants did not seem to indicate this liability on Fazal. The Sojhat kachedi changed the verdict, and advised the jati panch to adjudicate cases more carefully after examining relevant documents.[69]

Even when disputes moved from the relatively 'private' to the 'public' domain and litigants sought direct state intervention, collaboration with their respective jati panchayats was the norm. For, as notes Radhika Singha, the state was aware that 'punishments for certain offences were best left to the community for order could be better maintained through the organic institutions of social authority than through policing' and coercion alone.[70] When approached for direct intervention, the state often referred the dispute to pre-existing caste councils for resolution. To mention a few, the disputes over betrothal issues between julahas Badha and Nura of Nagaur,[71] between suthars Toghale of village Dhaharhin and Bhagwan of Taranki,[72] or between luhars Basta of village Lambiya and Gordhan from Devali,[73] were delegated to their respective jati panchayats to resolve. Given the proximity of the panch to their caste members, the state did caution them not to show any favour to anyone (*harkora rakhjo mati*), and to be totally impartial in the discharge of judicial obligations. Yet the state administration preferred to put faith in popular bodies embedded in local society than act totally independently. The prime concern of the state was to ensure social stability. Document after document records the state's repeated reiteration that the traditional customs of each community be respected. Age-old practices and customary laws were accepted as being of supreme importance in the disposal of disputes, and the state deliberated with all those who could help it determine the wajabi course of action, even if the reading and interpretation of wajabi was constantly manipulated to suit the state's immediate agenda.

This collaboration and consultation with the caste councils was prompted by the state's inadequacy on two counts: the lack of sufficient comprehension of customary laws observed by different communities, and their difficulty in collecting information and finding corroborative evidence to resolve the inconsistencies in the variable testimonies of rival claimants.[74] The stress on 'time-honoured' practices made it mandatory that the state consult the jati panchayats and abide by their advice. Precedents certainly helped to strengthen the verdict and made it widely acceptable, even if it hurt the interests, as it was bound to, of one of the litigants. In all cases, the state's attempt was to make an informed decision after adequate deliberation, such that the social disharmony generated by the conflict got settled.

Often the Jodhpur state approached the local caste councils for corroboration of evidence or information furnished by the litigants. Such was the situation in the case of Chhipa Isak, who appeared to have been boycotted by his community. The state authorities attempted to get complete evidence from the panch, and statements of witnesses from amongst their community, to settle the problem.[75] And this exercise revealed interesting facts about Isak, who was said to have lived in Pali earlier, where he committed homicide and took his victim's wife for his own. Then, fearing ostracization by the community, he moved to the neighbouring qasba Siharh.

His misdeeds, however, became known to his community, who decided to boycott him socially, and apprised the state authorities about these facts. Information furnished by the panch eventually helped the Pali kachedi in resolving the case.[76]

In yet another case, Pinjara Jalal raised objections on the validity of the marriage between the children of pinjaras Ali and Kesara on the ground that the customary exchanges and rituals had not been observed properly. Jalal's fuss led to a gunegari of thirty rupees being imposed by the Jalor chauntara on the two alleged defaulters. When Ali petitioned against these impositions and deposed that Jalal had stated untruths, the chauntara resolved the case after consultations with the pinjara caste council had enabled them to ascertain wajabi.[77] Consultations with the jati panchayats had therefore become a norm and the state had to reckon with and respect the pressure to recognize the authority of the panchayat regarding internal matters of communities.[78] In the case of property disputes too, the recommendation of the community leaders was an important input in the decision-making process.[79] Customary laws pertaining to adoption and inheritance were complex hence the state preferred to have the community Panch help resolve conflicts over these issues.[80] Numerous cases indicate that rather than immediate recourse to direct intervention and keenness to take matters into its own hands, the state preferred resolution of disputes through popular assemblies. Indeed, their local roots and fuller knowledge of customary practices made them a force to reckon with, one that the state could ill afford to ignore.

Direct involvement in 'petty' matters seemed both unnecessary and an inefficient utilisation of the limited resources of the state. Conservation of the use of its agencies for its own priorities while retaining the rhetoric of being judicious rulers was best served by referring civil cases to caste bodies and advising them to practise wajabi. It was therefore not merely expedient but mandatory that the state take cognisance of these locally embedded bodies. In fact, atleast as far as subordinate formations were concerned, the administration even invested their caste councils with 'further' powers to ensure social stability by repeatedly ordering that people approach their respective panchayats instead of taking the law into their own hands.[81] Thus rather than erode the authority of a competing centre of power, the state, atleast in routine affairs of artisanal society, encouraged them to approach their caste councils for the restoration of social harmony. As local grass-roots institutions for human and resource management at the community level, caste councils were participatory organs that effectively mediated state-artisan relations. Instead of attempting to disrupt entrenched customary power and thereby inviting popular protest, the rulers followed the policy of minimal intervention in civil suits that generally amounted to be non-issues for them. Besides, the endorsement or ratification of the authority of the jati panchayats to discipline their community helped organize and order society in an efficient and much less wasteful manner, that is economically, without having to incur great expenses in erecting full-fledged judicial mechanisms. More importantly, this participative, collaborative exercise of power through an agency internal to those governed, and therefore relatively unobtrusive and invisible, was crucial in determining wajib and making the whole system more acceptable.

TENSIONS AND MANIPULATIONS: THE ISSUE OF EX-COMMUNICATION

How wajib was read and interpreted was, however, open for negotiation and manipulation, often provoked by conflictual agendas and motivations of the parties in question. While considerations of expediency and realpolitik may have dictated collaboration between the state and caste councils, the two often pursued contradictory agendas and got locked in struggles over 'legitimate' levels of taxation, wage payments, and even customary conduct.[82] Caste affairs were ideally 'private matters' resolved internally through customary law. The decisions of the jati panchayats were, however, open to negotiation and debate once they became a more 'public' concern, where they had to be handled very delicately. The adoption of a threatening posture by the state was extremely rare, and records transcribed by the administration tended to underplay these confrontations; but that they occurred more than rarely is beyond dispute. When confrontation could not be avoided, the dispute, as in the following case, became a subject of detailed record-keeping.

Amongst the community of mochis, a bride's father was expected to provide a substitute in case he was unable to give in marriage the girl originally promised. Mochi Udiye of Nagaur had accepted bride prices and betrothed his elder daughter to a caste-fellow of Asopa, and his wife's unmarried younger sister (*sali*)—who clearly was in the guardianship of Udiye—to Mochi Pirag. His sali had already been betrothed to another mochi by her parents before she came into his care, and on learning that, Udiye tried to return the bride price he had accepted from Pirag. Pirag, however, insisted on having Udiye's already betrothed elder daughter as the substitute. Udiye then offered to give his younger daughter in marriage to Pirag but the latter was uncompromising. (The younger daughter was perhaps not old enough to be of productive or reproductive value early enough). The Nagaur panch supported Pirag's demand of the elder girl and in despair, Udiye approached the Nagaur kachedi. In an effort to settle the issue amicably without openly rejecting the verdict given by the Nagaur panch, the state authorities decided to consult the mochi jati panchayat of Merta too. The panch of Merta supported Udiye's stand, and with their backing, the state negotiated with the Nagaur panch. The controversy snowballed into a major issue that saw the state play politics between different factions of the community of mochis in an effort to help Udiye who had sought their intercession. The Nagaur panch adopted an aggressive stance and imposed a fine on Udiye, and then ex-communicated him as well. The Nagaur kachedi then asserted itself and ordered that their enquiry from the mochi community had revealed that adequate grounds for ex-communication were not present in this case. They also pointed out that Pirag's claims were inconsequential because a betrothal was valid only when it enjoyed the blessings of a bride's father. As such, the kachedi maintained that Udiye might marry his elder daughter to the mochi of Asop. Resistance from the Nagaur panch forced the state's adoption of a confrontationist posture, and it further ordered that the Nagaur panch be punished for unjustly ex-communicating Udiye. The Nagaur kachedi even imposed a gunegari fine on Pirag for his 'illegitimate' insistence on taking Udiya's elder daughter without Udiya's concurrence. Thus the defiant position of the Nagaur caste council was countered by the state with the support of the Merta branch. The deliberations between the Nagaur kachedi and the jati panchayats of Merta and Nagaur were recorded at length, and brought out the finer points of jurisprudence to help resolve the dispute.[83] Such tensions between the Rathor state and local caste councils were quite common though both preferred to circumvent these as best as they could.

More often, however, disputes arising over permanent ex-communication of individuals witnessed friction and negotiations between the administration and the caste council in question. Temporary ostracization by the community was not objected to, but in cases of long-term boycott by caste leaders, the state generally exercised its appellate authority in a more decisive way and often over-ruled the verdict of the jati panchayats. After all, once expelled from his caste, the only patron an individual could plead with was his king—the pater familias. After extracting fines and inflicting wajib punishments, the state tended to argue for reintegration of the outcaste. For this, it negotiated and if necessary, even threatened the caste councils to force them to reconsider their decision.

The state's proactive response in cases involving ex-communication, even at the cost of intensifying tensions between them and the concerned caste council, was prompted by the severe implications of boycott and ex-communication both for the individual as well as the state. An order of expulsion from a caste was like the passing of a death sentence that deprived the person of his only source of livelihood.[84] An expelled person could no longer practice the occupation of the caste from which he had been expelled. Neither could he become a member of any other caste since membership could be acquired only by birth, and the right to practice a particular occupation was hereditary. A person thus expelled lost his livelihood, and was socially ostracized to the extent that even if he did try to continue practising his vocation, the village folk refused to accept him as a client and he lost all erstwhile patrons. In fact censure was so strict that if despite the ban, a husband took back an erring wife or a father received home an erring son, they too were liable to be outcaste. It was this attitude that led the jati panchayat of Jodhpur to order the ex-communication of Chhipa Isak for allegedly helping his brother escape after raping a chhipi. Clearly, Isak was made to bear the brunt of his brother's misdemeanour.[85]

Ex-communications could be in the form of temporary penalties for a stated period, or for an indefinite time, subject to the performance of some expiation. Only in extreme cases was it for life. In the case of Darzi Kisora this extreme step had to be resorted to since, despite repeated warnings and milder forms of punishment, he refused to terminate his illicit relations with Darzi Naga's wife.[86] The fear of ex-communication helped to preserve the sanctity of the caste system over generations, the only recourse left open to an outcaste being the ability to muster resources for expiation and pardon from the state by paying a huge fine. This indeed reinforced the position of the state as the final arbiter of justice.

The state's interest in ensuring the reinstatement of ex-communicated individuals into their communities was dictated by a number of factors; the most important was that free-floating individuals bereft of a community identity were potential criminals who often took to breaking the law. Devoid of social ties and pressures, the likelihood of their refusal to abide by social rules and norms was high. As such, it was in the state's interest to have everyone fully integrated and well settled in his or her respective community. In the case of artisans in particular, every individual represented a productive resource that was extremely valuable to a labour-starved economy. As part of a community, every craftsman generated a certain surplus that the state valued and wished to extract, while an expelled artisan, in the absence of a source of livelihood, was a burden both on himself as well as on the authorities. He was likely to migrate, and this would mean complete loss of control over his surplus labour. In such cases therefore, the state generally chose to project its 'patriarchal' posture and rescue its pleading subjects from starvation and 'social death'.

Evidence from other regions like Bengal and Maharashtra also suggests similar concerns of the state since dispensation of justice had, as already noticed, a much larger role in local politics than mere implementation of righteous rule and enforcement of law and order.[87] It was as much a reflection of the ability of the strong to protect their clients. The dispute over the fate of Padam Kumhar Paima of Merta is a case in point. For the indiscretions of the younger son of Paima, the jati panchayat of potters ordered a punishment for the father. The potter regularly supplied clayware to the palace and thereby enjoyed proximity to, and patronage from them. His son had abandoned his wife, and on the complaint of her parents, the panch imposed a heavy fine of fifty-one rupees on Paima—the head of his family and accountable for the actions of his dependents. Paima's defence was that his son had separated from him after claiming his inheritance, and that Paima was therefore neither aware nor responsible for his son's improprieties. The case became a prolonged one since the panchayat insisted that Paima pay the fine though the state directive absolved him. Paima's privileged status became the site of conflict between the caste council and the state. Paima represents a clear case of multiple identities, those that came into play in this case involving bonds with the patron as opposed to caste affiliation. Frustrated, the panch then began to insist not only on the fine but that they would boycott Paima and even excommunicate him if he persisted in seeking state help. The jati panchayat's self-assertion provoked the state authorities further: They first threatened punishment, and then went ahead to order a gunegari on the panchayat. They also directed that the council must withdraw their expulsion of Paima from the community immediately. Asserting its sovereign authority, the Durbar declared that punishing Padam would be illegitimate (*gair-wajib*).[88]

Cases such as this one exemplify that multiple identities generated crosscutting loyalties, and these in turn tended to subvert the development of dualistic social conflicts. Thus even if statecraft discouraged the administration from offending the sensibilities of community organizations, discordant notes in their mutual interactions could not always be avoided. Specific contexts saw the two exerting to extend their respective prosecutorial jurisdictions, provoking stresses that otherwise lay relatively dormant.

CONCLUDING REMARKS

In the exercise of power, collaboration between artisanal jati panchayats and the Jodhpur state was mutually advantageous to both.[89] As an intermediary body between the people and the Rathor state, jati panchayats were a vital link that established close networks or contacts between the dominant and the subordinate. Their roots in local tradition and a semi-autonomous structure constituted the basis of jati panchayats' power and compelled the state to take cognisance of their authority. The two therefore often acted in tandem to administer justice and ensure proper social conduct. Official recognition and sanction to the mediation of caste councils in the dispensation of justice empowered them and helped to consolidate their position over community members. As for the state, coalescing with locally rooted jati panchayats was a way of enrolling acceptance of verdicts and thereby, popular support.

Popular consent and acceptance of authority was after all possible not through coercion and military might alone, but through consensus building. The Jodhpur state could not intervene effectively in the social assemblies of the artisans, but the panchayats could. Procurement of willing submission and co-operation through a partnership with local bodies was obviously more convenient in this exercise of social power than having the subjects perpetually in a recalcitrant mood. Also, the state tried to maintain a panoptic vigil over its realm through jati panchayats; the continuous surveillance that these bodies provided helped to discipline people in their specific environment, and worked towards ensuring that every individual adhere to the behavioural pattern prescribed by his caste.

This collaboration, however, did not imply that the perusal of divergent interests, accomodations and adjustments to reconcile pressures, the obligations inherent to patron-client relationships, and commitments to variable programmes of different loci of power did not cause repeated tensions. In fact occasional flashpoints also occurred intermittently, and these cannot be discounted. The practise of wajabi was hardly guided by idealism; it was neither consistent nor capable of eradicating perceptional and operational polarities. Maximization of administrative efficiency did still demand that constant conflicts, inherent in unequal relationships, be avoided. The dominant trend therefore still appears to reveal partnership and working in concert with one another for the preservation of the social order. This is not to suggest that the state or the jati panchayats consciously and deliberately 'chose' to support one another, but rather that the process of political governance and efforts at disciplining threw up mechanisms to ensure optimal efficiency. The administration and popular local bodies more often than not, collaborated and co-operated in the exercise of power not as a planned strategy, but because there existed a network of ties between the state and society of the region.

The two following chapters, Chapters 4 and 5 explore how the state discourse of wajabi and just rulership unfolded on the ground in the villages and urban centres of Marwar. It examines how, in normal times, the conflicts inherent to an essentially antagonistic relationship between the dominant and the artisanate were mitigated both due to the rhetoric of wajabi and pressures from below.

NOTES

1. Francisco Pelsaert, describing conditions in seventeenth-century India, wrote thus; see *Jahangir's India: The Remonstrnatie of Francisco Pelsaert* (Cambridge, 1925), translated by W.H. Moreland and P. Geyl.

2. Indeed, these questions merit much more than a mere section in the volume, but since my on-going project focusses on the patriarchal nature of the craft society, I have limited here my discussion of these issues here.

3. The spaces used for the transmission of skills were generally the openings in front of dwellings. The looms of the weavers were installed in the open space in front of their houses or in front verandahs which permitted adequate amount of light. The dyers and printers, the potters, the metallurgists, and the leather-workers operated from their houses, and used the open spaces in the front or backyards of their hutments as the working area. As for carpenters and tailors, apart from functioning from their homes for making items of standard sizes and shapes, they sometimes worked in their client's residence since observation of precise measurements was crucial to their trade. There were many disputes, both with private individuals and the state, arising out of encroachments on the weavers' open land in front of their houses where they worked on their looms; *JSPB* 34, 1843/1786, f. 123B, *JSPB* 36, 1844/1787, ff. 235A and 237A.

4. See *Mardum Shumari Raj Marwar*, pp. 451–2, 481–2, 484, 495, 545.

5. Kumharan Rupli of Pokaran village, district Pokaran, provided these details during a conversation on 29 December 1997.

6. Indeed, there were exceptions to this, as in the trade of blacksmithy that allowed negligible participation for women in the tasks of smelting and forging iron.

7. Illustrative of this tension is the case of Darzi Sukhiya's wife Jagari who used to return home late in the evenings, perhaps delayed in moving door to door to deliver clothes she and her husband tailored for their clients. Her nocturnal mobility invited suspicions about her character and she was not only admonished but even beaten for her 'immoral conduct' by Brahmin Motiya. She then escaped to her natal home but even her departure did not put to rest the fears of men of her marital village. Five of them followed her there, continuing to chastise her for bringing a bad name to her family. Jagari finally complained at the Phalodi kachedi against their harassment. See *JSPB* 45, 1793, f. 521B.

8. The wife of Kumhar Naga of qasba Pali complained that her husband and father-in-law had alleged her involvement in illicit relations, assaulted her, and thrown her out of the house; see *JSPB* 20, 1778, f. 193B. Such problems were normally faced by women if they were too ill to work and provide progeny for the family.

9. Only in the rarest of cases did the uniqueness of circumstance lead to a woman receive sufficient guidance in skilled work. For instance, Sunari Dipli of village Kudaki in Merta had become a child-widow. She, however, did not remarry like other young widows, and instead lived with her brother and assisted him actively to supplement household income. See *JSPB* 31, 1841/1784, f. 40A.

10. Devaluing women's work by seeing it as an extension of their housewifely role has been a common strategy to ensure their subordination; see Maria Mies, *The Lace-Makers of Narsapur: Indian Housewives Produce for the World Market* (London, 1982), 53–6.

11. That procreation and fertility of women and men was the primary *raison d etre* of marriage is apparent from several documents that reveal impotency of men and infertility of women as legitimate grounds for divorce. See, for instance, *JSPB* 11, 1771, f. 147A.

12. See Uma Chakravarty, 'Gender, Caste and Labour: The Ideological and Material Structure of Widowhood', in Martha Chen (ed.), *Widows in India: Social Neglect and Public Action* (New Delhi, 1998), pp. 63–92.

13. A sunari's complaint at the Merta kachedi was registered in the name of 'Sunar Natha's wife', see *JSPB* 13, 1830/1773, f. 149A. A khati woman registered her complaint at the Sojhat kachedi, but instead of recording her name, she has been identified as 'Khati Agada's wife'; see *JSPB* 20, 1835/1778, f. 168A. Nagaur chauntara too registered a silawat woman's complaint in the name of 'Silawat Hasan's wife'; see *JSPB* 20, 1835/1778, f. 56A. Pali kachedi registered a complaint in the name of `Kumhar Naga's wife'; see *JSPB* 20, 1835/1778, f. 193B.

14. *JSPB* 3, 1765, f. 391A.

15. *JSPB* 6, 1767, f. 64A. Numerous petitions record the sale of women and detail hardships they had to suffer thereafter.

16. *JSPB* 53, 1856/1799, f. 162A.

17. *JSPB* 10, 1770, f. 24A.

18. *JSPB* 13, 1773, f. 217A.

19. *JSPB* 12, 1772, f. 226A.

20. The wife of Darzi Ramray of Nagaur was charged with homicide, having killed his younger brother's wife. She was neither awarded capital punishment nor asked to pay 'blood money' as compensation, but merely thrown out of the kingdom (*desh bahar kadh devo*), and not allowed to resettle when she later returned to live in familiar surroundings. *JSPB* 26, 1781, f. 23A.

21. *JSPB* 5, 1766.

22. *JSPB* 22, 1779, f. 56A; *JSPB* 24, 1780, f. 122A.

23. *JSPB* 18, 1834/1777, f. 95B.

24. *JSPB* 14, 1831/1774, f. 47B.

25. *JSPB* 11, 1829/1772, f. 164B.

26. *JSPB* 23, 1836/1779, f. 121A.

27. See Shashi Arora's 'The Practice of Sale of Girls and their Position in Rajasthan, 1700–1800 AD', *Proceedings of Rajasthan History Congress*, Bikaner session, 1984, pp. 77–82.

28. Sumit Guha, 'A Penal Regime', pp. 116–17.

29. *JSPB* 6, 1767, f. 63B.

30. In a recent article titled 'Intermediate Realms of, Law: Corporate Groups and Rulers in Medieval India', Donald R. Davis, Jr. reiterated this position, arguing that the dharmasastras, in tandem with customs and conventions of corporate groups, constituted law as practiced in reality; see *Journal of Economic and Social History of the Orient*, vol. 48, no. 1, 2005, pp. 92–117.

31. Jorg Fische, *Cheap Lives and Dear Limbs: The British Transformation of the Bengal Criminal Law 1769–1817* (Wiesbaden, 1983), pp. 117–21.

32. For more on this, see Radhika Singha, *A Despotism of Law: Crime and Justice in Early Colonial India* (Delhi, 1998), pp. 1–35.

33. See Bayly's *Caste, Society and Politics* , p. 60.

34. For caste kachedis in eighteenth-century British Bengal, see Radhika Singha, *A Despotism of Law*. As discussed below, other regions too report similar phenomena.

35. Hiroshi Fukazawa, 'State and Caste System (Jati) in the Eighteenth Century Maratha Kingdom', *Hitotsubashi Journal of Economics*, vol. 9, no. 1, June 1968.

36. See Sumit Guha, 'An Indian Penal Regime: Maharashtra in the Eighteenth Century', *Past and Present*, no. 147, 1995, pp. 101–26; and Uma Chakravarti, *Rewriting History: The Life and Times of Pandita Ramabai* (New Delhi, 1998) p. 14.

37. Sumit Guha, 'An Indian Penal Regime', p. 126.

38. See 'A Farman of High Dignity Containing Necessary Commands and Prohibitions issued to Nazims', c.1588', in M.F. Lokhandwala trans. *Mirat-i-Ahmadi: A Persian History of Gujarat, Ali Muhammad Khan*, Gaekwad Oriental Series, 146, Baroda, 1965, p. 142, quoted in Radhika Singha's *A Despotism of Law*, pp. 10–11.

39. The jagirdar's version was that the kumhar had made a hole in the fortress wall with the intention of stealing, and that when the night watchmen saw him, they stabbed him on the assumption that he was a thief. *JSPB* 25, 1838/1781, f. 246B.

40. The unstated principle guiding state action was perhaps the Islamic law that a man could put a person to death if he caught him involved in sexual intercourse with his wife or female slave.

41. *JSPB* 16, 1776, f. 118B.

42. Radhika Singha, *A Despotism of Law*, p. xv.

43. *JSPB* 54, 1800, f. 39A.

44. *JSPB* 18, 1834/1777, f. 33B.

45. *JSPB* 14, 1831/1774, f. 87A.

46. *JSPB* 41, 1789. folio number is not clear.

47. *JSPB* 8, 1825/1768, f. 182A.

48. *JSPB* 12, 1829/1772, f. 243B.

49. Classical works on caste tend to convey the impression that it was caste affiliation that played the predominant role in people's lives. See, for instance, J.H. Hutton, *Caste in India: Its Nature, Function, and Origins* (Cambridge, 4th edn, 1963), pp. 111–12.

50. *JSPB* 19, 1777, f. 164A.

51. *JSPB* 25, 1838/1781, f. 92.

52. These amounts have been gleaned from the *Marwar Mardum Shumari Report*, part I, pp. 462–7. As such they are late nineteenth-century figures, but can still be used to make the point of varying bride price demands. Also noticeable is that most castes fixed a lower amount of bride price for nata than for byav except khatis and mochis.

53. *JSPB* 15, 1832/1775, f. 311B.

54. *JSPB* 3, 1822/1765, f. 39, and *JSPB* 26, 1838/1781, f. 92B.

55. For instance, kumhars in the Jodhpur region belonged to the kheteriya, banda, merh or jatiya sub-castes or sunars to the bamaniya, merh, and niyariya sub-castes, and luhars to the malwiya, maru, multani, and gadoliya sub-castes. Each sub-caste had its own distinct identity with different costumes, customs and practices, trades, dietary habits, marriage traditions, inheritance rights, etc., discussed at length in the late nineteenth-century source *Marwar Mardum Shumari Report*, vol. I, (1891); information here finds corroboration, however, in contemporary documentary evidence as well.

56. There are few full studies of a caste or segments of a caste in recent historical or anthropological literature. Instead, the general focus has been on the village, and hence there is much more data on inter-caste relations, organization of authority, and dispute settlement within villages than within a single caste either in villages or across supra-village boundaries. See, for instance, Morris Carstairs' 'A Rajasthan Village', in *India's Villages* (Calcutta, 1955). An important exception, however, is E.A.H. Blunt's study of the structure and process of caste panchayats in his work *The Caste System of Northern India with Special Reference to the United Provinces of Agra and Oudh* (London, 1931), pp. 104–31. Studies devoted to particular castes include A. Aiyappan's *Iravas and Cultural Change*, (Madras, 1944), P.G. Shah's *The Dublas of Gujarat* (Delhi, 1958), and V.B. Punekar's *The Son Kolis of Bombay* (Bombay, 1959).

57. *JSPB* 15, 1832/1775, f. 956B.

58. Parallels have often been drawn between the sphere of action and domains of these caste councils and the medieval guilds of the Islamic world. A close look however suggests significant differences between the two. For instance, in Safavid Iran of the seventeenth and eighteenth centuries, sources indicate that artisanal guilds focussed on resolving commercial disputes rather than sociocultural. In the case of jati panchayats of Jodhpur the concerns were far wider, more often pertaining to customary social conduct. In Iran the *naqib* performed the function of supervising customs and maintained surveillance over the moral behaviour of guild members. The latter was a government official who enforced the rules governing the guild's social conduct. See Mehdi Keyvani's *Artisans and Guild Life in the Later Safavid Period: Contributions to the Social and Economic History of Persia* (Berlin, 1982), p. 68.

59. For instance, caste councils insisted that caste members adhere to their traditional occupational trades to prevent dilution of jati identity. Hence the cotton-carders panchayat forbade Pinjara Ladu of Didwana from combining the manufacture of pillows and mattresses along with cotton carding; see *JSPB* 24, 1837/1780, f. 208B.

60. Sunar Harkisan of Ajmer, charged with minting spurious coins, offered to go through ghij pani to prove his innocence. *JSPB* 11, 1828/1771, f. 264A.

61. *JSPB* 34, 1843/1786, f. 9B.

62. *Marwar Mardum Shumari Report* mentions that maru luhars had to pay seven rupees to the caste council for their permission to remarry, while among maru kumhars, they collected two rupees from every member at the time of marriage; see *Marwar Mardum Shumari Report*, part I, pp. 463 and 520. Among churigars, the custom was that all of them would pay one-fourth of their income from cutting ivory bangles towards the maintenance of their panchayat. Churigar Umar of Pali complained at the Pali qasba kachedi that though the custom among his community was for each member to pay one-fourth of his income from cutting bangles to the jati panchayat, Khudabagas and some of his associates had refused to fulfil this obligation; see *JSPB* 36, 1845/1788, f. 398B. Also see *JSPB* 41, 1846/1789, f. 33B.

63. The case came to the Pali kachedi when churigars Khudabagas, Faizbagas, and Gazi did not fulfil their obligation and the kachedi ordered that the records of the caste panchayat should be checked and reasons for their failure to fulfil their obligations enquired into. See *JSPB* 36, 1844/1787, f. 262B.

64. Rangrez Nura of Merta was alleged to have taken thirty rupees in excess of the usual amount taken as bride-price amongst his community; when the case came to the caste council, it ordered Nura to feed grains to the pigeons from the extra amount; see *JSPB* 10, 1827/1770, f. 132B.

65. Among artisanal guilds of Safavid Iran too, 'reconciliation feasts' to the brotherhood were a common form of punishment for first-time offenders. But for habitual offenders, the Persian state came down far more heavily with extremely barbaric punishments like flogging, nailing by the ears to their own shop doors, immurement in red-hot furnaces, and even the death penalty; see Mehdi Keyvanis' *Artisans and Guild Life in the Later Safavid Period*, pp. 136–7. However, the Marwar state and even the jati panchayats rarely went beyond banishment of an individual outside the desh. Perhaps social death was the worst punishment that could be conceived within those social mores.

66. *JSPB* 10, 1827/1770, f. 132B.

67. *JSPB* 36, 1844/1787, f. 261B.

68. *JSPB* 15, 1832/1775, f. 197A.

69. *JSPB* 13, 1830/1773, f. 203A.

70. Radhika Singha, *A Despotism of Law,* p. 124.

71. *JSPB* 18, 1834/1777, f. 26A.

72. *JSPB* 36, 1844/1787, f. 34A.

73. *JSPB* 6, 1824/1767, f. 97A.

74. The case of Kumhar Sawantiye of Ghanerav, for instance, necessitated the co-operation and help of his caste council. Sawantiye complained that before his wife could join him at his paternal home, her parents remarried her to another kumhar, and despite his repeated efforts, she was not handed over to him. The matter was complicated since her second husband wished to retain her. The state, in its effort to decide as per socially sanctified norms of the potters, sought the view of his caste panch, and ordered that the case may be resolved

by conforming to established conventions: '*Jo wajabi hoy so karay dena*'; see *JSPB* 18, 1834/1777, f. 74B.

75. *JSPB* 36, 1844/1787, f. 289B.

76. *JSPB* 38, 1846/1788, f. 206B.

77. *JSPB* 13, 1830/1773, f. 172A.

78. Chhipa Rughe complained that his son-in-law's illicit affair with a jat woman compelled him to bring back his daughter from her husband's home and re-marry her elsewhere. Five years later, the errant husband began to assert his rights over his erstwhile wife, and harassed the family. The Sojhat kachedi ordered that the details of the case be verified from the panch, and the matter disposed accordingly; see *JSPB* 15, 1832/1775, f. 203B.

79. Conflicts between Pinjara Ahmad of village Rohirhn and his cousin, Luhar Murad of Merta and his nephew, between julahas Bahadi and Nura, between luhars Dipa and Pichajoga, and many more, were resolved after deliberating with their respective caste councils. See *JSPB* 10, 1827/1770, f. 102A; *JSPB* 10, 1827/1770, f. 136A, *JSPB* 8, 1825/1768, f. 107A, *JSPB* 11, 1828/1771, f.197A, respectively. .

80. Kumhar Siriya and his cousin Dupi of Didwana quarrelled over the appropriate candidate for adoption; see *JSPB* 9, 1826/1769, f. 171B. And similarly, when Khati Dhana of Sojhat fought with his step mother-in-law over a share in his father-in-law's property, the jati panchayat was asked to intervene and resolve as per the inheritance laws practised in their community. Dhana's father-in-law Paima did not have sons, hence Dhana was living with the latter; Paima then remarried and had a son born through his second wife. On Paima's death, Dhana bore the expenses of his father-in-law's funerary rituals, and took a loan to fund the same. But then, his step mother-in-law, in collusion with her son, refused to give him a share in Paima's property, and forced him to take the matter to court; see *JSPB* 5, 1823/1766, f. 167B.

81. In an interesting case, a darzi of village Bilu was punished when enraged over his sister's miseries when her husband brought another woman to live with him, the darzi murdered his brother-in-law. The Parbatsar kachedi, though sympathetic, punished him for defying the law instead of taking his grievance to his jati panch; see *JSPB* 5, 1823/1766, f. 236A.

82. For a fuller discussion on these issues see Nandita Prasad Sahai, 'Collaboration and Conflict: Artisanal Jati Panchayats and Eighteenth Century Jodhpur State', *Medieval History Journal*, vol. 5, no. 1, 2002, pp. 77–102.

83. *JSPB* 15, 1832/1775, f. 79.

84. Ibid. In Padam Kumhar Paima's case the jati panchayat not only ex-communicated him but also threatened to boycott him professionally, i.e., they ordered that none of the villagers would buy earthen vessels from him. The loss of market and therefore a livelihood was sure to bring any erring person to heel!

85. *JSPB* 11, 1828/1771, f. 184A.

86. *JSPB* 16, 1833/1776, f. 69B, and *JSPB* 18, 1834/1777, f. 52A.

87. For Bengal see p. 238 of Verelst's manual *View of the English Government in Bengal* composed in 1772; also see L.S.S. O'Malley, *Indian Caste Customs* (1932), p. 59. On Maharashtra, see Sumit Guha, 'An Indian Penal Regime: Maharashtra in the Eighteenth Century', in *Past and Present*, no. 147, 1995, pp. 101–26.

88. *JSPB* 33, 1842/1785, f. 38A, 40B, and 41A. The jati panchayat's aggression provoked the state authorities and they first threatened to punish, and then went ahead to order a gunegari on the panchayat, accompanied with the direction that they must withdraw their expulsion of Paima from the community.

89. Other studies have noticed a similar relationship of tensions, yet co-operation in the sharing of power between the multi foci of power and levels of authority; for instance S. Nurul Hasan argues for a competitive, yet collaborative relationship between the Mughal state and the different stratas of zamindars in his essay 'Zamindars under the Mughals', in R.E. Frykenberg (ed.), *Land Control and Social Structure in Indian History*, (Madison, 1969). But these studies generally focus on relations between different centres of elitist power.

4

Village Artisans, Landed Elites, and the State

A folk tale popular in the Jodhpur region is a vivid account of the abject miseries that artisanal castes lived in due to pressures from the dominant elites of the village. It reads:

A bhambi (leather-worker) in a village could not tolerate the combined burden of levies imposed by the *thakur* (village chief) and the revenues appropriated by the state any longer. The numerous exactions gradually made life unendurable, and forced him take the extreme step of jumping into a well to take his life. The splashing of the water and the commotion created by his fall disturbed a frog that lived in the well. The frog called out to the newcomer to identify himself. When the bhambi did so, the frog scolded him for pulling him out of deep slumber, and ordered him to clean the well immediately of all the accumulated dirt. The poor man was damned, even after death, to unremitting labour![1]

Was the life of village artisans a saga of unceasing repression and suffering with no respite or escape from the exploitative demands of the elites? Though the concentration of artisans was higher in towns and pargana headquarters, in terms of absolute numbers, rural artisans residing in villages were a larger body. Yet, very little is known about their world except that they catered to the requirements of the village community for agricultural implements and a range of other commodities. This chapter begins by examining artisanal strategies of survival in an environmentally precarious region, and tries to comprehend the artisans' life experiences in the rural world of caste hierarchy. The pre-colonial Indian state has been portrayed in the nineteenth-century imperial historiography as predatory and parasitic, and the toiling people as the prey.[2] Marxist historiography has also seen similar polarities and a schism between the despotic, extractive state and a continually suffering toiling class.[3] This chapter examines whether these formulations cover the entire range of interactions and whether a unilateral exercise of power by the former over the latter explains the entire truth. It also probes the logic and rationale that modulated their exchanges. Were the subordinate castes completely bereft of a political identity, and devoid of political consciousness, as well as the means to protect their rights?[4]

Focussing on the 1750s, 60s and 70s, contemporaneous with the early decades of Maharaja Vijai Singh's reign, this chapter explores routine interactions of village artisans with local authorities and rural elites—the hakims, jagirdars, bhomias, thakurs, and chaudhuries—all of whom constituted different levels of 'disciplinary agencies' that organized, structured, and regulated society in their local environments. Were the exchanges between them simply one of antagonism and conflict of interest, or one of complementarity and inter-dependence as well? And if there was both opposition as well as apposition, how did these manifest themselves on the ground? In the complex grid of rights and obligations, the chapter analyses the material and ideological criteria that set the limits of disciplining, and juxtaposes universal cultural principles against the specifics of each context that regulated their interactions. Was the practise of wajabi and supposedly 'legitimate' appropriations that it was meant to define, able to ensure harmonious relations by lubricating the mechanisms of extractions into a tension-free, well-oiled system? If it did not, what social praxis did the lower formations adopt to be, in Marx's words, 'the actors and authors of their own destiny'? How did their own ideas about legitimate norms of economic behaviour, duties of patrons and clients, obligations of masters and servants, 'fair' compensation for their work, and 'unjust conduct' that justified resistance and protest, influence the interface between village artisans and the Jodhpur state and its functionaries?

BLENDING OF CRAFTS AND AGRICULTURE

In Marwar, the ultimate reality for all artisans was the caprice of nature, recurrent visitations of droughts and famines often causing extreme poverty. Concurrently, the low position of artisans in the social hierarchy and consequent exploitation by the dominant castes added to their woes, and made life much more difficult. Many artisans, however, displayed considerable initiative towards containing their precariousness, reducing their servility, and generally ameliorating their conditions through self-effort. Devising specific mechanisms and strategies to protect and promote their self-interest was common.

One of the fundamental problems of rural artisans was the fluctuating demand for craft goods, given the frequency of natural disasters. Every such calamity occasioned a scarcity of resources and caused a fall in an artisan's ability to dispose his manufactured commodities. Inevitably, this intensified the vulnerability of an artisanal household and necessitated that an artisans supplement his income through optional sources. Limited economic opportunities, the small market for craft goods in villages, and limited resources with their local clientele encouraged many artisans to combine their hereditary occupations of craft production with agriculture. Living close to the margin, they opted for a safety valve that would help them tide over difficult times. Partial self-generation of subsistence needs in food was recognized as essential for the family economy, and while some cultivated foodgrains, others preferred to grow raw materials that they would require for craft work. Rangrez Fazal of village Lotoi, for instance, chose not to invest capital in procuring his dyeing raw material nil from the market; instead, he cultivated it on his fields and sold the surplus for additional income.[5]

Perhaps another factor that prompted artisans to blend craft pursuits with agriculture was the prestige attached to the possession of land. As one of the primary indices of influence, land was the plinth on which power and position rested. Many who earned their wealth in urban, commercial occupations, still sought to translate it into land. A large number of artisans possessed land, mostly gifted to them or their ancestors by the local landlords.[6] Land ownership gave them a better position than their landless counterparts, and provided relative economic security as well. Possession of means of production, such as ploughs, and access to irrigation facilities further contributed to strengthening an individual artisan's position within his caste, and vis-à-vis higher castes as well. Conflicts over irrigation facilities were numerous, several documents exemplifying such disputes.[7] In one striking case, friction between Khati Nandu of village Vararhn and the jats of his village persisted for over two years when the latter refused to remove the fencing they had erected on one side of the khati's ancestral tank, obstructing Nandu from maintaining his tank through periodic digging out of the sediments.[8] These indicate the economic and consequent social advantages they showered on their owners, and whether one agrees with Marx's characterization of India as a 'hydraulic society' or not, there is no denying that relations of production in predominantly agricultural areas were deeply implicated in access and control of water resources.

It may seem paradoxical that despite the influence of scriptural prescriptions that bound each artisan caste to perform definite functions assigned to it by the religio-legal system,[9] so many craftsmen took to cultivation and engaged in craft production only on a part-time basis, during the interstices of the annual agrarian cycle. But in fact this was not peculiar to Marwar; not only the neighbouring states of Jaipur, Udaipur, Kota, etc., but Himachal, Punjab, and even distant Maratha Deccan recorded similarly synthesized forms of rural production in the early modern period.[10] The cycle of production reveals an extraordinary capacity of Marwari artisans to turn nature's challenges to their advantage. The scorching summer heat of the desert seasonally walled in the villagers, and kept them away from the fields, more or less as winter did in Kashmir. Activities related to craft production such as dyeing and printing of textiles, baking and firing of pottery, or even curing of leather, were possible only when there was bright hot sunshine. As the sun beat down the parched sands during April, May, and June, artisans huddled indoors to engage in craft work, transforming the dry, monotonous landscape lacking in natural luxuriance, to come alive and constitute the 'colourbelt' of the subcontinent. These halted with the onset of the monsoons, and as soon as the rains came, many shifted to cultivation and outdoor work.

The state encouraged this pattern of production since it maximized the efficient use of labour.[11] By way of inducement, the state assessed cultivating artisans lightly as compared to other agriculturists. Differential scales of revenue assessment were in circulation, with concessional schedules of land revenue rates (dasturs) applied to those members of the non-cultivating castes who had adopted cultivation in conjunction with their hereditary occupations.[12] The state, for instance, defended the right of Kumhar Tohaman and Jaipal Sanwaldas to cultivate when the local jagirdar tried to have them vacate the fields on grounds of non-ownership.[13] Similarly, when Luhar Hasan of Jalor complained that the hakim had asked him to give the land he had been cultivating to a kallal of the village, the state rescued the luhar on learning that he had already ploughed his field.[14]

The annual agrarian cycle started at *Akhatij* (April), a festival that fell in the hottest season when the fields lay dusty and empty. The farmer's first task was to plough and break the soil, and mix in manure. The monsoon (unalu) crop was sown by early July as soon as there was a good rainfall. There was a lull in the activity between sowing and weeding and again between weeding and harvesting, when the artisans could attend to the maintenance and repair of their tools and implements.[15] The *chaumasa* crop was harvested from October to November, in the month of *kati*. Diwali, the new year in this region, was also a harvest festival, to be celebrated with new grain. If rains were delayed, sowing and harvesting were delayed, making for a dull Diwali. The day after Diwali was Govardhan Puja dedicated to livestock, and all households left hay at the centre of the village for passing animals to consume. Threshing and winnowing followed. Thereafter, the land-owning artisans were free to turn to the craft production that their caste traditionally specialized in.

But for those who had irrigated land, this was the busiest period since they could grow a winter (siyalu) crop as well; this implied the overlapping of harvesting of the monsoon crop and the sowing of the winter crop. A winter crop of wheat or barley could be had only if the fields could be tilled, watered, and sown in good time. Labour demand was highest in this period hence many landless artisans became tenants or agricultural labourers for the winter, and served the dominant landed castes who owned irrigated land. Crops began to be harvested around the festival of Holi in the month of March, and this was completed by April. Meanwhile, *khejri* trees and certain other bushes had to be pruned, the branches of trees that provided firewood and the leaves valuable as fodder for goats and camels had to be collected, and the heavy grasses and reeds separated for making huts.

For artisanal households which did not have irrigated land, as was generally the case, there was no agricultural work from Diwali till the monsoons, and even those few who did, found the period from Holi to the monsoons free from the demands of agricultural work. This was a period of respite from agricultural work that artisans utilized to attend to personal and social obligations like the performance of betrothals and marriages and making pilgrimages, etc. The cycle of public rites thus more or less accomodated itself to the agricultural calendar, and with agriculture an integral part of an artisan's work, craft production was practiced in the interstices of the annual agrarian cycle.

But how did artisans come to own land? In fact this happened as a result of a variety of historical circumstances: The khatis, luhars, and kumhars, who accompanied a bhomia in settling virgin land and bringing it under cultivation were recognized as the original colonizers of the village. Proprietary rights over plots of land were granted to them for their maintenance .[16] Known as *bapoti ri zamin*, these ancestral lands, whether in khalisa or jagir territories, gave to successive generations of their holders (bapidars) hereditary rights as well as several privileges and concessions over their inheritance. These rights meant that they could not be deprived of their ancestral holdings even if they left their village for, as explains Irfan Habib, 'ownership' amounted to hereditary rights of occupancy. Since land was freely available, the right of alienation—the essence of modern proprietary notions—was irrelevant.[17] Land could be reclaimed by an artisan even if the absence was as long as five years, and all efforts invested by him to increase the productivity of his land either through digging of wells or through other devices, was given due weightage at the time of assessment. Bapidars were also entitled to sell or mortgage their plots to tide over indebtedness or to overcome other financial difficulties. Their position and rights were regulated by the customary practices of the pargana, and as original inhabitants of the area they became important constituents of the village community.[18]

The same was true when artisans helped in the rehabilitation of a depopulated village, an oft-occurring phenomenon in Marwar where disruption of water supply meant abandonment of a settlement. The state and the elites were always keen on having thinly populated villages transformed into viable productive units because revenues would be minimal unless villages were vibrant with agricultural and craft production. Often, therefore, the administration induced or even coaxed artisans to settle in abandoned villages by giving them incentives. A record mentions that Darzi Asa was given land and encouraged to settle with his cattle there, and the authorities ordered that the villagers must allow his cattle to graze and drink water from the area.[19] Sometimes, instead of persuasion, coercion was employed by the superior castes to settle under-populated areas, as evident from Khati Jivan's complaint that he was originally of village Sirhli, but was forced to settle in village Kathedi by the local elite, ostensibly on the ground that his father had inhabited the village for 50 years.[20]

Besides, successive administrations rewarded artisans with plots from the khalisa because the land-man ratio was favourable to man, and huge expanses of land lay uncultivated. The Durbar, for instance, ordered that darzis Naga and Jaga of Nagaur to be given pattas of two plots of land from the khalisa in view of their exceptional talent.[21]Incentives in the shape of temporary tax concessions, immunity from the performance of *beth begar* protection from eviction even when the ownership title was not clear, were other methods the state employed to encourage non-agricultural castes to combine their occupational trade with cultivation.

Though a mixed profile of artisanal households that combined craft production with agriculture was common, it is difficult to quantify the numerical strength of the land-owning artisanate, as opposed to those who cultivated on others' lands or practised craft production to the exclusion of agricultural pursuits. For the majority, land holdings were too small and on relatively infertile soil to provide for more than subsistence needs. Effective irrigation facilities were generally lacking, and allowed them to cultivate only drought-resistant low-value crops such as jawar and bajra that could withstand water stress. Sometimes recourse was taken to inter-cropping, so that even if crops fetching better prices failed to survive, atleast those that could survive with less water could provide a cushion for the family. As such, even the land-owning artisan-cultivators lived more or less at the subsistence level, asking for no more than 'a hut that does not leak, a good *munj* cot, plenty of bajra bread, milk and curd'.[22] Worse still was the precariousness of those artisans who did not possess land, or possessed too little to meet their subsistence needs.

TRANSFORMATIONS IN THE BIRAT SYSTEM AND RELATIONS OF PATRONAGE

Differentiated local conditions such as those of settlement density, distribution of power, land/labour ratio and the availability of labour, commercialization level of the village in question and its access to markets, etc., constituted a multi-centric set of dynamics that saw a variety of exchange forms co-exist simultaneously. Cash-based transactions operated alongside exchanges in kind, based on the forging of patron-client relationships in some villages among certain castes. Known in Marwar as birat relationships, these contracts were based on dyadic relations with specific patron households, conceptually distinct from the demiurgic *baluta* relationships of village servants with the entire village community, common in villages of the Deccan region.[23] Known in Marwar as birat relationships, the latter appear to be the local variant of the much-debated jajmani that were supposed to establish harmonious collective interdependence among different constituents of a village caste hierarchy on the basis of customary rights and privileges.[24] In its pure form, the model suggested that upper-caste landed patrons established affective ties with artisanal and service castes to control their labour and in turn took upon themselves the obligation to meet the minimal subsistence requirements of clients through a customary apportioning of a part of their harvest as compensation. The latter, known in this region as *biratkaris*, entered these social arrangements to find protection against dearth and deprivation in difficult times, exclusive bonds with their birat households a guarantee of their support, and also meant to act as exclusive catchment areas for distribution of their produce. Depending on the size of the family, fundamental consumption needs were more or less irreducible. Meeting these subsistence needs in a reliable and stable way was indeed their central concern, and as an insurance against economic distress, these artisanal families saw insurance against starvation by having a fixed cluster of patrons. In doing so, they attempted risk-aversion through control over an exclusive market during years when consumer demand for them goods failed to provide them adequate income.

Unlike the ahistorical uniformity attributed to patron-client systems of relations in Wiser's traditional archaic model of jajmani, sources from Rajasthan, reveal a range of bonds set in specific historical circumstances. For one, the form of exchange between the 'patrons' and the 'clients' is far from being uniform or clear, with no evidence discernable in the records that indicates a customary portion of the harvest being bartered for craft commodities. It is neither evident whether the payments were made in cash or kind, nor is it indicated if the quantum of payments was along 'customary' lines or had some relation to the amount of labour expended or quantity of goods provided by the biratkari. Lending credence to C.J. Fuller's critique of the archetypal grain heap as the enduring symbol of a moneyless economy, petitions from Jodhpur suggest a cohabitation of the twin forms of exchange, foodgrains and cash prestations co-existing simultaneously even within the same village.[25] Also unclear is the conventional perception that clients forged such bonds with landed families alone. As noticed in the previous section, numerous artisans engaged in agriculture and did not practice their traditionally prescribed trade alone. This 'non-correspondence of ordained role ascription', as Simon Commander notes, was bound to generate practices that appear ambiguous and anomalous when compared with the classic construction of jajmani.[26] Again, the extremely high mobility of artisans in this region puts into question the classic rationale for the existence of this system, explained most commonly as an elite device to spatially fix productive labour in a period marked by the abundant availability of land and consequent migratory tendencies of labour. That out-migrations were a constant feature is undisputable; and what may reconcile the evidence for birat with mobility is the fact that often one member of a biratkari family remained in the ancestral village and performed his hereditary obligations vis-à-vis the patrons, while the others in the household took up employment elsewhere. That the nature of birat relations was therefore either rapidly transforming during the eighteenth century, marked increasingly by monetization, commercialization, and market logic, or had always been different from what Wiser and Dumont described, are difficult to state categorically. But what is more than clear is that a close scrutiny yields few commonalities between the 'moral' contours built by Dumont and material realities.[27] Sources from Marwar support the conclusions of Commander and Fuller, and caution us against accepting at face value wisdom received on the subject.

The consolidation of such reciprocal arrangements for the production and distribution of commodities followed a particular procedure in late eighteenth-century Marwar. The biratkari perceived it as a form of property right; he deposited a certain sum of money with the administration to get birat rights over his patron households, where he alone would have exclusive rights to offer certain commodities or perform fixed services. As a symbol of a patron's acceptance of his biratkari, the former placed a turban on the latter's head, the ritual called *pagh bandhai* in contemporary literature.[28] After pagh bandhai, the right to serve specific households and receive patronage from them passed down generations, and was viewed by artisans as a property that their descendants would inherit. It needs reiteration, however, that these birat ties produced no 'egalitarian utopia', and cannot be romanticized for creating harmony and well-being. Rather, they signified asymmetrical relations and consequent tensions, though the mutual needs of the birat households and dependent biratkaris prevented a complete breach in their mutual relations.

Hoping to secure a preferential treatment for himself as compared to other vulnerable families that might be suffering bad years of drought or famine, the closest descendant from the patrilineal line of a biratkari normally inherited the birat. Matrilineal relatives, too, sometimes contested and staked their claims. Khati Bhagwan of Merta, for instance, asserted his rights on his *nana*'s (maternal grandfather's) birat and property on the ground that his nana had lived with Bhagwan's parents and that his parents had hosted his funeral feast. Bhagwan therefore challenged the right of the patrilineal clan members of his nana when they tried to lay claim to the same.[29]

Cultural norms prescribed the patrons to adopt a paternalistic attitude towards their biratkaris;[30] hence, the compensations the biratkaris received were not given as payment for the goods or labour they supplied, but as results of the responsibility that rested on every patron for their welfare.[31] Their exchanges did not always involve a market transaction of quid pro quo. The biratkaris had the explicit hereditary right to serve their birat, which ensured their survival in an economy of scarcity and closely bound their fate with the power and well being of their patrons. Several documents record that the Padam Kumhar Paima of Merta offered clay lamps to Shri Huzur every Diwali and clay toys for the palace every Holi. The amounts of clayware that he gifted varied, but invariably the money presented to him by the ruler remained constant at ten rupees. Similarly, Mochi Mahmad brought leather goods and received fixed cash amounts irrespective of the nature and quantum of goods brought by him. These exchanges may perhaps be the vestiges of patron-client relationships between the ruler's household and the artisans mentioned in the records.[32] What is noteworthy, in any event, is that remuneration came in the shape of money and not foodgrains as Wiser's model would have us expect. Biratkaris were also entitled to get gifts on festivals and ceremonies, and these were given not as dues for work done, but under the garb of a paternalistic generosity and a customary obligation traditionally observed on such occasions.[33]

But this is not to say that all artisanal castes were uniformly and universally integrated in birat ties. In fact, artisanal castes were differentially involved in agriculture, and their integration in the birat ties varied accordingly, that is those who provided essential services relating to agricultural work such as blacksmiths, carpenters and potters, and service castes like genealogists, musicians, priests, barbers, and washermen were integrated far more closely within the birat system than those who crafted other utility items like textiles, and ornaments, etc. It is also erroneous to assume that major landlords were the archetypal birat, and that all other castes were only meant to perform for their rich patrons. Records document potters, weavers, and even cobblers as constituting birat, with exclusive rights on the services of certain craftsmen.[34] Even so, birat ties could not make for an egalitarian village community or create harmonious interdependence.[35] Unequal relationships continued to persist, and the birat system merely mitigated and softened the harshness of some of these inequities.

Also worthy of notice is that pressures from subordinate castes appear to have substantially altered the nature of the birat system by late eighteenth century. To start with, it perhaps aimed at fixing labour to a certain locality, and to specific patrons, by ties of mutual exchange. Not only had the artisans reversed the same ideology to their advantage by thrusting upon their patrons the obligation of providing sustenance and looking after the needs of their dependents, but insisting that failure to do so would generate resentment that could induce them to rebel.[36] As part of their role as dependants, they demanded patriarchal benevolence, asserted their rights to get financial aid when they needed it, as is evident in the threat given out by Kumhar Kusaliye to his bohra. Kusaliye warned that he would be forced to seek patronage with another bohra if the latter continued to neglect his obligations of providing funds for funeral feasts, purchase of bullocks, and other sundry needs of the kumhar.[37] By at least the third quarter of the eighteenth century, the biratkaris were clearly free to change their patron in case of dissatisfaction with the patronage and maintenance. Kumhar Kusaliye's threat was obviously motivated by the confidence that spurning his patron would hurt and offend the latter adequately to make him fall in line. Pressures from the subordinate castes thus worked towards introducing some accountability in elite conduct. Also integral to this document is the idea that the classic perception of status and hierarchy as crucial determinants of labour relations with the elites is not the entire truth; such relations were in fact equally implicated in an awareness of contractual engagements. They were neither based fully on consensus, nor—as claimed by Dumont—entirely integrative, but rather a site of tension and pressures.

Thus, though the birat ties were said to be permanent, inheritable by succeeding generations on the patrilineal line for both sides, and could not be ended even by death because they were not between individuals but between families, artisans did not adhere to this principle. At least under special circumstances, a change in one's patron on grounds of apathy and negligence was possible, and artisans were indeed using this to their advantage. In situations where the dominant caste patrons disregarded their obligations, or displayed laxity in providing help and relief, the biratkaris charged them with dereliction of 'duty', and asserted their right to claim patronage. Birat arrangements seem to have persisted only if they served the interests of both parties well.

Also clear in the documents is that artisans strove to maintain their hold and control over their patron households. They considered their birat rights precious, akin to property, and insisting on these being sacrosanct possessions, they resented all encroachments. Belief in a right to sustenance, and the confidence that their patron's sense of duty would ensure its practise, made artisans feel cheated and fight to have their birat restored in case of loss. In moments of crisis, these constituted the most ready and assured source of relief in a region plagued by frequent natural disasters, and provided the rationale for its persistence. For example, when Darzi Nathe of village Vasi of Parbatsar returned from Malwa, he found his house and

birat usurped by another darzi. For four years, Nathe tried in vain to per-
suade his caste-fellow to surrender what rightfully belonged to him. Finally,
he petitioned at the kachedi for the restoration of his family's right.[38] That
the birat right was precious is also indicated by the case of Kumhar Karme
of Lotodi, who was upset that, though he had adopted Bhopada and bestowed his entire birat on the latter, Bhopada did not provide for the kumhar's
maintenance. Acknowledging the impropriety of Bhopada's conduct, the
state ordered that Bhopada should either support the kumhar financially or
else the kumhar would be free to pass on his birat to somebody else.[39]After
all, in difficult times, when most artisanal households had negligible savings or reserves to fall back upon, it was those enjoying birat patronage who
could hope to survive.

Implicit in Kumhar Karme's petition is the fact that by the eighteenth
century, with increasing monetization, birat had rapidly taken on the form
of a property right that could be transferred or sold as other forms of property though initially birat could only be inherited. Corroborating this
impression is the case of Nai Lale of Merta, who had the cobblers of the
village in his birat. When he planned to emigrate for a few years, he charged
a fee from a caste-fellow, Jivarhiye, and transferred his birat to him. When
he retuned, however, Lale had to fight to get back his birat since Jivarhiye
refused to surrender it.[40] The fact that birat could be bought is also evident
from the case of Kumhar Bale of village Bhadaliya who, unable to muster
the resources himself, promised to mortgage six of his donkeys to Brahmin
Ramkisan for a loan to buy the birat right over six families. The material
aid he hoped to get from his patron households appears to have meant more
to him than the value of the donkeys.[41] Thus, rather than rigid principles
determining the contours of birat relations, flexibility and manoeuvrability
characterized the structure due to changing pressures and expectations.

Since artisans fought over birat rights, the administration sought to avoid
friction by making clear demarcations between the respective birat of two
artisans who dealt in the same craft. But when, in the absence of a certain
craftsman or service caste, the patron families entered fresh ties with another individual, conflict was inevitable if the original biratkari resurfaced.
In fact quarrels over birat rights were as common as property disputes and
conflicts arising over monetary transactions.[42] Despite efforts to accommodate both biratkaris by dividing the birat into shares in such situations,
tensions could not be avoided. The numerous instances of quarrels clearly
indicate that conditions in eighteenth-century rural Marwar made birat arrangements not just desirable but a necessity for some. In view of fluctuating
consumer demands for craft goods, and difficulties involved in transporting
goods to the towns for sale, the exceptionally vulnerable artisans preferred
to have a local distribution network.[43]

The popularity and frequency of these bonds is, however, not at all clear. The fact that in over a 1000 documents studied on artisanal issues, less than a dozen relate to birat relations suggests two possibilities—one, that the bonds ensured extremely harmonious interactions and generated minimal grievances that would occasion petitions; the second, and more likely seems to be that such relations were in disrepair, declining due to biratkaris' increasing preference for market exchanges. Cash, as noticed earlier, was neither alien nor peripheral or subordinate to birat transactions in eighteenth century-villages, rural settlements closely integrated with the commercial world and its monetary imperatives. What seems likely is that those engaged in manufacturing wood, iron, clay, and leather goods often forged birat bonds, while other relatively commercialized artisanal castes such as textile workers, goldsmiths and other metal workers, and construction builders were more market-oriented. Working as wage employees or participating in cash-based market exchanges, they do not seem to have been part of the birat network. Stone workers in particular, whose labour was required by elite employers at different locations, had to necessarily move from place to place in search of construction sites. Constant mobility could obviously not support any long-standing patron-client ties. Similarly, sunars mostly worked on a cash basis since few mahajan households could generate enough work for sunars to become long-term clients.

Economic rationalization appears to have nibbled through the bonds of 'paternalism', and many seem to have withdrawn from the birat system to commercialize. Though dating these developments is not possible, it is certainly arguable that sunars, thatheras, kaseras, pinjaras, julahas, rangaras, chhipas, lakharas, and churigars were outside the birat fold by the second half of the eighteenth century.[44] In all likelihood, this transitional phase of the eighteenth century brought about an enlargement of that sector of the economy that was independent of patron-client relationships, and increasingly a part of the monetized commercial world. Artisans who crafted goods for the market worked in their small cottages, owned or hired their tools, and either recived cash payments in their transactions with the village folk, or wages for their labour.

In any event, birat ties co-existed alongside forces of a wholly market nature. Though biratkari artisans largely depended on their patron families, they too occasionally visited the local haats, fairs, and qasba markets, combining their production for the market with their customary obligation to the village community or to specific patron families. Payments in kind or cash were not mutually exclusive. Different forms of transactions occurred in varying degrees of dominance in different sectors of Marwar's village economy, and it is impossible to construct a uniform profile or model that shows the predominance of one or the other form of exchange. These in fact depended on spatial factors of distance between the village in question and a commercial centre, its integration with the trade network of the region, the occupational caste in question and potential for out-migration. In their intensely fragmented form, however, birat bonds can hardly be treated as a template justifying the attribution of Indian village economy as 'traditional' and archaic, the opposite of a modern and dynamic one that characterized western rural conditions.

Efforts to Establish Trade Monopolies

As discussed earlier, the bargaining position and clout that the artisans enjoyed vis-à-vis dominant groups was contingent on their indispensability to the local economy, derived from the specialized skills that they exclusively possessed. The rigour of caste prescriptions as well as training ensured that specific tasks could be performed by particular groups alone, and would remain unaccomplished if none of their caste members were available to carry them out. Hence, many craftsmen, faced with the problem of a limited market for their goods in the countryside, took recourse to aggressive direct action to maintain their monopoly over the small village clientele. They tried to prevent over-saturation of the limited market by disallowing craftsmen of their own occupational group from immigrating and settling in their village.

Such aggressive responses on the part of artisans resulted from the fact that the craftsmen were as much dependant on the patronage provided by their consumers as the latter were on having their needs for both routine and special commodities met by the artisans. Precarious levels of income that were just about sufficient to provide for subsistence made them vulnerable to any fall in demand or withdrawal of patronage. The infiltration of other members of the same occupational group would imply the sharing of the market with a caste-fellow. More importantly, it would provide patrons wider options from whom they could pick the more docile worker for the performance of the necessary service, and this would cause the artisan to lose his bargaining strength born out of a refusal to work. Loss of income and support fostered by patrons would deprive him of this sustenance and negotiating power he otherwise enjoyed in a situation of monopoly over patron houses.

It was this sole right to provide for certain essential needs in the village that an artisan struggled to withhold and pre-empt any encroachment into his sphere of influence. Complaints against caste-fellows who had laid claim to his patrons were a manifestation of this problem and the anxiety to maintain exclusive control over patronage is manifest in numerous records. Business in gold and silver was, for instance, limited in villages, only a few families able to afford high expenditures involved in the purchase of precious metals. Consequently, it was not unusual for sunars to resist immigrants. A document records that Sunar Bhage of village Sankhwas resented Sunar

Bharomal's attempts to settle in his village and appealed at the pargana kachedi when the latter refused to relent and move out of Sankhwas.[45]

Others chose to take matters in their hands, and offered stiff resistance to any sunar's attempts at immigration and setting up business in their village. Repeated instances of such episodes created precedents that gradually gave rise to a custom that forbade the immigration of new sunars' without the permission of the original sunar. Contravention of this custom led to friction and disputes, desperation sometimes leading to violence and physical abuse as is evident in the following case:

Sunari Dipli of village Kudaki of Merta came here and reported that I have no sons; hence I have kept kept my son-in-law with me (*ghar-jamai rakhiyo hai*). I am not an original inhabitant of this village. Now all the sunars of the village—Khuspal, Sukhe, etc. came and assaulted me (*chot ghali*) and warned me against taking residence in this village. They claim that it is against norms for new goldsmiths to come and settle in a village that already has goldsmiths residing there. (It was ordered that) check the settlement customs of their community from the sunars in the neighbouring villages and resolve accordingly. [46]

Sunars of a locality also clashed with the mahajans because many goldsmiths, apart from crafting ornaments and essaying coins, were engaged in extending credit as well. Moneylending was an extremely profitable business, and often the two quarrelled to exercise complete monopoly over this trade. A document records that a sunar of Piparh had twice got pattas to open a shop in his village. He complained at the chauntara when the mahajan of the area repeatedly prevented him from starting his business. [47] Life at the margins was always a struggle, and survival strategies had to keep pace with new and ever changing developments.

Exactions, Extortions, and Intimidation by the Dominant

These strategies for self-preservation only partially mitigated the pressures that village artisans faced quotidinially. The negativities of ecological adversities multiplied manifold due to burdens generated by human agencies—the state and its ohdadars, and the locally dominant landed castes. Village society displayed considerable social stratification and economic differentiation, those like jagirdars, bhomias, chaudharis, *qanungos* (village accountants), *patwaris* (village record-keepers), etc., enjoying power and social status both due to their possession of superior rights in land, and due to their position in the apparatus of revenue administration, and resultant backing from the state.[48] Then there were substantial landlords from the rajput and mahajan communities who, too, exercised clout derived from a superior ritual status and material resources in land, which they often employed to transform free workers into servile labour. Still others, like brahmins, wielded power solely on the strength of their caste status, and intimidated socially inferior landed artisans. The subordination of artisans who owned land does not appear to have been as comprehensive as that of landless artisans who were forced to work on the fields of superior castes. Land ownership, however, could not eliminate the bhomia's access to their resources because the latter's proprietary rights over the village gave him control over the residents and their produce. Artisan-cultivators' ownership claims, therefore, did not imply the abrogation of elite claims on the produce of their land. And finally, those who possessed no land, a large proportion of whom were from the lowest service and castes, were totally dependent on patronage from the dominant castes, considerably vulnerable to their excesses. Even for them, landlessness in this period 'did not necessarily imply an absence of all 'property' and an entire reliance on the sale of 'labour power', as, to a considerable degree, it did later'.[49] Alliances with dominant individuals could ensure control over some resources, even a plot of land, as long as the subordinate were loyal and deferential. This continuum from 'free' peasant proprietors— the *khud kasht* , *pahi kasht*, and *muqarari riaya* to the 'bonded', 'unfree' *halis*, *vasis* and *golas* reveals differentiation among the lower formations, and consequent diversities in their rights, obligations, and experiences.

The morphology of rural settlements, organized along caste lines, generally reflected this intensely hierarchical social order, large villages possessing separate mohullas or *bas* for different castes. Upper castes were located in the core area, lower but 'clean' castes in their vicinity, and the 'unclean, impure' castes, especially those involved with preparing and working on leather, at the peripheries of the village. The settlement pattern was thus geared to maintaining a strict segregation of different occupational groups.[50]

One of the most vital of the artisans' pressures related to the plethora of revenue extractions they suffered, whether as full-time craftsmen or as part-time cultivators and part-time artisans. The list of exactions is unending, but the sources do not indicate the quantum of each incidence. They also fail to clarify whether each of the taxes was uniformly levied all over the territories of Marwar or only over certain specific parganas. Similarly, we remain in doubt about the specific communities from whom each was appropriated, rendering the likelihood of all attempts to gauge their pressure too erroneous to be of any utility. Table 4.1 lists some of the important taxes that find mention in secondary literature on this region, and documents on eighteenth century Marwar corroborate the imposition of the same.[51]

Taken together, all these levies constituted a huge burden on the already hard-pressed people impoverished by droughts and famines. These state taxes (*hukumat lags*), however, pale into insignificance when compared with some of those that the jagirdars used to levy on the people residing on their estates.[52] In addition, a major source of exploitation and oppression, apart from revenue exactions, tributes and miscellaneous dues, was begar or bethbegar. It implied the performance of unremunerated labour or provision of craft commodities free of cost, or in some cases, both. In eighteenth-century Rajasthan, the administration and the political elites requisitioned begar from the subordinate castes on a regular basis. In the Maratha Deccan such demands seem to have been restricted to villages alone. In Marwar, however, urban artisans and service castes too appear to have been subjected to unremunerated labour, enjoined to perform their duties in khalisa as well as jagir areas.[53] Begar was thus a legally recognized form of surplus extraction, free services expected to be performed when state officials visited the village.[54] Documents show that this practice was widely prevalent in almost all regions of the kingdom, and was levied either in lieu or in addition to revenue collections. The demand for begar labour was usually made in the artisan cultivators' slack season, from October to June. The records do not, however, suggest that artisans performed begar for the cultivation of state lands, for which normally share-croppers and tenant-farmers were employed.

Taxes were convertible into begar, and those who could not afford to pay revenues, or could pay them only partially, were allowed to compensate by performing unpaid labour in excess of their normal due. Once in a position to pay taxes and preferring to do so, however, they were entitled to withdraw from the performance of extra begar services.[55] Those from the service castes had to offer free labour, whether by working in state enterprises or at the homes of landed elites. Carpenters, ironsmiths, stone-workers, masons, and brick-layers were sometimes recruited to provide unpaid labour at the forts, palaces, royal gardens, and other construction sites for repair work. They were often asked to porterage grains, timber, and other goods for the government, cut fodder at the state meadows, serve at the government stables and provide free service of watchmanship at market places. As part of domestic chores they were expected to sweep and clean the mansions of the lords, water their animals, and help with different household errands when guests arrived on special occasions. For instance, Nai Paimle of village Behad of Jaitaran was asked to send his wife for making rotis at the jagirdar's mansion (*kotri*) when he had guests; on the nai's refusal, the jagirdar was enraged, and as a punishment, prevented him from continuing to enjoy patronage of his birat houses in the village.[56] *Begar kotri ki* at the bhomia's or jagirdar's establishment was a demand that craftsmen had to contend with, especially on special occasions when labour was needed during the harvesting season, at the time of marriage in the lord's house, or when a guest visited him. On such occasions they had to provide routine consumption goods and items of daily use, as happened in the case of a mochi from whom the state servants (*mahindar chakars*) of the chauntara took away twelve cots without paying.[57]

Table 4.1 Some Important State Taxes in Eighteenth-century Marwar

Type	Tax	Purpose
1. On Agriculture	Bhog	Land revenue
	Kharach-bhog	To meet the expenses made towards the collection of revenue
	Lag-bag	Miscellaneous irregular taxes for the upkeep of local and revenue administrations
2. On the Use of Natural Resources	Ghasmari	On grass-eating cattle (cows and buffaloes)
	Pan-charai	On leaf-eating animals (camels and goats)
	Kabada bab	On the use of forest timber
3. On Commerce	Rahdari	On merchants, for providing safe movement of merchandize on roads
	Nikal-pesar	Customs duties levied on the entry and exit of goods
	Mapa	On the import and export of goods
	Baithak	On sitting space in a market-place
	Singoti	Sales-tax on cattle
	Vatvali	For the maintenance of the collectors of mapa and rahdari
	Kayali	For the maintenance of official weighers in a market or mandi
	Parkhai	For the mint officials who essayed coins deposited as tax
4. On Ownership of Major Assets	Ghar-ginti	House tax on house-owners
	Balad-bhainsiya-ri-bab	On cattle owners
5. On Income of Professionals	Sahukara-ri-bhachh	License fee on merchants for permission to ply their trade
	Pinjar bab	License fee on cotton-carders
	Chautha	Obligation of Churigars to deposit one-fourth of income from cutting bangles to the state
	Sarh bab	License fee on weavers, for permission to install pitlooms
	Sarhawi Sarhe	License fee on weavers and tailors
	Dand Kholarhi	License fee on potters
	Jhunki	License fee on khatis and sunars
6. On the Provision of Security	Fauj-kharach-ri-bab	Levies for the upkeep of royal armies
	Ghoda-kambal	Levies to finance warm covers for royal horses

(Table 4.1 Cont'd.)

(Table 4.1 Cont'd.)

	Kharnal-bab	Levies for the provision of horse-shoes for the royal stables
	Rasad bab and Khichdi	Obligation to provide rations and food to royal troops passing through a village
7. On Villagers	Peshkash	Contributions made by villagers towards the amount paid by jagirdars and senior officials to the maharaja
	Nazrana	Contributions made by the subjects towards payments made by elites on occasions of birth and marriage in the royal family
	Chaudhar bab	Contributions by villagers towards the payment of the village headman's emoluments
	Qanungo dastoor	Contribution by villagers towards the qanungo's emoluments
	Likhawani	Contributions by villagers towards the accountant's emoluments
	Talbana	Contributions towards the salary of royal summon-carriers
	Malba	Contributions by villagers towards the maintenance of communal resources of the village
	Deorhi Dastoor*	Contributions made by villagers to the nazrana paid by the village chaudhuri for the maintenance of the maharaja's personal staff
	Kewari*	A tax paid by each household to assist Maharaja Vijai Singh regain his throne from Ram Singh
	Habub*	Contributions for royal maintenance in the face of Maratha pressure
8. On Important Social Occasions in the Lives of Subjects	Chanwari	To procure the legal recognition of a marriage
	Nata	To ensure the legal recognition of a remarriage
	------------	Contributions towards the mainte nance of temples
	------------	Contributions towards the celebration of festivals

Note: * New taxes imposed during Maharaja Vijai Singh's reign.

Rates of begar, pertaining to different castes in different parganas, were fixed, and craft castes were accustomed to extending these as per tradition. Such customary begar, which was not in contravention of established practice, was by and large not questioned by those affected. But when local authorities attempted to exact additional begar, either in the form of goods or services, artisans felt harassed and violated, and were resentful of the new levy and its perpetrator. In one case, the chaudhari of village Phidoth demanded water pots in begar from Kumhar Amare of the village. Claiming this to be an illegitimate demand, the kumhar refused to part with the same without payment. The chaudhari, in retaliation, assaulted him and took away his pots and pans forcibly.[58] The demand for unpaid goods and services exceeded the capacity or willingness of the artisanate, and frictions due to the use of force were common, especially during war and famine. The abjection of forced labour was a major part of the wretchedness experienced by subordinate castes. Even in the present-day memory of the subjects of the region,[59] this is clearly evident.

In an economy of scarcity, efforts at maximization of material resources formed the crux of the mutually conflictual relationship between the dominant and the subordinate, and forms of exploitation were often economically determined. Extraction of unremunerated labour, inflicting fines by making false allegations of theft, usurpation of dwellings, extortion of live-stock, disruption of irrigation facilities, etc., constituted routine forms of harassment in the lives of the subordinate, provoking them to resort to different forms of protest as per their resources and bargaining ability. It was not merely those dependent on their patrons who suffered oppression; even the relatively commercialized castes did not fair much better. The sunars, julahas, chhipas, rangrez, and lakharas, as susceptible to subsistence crises as the others, were subjected to extortions by the superior castes. For instance, Sunar Bholiye of village Thanwala was arrested and forced to go through the *ghij pani* ordeal of having hot oil poured on him by the jagirdar's men. The false charge they framed against him was that he had stolen from Bija of Dungarwal. Despite emerging innocent, and despite discovering that Bija's nephew was the culprit, they extracted hundred rupees from him.[60]

These pre-bourgeois techniques of subordination were endured in a context where caste rendered artisans socially inferior, even if they compared favourably in terms of material resources. This is starkly borne out by the case of Sunar Jete of Jawala in Parbatsar who, despite being well-off, was exploited by the local jagirdar due to his inferior caste. The jagirdar stood guarantee, and asked the sunar to lend 60 man grains and fifteen rupees to a neighbour in the village. But instead of aiding the sunar in the recovery of the loan, the jagirdar levelled a false allegation of theft on him, and confiscated his house.[61] In another similar case, a darzi who had been promised six man of foodgrains for watering the local jagirdar's fields, found that instead of being remunerated, he was falsely charged with stealing an ornament from the jagirdar's house. For this alleged crime, he was not only detained but forced to pay a fine of four rupees.[62]

The state, caste dominance, and customary traditions vested the jagirdars with powers to impart justice in their territories, but more often than not, they joined in the exploitation and were partial towards their supporters and clients. Pinjara Nure of village Thure was helpless when the local jagirdar refused to pay him for the buffalo he had forcibly taken from him. In addition he imposed a *pinjar bab* (a tax levied on the profession of cotton-carding) higher than the going rate. Worse still was the jagirdar's failure to provide justice in the face of gross abuse committed against the pinjara by a *rebari* (camel-herder). The latter not only misbehaved with Nure's wife, but also took away a sackful of sesame seeds from his field. Yet the jagirdar did not punish the rebari. Ultimately the Jalorgarh kachedi ordered that justice be meted out to the aggrieved pinjara by punishing the guilty.[63] Another complaint recorded that the jagirdar of village Itawa illegally took away several valuable possessions from a lakhara, and prevented the latter from using his Persian wheel.[64]

As noticed earlier, wealth in cattle was extremely precious to the economy of the region, with camels of special value as a mode of transport in the desert terrain. Bhomia Tej Singh therefore took away two camels of Kumhar Dane of village Belu of Bikaner on the false charge that Dane had borrowed money from the rajput two decades ago.[65] Usurpation of houses was another common form of harassment that temporary artisanal emigrants had to often face. Bhomia Nawal Singh is recorded to have usurped the houses of julahas Kheru and Mheru of Harsor while they were in Malwa, and refused to return them even after the julahas came back and demanded their dwellings to be returned.[66] The kumhars of village Anandpur had migrated out during the famine years, but on return, found that the village chaudhari, Ramchand, had usurped their houses.[67] Even a blind kumhar was not left in peace, and was harassed by his village chaudhari to perform his share of the work though he was living with his brother and was maintained by the latter.[68] The inferior status of the artisans emboldened the other well-to-do castes of the village, even the unprivileged ones, to take advantage, abuse, and manipulate them in different ways.[69] Of the middle-level agriculturists, conflict with the jats seem to predominate, especially over access to irrigation facilities. In one case, a mali who had been using the ancestral Persian wheel of a kumhar while the latter was in Malwa, refused to let the kumhar claim ownership of it on his return.[70]

Clearly, exploitation, intimidation, and coercion from the landed elites was a reality that the artisans had to routinely contend with, and these were

an extension of not only economic but also social superiority that they enjoyed over those down below. This specific blend of socio-economic
superiority leading to material extortion and extra-economic coercion saw
frequent episodes of corporal punishment being inflicted on the subordinate, whether landed or landless artisans. Levels of vulnerability varied, but
that a majority were susceptible to occasional abuse is not what this study
tries to challenge. It notices, in fact, the extreme subordination of some artisans into variable degrees of servility as a consequence of financial crises.

MERCHANTS, LANDLORDS, DEBTS, AND AGRESTIC SERVITUDE

In the face of substantial demand for revenue and begar, coupled with illegal extortions, artisans often took recourse to loans from the mercantile
classes—the mahajans, baniyas, bohras, or sahukars. The much-maligned
merchants and moneylenders in fact played a critical role in the precarious
household economy of the poor. In moments of crisis, their role was crucial in funding the indigent and thereby rescuing them from immediate
ruin, starvation, and death. The frequency and magnitude of loans varied
both spatially and circumstantially, depending on a variety of factors such
as the size of the family and the land holding, the commercial value of
crops sown, local agricultural prices, and whether they owned a plough
and agricultural implements or not. Artisans usually took loans to meet
heavy expenditures they incurred over life cycle rituals of birth, marriage,
and death, invariably compelled to spend far beyond their means. Constant
privation and precariousness of their household economies got aggravated
by such occasions in the family, with documents recording several cases
where loans were incurred when a boy was betrothed and his father had to
pay a bride price.[71] Such festivities were extravagant, requiring the hosts to
feast not only the community but often the entire village. Funeral rites, called
ausar-mausar in the region, also involved pilgrimages, charities, and feasting
of clansmen over several days.[72] The stranglehold of these customary obligations was so strong that despite being ill-equipped to afford such
immoderate expenses, the poor saw loans as the only way out.

While such loans saw artisans through moments of crisis, they also forced
them into indebtedness and subordination. An examination of the eighteenth-century archive suggests that evidence from Marwar can only partially
support Prasannan Parthasarathi's findings, and that contrary to his claims
about (south Indian) labourers having experienced neither poverty nor oppression due to a high level of financial security in their pre-colonial past,
artisans in Marwar suffered grave deprivations and frequent subsistence
crises due to revenue and labour exactions that transferred a bulk of their

surplus to dominant groups.[73] Default in repayment of loans was more than common, and resulted in the loan being serviced through labour for the creditor, the debtor thereby entering into a spiral of dependence and servility from which extrication was near impossible. Indeed, there was no way merchants could enforce repayment, and one would agree with Prasannan Parthasarathi's view that often the only way for merchants to 'recover their money was to make further advances and to allow weavers to gradually work off the sum'.[74] Since compensations or wages that the indebted artisans received for their services were very low, their chances of discharging their debts were negligible. Parthasarathi's findings, however, that the 'accumulation of weaver debts was potentially disastrous for merchants as there were no legal or institutional mechanisms with which they could enforce repayment' and that 'it was not uncommon for weavers who had accumulated debt to simply pack up their looms and possessions and move elsewhere' seems an overstatement of the reality, at least as it appears in early modern Rajasthan.[75]

Contrary to his view that creditors in pre-colonial south India had no control over indebted weavers who were free to emigrate out of bounds, evidence from Marwar suggests that once caught in the quicksand of indebtedness, getting out of it was highly improbable due to coercion from the dominant, especially in areas where labour was not easily available. For instance, Kumhar Sarupe sought a loan for his marriage from two charans in 1747. They not only compelled him to serve them for the next twenty-five years, but later, when he tried to break away from them, the charans forced him and his children to accompany them back to their village. They insisted that since their beneficence had supported the upbringing of the children, they would retain Sarupe's children too as servants. The kumhar's attempts to opt out of this arrangement and rejoin his community by paying the charans five rupees failed, and they refused to release him even after deriving thirty years of service.[76] Khati Champekhete of village Bhagsar in Jalor had borrowed a pot of grains twenty-two years ago from Laghar Singhvi (a bania). Despite working to repay it for over two decades, the latter's demands did not end.[77] Such coercions became necessary to prevent an artisan from migrating away.

Equally, insufficient resources and agricultural inputs disabled many artisan-cultivators from being able to cultivate independently despite the abundant availability of cultivable land. They were dependent on advances from their bohra, a small merchant who fulfilled a variety of credit needs of the village folk. Bohras generally owned a shop stocked with grain, cloth, vegetable oil, salt, ironware, and other necessities of daily life, which they advanced to the artisans and cultivators—along with small sums in cash when needed.[78] Larger loans were provided to cover the state demand for land tax, to pay for new livestock or agricultural equipment, for the celebration of births and marriages, to meet mourning expenses and funerary rituals, and for religious rites. The bohras advanced seeds for the cultivators to sow in their fields, but were careful to ration them. This was prompted by their calculation that the size of the harvest should not be large enough to render the peasants independent of the bohras, because more seed-grains would mean a profuse harvest. If their dependents managed to meet their loan obligations and became free, the business and affluence of the bohras would collapse.[79] These advances were pledged against crop security, and at the time of the harvest, the bohra went with his cart to the client's threshing floor and demanded that he be handed over a greater proportion of the harvested crop. He thereby maintained large stocks of surplus grains. Thus, though their produce had to be hypothecated to their creditors, the need to maintain financial aid in future caused artisans to comply. Generally unable to repay the loan soon, they remained yoked to the arrangement for generations.[80]

With the bulk of a peasant's crop thus taken away by the bohra or the bania, the indebted ended up mortgaging his 'freedom' partially, if not wholly. A proverb popular in this region reads to the effect: *kuro karsa khai, gahun jime bania*, that is, the cultivators are reduced to eat coarse grains while the baniyas enjoy wheat (a relatively costly cereal in this region).[81] Moneylenders felt comfortable about this personalized arrangement because they did not have to worry about competition from other usurers, and could impose harsher terms on their clients. This was particularly true if all the business of a village was in the hands of a single moneylender, as was often the case. Credit was given both in cash and in kind, and the interest rates were high. A seventeenth-century Jain traveller reported that loans sometimes rose through compound interest to five times the original sum advanced.[82] In many cases the mahajans purchased the agricultural land of those in need of a loan, and then leased out the same to the erstwhile owners on a share-cropping basis. Alternately, credit was advanced against a surety furnished by the village bhomia, chaudhari, patel, or even a respected caste-fellow.

Most creditors extended loans against the security of mortgage, either of the debtor's house, land, harvest, or labour, for a specified period of time. Both parties to the agreement tried to push their self-interest, and the more powerful obviously had an edge over his weaker counterpart.[83] When Khati Khwajbagas Rehman took a loan by mortgaging both his houses to yatis Akhaychand and Birghichand, he felt relieved at having tided over the immediate crisis. But the yatis soon declared that he must either return the entire amount with interest or vacate the property. Unable to repay, the khati petitioned the state to resolve the matter.[84] Chhipa Nanag of Bagadi had to mortgage his house with Mahajan Harakha for a loan of rupees hundred and fifty. He failed to repay the amount though the capital, with interest, had doubled. Harakha therefore went to the Sojhat kachedi and insisted that Nanag vacate the house, and that the kachedi register the same as his property. Nanag petitioned that he would pay a rent of five rupees annually till he was unable to service his loan, but till then, he must be allowed to continue living in the house.[85] One of the strategies creditors employed to take control of mortgaged property was to invest on it. Khati Narsingh of village Gangawas had difficulty in getting his house released from the mahajan, the latter staking his claim on the ground that he had sunk his money into it.[86] A popular folk tale among the villagers neighbouring Jodhpur shows the vile manner in which banias operated against their victims. The story runs thus:

Irritated with the slyness of a bania, a thakur of a village punished him by settling a bhambi (leather-worker) as the bania's neighbour. The thakur presented the humble bhambi with a large plot of land. The stink from the bhambi's leather-processing bothered the bania, and aghast at finding himself in such poor company, he decided to appropriate the bhambi's land by fair or foul means. He therefore began to scheme and plot to get rid of his lowly neighbours and usurp their land. To this end, he set about generating friction between the bhambi and his devoted wife, and sowed seeds of suspicion vis-à-vis each other, in their minds. Every time either of the bhambi couple went to perform *begar* at the thakur's *garh* (mansion), the bania visited the spouse who had remained at home, and planted untruths to create suspicions. Eventually the bhambi husband and wife began to despise one another, and their anger against each other knew no limits. Uncontrollably provoked, the bhambi assaulted and killed his wife and for this heinous crime he was imprisoned, and then sentenced to death by the Durbar. This gave the bania the opportunity he had been scheming and waiting for, and he asked the thakur to make the *patta* for the bhambi's land in his favour. After all, the bania had ensured that there was no living claimant to it![87]

The dearth of labour, rather than land, however, generally ensured that artisans were practically never evicted from their fields. Since labour was not easy to obtain, it was in the interest of mahajans to respect the *bapoti* (ancestral rights) of artisan-cultivators and keep them attached to the land rather than sell it.[88] Even when they took loans on the security of land or a house they owned, and were unable to repay for generations, their title to the ownership generally remained unaffected. Records do not indicate forced evictions, and sale proceedings occurred only when artisans in need of capital preferred to sell and emigrate rather than remain indebted.[89] More often than sale, documents reveal a transfer deed whereby, in return for money borrowed, the landholder would give possession of a portion of his field for some years till he was able to service the loan. Mahajans were obliged to allow the artisan-proprietor who owned the land to continue cultivating it, merely reducing for some years, his status was from a full proprietor to a share-cropping tenant.

Also, it was not in the interest of moneylenders to have clients so enfeebled by hunger that they abandoned agricultural operations and were rendered unable to service their debts. If the poor starved to death, or fled from the village never to return, the long-standing debt would be worth no more than the paper on which it was written. To secure future debt payments, usurers readily rescued their clients in times of dearth. During a drought in neighbouring Ajmer–Merwara in 1848–9 the banias provided food for their clients at—so they claimed—considerable expense to themselves. As a result, the impoverished residents of the region did not migrate out of the area in search of food.[90] The exploitation by mahajans was constrained by such fears, and tended to respect the limits of wajabi as set by custom.

As a result, despite oppression, the bohra seems to have been regarded by the poor as a patron under obligation to extend subsistence to his clients, bound by duty to provide for their sustenance. The motive of the economically weak in entering such relationships was the sharply fluctuating demand for labour, sometimes far from adequate in providing wages during lean periods in the annual agrarian cycle. The matter was of hard interest on either side. It was not to the advantage of a moneylender if a client household became perilously destitute, making it impossible for them to service the loan. And as for the poor, it was a matter of survival in an inhospitable environment. Bohras who could not protect their clients could lose standing in their community. Conversely, a bohra bestowed status upon his dependent, perceived among the village folk as one backed by a valuable benefactor. David Hardiman's characterization of their mutual relationship as that of a child with his parents who are both beneficent and nurturing as well as harsh and punishing[91] appears an exaggeration, the affective quality of the relationship relatively missing. The prescient need to indulge the clients by adopting a parental posture was, however, by no means absent.

Once craftsmen went in for a loan, they experienced subordination not only from their creditor but also the guarantor, often the bhomia or chaudhari who had given surety at the time of borrowing the money from the mahajan. While many artisans got ensnared in the vicious circle of indebtedness to celebrate the rites of passage, abnormal years of wars and famines were equally responsible in encouraging those on the margins of subsistence to sell themselves or members of their families into 'debt bondage'.[92] The fear of starvation was more than real in such conditions, and more important than the loan itself was the 'guarantee of maintenance' implied in these relationships. Subsistence crises could not always be eradicated through migrations, especially in areas lacking adequate means of transport and communication and inability to ascertain alternate locales where one might move for patrons. A drop in demand for labour, either during slack phases of the agricultural cycle, or circumstances of exceptional hardship, easily jeopardized sources of livelihood, and made the need for security outweigh restrictions on movement implied in a relationship of 'unfree' bonded labour.

In additions, as Jan Breman rightly notes that servitude has generally been studied as arising either from a need for labour leading to forced attachment, or from a need for security leading to voluntary acceptance of bondage.[93] In fact neither interpretation covers the entire gamut of factors, unless the total context of hierarchical social relations and cultural mindset is taken note of. The fact that agricultural labour, especially handling the plough, was considered demeaning and defiling by the upper castes, forcing them to maintain a distance from lowly despicable work by employing others for it, explains as much the prevalence of servile labour as economic determinants . It was a means of enhancing ritual status, and thereby power, even if the economic rationale for it was negligible. Tensions between creditors/masters and servile artisanal labour were plenty, and especially in better times coercion had to be used to hold back one's clients from migrating. Even so, in specific contexts, 'an obligation to work could be construed as a right to employment'[94] and appeared as the preferred option than unlimited freedom with no patron.

Hereditary servitude through institutionalized bondage appears to have tied down a substantial proportion of the landless artisanate, 'unfree' labourers categorized as halis and vasis. Since 'unfreedom' was so deeply enhenched in the Indian ethos, Gyan Prakash's insights about the irrelevance of the 'free' 'unfree' dichotomy appears true.[95] Unlike other issues such as familial morality or political loyalty being emphasized in the literature of this period, there is no discourse condemning the suspension of 'natural' rights to freedom, whether as halis, vasis or golas. By succumbing to different forms of servitude, artisans bargained their independence and labour against material security and protection. The dependant relationship usually resulted when an impoverished artisan, either of his own volition or under coercion from the superior castes, forfeited his freedom and accepted bondage in exchange for a loan in kind or cash, most often to meet the expenses of his marriage or the funeral rites of a family member.[96] Advances were contingent on the borrower accepting, wittingly or unwittingly, suspension of rights to migrate or to offer services to other masters. The halis, essentially landless agricultural labourers dependent solely on the wages they received from their employers, enjoyed relative freedom. Their relationship with their masters was that of contractual service, which theoretically implied freedom after serving the master with labour services for a specified period. But generally, the inadequate remuneration they received for their labour meant a lifetime of unremitting misery and subordination. Kumhar Sarupe, who was unable to buy his freedom even after serving his creditors for over thirty years, is a case in point.[97] The terms of service were put in writing, and the hali contracted to serve as a farm servant to a wealthier landlord for one to three years, until he had paid off his debt. The loans had to be paid back in instalments, and one or two of the junior members of the family in debt were made halis to serve the master and thus facilitate the repayment of the loan. Some young orphans brought up by the landlords in their houses also had to become halis of their benefactor, as in the case of Kumhar Devale who, on his father's death, was brought to the shelter of the local jagirdar by his mother. He initially looked after his patron's cattle, and later cultivated his fields to repay the money spent by the master on getting him married.[98] But because of the low emoluments he received for his services, his chances of discharging his debt were negligible. The debt tended to increase in the course of time, and the farm servant, with few exceptions, remained in bondage for the rest of his life. The attachment continued into the next generation when his son also married at the expense of his father's master, and thus in practical terms, the agreement between landlord and agricultural labourer implied a lifetime of bondage.

The term hali literally meant one who wields the plough, but in eighteenth century Marwar it referred only to servants so engaged and not to permanent ploughmen or halwaha, as often thought to be.[99] Given their traditional bias against ploughing themselves, brahmans and rajputs generally employed halis. Thus, in various ways and in varying degrees the land-owning castes managed to establish considerable control over the economically and socially weaker groups of the village, and to monopolize their labour periodically or sometimes, even permanently.

A more permanent form of servile labour was that of vasis, who were driven to become dependants of a jagirdar, and settled by him on his land as tenants, free of charge. Known as vasidars or vasi in contemporary records, their relationship was considered unlimited and the mutual obligations inviolable. Vasis were not free to leave, and their masters were not permitted to expel them. Unlike halis, vasis were enjoined to reside on the master's land, and they appear to have been paid more than the halis. The primary objective of the landlords was to ensure themselves enough help at the peak phases of the agrarian cycle when hiring labour became difficult. Their need for farm labour and the resultant elevation in status it brought, sometimes saw the employment of coercion in recruitment, as in the case of Kumhar Kusale who had migrated out to Bikaner due to the *Dakhani* (Maratha) threat. When he returned to village Bua near Nagaur, and accepted Bhomia Daulat Singh Karamsot's shelter, the rajput forced the kumhar to become his vasi.[100] The usual scarcity of labour was a strong incentive for high caste landlords to employ labourers in hereditary bondage, and bonded labour relationships thus constantly reproduced themselves.

Years of peace and good harvests certainly encouraged artisans to opt for wage labour, but the picture changed dramatically in times of crisis when bondage ensured survival. Recurrent subsistence crises imperilled the lives of petty commodity producers more than bonded labourers, whose masters were not only committed ideologically but also had a vested interest in supporting their debtors, servants, and slaves.

The 'servant' entered the master's services through a deed which appears to have been recorded on paper. The vasi's monetary gratification was minimal, his compensation mostly in the shape of a share of the produce, and often the allotment of a piece of land. The amount of land the masters gave their vasis was never sufficient to meet their subsistence needs, or match the labour potential of their families. Thus, some of the family had to provide agricultural labour or render domestic help at the jagirdar's kotri. As such, they became retainers of the jagirdars, who allotted them uncultivated lands to cultivate. The vasidar paid land revenue to the jagirdar, and perquisites to the hereditary village officials. For his services he was 'reared and fed in years of scarcity and the charges for settling him in marriage' were also borne by the master.

Since economic methods of trying to retain labour through wage incentives expensive, the employment of extra-economic means of retention were expected to keep at bay the intense competition for skilled labour. For instance, the pattayat of village Bua in pargana Nagaur, Rajavi Daulat Singh, forcibly took away all of Kumhar Ladu's valuables from his house, on his refusal to become a vasi, The Rajavi demanded that the kumhar either become his vasi or pay twelve hundred rupees to get his belongings back.[101] The collection of this astronomical amount was clearly not the objective; Daulat Singh was harassing the kumhar to force his submission. The labour-intensive agricultural technology in a period of labour scarcity necessitated these contractual arrangements, and consequent efforts to bind them to the rural elite. The jagirdars and zamindars compelled the subordinate groups to reside on their vasi or personal settlement, and such dependants were not permitted to leave at will.

This clause of the agreement that put a moratorium on their mobility caused considerable resentment among artisan-cultivators, and they often preferred to be temporary contractual labourers rather than permanent servants of the master. Kumhar Durga of village Karmawas had ploughed the jagirdar's brother's lands for years, but even after being released of this obligation, he was prevented from leaving the jagirdar's settlement on the claim that he was their vasi. The kumhar clarified in his petition that he was serving on a patta contract, and not as a permanent dependant servant.[102]

Since the vasis did not possess an independent establishment, they were exempted from paying house-tax. They were not treated as members of the village community, although their special link with the jagirdar was well-recognized. The numerous instances when they were coerced to settle on the lands of the big landlords seem to suggest that there were not many takers for this kind of arrangement. Compared to other craft castes, the kumhars of Marwar appear to have entered, voluntarily or under coercion, such relationships in larger numbers, though the reasons for their submission are difficult to fathom.[103] Interestingly, judging by the documents on birat disputes, patron-client bonds also seem to have been more common among kumhars than among other castes.

Apart from artisans having to become halis and vasis and living their lives as bonded labourers, agrestic slavery with the master as the private proprietor of his gola whom he could sell, mortgage or rent out, and whose productive and reproductive capacities he was entitled to exploit, is also recorded. The practice of agrestic slavery may appear to contradict the argument offered earlier that the artisans' bargaining position was fairly strong in this period. Evidence for this form of subordination among males, however, is extremely scarce—documentation on female slaves being far more common. One may hypothesize that perhaps artisan labourers entered such relationships in periods of war and famines when alternate sources of subsistence failed and dramatically low standards of living made all reservations against denial of freedom irrelevant. Even when provided extremely sparing allowances, slaves enjoyed relative material security compared to those without patrons. The possession of slaves conferred status on their owner, and with their help, masters were continually busy enlarging their influence by damaging, sometimes in coalition with others, the power and prestige of their peers.

Without doubt, the presence of a core of clients that helped in dealing with relationships of competition and permanent rivalry among the dominant castes in the countryside, placed a premium on them. Subordinate-superordinate dialogues were far from harmonious with neither the master meeting his obligations with munificence, without stint or chicanery, nor the servant/slave providing loyal service. The distance between pretensions, between the rhetoric and the reality, was a source of persistent tensions, met by a range of responses from either side. All relationships of servility were not based strictly on the labour motive that may have been the dominant, though not the sole, determinant. They had as much to do with the ideology of status and rank, and their function in perpetuating the value system of social hierarchy, and of enhancing the lord's prestige and gratifying his self-esteem is equally important. This gave masters a vested interest in wowing their dependents, an equally significant dimension worthy of notice.

The State and the Question of Artisanal Agency: Petitions, Migrations, and Protest

Apparent from the discussion above is the conclusion that routine interaction between the state and the lower formations were pervasive ,and relations between the subordinate and the superordinate were not merely repressive, even if an influential body of recent literature has privileged the role of the state as an autonomous actor in and on society.[104] The crucial question is not whether the state aspired to be absolute but whether it could actually accomplish its ambitions. Equally, not just the role of the upper strata but also that of the underbelly needs to be examined to comprehend the myriad processes at work in early modern state formation in India. Instead of assuming the acquiescence of the lower castes in their abuse, their agency, or the lack of it, in determining social relations needs to be empirically explored and theoretically conceptualized. Were Marwari craft groups able to cope with their pressures, deal with unjust demands, and resist or protest against exploitation? Did structures and channels of communication and manipulation exist that helped to mitigate and alleviate their sufferings? This section examines some of these questions to interrogate the stereotypical characterization of artisans as silent spectators of their destiny, and emphasizes the moral underpinnings of justice that the lower formations invariably drew attention to while asserting their rights. It also explores the role of cultural hegemony of the dominant in constraining artisanal struggles, aimed at bargaining and negotiating with the 'powerful' to minimize their disadvantages. What was the nature of artisanal politics and potential for rebellions in this scenario?

The state in early modern India was close in pattern to the 'contest state' model, unable to prevent subject groups from evolving defence mechanisms to protect their interests.[105] Central to this form of political organization was rule by a king who claimed a monopoly of power and authority in a given society but whose effective control was in reality severely restricted by rival power centres among the elite, by weaknesses in administrative organization, by poor communications and, of course, by a low population density ratio that placed a premium on manpower retention and regulation. The early efforts of the Rathor state at enumeration of caste data, such as in Nainsi's *Vigat* suggests, as noted earlier, an agenda of 'knowing the country', and thereby disciplining it. Peabody and Arjun Appadurai have argued that such computations of human inventories were 'tied, in these pre-colonial regimes, to taxation, to accounting, and to land revenue'.[106] Making a distinction between the logic of taxation and social control, Peabody asserted that caste-sensitive lists of households (*gharam ri vigat*) tabulated by Nainsi were for fiscal purposes while Sumit Guha argued that these are indicative of the state's interest in policing and social control.[107] Whether geared primarily to the goal of revenue collection or social governance, these census operations were mired by primitive methods of a state whose information system was dependent on the collaboration of local elites to keep the news runners moving and the newsletters flowing in. Political surveillance had not developed too far, backward means of transport and communication disabling the state from being able to predict and monitor labour activism and signs of agitation.

These conditions of a relatively low level of administrative control and coercive capacity facilitated suppressed groups to develop strategies to buffer elite demands on their production and labour. Inadequate capacity for policing resulted in low levels of repression. Thus, though the state inherently attempted aggrandisement of power, material constraints and those of realpolitik forced it to concede and relent to pressures.[108] Adjustments and accomodation towards pressures from below had to be made, and the rhetoric of wajabi came in handy in camouflaging the state's lack of means and competence to coerce beyond a point. The cultural ideology of the state therefore led the dominant to extend protection and patronage and the state's weakness could easily be projected as a generosity towards, and as 'concessions' for the 'weak'. Adas discounts the importance of ethics and morality acting as a check on states from making 'excessive' demands from their subjects. Retrieving the reality from the rhetoric and gauging the role of moral pressures is, of course, a complex task. It seems reasonable to argue, however, that the material reality of the distributive nature of state power, the cultural underpinnings of wajabi kingship, and the contestatory propensity of socially valued skilled castes such as artisans together ensured general adherence to social norms and customs.

These conclusions emerge from a mass of petitions made by the subjects of the Jodhpur state to their rulers, complaining against those heedless of wajabi. The nature of the documentation itself demonstrates that artisans petitioned frequently, and one might in fact argue that, given the larger outlines of power, caste status, and political authority, the act of petitioning, often against the officialdom, was an explicitly pro-active move in itself. Quite expectedly, such petitions address only one aspect of their lives directly—viz, exploitation, indigence, pressures and precariousness, illuminating the inherently adversarial nature of interaction between the dominant and the subordinate. Equally visible in the documents, though usually ignored in historical scholarship, however, is the fact that craftsmen were resentful about their plight and complained against the 'excesses' in terms of revenue and begar demands that were inflicted upon them. The standard of wajib provided the template against which the moral performance of elites was judged, and the central assumption of the artisanate appears to be that, whatever their social disabilities, they had the inviolable right of subsistence, and any claim by the elites or the state that infringed on their basic needs was neither wajib nor could it be justifiable. An 'against the grain' reading of these documents is reflective of the fact that, in response to what artisans recognised as violations of their customary rights, they evolved a range of strategies to counter their disadvantaged position. Rather than passive docility and inertia as usually imagined, what we see here are artisanal initiatives constantly engaged in a struggle to secure their influence in a niche area. Craftsmen were aware of the acute demand for their skills, for the resultant criticality of their presence to the region of Jodhpur, and of their privileged position in the elitist discourse. They leveraged upon the same in their dealings with the state and the elites, and the latter, equally conscious of the indispensability of these lower castes, felt compelled to concede to their pressures.

Indeed, most petitions were against state functionaries, and given the administration's propensity of being 'hard with the soft and soft with the hard', one would expect that justice would never get done. Farhat Hasan, in his recent study, tends to conclude that imperial sovereignty (in the case of the Mughal rule in Gujarat) served to buttress the local structures of power, its overall effect being that 'the subalterns, in their resistance to local power relations, did not have to confront the local power-holders alone, but a configuration of forces represented by the state and local power system together'.[109] One might then ask: Did the imperial and the local not counterpoise one another? Was there sheer collaboration and no conflict of interest between the centre and the locality that subordinate groups could exploit?

Records from the Jodhpur state reveal that, in fact, the elites themselves were not a monolithic body but a hierarchy of disparate interests, competing and clashing for resources. Petitioners appear to have been cognisant of the fact that the government was a multilayered formation in which one layer could be encouraged to operate against another, using perceived fissures within ruling classes to win justice.[110] The rapacity and abusive conduct of the officials was a universally recognized fact, and by forcing the authorities to react against its men, petitioners set political agendas, seeming to have both desired and trusted the rulers' mediating capacities. While numerous instances of the administration protecting the powerful are visible, there is absolutely no consistency in this pattern, and there are just as many disputes where circumstances specific to the case ensured full or partial justice for lower groups.

The fact that the state made the instrument of petition available to the subalterns is also worthy of comment. Petitions and record-maintenance of the same were new and unique to the eighteenth century, a result of a calculated move on the part of the state towards the achievement of twin purposes. For one, popular petitions offered the state an opportunity to outmanoeuvre rival local elites by providing occasions to take action against them in response to the people's demand for justice. To that extent, petitions helped rulers in their pursuit of centralization and eroding the power bases of competitiors. Petitions also provided a window into the mindscapes of the subjects, and thereby ensured that legitimate demands did not remain unheeded. As safety valves for ventilating grievances, they were adopted by the state as a matter of deliberate policy. That the rulers responded to petitions, even from those without money or influence, was not due to their inherent benignity and compassion, but because it made good sense for them to keep these channels open. The artisans, on their part, learnt quickly about the inherent value of petitioning to remind Shri Huzur of his paternalistic responsibilities!

In the face of transgressions of traditionally sanctioned norms, artisans—rather than undermining the foundations of society organized hierarchically according to an ideology that they had got acculturated into—promptly resorted to a spectrum of devices that would help them protect their subsistence. Petitions tended to be the first act of protest employed by dissident artisans since it was one that was sanctioned by custom and enjoyed official approval too. Acts of evasion, change of patrons, and often migration constituted other forms of protest and, failing all these, artisans indulged in defiant confrontations, strikes, and open protest as discussed in the next chapter. Even in doing so, they were merely trying to retrieve what had for long rightfully belonged to them.[111]

The Gramscian notion of 'false consciousness' argued that the symbolic hegemony of the elites had allowed them to control the very standards by which dominant rule was evaluated. He had argued that the elites controlled the 'ideological sectors' of society and could thereby engineer consent for their rule. By creating and disseminating a universe of discourse and the concepts to go with it, by defining the standards of what is moral, fair, and legitimate, they built a symbolic climate whereby the proletariat was more enslaved at the level of ideas than at the level of behaviour. In such circumstances, the question of protest and resistance did not arise. Such interpretations have been invoked to account for lower-class quiescence, particularly for Indian subordinate groups. Identifying caste stratification as the singular factor responsible for the complacence of the lower formations in India, theorists from Hegel, Weber, and Dumont, to historians Moore, and Wallerstein—and even developmental economists like Myrdal—are agreed about the hegemony of the hierarchical ideology of caste and the Hindu theory of reincarnation as responsible for the self-repressive mentalite of Indian lower formations. While the *Subaltern Studies'* scholarship has been at pains to argue for the autonomy of the subordinate, it does not appear germane to the argument here to identify those who had set the standards of behaviour and the nature of exchanges between the rulers and the ruled. Eighteenth-century sources do not help to comprehend the processes that set moral standards and notions of wajabi norms, and any attempt to discern the former would be in the realm of conjecture.

What is important and significant for this study is that there is no dearth of contestation on the part of subordinate groups to elite acts of commission and omission. Subaltern groups displayed an autonomous consciousness not only vis-à-vis their socio-cultural customs; their interactions with the state and dominant groups were also largely determined by their perceptions of propriety and mutual rights and obligations, though interpretations of what constituted 'legitimate' and proper sometimes varied. And readings of wajabi that were contrary to their expectations were perceived by them as breaches in the 'contract', not to be suffered resignedly. Petition after petition from artisans asked for justice, and this 'moral economy' widely impinged upon eighteenth century government and thought in Jodhpur.[112]

In studies on European, African, and Asian societies, research on subaltern resistance reveals an array of culturally acceptable forms of protest typical to different regions. Historical studies such as those of Hobsbawm focussed on social banditry as a traditional response to violations of accepted norms. Charles Tilly discussed ritualized protest among French peasants; Rodney Hilton and Jerome Blum noticed similar forms of resistance in feudal Europe and Russia respectively.[113] For South-East Asia, too, Adas's work on Burmese peasants mentioned a traditionally sanctioned repertoire of unrest including petitions to officials, transfer of allegiance to new patrons, flight from unacceptable situations, millenarian movements and entry into religious groups, co-operation with bandits and gangs, all of which he calls 'avoidance protest'.[114] And the anthropological perspective on rural Malaysia, the focus of James Scott's celebrated study, noticed the forms of 'everyday resistance'—from mockery and sarcasm to pilfering and arson—that subordinate groups employ to combat the hegemonic claims of dominant elites.[115] These 'resistance studies' have already established the effectiveness of 'everyday' methods of protest, and it is interesting to note that many of the responses from Marwari artisans run parallel to those mentioned above. While social banditry and millenarian movements, emphasized by Hobsbawm for the West and by Adas for the East, are not evidenced in Marwari documents, it is clear that rather than reticence and fear in engaging with the authorities, subordinate groups like the artisans come across as not only conscious about their rights but assertive in their insistence on wajabi conduct on the part of the state. In fact, one finds a wide range of direct responses from artisans, not merely evading elite demands, but openly questioning the conduct of the dominant; and that too by identifying themselves through petitions, rather than offering clandestine anonymous resistance. Such direct protests on the part of the subordinate suggest that the state that sought to structure the options available to the subordinate was not quite as is repressive as is usually assumed.

Petitions were expressed in submissive terms like '(He/she) brought the petition to His Majesty's notice' (*araz malum karai*), and through them artisans evoked the rajdharma ideal, continually appealing to the paternalistic basis that their relationship with the state ostensibly rested on. Their meekness and show of deferential submission was a strategy that was ultimately calculated to contribute to their benefit. It did in the process create, recreate, and thereby perpetuate the values of their own subordination. Artisanal consciousness of the social imbalance of power, however, and the resultant calculation that confrontationist outbursts would be dangerous, if not suicidal, inhibited them.[116] In fact, there was a clear realization that tangible advantages could be gained by soliciting the favour of the powerful. Hence, though struggling to break free from exploitation, they still maintained obsequious appearances in their negotiations for space.

The petitions symbolized, all the same, a rejection of the principle of dormant unquestioning acquiescence in their own abuse. Since the Jodhpur state itself had extended this instrument as an outlet to channelize popular will, they were committed to entertain petitions and respond to popular grievances. While revenues were imposed on practically every aspect of the people's lives, it is equally true that artisans did not hesitate to question unconventional levies transgressing sanctioned levels of appropriation. Darzi Aso of village Loharji Bari complained that earlier, under the rule of the *Karnat*s, land revenue assessment had come to a smaller amount than the current one, but now, an enhanced amount was being demanded. He petitioned against the increase, and the state relented on grounds of past practice.[117]

The insubordination of Nai Paimle of village Behad of Jaitaran is remarkable in this context, and suggests a tremendous degree of fearless defiance that seems to assert that retribution could not be far worse than submission before the endless exactions of the jagirdar. As discussed before, the nai's refusal to concede to unprecedented demands beyond customary sanction saw the jagirdar perceive it as an act of treason and disloyalty and, enraged, he ensured that Nai Paimle's birat households withdrew their patronage to him.[118] Even so, Paimle's defiant stand supports Gautam Bhadra's assessment that '...subordination or domination was seldom complete, if ever', and is evidence enough to question the notion of plebeian groups' consciousness being totally overwhelmed by dominant standards.[119]

Often, petitions were made collectively, harnessing caste and community networks, a particular artisanal community from a certain pargana negotiating as a group to put pressure on the administrative authorities. Documents record that they reported their grievance jointly as a single body (*samsat*) when seeking redressal, arguing for custom and convention to be adhered to. Joint petitions against enhanced taxation indicate that the capacity for organization in pursuit of demands for tax concessions arose naturally from the day-to-day experience of life. Artisan-cultivators, as well as full-time craftsmen, developed solidarities by living and working together, contacts during communal feasts and other life cycle rituals considerably countering the isolation that some individual artisanal households may have suffered if they were the solitary representative of their caste in a village. Shared experiences of oppression and injustice cemented and promoted caste collectivity and encouraged joint action.[120] The khatis of Sojhat, for instance, claimed they had enjoyed exemption from paying *kabada* tax. When asked to pay the same, they requested the authorities to desist from flouting traditions. Their joint petition found a favourable response, and the authorities ordered that the convention in this matter should continue to be honoured.[121] Similarly, the darzis of Merta complained that the kotwal of Merta was harassing them with demands for food on certain ceremonial occasions (*kansa*) though the practice did not enjoy sanction as per custom. The Durbar immediately forbade the kotwal from making new exactions from the community of tailors.[122] Again, when there were demands for higher taxation in the 1770s for instance, the rangrez, silawats, and kheradis of Sojhat came together individually as cohesive communities and protested. The administration relented and ordered that they need not respond to the demand for higher taxes.[123] The kumhars of village Ghanawas complained at the Sojhat kachedi when Khate, a landed elite of their area, asked them to fill water at his house. They refused on the ground that customarily they had performed this task for the local jagirdar only.[124] As in other cases, these kumhars, too, were able to muster the strength to refuse Khate due to their collectivity. Close contacts established through the jati panchayats and the intermixing of caste members helped them consolidate as a cohesive group. Darzis of Siwana and Jalor came together when taxes were demanded of them in 1775. They had been performing extra begar in lieu of taxes since Maharaja Ajit Singhji's days. Since taxes were convertible into begar, and the subjects who could not afford to pay taxes were allowed to compensate by performing extra free labour, the darzis petitioned that, despite their willingness to perform extra labour, the local administrative authorities were again harassing them unnecessarily for taxes.[125]

In cases where efforts at compromise and reconciliation failed, artisans took recourse to more severe forms of resistance. Some amounts of excesses were tolerated, but if in their perception the threshold had been crossed, they questioned it.[126] Faced with excessive demands, they sometimes deserted their villages if the local authorities did not relent and lighten their burden, and petitions failed to provide relief. The presence of large tracts of unoccupied land and vigorous elite competition for limited supplies of manpower reinforced this predominant characteristic of artisanal behaviour.[127] Control over manpower or labour, rather than land, was the basis of surplus extraction; hence artisans were confident that they could find generous patrons for themselves. Desertion of ancestral villages and emigration also occurred when production declined due to a natural calamity. Migration was thus the predominant safety valve that opened possibilities of survival not only in the face of elite extortions but also to escape frequent droughts, famines, and debt bondage.[128] Such desertions, as noticed earlier, constituted a major threat to the economic stability of the region, and the administration was by and large careful about ensuring that the level of demand for revenue, begar, and other burdens was not so high as to harass the artisans into abandonment of their home and hearth.

The landed aristocracy, local officials and their subordinates were sometimes not as cautious, and tended to focus on short-term gains. Often their appropriations became so heavy as to cause artisans to flee *en masse* from their village.[129] For instance, kumhars and nais of village Khatu had a conflict with their jagirdar over his demand for beth begar, and threatened to leave their homesteads.[130] Kumhars of Sambhar did not merely warn but actually implemented their threat by abandoning their homes and moving away to Parbatsar. The provocation for this extreme step was the persistent harassment they were faced with due to ceaseless forced extraction of clayware by the local gentry.[131]

Crucial to this decision of emigration was an artisan's awareness of his indispensability to the local economy, and consequent 'power' he enjoyed in the village. Those prepared and trained to till and toil were confident that they would manage to bargain for themselves attractive terms of settlement in a new region. Villages that were small often had no more than one luhar or kumhar, and if he migrated, the absence of substitutes would mean that the job would remain undone; or even in large villages that had several luhars, the demand was proportionately higher which one luhar could not meet. Hence, the emigration of an artisan from a locality implied serious adversities for the local inhabitants. In the case of Kumhar Kaliyo of village Virami in Desuri, for instance, the state made every effort to resettle the kumhar in his original home when the Solankis took away all his belongings and injured his family members during his return journey from Malwa. In an attempt to restore his rights and thus prevent migration, the administration ensured that his ancestral house, field, and potter's wheel were returned to him. In addition, they ordered for a pair of bullocks to be provided to him from the state cattle-shed, and a bohra appointed who would meet Kaliyo's credit needs.[132] These realities served as an automatic check on oppression levels. By and large, the apprehension that the toiling sections may flee was enough to make the dominant castes pay heed, and limit their propensity to indulge in 'excesses'.[133]

The fact that many artisans had extremely modest belongings that comprised of no more than their craft tools and a minimum of domestic goods, facilitated their migration. Unlike pure agriculturists, whose ties to land were much stronger and weighed them down, the fact that not all craftsmen possessed agricultural land meant that at least the landless ones had little to tie them and prevent mobility. Even in situations of debt bondage, as halis and vasis, an individual got tied to his master, but the rest of the family was free to migrate. Spatial mobility on a large scale was therefore a characteristic feature of Marwari artisans, and their constant flow between different settlements finds frequent mention in the records. Local short-distance emigrations from a village to a city or from one city to another were common, but sometimes an artisanal family or a whole group belonging to one community emigrated en masse to a distant destination. In case of long-distance relocations, a favourite destination appears to have been the more fertile Malwa[134] though on certain occasions Hyderabad (in Sind),[135] and the neighbouring kingdoms of Bikaner or Mewar, too, seem to have attracted artisans. In such cases the artisans were generally away for long durations of time, and sometimes there was a permanent change of residence.

This floating population of rural migrants, some of whom set up business in cities to engage in craft production, often continued to maintain links with land and cultivation.[136] Sometimes, their families remained in the village to manage the fields there, while an adult member of the household moved to the city to supplement family income.[137] But attachment to their native villages often saw them return once conditions improved in their village.[138] On returning home, many faced a host of problems. Sometimes, their land was given away by the superior castes to other members of the same community. Very often, they found their houses usurped, or their families dispersed as a result of hardships during their absence.[139]

More often than not, sub-units of a family, either single male adults or nuclear families, emigrated while the remaining members of the joint family continued to reside in the same village, carried out their traditional occupations, and fulfilled obligations of revenue payments and begar towards the authorities and superior castes. Those who had relocated themselves temporarily did so to earn additional income and, if problems with their exploiters persisted, they assessed possibilities of complete abandonment of their original homes. If conditions improved, they either returned immediately, or after accumulating some surplus income to improve the standard of living of the family. En masse desertion of a village occurred only during famines and droughts, or in severe cases of oppression due to unusually excessive pressures.

Artisans were aware of their indispensability as providers of labour, but equally mindful of the superior status and resources of the dominant castes. Realizing that direct attacks and defiance could invite the coercive might of the 'powerful', they preferred not to provoke the powerful, and opted for more non-confrontationist forms of resistance. In any event, such situations arose in the rarest of rare cases. More often, artisanal petitions received a response and succeeded in partially undoing the justice.

Nor should apparent deference be taken at its face value. Although it was generally in the interest of subordinate groups to make a public show of accepting the self-image of their patrons, they tended to have their own thoughts on the subject that they kept to themselves, or shared with their brethren.

This comprised the 'hidden transcript' of dissident popular opinion,[140] and can be found in folk tales, popular songs, and proverbs. Debtors, for instance, were deferential towards moneylenders due to the force of circumstances, but were fully conscious of their exploitative proclivities. Hence, a popular proverb from the region reads: *Hit mein, chit mein, hath mein, khat mein, mat mein khot. Dil mein darsawe daya, pap liya sir pot.* It translates as: Deceitful in friendship, in thought, deed, accounts, and promises; he may appear merciful, but in fact is always full of sinful immorality.[141] And, again, another sums up the pressures on the impoverished: *Pehle pet ne pache Seth, Pehle raj ne pache Biaj* (A debtor plans to first provide for his own needs and then settle his debt to the creditor; but finds that he has to first pay the state's revenue demands, and then the interest on the loan he took).[142] Clearly, they perceived elites as exacting and scheming, but found their presence indispensable.

Equally, the folk tales recounted in this chapter also provided counter-perspectives to the one offered by the state regarding their dealings with the subordinate.[143] Oral traditions of the lower castes often claimed that they once possessed a high status. Origin often myths recounted by different artisanal castes focus on their descent from a superior group in some remote past. Gadoliya luhars (vagrant blacksmiths) for instance, recount that they were rajputs till the early thirteenth century when the Muslim sultan Alauddin Khalji invaded Chittor. Their ancestors were vanquished in the battle, and to save themselves from the Muslim king's ire, they adopted the trade of blacksmithy. Humiliated, they pledged to themselves that till they did not succeed in defeating the enemy, they would not set up home and rest, but keep travelling in their carts. Since then, they claim, they have remained on the move.[144] Through this myth, they questioned the legitimacy of their low ritual status, and also sought to confer the superior virtue of commitment to themselves, drawing attention to their unremitting mobility and its associated discomforts as a proof of their being 'true to their words'.

CONCLUDING REMARKS

Contrary to the immensely consistent nationalist depictions of immutable, primordially harmonious village life in 'traditional' India, evidence from eighteenth century presents a puzzling inconsistency, and supports neither integrated nor consensual relations. At first sight, it appears paradoxical that patron-client relationships co-existed with commercialization, monetization, and an increasing penetration by the of market, that the position of caste bodies got more entrenched alongside the state's assertion of its power, that artisanal groups were part of this whole process—and yet continued to choose 'unfree' forms of labour as servile and bonded agricultural workers. The extent of social transformation was clearly dependent on the social praxis of the various historical agents and their competing agendas.

The interplay of forces between the ruling elites on the one hand and lower formations on the other has generally been studied and understood in two ways: By and large, the 'haves' and the 'have-nots' have been perceived in perpetual antagonism, plagued by an inherent contradiction. An alternate position insisted that patron-client relations constituted the foundation of their relations, and that it was a harmonious system of give-and-take rooted in reciprocity, and in 'traditional culture'.[145]

Evidence from Marwar confirms neither of these formulations. Rather, it suggests that the engagement between the elite and the subaltern was a far more complex two-way traffic of power, demonstrating neither sheer conflict nor complete harmony. The patron's own self-interest was his paramount concern, but the promotion of this end was not possible without winning the loyalty of his clientele through measured levels of appeasement. Both were aware that they needed each other, and especially given the acute competition for labour in eighteenth-century Marwar, the elites felt compelled to accommodate and adjust to the pressures from below. The generosity enjoined on the rich in their discourse of wajabi was not without its compensations. It redounded to their prestige and served to surround them with a 'grateful' clientele that helped validate their position.

What also needs to be understood is that the artisans at the receiving end of oppression from the state and the superordinates did not have a universal experience that can be labelled as positive or negative. In fact, it would be pertinent here to note that the state or the ruling class was not one single entity that adopted a uniform policy towards all artisans at all times. It, in fact, comprised of a complex structured hierarchy where different groups of those invested with power often had a relationship of friction with one another, and worked at cross-purposes in a struggle to check the other. Given this multi-centred diffusion of power, the manufacturing and service castes found themselves confronted with oppression from certain state authorities and patronage or protection from those trying to counterpoise them. The 'checks and balances' mechanism of the administration, and the mutual rivalries among members of the ruling class ensured that the undue demands and deviations of errant officials would be corrected by other power centres. The central administration tended to be vigilant about the conduct of the local officials, true in the case of other medieval empires as well. An account describing the seventeenth century Ottoman administration, for instance, argues: 'The very fact that tax officials complained to the court against ordinary people but did not always win, shows that the notion that the court would automatically back the state official against ordinary people is false'.[146] The picture that emerges, therefore, was far more knotty and intricate than generally admitted, and it is quite meaningless to talk only in terms of an exploitative state relentlessly tyrannizing the artisan.

With power fractured and diffused, both the dominant and the dependent wielded it in their interaction with each other, though in nasty different
degrees. The elites controlled land and patronage that the impoverished
artisans greatly prized, while the craftsmen possessed specialized skills and
provided the much-needed labour services that the upper castes of the village were always in need of. The persecution of artisans and other
subordinate groups at the hands of the dominant was commonplace, and
they were indeed regularly harried and hounded for more revenue and labour
services. However, equally visible though generally ignored is the fact that
artisans continuously challenged the harassment and victimization thrust
upon them by the superior castes.

Biratkaris, halis, vasis, and golas were all complicit in the perpetuation
of social hierarchy, their respective states representing different degrees of
'unfreedom', sometimes chosen by the dependents themselves. To argue
that relationships of bondage, as between a birat and biratkari, or between
halis, vasis, and slaves with their masters, were, simply a response to agricultural needs would trap all in an overly deterministic agro-economic
discourse when the agrarian economy in fact was created under social relations of production secured and reproduced by power.[147] The essential
difference between biratkaris and halis/vasis was that the former had several patrons, hence their dependence and loyalties were spread over and
their patrons, relatively uncertain of their support, had to strive harder to
keep them content. As providers of specialized services, artisan biratkaris
had a greater sense of their indispensability as compared to farm servants
attached to a single master, making them entirely vulnerable to the treatment meted out by their landlord. The latter felt bound as much by contract
as by differential social status between them and the master. Inscribing them
as bonded and 'unfree' seems unnecessary when viewed in the context of
contemporary subjectivities.

Petitions and state responses strongly indicate that the elite-artisan dialogue was still open, constant negotiations constituting and reconstituting
it. Insubordination was inherent and integral to the dialogue between the
two. Petitioners in early modern Jodhpur self-consciously categorized their
identities under neat labels, in terms of village/city they hailed from, their
name, caste, gender, etc. Identity assertion and widespread wrangling over
caste identities, their privileges and customs, ensured their politicization.
They framed their petitions using definite categories as a way to empower
themselves, and directed the attention of the administration to the specifics
of their grievances. The 'agency' of the artisan that constantly assessed,
worked towards the promotion of its self-interest, and bargained with the
support of its caste group, becomes increasingly evident, as do the state's
efforts to maximize its own benefits without having its labour turn their
backs and move elsewhere. The situation was not one of grim, unques-

tioned repression, with power exercised from top down, but a far more intricate situation of 'adversaries' assessing their relative strength, and leveraging upon it.

What seems clear is the compatibility of subaltern autonomy with elite domination or hegemony and the dialectical nature of their relationship.[148] After all, domination could not have existed in isolation; its perpetuation was possible only within a relationship. One cannot disagree with Partha Chatterjee that the dominant groups, in their exercise of domination, 'did not consume and destroy the dominated classes, for then there would be no relation of power, and hence no domination'.[149] Without their autonomy the subalterns would have no identity of their own, no domain where they might have resisted at the same time as they were dominated. They would simply become integrated into the networks of the dominant classes.

Strategies employed by rural artisans were distinct and in sharp contrast to those used by artisanal groups resident in urban areas. Settlement of rural artisans was dispersed, and their access to the dispute resolution mechanism of the state was proportionately more difficult. As a result, they worked to strengthen their bargaining position by establishing trade monopolies and disallowing caste-fellows to serve as substitute labour. In case this did not solve their problems of elite violations they threatened to migrate, again hopeful that non-availability of necessary skills that they possessed would bring their exploiters to heel. As opposed to them, city artisans lived together in large numbers and sought to fight and resist oppression through collective action. It is the dissimilarities of artisan-state interface in the urban context that are discussed in the following chapter.

NOTES

1. Vijay Dan Detha's Marwari folk tale entitled 'Bhambi ri Begar', in Komal Kothari (ed.) *Batan ri Phulwari, Rajasthan ri Kadimi Lok Kathawan, bhag 3* (Borunda, 1962), pp. 41–2.

2. One of the earliest to build the Orientalist perception of the pre-colonial Indian state was James Mill in his *History of British India*, (ed.) Horace Hayman Wilson, (London, 1858); then followed the works of Macaulay, and then Henry Summer Maine's *Village Communities in the East and West* (London, 1871). Also see William Wilson Hunter's *The India of the Queen and other Essays*, (ed.) Lady Hunter, (London, 1903).

3. For instance, Tapan Raychaudhuri characterized the Mughal state as a 'Leviathan' with an insatiable appetite, 'its impact on the economy was defined above all by its unlimited appetite for resources', which it extracted from the agricultural society; see his 'The State and the Economy', in *Cambridge Economic History of India*, vol. I, p. 173.

4. Ranajit Guha, in his classic work *Elementary Aspects of Peasant Insurgency in Colonial India* (Delhi, 1983) noticed peasant consciousness and peasant political participation as fundamental features of rural society in colonial India. Was the situation any different in the case of artisans just a few decades earlier?

5. This asset enabled Rangrez Fazal to get a loan from Rangrez Sirichand of another village by mortgaging his indigo. See *JSPB* 36, 1779, p. 181A.

6. Khati Sriram Sukhe had agricultural fields in village Didkhawada, pargana Nagaur, and so did kumhars Tohaman and Jaipal Sanwaldas, Luhar Hasan of Jalor, and Julaha Guman of Soghawas in Merta; see *JSPB* 13, 1830/1773, f. 25A; ibid.11, 1828/1771, ff.203A, and 145A, respectively. Also see *JSPB* 38, 1845/1788, f. 95A.

7. Silawat Dole of Makrana inherited a well from his ancestors, but while he was in Malwa, the local jagirdar took possession of it and refused to return it even after the silawat's return; see *JSPB* 21, 1835/1778, f. 132A.; *JSPB* 20, 1835/1778, f. 2B. Yet again, there was a lot of resentment when a brahmin closed the path leading to a well on the jagirdar's land, from which the village folk and cattle had been quenching their thirst; *JSPB* 38, 1845/1788, f. 113. Also see *JSPB* 15, 1832/1775, ff.183B and 186A. A ghanchi complained when the village chaudhari diverted a water channel that used to earlier irrigate his fields; see *JSPB* 31, 1841/1784, f. 61B.

8. *JSPB* 20, 1835/1778, f. 2B; *JSPB* 22, 1836/1779, f. 14B; *JSPB* 22, f. 25B. In another case a julaha of Sojhat was given an alternate piece of land from khalisa when he tried to construct a house on his land which blocked the pathway to the village pond.

9. Studies such as those of G.S. Ghurye, J.H. Hutton,Wiser, and Dumont, etc. insist that every caste practised none but the trade prescribed for it in the scriptures. See G.S. Ghurye, *Caste, Class and Occupation in India* (Bombay, 1957); J.H. Hutton, *Caste in India: Its Nature, Function and Origins* (Cambridge, 4th edn, 1963); William Henrick Wiser's *The Hindu Jajmani System: A Socio-Economic System Interrelating Members of a Hindu Village Community in Services* (Lucknow, 1958); and Louis Dumont's *Homo Hierarchicus* (Chicago, 1980).

10. For similar evidence on the Jaipur region, see Dilbagh Singh, *The State, Landlords and Peasants: Rajasthan in the 18th Century* (Delhi, 1990), p. 29; for Himachal, see Laxman S. Thakur, 'Artisans in Himachal Pradesh, circa AD 700–1440: A Study Based on Epigraphs', *IESHR*, vol. 23, no. 3, 1986, p. 311; For the Maratha territory see Hiroshi Fukazawa, *The Medieval Deccan, Peasants, Social Systems and States, Sixteenth to Eighteenth Centuries* (Delhi, 1991, rpr. 1998), p. 201; and for erstwhile Vijaynagar see Vijaya Ramaswamy, 'Artisans in Vijaynagar Society', *IESHR*, vol. 22, no. 4, 1985, pp. 417–44.

11. Its issuance of specific instructions that the telis of Nagaur must cultivate instead of producing oil during the chaumasa, and that they would be exempted from the obligation of paying hasil for the same, is a clear example; see *JSPB* 28, 1839/1782, f. 61A.

12. For the neighbouring Jaipur state, Dilbagh Singh has conclusively shown that the land revenue demand on such kamins as khatis, nais, luhars etc., as per the *Dastur-ul-Amals* of parganas Niwai and Gijgarh, and of Antela, in 1791/ 1734 and 1784/1727 respectively, ranged from 33 per cent to 40 per cent of the gross produce, whereas the raiyatis had to pay at the rate of 40 per cent to 50 per cent See Dilbagh Singh's *The State, Landlords and Peasants, Rajasthan in the Eighteenth Century* (New Delhi, 1990), p. 40. Kumkum Mahobiya, in her article 'Bikaner Rajya ke Gavon ka Swarup: Satravin-Atharvin Shatabdi Mei', *Rajasthan History Congress*, 1975, confirms that artisans engaged in cultivation paid taxes at concessional rates.

13. *JSPB* 11, 1828/1771, f. 203A.

14. *JSPB* 11, 1828/1771, f. 145A.

15. The annual agrarian cycle was outlined for me extremely coherently by Mochi Sukhdev from village Kotara, P.O. Kotara, District Ajmer, during his visit to Delhi for the Dastkar Mela on 19 January 1998. Kumhar Ghanshyam visiting the same mela, who had come from a neighbouring area with his wares, corroborated the information supplied by Sukhdev.

16. For example, the ancestors of Darzi Bhade of village Paladi Khoja of Merta had been given land to live on by the ancestors of Bhomiya Sultan Singh; see *JSPB* 18, 1834/1777, f. 38A. sultan's cousin Dhiraj Singh was trying to get the darzi to vacate the plot.

17. See Habib, *Agrarian System of Mughal India* (London, 1963) p. 115. Land belonging to Kumhar Paimle of village Thanwala had been usurped by his *kabila bhai*-clan brother Tinku while Paimle was in Malwa. Paimle was able to have his land restored through orders of the Parbatsar Kachedi on returning after five years; see *JSPB* 16, 1833/1776, f. 141B. This is evident from the attempt of Chhipa Kaise of Ladarhun to first sell his land off to Singhvi Sagarmal, and then when he changed his mind, he bought it back from the Singhvi; see *JSPB* 24, 1780, f. 18A.

18. Dilbagh Singh, 'Caste and the Structure of Village Society in Eastern Rajasthan During the Eighteenth Century', in Ghanshyam Lal Devra, (ed.) *Some Aspects of Socio-Economic History of Rajasthan* (Jodhpur, 1980), pp. 149–70.

19. *JSPB* 8, 1826/1769, f. 263B.

20. *JSPB* 15, 1832/1775, f. 1041.

21. *JSPB* 44, 1849/1792, f. 184A.

22. Col.Archibald Adams, *The Western Rajputana States: A Medico-Topographical and General Account of Marwar, Sirohi and Jaisalmer* (London, 1900), pp. 438–9.

23. See H. Kotani's essay 'Dyadic Relationships at Work within the Vatan System with Special Reference to the Jajamani System', in Kotani (ed.), *Western India in Historical transition: Seventeenth to Early Twentieth Century* (Delhi, 2002), pp. 52–61 for an elaboration of the distinction between the two. H. Fukazawa's discussion on the subject is of course enlightening; see his 'Rural Servants in the Maharashtrian Village: Demiurgic or Jajmani System?' in Fukazawa (ed.),

The Medieval Deccan: Peasants, Social Systems and States, Sixteenth to Eighteenth Centuries (Oxford, 1991), pp. 199–244.

24. The classic model of the jajmani system, as constructed by William Henricks Wiser's *The Hindu Jajmani System: A Socio-Economic System Interrelating Members of a Hindu Village Community in Services* (Lucknow, 1958, first published in 1936) has already been exposed as idealistic rather than one that reflected ground realities. It makes several assumptions that the evidence, atleast from Marwar, does not corroborate. He wrote that jajmani ties created a community where all castes existed to serve each other, thus making for a self-sufficient village order. Wiser writes that jajmani ties created an integrated organic society in contrast to the atomistic society of the West. But in fact the inter-caste ties prevalent in the villages of Marwar did not even cover all the artisanal castes-considered the essential and typical members of the system—let alone including landed elites as servants or clients. Dumont agreed when he said that the ideology of pure and impure was the inherent principle that structured the caste system, which in turn determined jajmani ties. The economic ties reflect the ideology of pure/impure through an exchange of prestations and counter-prestations. Caste restricted people from employment outside their traditional occupations thus forcing villagers to recruit people of other castes to do many jobs; see Louis Dumont, *Homo Hierarchicus* (London, 1972), p. xviii.

25. C.J. Fuller, 'Misconceiving the Grain Heap: A Critique of the Concept of the Indian Jajmani System', in J. Parry and M. Bloch (eds) *Money and the Morality of Exchange* (Cambridge, 1989), pp. 33–63.

26. Simon Commander, 'The Jajmani System in North India: An Examination of its Logic and Status over Two Centuries', in *Modern Asian Stdudies*, vol. XVII, 1983, pp. 283–311.

27. Louis Dumont, *Homo Hierarchicus* (Chicago, 1980), p. 102. Dumont argued that *jajmani* was an economic system subordinated to religion, based on the ideological opposition of purity to impurity, which 'underlay division of labour because pure and impure occupations must ... be kept separate'. This opposition restricted services that castes could perform because they would get polluted by the task required or they were too impure to perform the service. This religious ideology forced castes to obtain necessary services from other castes, and underlay caste specialization, not the advantages of economic specialization. This ideology got reflected in economic exchanges within a specific social context.

28. *JSPB* 53, 1846/1789, f. 40B.

29. *JSPB* 13, 1830/1773, f. 154B.

30. The birat system of Marwar has been studied by Padmashri Komal Kothari in his article 'Patronage and Performance', in N.K. Singhi and Rajendra Joshi (eds), *Folk, Faith, and Feudalism* (Jaipur, 1995), pp. 55–66. Though his focus is on patronage in the field of performing arts, he traces the relations of mutuality and obligations of the patron and the performer towards each other.

31. Late feudal Western society too recognized the prototype of such structures of obligation. See Marc Bloch, *Feudal Society*, trans. L.A. Manyon, vol. 1, pp. 163, where he shows that the feudal bond implied a comprehensive duty on the part of the lord to see that his men were protected and taken care of.

32. See *JSPB* 1, 1821/1764, 62B, *JSPB* 2, 1822/1765, f. 54A, *JSPB* 13, 1830/1773, f. 153A, etc.; and *JSPB* 1, 1821/1764, f. 37A; *JSPB* 2, 1822/1765, f. 202A; *JSPB* 9, 1826/1769, f. 58A; *JSPB* 10, 1827/1770, f. 69A; *JSPB* 15, 1832/1775, f. 363B respectively.

33. *JSPB* 16, 1833/1776, f. 67B.

34. *JSPB* 6, 1825/1768, f. 133B; *JSPB* 53, 1846/1789, f. 40B; *JSPB* 20, 1835/1778, f. 95A, respectively.

35. Wiser and Radhakamal Mukherjee would like to have us believe so. After all, Wiser went to the extent of saying that 'Each in turn is master. Each in turn is servant' see Wiser, 1958, p. xxi. In fact what appears more than apparent in Marwar was that large land owners were generally masters, not servants, and instead of supplying services or commodities, only received them.

36. Though the contexts were different, and the responses of the subalterns too varied as per circumstances, E.P. Thompson, and following him, James Scott saw similar obligations imposed by the poor on their rich patrons. See E.P. Thompson's article 'The Moral Economy of the English Crowd in the Eighteenth Century', *Past and Present* 50, February 1971, where he discusses this concept and its implications.

37. *JSPB* 12, 1830/1773, f. 172B. The sources, however, do not indicate that the patron too could change his biratkari on the charge of incompetence or negligent quality of work.

38. *JSPB* 16, 1833/1776, f. 139B.

39. *JSPB* 31, 1841/1784, f. 81B.

40. *JSPB* 20, 1835/1778, f. 95A.

41. But when he later backed off from sending the donkeys, his claims to the birat were questioned; *JSPB* 20, 1835/1778, f. 132B.

42. When there was a conflict between Suthar Tile and Suthar Devalo of village Chhapri for having worked for the same jat patron, the state ordered that in future both must work for their respective birat; see *JSPB* 38, 1845/1788, f. 82A. Bhats of Bikaner and Mewar approached the Durbar which appointed the Bilarha bhats to settle their dispute regarding birat rights over the Kaseras of the area; *JSPB* 21, 1835/1778, f. 180A. Luhar Jamal and Luhar Khushal Khan were able to resolve other property disputes between them but their conflict over birat rights persisted for long; see *JSPB* 13, 1830/1773, f. 154A. Similarly Bhat Sahu Khuspal and Bhat Ramla of Jalor quarrelled as to who had the birat right over the kumhars of the area; see *JSPB* 20, 1835/1778, f. 128A.

43. Jan Breman offers a similar rationale for the continued popularity of patron-client ties in the villages of southern Gujarat; see his *Patronage and Exploitation: Changing Agrarian Relations in South Gujarat* (India, 1974), pp. 10–23.

44. Sunars are recorded to have had shops in the village and did not work for a birat; see *JSPB* 11, 1828/1771, f. 22B. Julahas, chhipas, and rangrez are recorded to have visited the local haats regularly and no document reveals any of them enjoying birat bonds with any patron.

45. *JSPB* 16, 1833/1776, f. 13A.

46. *JSPB* 22, 1779.

47. *JSPB* 11, 1828/1771, f. 22B.

48. See G.S.L. Devara, 'Position and Role of the Intermediaries in the North-West Rajputana, (AD 1650–1800),' in G.S.L. Devara (ed.), *Some Aspects of Socio-Economic History of Rajasthan* (Jodhpur, 1986), pp. 90–102.

49. David Washbrooke, 'Land and Labour in Late Eighteenth Century South India: The Golden Age of the Pariah?' in Peter Robb (ed.), *Dalit Movements and the Meaningss of Labour in India* (Delhi, 1993), pp. 69–70.

50. See Col.Archibald Adams, *The Western Rajputana States: A Medico-Topographical and General Account of Marwar, Sirohi and Jaisalmer,* (London, 1900) pp. 429–30. Also see Brij Raj Chauhan, *A Rajasthan Village,* (New Delhi, 1967), pp. 85–6. There may have been occasional exceptions to this rule, as implied in the folk tale *Baniya ra Pardos,* where a bania was forced to suffer a bhambi next to his house due to the local thakur's wish to harass the bania. See Komal Kothari (ed.), *Batan ri Phulwari: Rajasthan ri Kadimi Lok Kathawan,* bhag 4, pp. 280–95, (Borunda, 1964).

51. I have compiled these from a variety of sources, including G.D. Sharma, 'State Land Revenue Demand in Marwar During the Seventeenth Century', *Proceedings of Rajasthan History Congress,* Pali Session, 1974, pp. 69–73; G.D. Sharma, 'Some Agricultural Taxes in Marwar', *Proceedings of Rajasthan History Congress,* Beawar Session, 1973; B.L. Bhadani, *Peasants, Artisans and Entrepreneurs* (Jaipur, 1999), p. 217; and numerous documents.

52. This is the reality most easily accessible and discussed by historians. See for instance, Harbans Mukhia 'Illegal Extortions from Peasants, Artisans, and Menials in Eighteenth Century Eastern Rajasthan', *IESHR,* vol. 14, no. 2, 1977, pp. 231–45. Gautam Bhadra also notes in his 'The Mentality of Subalternity: *Kantanama* or *Rajadharma*' in Ranajit Guha (ed.), *Subaltern Studies VI:* pp. 54–91 that rules governing economic arrangements between peasants and land owners in Bengal were exploitative to the extreme since 'there was no legally defined limit to how much the landlord could demand of the peasant: there was nothing written or definitive about it. It was kept vague and judged by custom; See p. 71.

53. Compare Hiroshi Fukazawa, *The Medieval Deccan* (Delhi, 1998), p. 133, with documents cited below.

54. *JSPB* 1, 1821/1764, f. 21.

55. Chhipa Nimba of Merta, for instance, was able to revert to past practice when he asked to do so; see *JSPB* 13, 1830/1773, f. 153B.

56. *JSPB* 20, 1835/1778, f. 183A.

57. *JSPB* 23, 1836/1779, f. 50A.

58. *JSPB* 13, 1830/1773, f. 49A.

59. See Ann Gold and Bhoju Ram Gujar's *In the Time of Trees and Sorrows*, pp. 93–104 for an elaboration of this point.

60. *JSPB* 12, 1829/1772, f. 230A. Sunar Likhama too was beaten till unconscious by the jagirdar's bhambi when he objected to having their cattle graze in his fields; *JSPB* 13, 1830/1773, f. 26A. Mahajan Kesara of village Paduwadi felt justified in thrashing Sunar Gule when he failed to repay a loan taken from the mahajan; *JSPB* 14, 1831/1774, f. 67A.

61. *JSPB* 24, 1837/1780, f. 174B.

62. *JSPB* 16, 1833/1776, f. 88B.

63. *JSPB* 13, 1830/1773, f. 165A.

64. Four *man* grains, ten *ser munj* (with which ropes were made), a spade and grass were forcibly taken away by the jagirdar from the lakhara; see *JSPB* 18, 1834/1777, f. 38B.

65. *JSPB* 16, 1833/1776, f. 154A

66. *JSPB* 15, 1832/1775, f. 807.

67. *JSPB* 1, 1821/1764, f. 55A.

68. *JSPB* 18, 1834/1777, f. 33A.

69. Mahajan Tilo of village Kharchiya of Sojhat pargana took away Chhipa Dole's *karhaw* (large dyeing vessel) and refused to return it even when the chhipa returned from Malwa; *JSPB* 22, 1836/1779, f. 116A. In another case, a jagirdar took away a kumhar's cows without any provocation; *JSPB* 26, 1838/1781, f. 149B. Darzi Durge of village Khanpur was also able to recover his Rs 110 from Deval Abhay of village Lai but not without the help of the Bhinmal Kachedi; *JSPB* 10, 1828/1771, f. 150A.

70. *JSPB* 15, 1832/1775, f. 183B.

71. Chhipa Bharundawar of Harsor had to contract a loan from the local mahajan for his son's betrothal. A caste-fellow, Chhipa Dole stood guarantee, but later they had a conflict when the creditor began to pressurize, and Bharundawar was unable to repay; see *JSPB* 15, 1832/1775, f. 535.

72. Khati Bhagwan of Merta had to take a large loan to meet the community obligations on his maternal grandfather's death; he therefore felt entitled to inherit the latter's property, especially since he had not been able to service the loan for long; see *JSPB* 13, 1830/1773, f. 154B.

73. Prasannan Parthasarathi, 'Rethinking Wages and Competitiveness in the Eighteenth Century: Britain and South India', *Past and Present*, vol. 158, 1998, pp. 85, 89, 92, 101.

74. Parthasarathi, *The Transition to a Colonial Economy: Weavers, Merchants and Kings in South India, 1720–1800* (Cambridge, 2001), p. 28

75. Parthasarathi, *The Transition to a Colonial Economy*, pp. 28–9.

76. *JSPB* 18, 1834/1777, f. 33A.

77. *JSPB* 8, 1825/1768, f. 120A.

78. See David Hardiman, *Feeding the Baniya : Peasants and Usurers in Western India* (Delhi, 1996) for an in-depth study of the interplay of complex elements within the relationship of domination and subordination born out of usury, the extension of loans by the sahukar to the peasant.

79. See the *Report on the Administration of the Marwar State for the Year 1896–1897,* (Jodhpur, 1898), p. 25.

80. See David Hardiman, *Feeding the Baniya : Peasants and Usurers in Western India* (Delhi, 1996).

81. A report of AD 1900 states that the baniyas took away the entire wheat crop, valued at a high rate, leaving the peasants some of the less valuable maize and barley; see Sukhdev Prasad's *The Final Report of the Famine Operations in Marwar during 1899 and 1900* (Jodhpur, 1900), p. 157.

82. Quoted in B.L. Gupta's *Trade and Commerce in Rajasthan*, p. 15.

83. For more on the subject, read G.D. Sharma, '*Vyaparis* and *Mahajans* in Western Rajasthan During the Eighteenth Century', *Proceedings of Indian History Congress*, 41st session, Bombay, 1980, pp. 377–85.

84. *JSPB* 41,1846/1789, f. 103A.

85. The kachedi ordered in favour of Nanag, with the stipulation that if he failed to pay the rent, Harakha may take over the property; see *JSPB* 24, 1837/1780, f. 128A.

86. *JSPB* 26, 1838/1781, f. 89A

87. Marwari folk tale penned by Vijay Dan Detha, titled 'Baniya ra Paros' in Komal Kothari (ed.), *Batan ri Phulwari: Rajasthan ri Kadimi Lok Kathawan*, bhag 4, pp. 280–95, (Borunda, 1964).

88. For an elaboration of this aspect, see Imamuddin, extra assistant commissioner, Ajmer District, 9 June, 1896, RSAB, Ajmer Commissioner's Office, Register 1, SN 216, file B(5)6, basta 19, 1893. Reference quoted from David Hardiman's *Feeding the Baniya: Peasants and Userers in Western India* (Delhi, 1996), p. 193.

89. Chhipa Nanag of Bagadi was not ousted from his house even though over years his failure to repay the loan had led to the doubling of the principal. Ultimately he became a tenant in his own house, and promised that he would pay a rent of rupees five till he managed to service the entire loan; see *JSPB* 24, 1837/1780, f. 128A.

90. C.G. Dixon, 22 October 1849, in the author's *Report on Ajmer and Mairwara, Illustrating the Settlement of the Land Revenue and the Revenue Administration of those Districts to 1853* (Agra, 1853), pp. 19–20, quoted in David Hardiman's *Feeding the Baniya*, p. 156.

91. David Hardiman, *Feeding the Baniya*, p. 126.

92. See Dilbagh Singh, 'The Role of the Mahajans in the Rural Economy in Eastern Rajasthan During the Eighteenth Century', *Social Scientist*, May 1974, pp. 20–31.

93. Jan Breman, *Patronage and Exploitation: Changing Agrarian Relations in South Gujarat* (Berkeley, 1974), pp. 14–15.

94. See Dharma Kumar's 'The Forgotten Sector: Services in Madras Presidency in the First Half of the Nineteenth Century', *IESHR*, vol. XXIX, no. 4, 1987, pp. 367–93.

95. For an elaboration of the ideology and mechanics of servitude, see Gyan Prakash's *Bonded Histories: Genealogies of Labour Servitude in Colonial India* (Cambridge, 1990) where he probes the *kamiauti* contracts that *kamias* of southern Bihar entered with into local *maliks*.

96. *JSPB* 18, 1834/1777, f. 33A.

97. Ibid.

98. *JSPB* 26, 1841/1784, f. 149B.

99. Bernard S. Cohn, while discussing the chamars of village Madhopur in the Jaunpur district of Uttar Pradesh, refers to them as such; see Cohn, 'The Changing Status of a Depressed Caste', in McKim Marriott (ed.), *Village India* (Chicago, 1955), p. 56. Existence of a similar institution as the *hali* has been noted by S.C. Dube for Shamirpet where 'rich landowners employ labourers on the basis of an annual contract. Rates of payment vary with age, ability and experience of the person employed, and also partly with financial position of the employer'; see S.C. Dube, *Indian Village* (London, 1955), p. 78.

100. *JSPB* 13, 1830/1773, f. 54A.

101. Ibid., f. 36B.

102. *JSPB* 15, 1832/1775, f. 228B.

103. All three instances mentioned above pertain to potters.

104. See T. Skocpol, *States and Social Revolutions: A Comparative Analysis of France, Russia, and China*, (Cambridge 1979); also P. Evans, D. Rueschemeyer, and T. Skocpol, (eds) *Bringing the State Back In* (Cambridge, 1985).

105. Michael Adas constructed the 'contest model' to describe pre-industrial political formations; see his essay 'From Avoidance to Confrontation: Peasant Protest in Precolonial and Colonial Southeast Asia', *Comparative Studies in Society and History*, vol. 23, no. 2, 1981.

106. Norbert Peabody, 'Cents, Sense, Census: Human Inventories in Late Precolonial and Early Colonial India', *Comparative Study of Society and History* 2001, pp. 819–50; and Appadurai, 'Number in the Colonial Imagination', in Carol Breckenridge and Peter van der Veer (eds) *Orientalism and the Postcolonial Predicament: Perspectives on South Asia* (Philadelphia, 1993), pp. 329–30.

107. Sumit Guha, 'The Politics of Identity and Enumeration in India c.1600–1990', *Comparative Study of Society and History*, 2003, pp. 148–67.

108. Similarly, resistance was also small scale because larger levels of organization were not possible.

109. See Hasan, *State and Locality in Mughal India*, pp 52–3.

110. Nandini Sunder too, in her work *Subalterns and Sovereigns: An Anthropological History of Bustar 1854–1996* (Delhi, 1997) noticed that the Raja himself was not blamed for maladministration, only his corrupt officials.

111. Many of these responses from Marwari artisans run parallel to those discussed by Michael Adas in his essay 'From Avoidance to Confrontation: Peasant Protest in Precolonial and Colonial Southeast Asia', *Comparative Studies in Society and History*, vol. 23, no. 2, 1981; and 'From Foot-dragging to Flight: The Evasive History of Peasant Avoidance Protest in South and Southeast Asia', in James C. Scott and J. Tria Kerkvliet (eds), *Everyday Forms of Peasant Resistance*, *Journal of Peasant Studies*, vol. 13, no. 2, 1986, pp. 64–86.

112. Concessions conceded in the past were seized upon by the lower orders as a 'right' which they fought to protect. The Jodhpur Durbar, for instance, sent an order (*parwana*) to the officers of the Jalor customs' treasury (Sayar) not to collect the *chothai* tax from the churigars on their insistence that the previous administration had exempted them from this payment; see *JSPB* 14, 1831/1774, f. 135. Rangrez Misari had not been asked to pay *rahdari* while transporting his dye materials (kasumba, gul, and nil) from village Arhandpur to Jaitaran earlier. On his complaint about the sayar's new demands, the latter were told to follow past practice and not charge indiscriminately; see *JSPB* 52, 1855/1798, ff. 52B.

113. See E.J. Hobsbawm, *Primitive Rebels* (New York, Norton, 1959); Tilly, *The Contentious French* (Glencoe, Illinois, 1988); Blum's *Lord and Peasant in Russia* (Princeton, 1961), especially chapter 14; also Hilton's *Bond Men Made Free* (New York, 1973), respectively.

114. See Michael Adas' 'From Foot-dragging to Flight: The Evasive History of Peasant Avoidance Protest in South and Southeast Asia', in James C. Scott and J. Tria Kerkvliet (eds), *Everyday Forms of Peasant Resistance, Journal of Peasant Studies*, vol. 13, no. 2, 1986, pp. 64–86.

115. See James Scott, *Weapons of the Weak* (New Haven, Connecticut, 1985).

116. Their fears were valid, as is evident from examples of confrontational outbursts by subordinate groups elsewhere in the pre-modern world. Charles Tilly's study of the Lustucru peasant rebellion against taxation in mid-seventeenth century France is a case in point. He records that in the aftermath of a rebellion, the commander of the rebels was hanged, and more than 360 of the rebels sent off in chains to serve their lives as galley slaves. See Tilly, 'Routine Conflicts and Peasant Rebellions in Seventeenth Century France', in R.P. Weller and S.E. Guggenheim (eds), *Power and Protest in the Countryside* (Durham, N.C., 1982) p. 15.

117. *JSPB* 1, 1821/1764, f. 13A.

118. *JSPB* 20, 1835/1778, f. 183A. Read Eugene Genovese's *Roll, Jordan, Roll: The World the Slaves Made* (New York, 1972) p. 52, for an elaboration of this

psychology on the part of patrons, when they feel spurned and angry on find-ing their clientele in an insubordinate mood.

119. See Bhadra, 'The Mentality of Subalternity: *Kantanama* or *Rajdharma*', in R. Guha (ed.), *Subaltern Studies VI* (Delhi, 1989), p. 54.

120. Douglas Haynes and Gyan Prakash too emphasize that shared experi-ences of the subalterns in particular relationships generated autonomy and resistance in that specific context; see the 'Introduction' to their jointly edited volume *Contesting Power*.

121. *JSPB* 6, 1824/1767, f. 88B.

122. *JSPB* 20, 1835/1778, f. 43A

123. *JSPB* 14, 1831/1774, f. 227A, and *JSPB* 19, 1834/1777, f. 82A, respec-tively.

124. *JSPB* 8, 1825/1768, f. 155A.

125. *JSPB* 15, 1832/1775, f. 63 and *JSPB*., 16, 1833/1776, f. 86B respectively.

126. Kumhar Chhad of village Bithohra migrated due to due to the jagirdar's oppression; see *JSPB* 15, 1832/1775, f. 174B.

127. Conditions in pre-colonial Jodhpur seem to run parallel to those outlined by Adas as responsible for encouraging the widespread trend of migratory labour. As an emergency remedy in times of famine, and as a weapon of protest against oppression, it was popularly used in other parts of the subcontinent also; for instance, Ranajit Guha writes about eighteenth century Bengal, 'The primitive or one might say natural method—the only method infact—yet known to the *ryot* for enforcing a bargain was migration'; see his *Report on an Investigation of the Gauripur Raj Estate Archives* (West Bengal, 1955–6) p. 29. This reference has been cited in Gyan Pandey's 'Economic Dislocation in Nineteenth Century Eastern Uttar Pradesh', in Peter Robb (ed.), *Rural South Asia: Linkages, Change, and De-velopment* (London, 1983), p. 112.

128. *JSPB* 1, 1821/1764, f. 55A.

129. Brouwer, in his *Makers of the World*, as also numerous other studies on south Indian artisans, notices emigration as a popular form of escaping what was perceived as over-taxation; see pp. 205–7.

130. *JSPB* 22, 1836/1779, f. 18A. For an elaborate discussion on this issue, see G.S.L. Devara, 'Bikaner Niwasi aur Deshantar Gaman Pravarti: Satrahavin avam Atharvin Shatabdi mein', in *Proceedings of Rajasthan History Congress* (1974), pp. 42–8.

131. *JSPB* 16, 1833/1776, f. 151A.

132. *JSPB* 15, 1832/1775, ff.257A, and 260A.

133. For an elaboration of plebeian strategies to combat exploitation, see Michael Adas, 'From Avoidance to Confrontation: Peasant Protest in Pre-Colonial and Colonial Southeast Asia', *Comparative Studies in Society and History*, vol. 23, no. 2, 1981, pp. 217–47.

134. Chhipa Mahmad of Piparh, Nilgar Fazal of Nagaur, Darzi Mohan of Jaitaran, Khati Dhaniye of Village Saisada, Julaha Jivadan of Didwana, Luhar Rohtas of Village Sihat, and many others are recorded to have spent several years in Malwa. In each of their cases, property disputes arose due to their prolonged absence; see *JSPB* 8, 1826/1769, f. 2B, *JSPB* 9, 1827/1770, f. 62A, *JSPB* 11, 1829/1772, f. 175A, *JSPB* 15, 1832/1775, f. 561; *JSPB* 16, 1833/1776, f. 127B, *JSPB* 18, 1835/1778, f. 18B, respectively.

135. *JSPB* 10, 1827/1770, f. 70A.

136. Rangrez Nure of Bilarha cultivated indigo on his fields in the countryside; *JSPB* 11, 1828/1771, f. 197B. Darzi Dharam of Phalodi inherited ancestral revenue-free fields which his uncle (*kaka*) rented out on muqata; *JSPB* 6, 1824/1767, f. 109B. Darzi Suja and Nai Chanda of Phalodi also had a dispute over a field; *JSPB* 7, 1824/1767, f. 18A.

137. While Rangrez Misari was living in Jaitaran, part of his family was in village Arhandpur. He therefore regularly commuted between these two places with his dye stuffs; *JSPB* 36, 1844/1787, f. 199B.

138. *JSPB* 15, 1832/1775, f. 807, *JSPB* 21,1835/1778, f. 132A, *JSPB* 22, 1836/1779, f. 116A, *JSPB* 15, 1832/1775, f. 183B, etc.

139. When Kumhar Dede of Balatu returned after spending five years in Malwa, he discovered to his dismay that the jagirdar and chaudhari had settled another kumhar on his land; see *JSPB* 38, 1845/1788, f.3A. While Khati Dhaniye of village Saisanada was in Malwa, Khati Natho occupied Dhaniye's ancestral house and refused to vacate it even when the former returned. Such incidents bred disaffection, and gave rise to tensions which the administration had to tackle and resolve.

140. For an elaboration of this point, see James C. Scott's *Domination and the Arts of Resistance: Hidden Transcripts* (New Haven, 1990); also see Ranajit Guha, 'The Prose of Counter-Insurgency', in Ranajit Guha (ed.), *Subaltern Studies* (New Delhi, 1983), vol. II, pp. 1–42.

141. Maharaja Sardar Singhji's *My Pali Tour Diary* (Chaupasani, Jodhpur) p. 141, (quoted by Jagdish Singh Gehlot in *Marwar Rajya ka Itihas*, p. 268).

142. See Col.Archibald Adams, *The Western Rajputana States: A Medico-Topographical and General Account of Marwar, Sirohi and Jaisalmer*, p. 97.

143. A pioneering attempt in using sources of the oral tradition for constructing an aspect of medieval history has been made by Vijaya Ramaswamy in her article, 'Weaver Folk Traditions as a Source of History', *IESHR*, vol. 19, no. 1, 1982, pp. 47–62.

144. See *Marwar Mardum Shumari Report*, pp. 463–4.

145. The nationalist historiography seems to suggest harmony and communal accord as the hallmarks of village communities in the pre-British Indian state.

146. Demirci, p. 472.

147. Gyan Prakash rightly cautions against such materialistic approaches; see his *Bonded Histories*, pp. 31–2. In a more general sense, Karl Polanyi too emphasizes that the economic was embedded in the social in pre-capitalist formations.

148. David Arnold, in 'Gramsci and Peasant Subalternity in India', *Journal of Peasant Studies*, vol. 11, 1984, pp. 155–77 also argued that domination and hegemony, however strong, were never absolute.

149. For more on this, see Partha Chatterjee, 'Peasants, Politics, and Historiography: A Response', *Social Scientist*, no. 120, 1983, p. 59.

5

City Artisans, Merchants, and Urban Administration

Pur hai luhar ka pohlak, budhh sudhh karigar bahulak,
This is the colony of blacksmiths where reside numerous skilled ironworkers,
Tikha bhal gharh talwar, aur hi tuppak nal apaar,
They craft sharp-pointed spears and swords, horseshoes, and other arms,
Chhala chhipiya ki chump, ik ik cheez gharhat anoop,
The printers have their own corner where they fabricate unparalelled textiles
Jud bal jar gharhat jiwar, pura sughat gharh prakar,
Metal-workers are busy crafting a variety of weapons,
Chhinpa chanchi mochi chhaj, soni bharawa sirtaj,
Also active in the bazaar are, cobblers, goldsmiths, and bronze casters,
Darji dabgara dekhyak, pun kas lakhara pekhyak,
Tailors, drum-makers, and laquer bangle-makers ply their trade,
Kheradi, khararhiya, khagdwar, kai kah kam kai lohkar
Turners, blacksmiths too abound,
Sawarhn garhasi singar, teli tamboli arhnpar,
Oil-pressers manufacture cosmetics and toiletries for ornamentation,
Dhobi, kalal, kumbhakarak, kabarhingar vasay hai sarak,
Washermen, liquor distillers, and potters all live here,
Chhajat pavan hai chhattis, varnya kai vishwabis.
In fact all thirty-six pavan jat have thronged to the city.[1]

Contrary to European discourses on Indian polities that have continued to blinker modern interpretations, the above passage penned by a Jain saint showers praise on an early modern indigenous regime for being able to ensure the comfort of artisans such that a vast range of them had chosen to settle in Marwar and make for the prosperity of the area. The presence of bustling bazaars in the different cities of Marwar is vividly reflected in other ghazals as well, drawing attention to merchants, banias, artisans, and service castes, all of whom lent vibrance to the urban economy of the qasbas and urban centres of the kingdom. At the same time, exploitation is indisputably attested in contemporary records. This chapter examines the nature of exchanges in pre-colonial cities, positing artisanal autonomy both in the context of urban markets and mercantile control over them, as well as vis-à-vis artisanal-State dialectics. Probing the factors that ensured substantial artisanal concentrations in the cities, it describes urban morphology and settlement patterns, and discusses the rationale for artisanal localization into caste colonies (muhalla or *pur*). It examines close living as caste brotherhoods and how this effected alterations in subaltern subjectivities and capacity for organization. Focussing on the political logic and imperatives of the Rathor state in the early decades of Vijai Singh's reign, it examines how caste solidarities helped artisans bargain and negotiate for greater space, whether as tax-payers or as wage-earning state employees. Can the role of the caste system, indeed a divisive and limiting force, also—paradoxically enough—be interpreted as one that helped in the mobilization of the community, and thereby act as enabling and empowering?

Cities and their 'Pull' for Artisans

Rajput chieftaincies, including Marwar, were kin-based segmentary political systems where perennial conflict between the crown and the prebends was a structural feature of the polity.[2] As noticed earlier, the eighteenth century saw the gradual collapse of Mughal imperial power while Marwar achieved a new level of autonomous political standing. But the absence of an overarching paramount authority that could ensure stability led to the resurgence of tensions inherent in Rathor kinship relations.[3] Appanaging and the theoretical notion of a corporate state, where segmentary Rathor lineages enjoyed co-equal rights to participate in and share the power and resources of the lineage territories, resurfaced in the eighteenth century. Many of these lineage chiefs, known locally as thakurs, became for all intents and purposes small kings in their own right. Though on a reduced scale, their thikanas with independent durbars reflected the pomp and grandeur of their masters.[4] The combined resources of the thakurs were greater than that of the maharajas, evident from the fact that only 15 per cent of the land belonged to the crown, the remaining areas alienated as appanages to the prebendal chiefs and their dependents.[5] The thakurs repeatedly challenged the primacy of the rulers, and there was a continual struggle for power amongst them.

These political forms reflected on the pattern of urbanization and forms of artisanal productivity in the cities. A majority of urban centres, whether Jodhpur, Nagaur, Merta, or Pokharan, were administrative bases, homes to the subordinate lineages of the Rathors. As ruling centres, they reflected the political culture of the region where ritual display marked by conspicuous consumption had a significant role. 'Conscious ritualization of everyday life' resulted in a complex proliferation of service communities and functionaries required to fulfil courtly 'luxuries' and the kingly style.[6] Along with piety, royal descent and valour, pomp, display, and patronage were fundamental to legitimate power.

In their competitive political dynamic, the Rathor kings, while negotiating their gradual transformation to increasing autonomy, could secure themselves only through careful use of these prevailing norms of kingship. To secure and maintain their superiority, the rulers had to distinguish themselves from their kinsmen and potential rivals by embracing the entire arsenal of emblems associated with power and rule.[7] Notions of Marwari honour had come to include patronage of the arts and artisans as one important way by which power and status could be legitimized and enhanced. It was seen as a means by which the rule of a particular individual could be validated, and it constituted an important symbol for garnering support for the ruling dynasty. A patron's ability to award, augment, or revoke land grants and Durbar honours thus went beyond simple economic considerations because status and honour (*izzat*) had become critical to the rajput system by the eighteenth century.[8] Marwari ghazals, as a genre, may be somewhat hyperbolic in content, but they did certainly indicate contemporary ideals, notions of 'greatness', and the standards and indices that went into making a ruler 'eminent'. As evident from the stanza cited from the Nagaur ghazal at the beginning of this chapter, the extension of patronage to artisans and their presence within the territories of the kingdom was an important yardstick indicative of the prosperity of the state.

The expectation that the king should support artists and artisans was implicit not merely in Hindu but also in Indo-Persian theories of kingship.[9] A ruler was traditionally expected to be generous in his patronage to artists and artisans, such patronage viewed not only as his responsibility but also as an emblem of his status. Moreover, such patronage was seen in both traditions as a visible indicator of the ruler's superior lineage, and presumably, of his worthiness to rule. As a powerful reinforcement of his right to rule, patronage therefore had a larger social and political function, and had become an extension of political culture. Local and regional rulers were, therefore, expected not merely to provide leadership on the battlefield, or dispense largesse to their followers and kinsmen—they were also expected to be active patrons of artists, artisans, and cultural performers. Court ceremonials and public rituals gave them an opportunity to act out the relationships with the elements that supported the organic structure of the state. Indeed, in an effort to appear as sumptuous patrons and consumers of fine goods, Rathor maharajas and their lineage chiefs organized lavish public rituals and court ceremonies, especially during festivals. These were legitimizing symbols that were meant to provide an additional buttress and confirm the primacy of the maharaja or thakur in his respective territory.

This concern finds reflection in a proverb popular in this region, which reads: *Kai nanv gitaran, kai bhintaran,* and translates as 'One's name can be perpetuated either in ballads or in buildings'.[10] Large-scale building construction was undertaken by the ruling elites throughout the period, and artisans invited to work for it. In fact, the beginning of a new record series titled *Kamthana Bahis* is testimony to this increased building activity during the eighteenth century. Other forms of conspicuous consumption were also recognized as hallmarks of high status, and necessitated the availability of skilled labour to craft out fine artefacts.

Equally, rajput potentates were aware of the potential value of commerce for their regimes, and, eager to realize that potential, they strained to attract productive forces to their territories.[11] Competition for merchants and craftsmen was keen, and sources indicate that to meet these requirements, scores of artisans were invited to settle in towns, a large majority of them residents of the over two dozen cities and qasbas in the fertile eastern parts of the kingdom. Disaggregated political structures acting as elite bases saw the emergence of a large number of court and consumer-oriented urban centres. Artisans were drawn to these cities due to the availability of elite patronage and facilities extended by the aristocracy. The capital city of Jodhpur and other pargana headquarters such as those of Nagaur, Merta, Pali, Sojhat, Jaitaran, and Jalor, became home to not only administrative officials but also an array of artisans, merchants, and servants of the elite. A primitive 'census' attempted by Nainsi reveals the distribution of artisanal concentrations in the different pargana headquarters during the late, seventeenth-century (Table 5.1).

The pomp and grandeur of the Mughal emperor served as a template keenly emulated by the Rathor maharajas, the lifestyles of the latter, in turn, shaping those of the subordinate chiefs. What they achieved was a near, sometimes poor duplication of some of the attributes of their superiors' headquarter.[12] The fortress (garh) of the thakurs was the locale for the administration of the thikana, encompassing within it a court, revenue offices, police post, jail, petty thakurs' havelis, officials, servants and retainers, artists and artisans, and many others.[13] The presence of the elites, and that of a hierarchy of administrative officials enhanced the economic potential of these administrative-cum-commercial centres. Other than their feudal masters, they were the home of a huge floating population, particularly craft and service castes. The artisans, in particular, were markedly mobile,

Table 5.1
Pavan Jat Households in Pargana Headquarters by Late Seventeenth Century

Cities	Total Houses	Pavan Jat Occupied Houses	Percentage (%)
Sojhat	2254	625	27.72
Jaitaran	1839	389	21.15
Phalodi	659	88	13.35
Merta	5860	2124	36.24
Siwana	283	33	11.66
Pokharan	557	66	11.84

many possessing strong rural roots, often tending to treat towns as a temporary home in crisis situations of famines and droughts, or 'transit' markets where their commodities fetched a better price. These were centres that generated a high demand for luxury goods, as well as a considerable demand for goods of daily consumption.[14] The morphology of these settlements, with their royal palace, jagirdars' kotri, or a thakur's thikana at the centre, and the township of lower functionaries of the state, merchants, artisans, and service castes settled around it, reflected the relationship between the masters and their subordinates.[15]

MUHALLA-LIVING AND CONCEPT OF BIRADARI

On migrating to urban centres, artisans usually settled in segregated streets or caste colonies, called muhallas.[16] As is well-known, the segregation of people on the basis of caste based on normative prescriptions of ritual purity, determined settlement patterns in cities as much as in villages. The convenience of both artisanal communities as also that of the state administration together ensured that caste specific congregations of craft groups live together.[17] In Nagaur, for instance, sources mention that luhars resided in Luharpura, khatis in Khatripura, and julahas in Samadhipura, moving *en bloc* to Khatripura in the 1770s.[18] Such muhallas became highly integrated units because almost all the kinship and affinal relationships of an individual were confined to his muhalla, and most of the members practiced more or less the same occupation. They resided on a single street, often possessed joint property, regulated their corporate affairs through a jati panchayat, and worshipped a common tutelary deity. This was probably true for large villages as well, where a few occupational craft groups lived in concentrated pockets. In either case, as discussed below, close living led to the development of 'social capital' within communities.

Administrative policies of the state reflected as sensitivity to such community and caste divisions. In its interface with these social groups, the state appears to have been extremely receptive to the norm of hierarchical segregation and responsive to caste preferences for residing together.[19] At the ideological level, the administrative policies of the state were geared towards the realization of its role as the supreme regulator of society. As such, it deemed it fit to enforce ritual stratification that divided society into clean and unclean castes. In case two communities lived close to each other, an open courtyard or large platform (called chauntara in local parlance), served to separate them.[20] From the state's perspective, equally, if not more important a rationale for this practice was that most taxes were assessed on the basis of the number of houses of a caste in the muhalla, and collected accordingly. Individual members made contributions to a common pool, and any changes in the quantum of tax were notified jointly for a caste.[21] Hence, the state's interest in implementing this settlement pattern along muhallas made for a lot of administrative convenience. When the rate of a particular tax was raised, or when exemption was granted to a certain community, a single Durbar order or proclamation applied to all its members. Any infiltration of other caste groups would cause difficulties to not only the state machinery but the tax payers as well.[22] Revenue policies, therefore, confirmed and consolidated ritual segregation, and rendered it 'official'.

Another aspect of this regulatory role of the state was its effort to maintain social discipline, and closely monitor the intra-caste as well as inter-caste behaviour of different communities. The preservation of order was indeed facilitated by having them settle in close proximity, and then intercede either through popular local bodies like the jati panchayats, or directly, when required. Segregated settlement also helped during the celebration of festivals, especially Holi, which became an excuse for the abandonment of all forms of orderly behaviour. Unpleasant exchanges and unruly behaviour between members of different castes was common during Holi and many complaints came to the state in this regard. The Holi *gahar* (caste-wise processions with dancers and singers) of the *kharol*s (salt-makers) of Bilarha inevitably clashed with the *daphariya*s (drum-beaters). In an effort to bolster their image as the upholders of 'dharma' and the 'great regulators', the state stipulated that the day following Holi, all castes were obliged to play in their own caste muhallas only.[23] The daphariyas were instructed not to force their entry into the kharol muhalla. Besides certain castes were 'traditionally' hostile to specific groups, and keeping them apart was one way of preventing disruptions of law and order.[24]

From a artisan's perspective, it was always preferable to settle with his kin in his jati muhalla when he immigrated to a city. Conscious of his low position in the ritual hierarchy, he felt secure living with people with whom he shared bonds, whether professional or personal familial ones.[25] Old links between caste-members in towns and villages facilitated the process of relocation, and the new entrant did not feel like a total stranger. He came through pre-existing links, and was absorbed into the world of caste and kinship of the town. The converse was equally true: Often, communities resented infiltration into their colony, and by reporting such cases to the state authorities, ensured segregation.[26] Outlines of caste segregation were still incomplete, and 'mistakes' did happen, though the ideal for both craft communities and the state was to have people settle in their own colonies.

As noticed earlier, shared cultural beliefs and related behavioural patterns knit occupational groups into closed castes or communities called nyats. Each of these developed their own culture, rituals and festivals, commensal practices, marriage customs, and funerary rites, and—thereby—a distinct identity.[27] Common religious beliefs meant that castes could have their own temple, mosque, or shrine in the vicinity, worship common deities and saints (pirs) together, and visit shrines, or go for holy dips as a communal activity.[28] In addition, caste members found it mutually beneficial to settle together in view of basic material considerations. For instance, several rangrez could share a dyeing tank, or kumhars take turns to bake their pots in a co-operative manner in a kiln.[29] Practical concerns such as using the same raw material, and therefore finding a ready source in the neighbour in case one's own stocks got over, also had a role to play in determining the settlement pattern of the artisans in caste colonies in urban centres. The sense of shared identity provided a feeling of security and comfort, particularly in a period when patron-client relationships were beginning to dissolve. Strength and sustenance had to be found now in caste solidarity rather than other kinds of formations. Self-identification of an eighteenth-century Marwari artisan therefore largely merged with that of his communal identification. The solidarity and brotherhood born out of an awareness of belonging to a common biradari was a great source of strength in moments of crisis, whether droughts, Maratha depredations, or increasing skirmishes with the ruling elite during the latter decades of the century.[30]

The closely spaced construction in the lower-caste colonies was not without its own share of problems, however. For one, it posed innumerable tensions due to crowding, and resultant property disputes.[31] Most cities had walls surrounding them as a defence against external attacks—and settlers, keen for protection and patronage—preferred to settle within the city ramparts. While the upper castes enjoyed greater open space to spread outwards, artisanal muhallas were densely settled, and tended to get excessively crowded over time, each new migrant pushing into the limited spaces allotted to his community. In a colony teeming with small houses, separate approaches to a dwelling were often difficult to carve out, and property disputes were a recurrent problem.[32] Possession of an ownership deed delineating clearly the boundaries of a property helped but, in the absence of it, there was scope for fraudulent claims being pushed.[33] However, pattas also lost validity after a certain period, and had to be renewed, failing which there was further confusion.[34] Close living in colonies often created other irritants, especially if the nature of the trade a particular community engaged in resulted in large amounts of waste. Given the primitive standards of civic amenities, the disposal of these had to be arranged to avoid friction. Chhipa Kamal of Pali had been residing and carrying on his trade of dyeing and printing textiles for a long time. Disposal of large quantities of dirty water carrying dyes did not pose a problem then, but eventually some of his caste members living near-by began to object. To resolve this clash with the community, Kamal approached the Pali chauntara.[35] Competition and rivalry was generated where too many services of a kind were together available at one place. Early settlers sometimes tended to be hostile towards those who came later.[36]

Even so, the overall impact of settlement in artisanal caste colonies where members of a community lived and worked closely, ensured the emergence of strong ties and biradari or brotherhood solidarity. Inter-personal tensions were indeed there, and these surfaced every now and then in routine interactions. But the over-riding sentiment was of a shared identity, and consequent unity. These helped in the emergence of a network of social relationships, a web of connections through association. Termed 'social capital' in recent literature, the links were constructed just as much intangibly, through ethos, ethics, and a variety of other socio-cultural attributes binding people together within a particular group or community. Together, these facilitated the group's propensity for mutually beneficial collective action.[37]

Urban Artisans, Merchants, and the Market

While some city-based artisans worked independently, others took employment with the state. For many, the two categories overlapped rather than being mutually exclusive. They set up shop and catered to the market demand and, on attaining exceptional skills and fame, were sometimes commissioned by the state or its agents to work for them. Alternating between production for the market and for the state and its elites at different points of time was common. Sources from Marwar therefore do not quite subscribe to the picture constructed by Stephen Blake for Delhi and Agra, where he found that 'there were very few independent artisans producing for the market'.[38] Even if Blake's rather extreme interpretations were accurate for the twin imperial capitals at the core of the Mughal empire, they do not apply to Marwar. Those in state service often used their own tools, though raw materials were provided or paid for by the state. A considerable part of artisanal production was geared towards consumption by the state, alongside the independent manufacture of low-quality goods for common use.

The characteristic form of artisanal organization, even in cities, was family-based, with a large number of artisans setting up small autonomous residence-cum workshop-cum sale units for plying their trade. Some affluent artisans who could afford double-storied houses had their workshop and the sale section on the ground floor and the residential area on the first floor.[39] Though differences in income were common, the polarization between master-artisans and journeymen apprentices as distinct categories, so typical of pre-capitalist European society, and also evident in south India, is not indicated in this region.[40]

A common assumption is that artisans in the state's employ alone were the ones able to achieve any degree of competence in their craft. Drawing a distinction between the fortunes of permanently employed karkhana artisans who enjoyed state patronage, and independent bazaar artisans in Shahajahanabad, Bernier wrote: 'The artists, therefore, who arrive at any eminence in their art are those only who are in the service of the king or some powerful Omrah, and who work exclusively for their patron'.[41] He further pointed, 'workshops occupied by skilful artisans will be vainly sought for in Delhi'.[42] Implied in this statement is that in terms of quality of commodities manufactured and the skills developed, independent artisans could not match their counterparts who enjoyed state patronage. Given the modest resources available to independent self-employed artisans, and their reliance on cheap raw materials and tools, the logic in Bernier's observations seems unexceptional. Eighteenth-century Marwar records, however, provide reasons to doubt this generalization. There are specific instances of artisans who excelled in their particular craft and gained sufficient renown to warrant summons from the state for the manufacture of quality artefacts.[43] Though most independent craftsmen possessed mediocre skills and lived in modest huts, their proficiency in their trade does not appear as low as is generally imagined. The reasons for this are, of course, hard to discern. By the eighteenth century, urban craftsmen had been largely weaned away from non-monetized to cash-based market transactions. The profit-motive had become an integral part of urban culture and monetary disputes prompted by the impulse to enhance profit margins rather than land-related disputes were more common in cities.

Scholars have argued that by at least the eighteenth if not the seventeenth century, manufacturing fell under the total subjection and control of merchant capital. They reiterate that the system of advances (dadani) of credit or raw materials, or both, had become universal and artisans had lost their economic independence. According to this formulation, the local middleman was the only person to whom the small producer could sell his goods, thereby exercising a monopoly position to substantially press down the price he paid to the craft producers. The producer inevitably fell into

dependence upon the creditor and sank into bondage, with such an economic dependence inevitably growing into a personal subjugation of the
artisan. Independent artisans were thus assumed to have eventually transformed into wage earners, working for their employers as per their directives
rather than carrying out autonomous production.[44]

Marwar, however, reveals a dramatically contrasting situation, largely
because it followed a historical trajectory quite distinct from that of the
coastal regions that were the first homes to commerce sponsored by the
European East India companies. In Marwar, instead, artisans by and large
produced and sold goods in their independent establishments, and the merchants played a negligible role in the process. At least as far as small and
middle-level urban centres were concerned, artisans operated freely, with
negligible mercantile intervention in the process of production. As for distribution, the artisan was free to decide whether he preferred to have the
local merchant market his produce, or personally engage in the distribution
process. Artisans also rarely seem part of the dadani system of advance
from the buyers or middlemen.[45] In fact, they were actively engaged in the
supply of timber, iron, or even textile yarn to their employers and patrons,
whether the local authorities or state officials. The involvement of merchants is not indicated in the procurement of raw materials.

In regions where it was normatively practiced, the basic raison d'être of
dadani was the inadequacy of the artisans' capital reserves for the requirements of a rapidly expanding market. The need for money for large
quantities of raw materials to manufacture huge amounts of commodities
ordered for by the European companies, led artisans in south and east India to turn to merchant capital.[46] But in the case of Marwar, as demonstrated
in the last chapter, rather than taking advances for production work, artisans contracted loans from moneylenders for funding their social
commitments such as marriage expenses or funeral feasts. Dadani was also
a way of binding producers to creditors in the face of competition from
other European companies and Indian merchants.[47] It was a device to ensure control over artisans and their skilled labour, to prevent them from
offering their commodities at higher prices to other buyers. Profits would
obviously be jeopardized if rival merchants succeeded in procuring commodities that had a high marketability and, especially in a situation where
there was a dramatic spurt in demand, it would lead to artisans pushing up
their prices. All these were indeed regions that had seen a sudden rise in
demand due to the arrival of European traders with elaborate preparations
for taking over local commerce; hence dadani was forced upon artisans by
the combined might of the Company traders.

But both these considerations were not applicable to Marwar, since it
neither experienced a rapid growth in demand, nor the sudden generation

of competition necessitating a need among buyers to monopolize or control the producers. Areas that did not get fully incorporated in the commerce of the European East India Companies clearly did not experience developments true for the Company-controlled regions. Records show that weavers of Jodhpur sold textiles in the city cloth-market independently, and deposited hasil in the sayar—the treasury where non-agricultural taxes were deposited.[48] Since the domestic market was expanding only gradually, the small producers generally limited themselves to disposing their wares in local markets often selling them directly to consumers. Such artisans therefore did not require advances of raw material or cash from merchants along the lines of the well-known 'putting-out system'.[49] The price they received for their commodities gave them some savings and, given primitive technology and the employment of simple tools, this limited capital was adequate to operate their small units of production. They essentially catered to the mass of city dwellers, and were exposed to the fluctuating vagaries of the market forces. The nature of the market was essentially oriented to meet the local, rather than the foreign demand, and enabled craftsmen to handle the production and sale on their own. There was no sudden opening of markets, and no dramatic rise in demand. This had happened in the case of regions integrated in the export trade handled by the European East India Companies, with its attendant consequences.[50] But Marwar largely remained out of the orbit of export trade, and its artisans did not witness the growing control of merchant capital, so much in evidence in the coastal areas from where the companies made their purchases.

A relatively high increase in the volume of sale occurred in textile production, where Marwar's integration in Gujarat trade had enlarged the market. In this single sector alone, and that too in large towns, there is evidence that a few middlemen bought goods for resale and took commission for providing marketing services. Usually in the range of 1 per cent of the cost price from the producer and 0.5 per cent from the buyer, these commission agents distanced the small weaver, dyer, or printer from the market, rendering him somewhat defenceless in the face of the power of merchant capital.[51] In these stray cases, artisanal autonomy in production was thereby inhibited. A record, for instance, states that a chhipa of Pali supplied sixty lengths of cloth (three *korhis* of *thaans*, each a set of twenty) he had printed to Sevo of Sojhat, a middleman (dalal). Sevo was supposed to market thus for the chhipa, and pay him Rs 103 for it. However, the dalal deceived him twice by claiming that the chhipa had given him only forty lengths (two korhis), and paid him less than the due.[52] The chhipa complained to the Pali authorities, who imposed a fine on the merchant and observed that such malpractices in trade would not be allowed to go unpunished. Evident from this case is the fact that such instances were not common, and invited stringent penalty. A majority of the artisans were, however, free from merchant control and handled their business single-handedly, with no merchant monitoring the operations at any stage.[53]

Subjugation to merchants is supposed to have inhibited mobility among artisans. As noticed in the previous chapter, however, documents from eighteenth-century Marwar show that artisans migrated from one place to another freely and frequently, discounting any possibility of being shackled in economic bondage to any moneylending merchant. Whatever the motivation or provocation, their frequent and habitual relocation to explore possibilities every now and then is undisputed. With a minimum of belongings comprising primarily of their cheap and simple tools and implements, they were the first to abandon a home to make another at a place of their choice, and mercantile pressures do not seem to have inhibited them in any way.

This is not to say that extra-economic domination of the moneylending castes on the craft groups was absent; in fact that was very much a reality, both in the cities as well as in the countryside.[54] Social superiority and greater economic strength facilitated mercantile coercion and oppression, and this was manifested in a variety of ways. Riding a horse was a privilege that was by and large enjoyed by the higher sections of society; hence, the mahajans objected to the low-born artisans assuming such pretensions.[55] Cases of forcibly appropriating artisans' belongings also abound.[56] To the extent that artisans had dealings with the merchants, the latter suppressed and exploited them, but by and large, a majority of urban artisans managed to keep free of mercantile intervention in the practice of their trade. Mostly, the direct producer used his labour in accordance with the market demand rather than the merchant's orders. He retained his right of ownership on the commodity manufactured by him, and sold his products himself instead of having to turn them over to the merchant in return for the organizational and financial backing provided by the latter.[57]

Rather than mercantile intervention, it was regulations from the state that were by and large more noticeable. For example, in 1766, when not enough skilled manpower was immediately available for crafting certain high quality textiles, the state ordered the julahas and *banawat*s of Nagaur to weave for the Durbar alone.[58] The kumhars of village Bhadarhan had regularly visited neighbouring towns to sell their wares, thereby making a good profit. But, in 1777, the state administration served them written orders to stop this practice, perhaps to ensure better control of the local elites over their labour.[59] Pinjara Ladu of Didwana was forbidden by the state from fabricating pillows with the cotton he carded, and compelled to limit himself to his original occupation of carding alone.[60] Indeed, the nature of the sources, which are essentially communications to and from the state, have ensured that they document the pro-active role of the state in regulating production. However, this would not skew the evidence regarding mercantile control, because in documentation of this nature, one would expect to find references to conflicts between artisans and merchants arising out of the subjection of craftsmen to merchant capital. After all, conflict between artisans and other dominant groups is amply reported. The near-complete silence on merchant control, and information indicating artisanal independence from merchant capital with regard to production, suggests that a rethinking of the commonly held proposition of crafts falling prey to mercantile control is required.

Also important to notice is the ambiguous relationship between the possessors of capital and the authority of the state. On the one hand, it was plainly in the interests of the emergent mercantilist states of this epoch to more firmly secure the control of merchants over producers and production since capital had become central to the maintenance and reproduction of military power. The ruler's concern, however, was to maximize his own returns from the development of commerce, not the levels of profits retained by the merchants. Hence, there was not only co-operation between rulers and merchants but much conflict as well. Given this conflict of interest, merchant sensibilities, as much as that of landlords noticed in Chapter 4, did not always prefer to maximize the powers of exploitation notionally lent them by the state, and the artisans' space to negotiate expanded in the interstices of this conflict.

Artisanal Wage Labour and the State

Artisans who acquired exceptional proficiency in their trade were often recruited by the state to meet the demands of the elites. They could either exercise operational autonomy or accept employment with the state. Indeed, many craftsmen alternated between working temporarily for the state authorities, and then revert to crafting commodities for sale in the market. Employment with the state administration was perceived as a matter of honour, a recognition of the skill and expertise of the artisan in his craft. While in state employment, craftsmen concentrated on the production of luxury goods and those of conspicuous consumption as per the directives of their employers and on returning to their shops, they fabricated commodities according to the market demand.

Mughal-centred historiography on medieval states has noticed the widespread existence of state workshops (karkhanas) geared towards the manufacture of commodities that would help maintain the splendour and pageantry of the royal court and household, and meet the needs of quality weapons for the army. Stephen Blake mentioned that karkhanas of the emperors, princes, and great Omrah 'were dominant and accounted for the lion's share of production. As a result, the productive process in Shahajahanabad was oriented towards the great households (and) not the marketplace, and the bulk of production did not reach the open market'.[61]

He noticed that a majority of urban artisans in Shahajahanabad 'seem to have worked with the materials and, in many cases, the equipment of some-one else'.[62] The neighbouring state of Jaipur also lists no less than twenty-four karkhanas in its Karkhanejat Records.

In the case of eighteenth-century Marwar, however, the meagre documentation on centralized in-house manufacturing units raises doubts about the universality of their presence and operation. The evidence suggests a combination of in-house production supplemented with goods produced on a contractual basis for the state and the royalty. The only karkhanas the records mention are the kilikhana (iron-cum-wood workshop), *palakikhana* (manufacturing unit for sedan-chairs), *khema karkhana* (tent workshop), *barudkhana* (gun-powder store), *tankshala* (mint), and the *kaparha ka kothar* (textile warehouse).[63] The last of these suggests storage rather than manufacturing or workshop functions.[64] Even for these units that find mention in the records, the documents are silent on the process of recruiting artisans, the terms of service offered to them, the organization of production within the karkhana, and the forms of supervision and bureaucratic management. Frequent references are available for the kilikhanas alone, and these seem dispersed all over the state instead of being confined to the capital of Jodhpur alone.[65] Hence, a belief in the universality of such karkhanas in every pre-modern state able to meet the entire needs of the royalty for luxury goods, seems ill placed. Such states, in fact, had their requirements met through a variety of arrangements, karkhana production being only one of them.

Occasionally, the state effectively bound the producers into a monopsonistic arrangement, and through the use of extra-economic coercion combined with concession, became the sole buyer. This was generally done for the production of commodities of high standard for which not enough skilled manpower was available, or when there was an urgency to meet a certain demand. In such situations an entire community was hired to manufacture for the Durbar alone, and was forbidden from selling in the open market. Since this arrangement could invite resistance, willing compliance from the artisans was sought through sanads that offered concessions and inducements.[66]

More often, Marwari elites tended to meet their needs for luxury goods by commissioning contracts to independent artisans. Whenever a specific need arose, renowned craftsmen who could perform the job were summoned for a fixed period and given wage employment on terms settled according to a contract.[67] Artisans of proven skill and accomplishment were specifically asked for by name, and the state acknowledged their expertise in a particular craft, whether in construction work at the fort, or in fabricating specific luxury commodities.[68] Most craftsmen in state employment were not kept on the rolls permanently, but only recruited for certain periods and

then disbanded when the job was completed. Such project-oriented contracts had the benefit of allowing the employer and the employee freedom
to enter into other relationships with suitable partners in the future.

The state administration appointed as mehatar a senior person from
every caste, who discharged the responsibilities of caste panch and was
considered respectable by his community, and asked him to work as a representative of his caste. The office was generally hereditary in nature, but
the sources do not offer explicit details on the process of recruitment, the requisite qualifications, and the precise functions of the mehatar as we have
for the *bashi* of contemporary Iran.[69] To maintain their superiority over their
caste-fellows, mehatars were allowed to realize certain cesses from biradari
members, on payment of a commission to the state, as per their resources.[70]
In case an artisan failed to pay his contribution to the caste mehatar, the
authorities deducted this amount from the wages due to the artisan. Or, in
some cases, the mehatar intercepted and claimed his share before the wages
reached the artisan. The latter is recorded in the case of Luhar Buddhe,
half of whose wages sent by the Durbar for the ironwork he had done for it
was intercepted and taken away by the Luhar Mehatar of Nagaur.[71]

Though the functions of mehatars are not clear, more often than not,
they appear to have collaborated with the state. They were expected to help
the government control and tax the artisans of their respective castes.[72] In
Marwar, their help was definitely solicited in procuring skilled manpower
for the performance of specific jobs. When the state wanted certain specific tasks accomplished, they sought the help of these caste mehatars to
utilize their nexus with the caste in locating the appropriate person, and
thereby providing the state assistance in recruiting labour.[73] In this sense,
mehatars represented the state's interest, and their frequent interactions and
close contacts with the authorities helped them wield considerable power
over their caste. The logic of the culture of hierarchy, inequality, and asymmetry made inevitable that the mehatar, conscious of his relatively influential
position and as leader of his caste, unwittingly assumed the role and
behaviour of a master rather than a representative of his community members.

That caste solidarity was therefore not without its own share of fissures
needs to be taken cognisance of. Luhar Ajmeri of village Rohal complained
at the kachedi when the Luhar Mehatar unnecessarily got a fine of Rs 41
imposed on him on grounds of non-obedience. Ajmeri explained that the
mehatar had arrived in the evening with summons for work at the Nagaur
kilikhana. Since the mehatar asked him to furnish the raw materials, Ajmeri
deferred his departure for the kilikhana till the next morning, and this delay
provoked the mehatar to complain against him.[74] As expected, the disciplinary propensities of the state coincided with those of the mehatar, and
the kachedi placed greater faith in the latter's version than on that of Ajmeri.

The fine on Ajmeri was merely reduced, but not withdrawn. In another case, Luhar Mehatar Ali of Luharpura in Nagaur usurped the land of Luhar Alabagas Karim when the latter migrated to Mewar during a famine. When Karim returned, Mehatar Ali refused to surrender the land to its owner, and provoked Alabagas to complain at the Nagaur chauntara.[75] Clearly, despite caste affiliation, a relationship of friction between mehatars and their caste members was common.

That a mehatar's functions were ambiguous and ill-defined is also obvious from evidence, though meagre, that points towards mehatars' support of their caste-fellows in the face of injustice meted out at the behest of the state. The solitary document to this effect suggests a regional caste head's mediation on behalf of his brethren. A *musraf* (petty official) of Sojhat denied a carpenter remuneration for work he had already completed. The khati, in frustration, approached Mehatar Sawant, who took the matter up with the Sojhat chauntara, and ensured justice for his caste-fellow.[76] Such documents indicate that while differences and tensions between mehatars and caste-fellows were pervasive, the two inhabited essentially the same cultural space.

Mehatars thus clearly possessed plural identities, and their worlds were internally fractured, generating a need for complex and cross-cutting liaisons both with the elites and caste-fellows. As accomplices of the dominant in the subjugation of their caste-fellows, their lives represented multifaceted encounters with several social spheres, their network with the state helping in lending a status by no means commensurate with their caste position, without at the same time completely dissolving their caste bonds.

Provision for the means of production was, on occasion made by the state, though just as often craftsmen were asked to come with their own tools and implements.[77] The responsibility for the provision of raw materials resided with the state, though often they delegated the artisan to aid the royal agents find those of appropriate quality. For instance, the state ordered Khati Paima to procure four man(forty kilos) of sandalwood for the Durbar, and directed the local musraf to pay for the same from the treasury.[78] The latter arrangement served to enlist a specialist's services for proper identification of the quality of raw material. In either case, the cost of the material was shouldered by the state, and the craftsmen were expected to offer their labour and skill and receive in return, 'suitable' wages. After the artisan's tenure at the royal project came to an end, he simply collected his dues and moved ahead to seek other avenues of income.

To an extent, therefore, not withstanding the rejection of these terms in the Indian context, one may label such 'wage labourers' as 'free'.[79] A cursory examination leads to the impression that artisanal labour relations in cities were primarily contractual, forged between formally equal parties, starkly contrasting those in the countryside. Historians who have explored these questions for south India have occasionally drawn such binary oppositions between rural and urban settings. But was this 'wage labouring artisanal class' actually free from extra-economic coercion at the instance of the state and its senior functionaries, responding merely to market forces, and in a position to exercise voluntary choice in matters of employment? Marx, and even Max Weber, recognized that wage labour was formally free only when the worker could decide himself the employer whom he would choose to sell his labour power to. Innumerable examples indicate that such 'freedoms' were not available to artisans in early modern India, whether, as cited earlier, it was Nai Paimle of village Behad and Luhar Ajmeri of village Rohal, or stone-workers of Makrana whose fight in the face of coercion to work for the state has been discussed in the next chapter.[80] There is ample evidence that artisanal labour relations in this period combined aspects of bondage with those of wage labour. Though sources do not indicate whipping and flogging, even as deterrents, they certainly cannot support these artisans' qualifying as the archetypical wage labourers. In fact, as Ravi Ahuja argues,

...a continuum of 'free' and 'unfree' forms of organizing labour had been created in rural society in a process of commercialization covering several centuries. This continuum extended to the...city although the specific pattern of labour relations in (these) commercial and administrative centres was of course considerably different...[81]

These relationships had to be atleast partially voluntary if mass desertion was not to jeopardize the state's interests. Artisanal concurrence seems to have been presumed rather than sought in most cases. Unlike villages where artisanal labour was sometimes paid in kind on the basis of patron-client relations, urban artisans were paid wages in cash. This was linked to the greater commercialization and monetization in cities. In most cases, in addition to their wages, they received different kinds of allowances in cash or kind (petia) as well. But even here, the growth of the wage system within the confines of feudal relations meant that the remuneration of such labour was strictly regimented by the state instead of market forces of demand and supply. Numerous instances of monthly wages paid to such artisans are quoted in contemporary documents, and petitions recorded in case there was a delay in having salary dues discharged from the state treasury. Rates differed not only for different types of work, but also for different grades of skill and competence.

Artisans who had acquired greater expertise were naturally entitled to a higher remuneration in consonance with the superior skill and talent they possessed. Specialization and internal differentiation among craft castes residing in urban centres led to the emergence of a nebulous sort of hierarchy among them. Though sources do not offer much evidence on wage statistics, it appears that the general range of wages stretched from Rs 2 to Rs 7per month. Among khatis and suthars those who catered to lesser offi-cials and commoners possessed just about adequate competence to fabricate building parts such as windows and doors, basic furniture like cots (charpoys), wooden utensils, agricultural tools, etc. Ordinary khatis received a monthly salary of Rs 3, while those considered skilled were employed at Rs 4 per month.[82] Luhars were usually paid Rs 2, and often complained about inadequate remuneration; but the more skilled among them com-manded higher rates. Among stone-workers, unskilled labour who engaged in rough hewing and shaping of stones were paid no more than Rs 2 per month, while the expert sculptors (the mistri and karigar silawats) com-manded much higher rates. The prefix of karigar attached to the name of any craftsperson indicated his higher level of accomplishment compared to others of his community.[83] In the case of chitaras, sources indicate that their wages could range from Rs 4 to Rs 7 per month.[84] Even so, if the maximum wages of artisans are any indicator, such incomes afforded mini-mal scope for savings that could lead to accumulation of capital.

Artisanal wages, thus, in real terms, could vary from bare subsistence to a reasonable degree of comfort. Unfortunately, even these wage statistics are not wholly reliable, and the statistics which are, have to be analysed in light of the facts that the demand for labour as well as wage rates were subject to dramatic seasonal shifts. Also relevant is the fact that since money wages were generally augmented by allowances in kind, and there is no an accu-rate idea of their quantum, real earnings of craftsmen are difficult to assess. Many were abysmally poor, unable to meet their most basic subsistence needs. Numerous documents reveal their impoverishment and the inad-equacy of resources they could accumulate even when in the state's employ.[85] Those slightly better off managed loans by mortgaging their house and tak-ing accommodation on rent to fulfil social obligations relating to life-cycle rituals. If unable to muster resources to repay the loan in time, they were rendered homeless.[86]

However, some artisans were comfortably off and sometimes turned the tables on those who traditionally oppressed them. Interestingly, in one instance, a sunar is recorded to have lent money to Mahajan Gangaram of Nagaur to buy some land.[87] The most impoverished of them all, the mochis also gave loans to cultivating castes, as in the case of Mochi Hame of Bilarha, who lent Siravi Panche forty rupees. Panche had to mortgage 2.5 bighas of his land with the mochi, and the latter laid claim to it when Panche was unable to have it released even after nine years, the stipulated period during which he was supposed to repay the loan.[88] In fact, in cities the superior castes did not always enjoy the control over lowly artisans as they did in villages; hence, many of them were as impoverished as the lower castes.[89] In villages, but even more in cities, varied levels of specialization and resultant economic differentiation were indeed true, but more pronounced was the fact of caste coherence borne out of a shared socio-ritual status and religio-behavioural culture.

POLITICS OF LEGITIMATION AND ARTISANS

Since legitimation and control was predicated as much upon political incorporation as on disciplining the subjects, state interactions with artisans reveal a relatively solicitous approach in the early years of Vijai Singh's reign. As discussed earlier, the decades of the 1750s, 60s, and early 70s were for the ruler a phase of consolidating a precarious regime facing external threats from the Marathas and internal challenges from collateral lineages. Therefore, harnessing the entire arsenal of symbols of kingship to fortify his fledgling authority, Vijai Singh and his administration felt constrained towards a generous reading of wajabi practices in relation to subordinate groups, especially skilled groups such as artisans.[90] Acute competition for labour was, after all, a pervasive concern in the pre-industrial period, rivalries among successor regimes between rival lineages, between the state and its landed potentates, and between the state and merchant capital resulting in each trying to ensnare productive forces to enhance the stability of their respective regimes. Both in content and the idiom in which they were expressed, the Rathor administration and judicial orders therefore projected vigorously their patriarchal discourse, and with few petitions complaining against tax appropriations, the state in this phase comes across as a cautious extractor of revenue and begar, and a relatively merciful employer. The rhetoric of 'legitimate traditions' underwrote its dealings with its subjects, lending the veneer of an unusually generous and even indulgent patron. Darzis of Merta, for instance, complained that the city kotwal had demanded of them a new tax in the shape of food (*kansa*) on certain ritual occasions. The tailors objected, and invoked past (non) practice to support their objections against this new demand. The state forbade the kotwal in view of lack of precedence.[91] Though alternate readings of the concept of wajabi, depending on context-specific considerations disallow the discernment of any neat patterns, it still remains possible to argue that a more pronounced paternalist hue coloured state policies during this period.

The new ruler and his subordinate lineages engaged in patronizing the skilled workforce in their respective territories in an attempt to gain legitimacy and reinforce their position. Rallying the largest possible range of elements behind them, they employed every possible device to mobilize support for their rule. Timely disbursement of wages was certainly on the agenda, as numerous records testify to the Durbar's concern in this regard.[92] Even when some silawats went away without completing the work they had been commissioned for, the Durbar summoned them to pay for whatever proportion of the work they had completed.[93] Complaints of salary dues, or fall in the amount paid as compared to the previous reign, were immediately redressed to ensure the observance of wajabi. When Khati Rehman employed at the kilikhana petitioned that his dues had mounted for almost a year, orders for immediate disbursement of his salary arrears were issued.[94]

In addition to wages, allowances in kind, mostly in the shape of grains, were a critical element in the strategy of legitimation.[95] Termed *petia* (from the generic word *pet* or stomach), this gift of grains (*anna*) represented the touchstone of royal character, and constituted an emotional and symbolic investment towards close bonds in a patron-client relationship. The embedded meaning in this gift of grains/food from the master carried immense significance in an environment of hunger and dearth, reinforcing the equation between the 'giver' and the 'recipient' as one of 'nurturer' and 'nurtured'. It was a structured and institutionalized form of *annadana*, and though its economic rationale of facilitating distribution of produce cannot be ignored, this ideological basis of symbolically buttressing the relationship between the employer and the employee needs as much reiteration. A record of 1768, for instance, states:

Mochi Mohammad used to receive grains and allowances (petiya) (from the government). After he died, (*faut huvo*), the grant of allowances is reported to have ceased. Mohammad's son Kamal has petitioned for these to be resumed. Shri Huzur has therefore ordered that the amount of grains and allowances that Mohammad was granted may now be given to his son Kamal. The same may be drawn on the Chauntara accounts.[96]

Rao, Shulman, and Subrahmanyam draw attention to the shift from land-based *dana* in earlier periods to this 'gift of grains' as representing a changing context where the gift is consumed soon after it is given. It leaves no residual that would support further claims on the donor or encourage a binding web of bilateral relations between the donor and the donee. Though their analysis has emerged from a different context of late sixteenth-century Nayaka period south India, it resonates with developments in Rajasthan, and requires further investigation.[97]

Wages and petia allowances were combined with liberal doles to attract artisans to participate in state service as and when required, and to encourage them to continue in service. Artisans in state employment often pleaded for material assistance during life-cycle rituals, and many had the government rescue them in moments of need. The state, for instance, ordered the Merta kachedi to grant Darzi Dolo twelve rupees for his marriage.[98] Again, the state ordered the Nagaur sayar to give hundred rupees for the marriage expenses of Darzi Asa's daughter and thirty for Khati Rupa's daughter.[99] Generosity was shown not only towards currently employed craftsmen but ex-employees as well. A khati was given re-employment with all the allowances, and an advance salary was extended so that he could meet the marriage expenses of his daughter comfortably.[100] Darzi Rupo, who had been a *gajdhar* (those carrying out measurements on land, etc.) with the state, continued to receive a small daily allowance even when he injured his eyes and could not serve the state any longer.[101] The ideology of wajabi therefore impregnated not just social exchanges, but also mediated economic transactions between the artisans and the elites.

Artisanal manipulation of the state's discourse of paternalism is interesting, suggesting that even without questioning domination, they were constantly pushing their agenda of promoting their well-being. Failure of a favourable response from the rulers would be labelled as non-conformity towards established ideals and, since these ideals were vague and ill-defined, the potential for a shrewd manipulation of them was always possible.

Even if rarely, attempts at enhancing revenue extractions were indeed sometimes made. But claims of customary prerogative, and refusal to accept new inflictions saw the state retract. The khatis of Sojhat, for example, were asked to deposit taxes for bringing timber from outside. They refused, claiming that they had always (*sadamad*) brought cartloads from the neighbouring regions, and never been told to pay hasil. Their *en masse* refusal and collective resistance led the Sojhat sayar to withdraw the demand.[102] Considerations of legitimacy also ensured that previous commitments regarding tax exemptions be honoured, as is evident from a parwana sent by the Jodhpur Durbar to the officers of Jalor sayar not to collect the *chothai* tax from the churigars since they had been exempted from this payment earlier.[103] Rangrez Ladu had his own shop in Jodhpur. This shop was taken into possession by the government when he had gone to Sindh. On his return, he urged the administration to return his shop, and in pursuance of 'appropriate conduct' (wajabi) the Jodhpur Durbar issued an order for necessary compliance.[104] Besides, as noted before, the rulers were extremely generous with grants of land as religious charities to artisans.[105] Patriarchal postures to validate their rule softened the stark material interest of the rulers, and led them to adopt a liberal reading of the discourse of wajabi in their struggle to contain the inherently tension-ridden relations between the dominant and the subordinate.

This is not to say that the Jodhpur state was not extractive or exploitative in these years, or that artisans did not suffer persecution, victimization, and violation of rights by the officialdom.[106] In addition to state officials even caste mehatars, appointed by the state to supervise their communities and report any misconduct or evasion of taxes, often tormented their caste-fellows. They enjoyed close access to the Durbar, and exploited their advantageous position to the detriment of their 'bretheren'. Financial strains due to Maratha demands of tribute began to reflect gradually in the Rathor government's policies towards the labouring groups. The administration began to demand extra labour from the artisans with as minimum a drain on their own resources as possible.[107] In a majority of the cases, however, 'politics of legitimation' appears to have left its imprint on elite-subordinate relations in the cities.

It is indeed difficult to draw sharp distinctions between the ideological and economic functions that were embedded in the state's patronal practices during this phase. Munificence was intertwined with the need to acquire merit, thereby power, and also maintain social harmony. It was, to that extent, an exercise in state-building. Patronage, however, was not denied to someone who did not work for the state in a strictly economic sense, or had never served in the administration. Those incapable of earning a livelihood to support themselves, be they the sick, the disabled such as the visually and mentally challenged, and others considered socially unfortunate like widows and orphans, received charity from the state.

In villages, as noticed earlier, inter-caste tensions were extremely pronounced and, given the highly stratified rural society, relative persistence of non-monetized exchanges, and lesser access to the judicial mechanisms of the state, subordinate subjects were more susceptible to any discretionary politics of the dominant. The Rathor state had not achieved vertical penetration to the extent where they could forge a direct relationship with the lower formations in the countryside. As a result, landed elites sometimes oppressed relatively, indiscriminately, confident that superior authority that might check their extortions was not within easy reach of the village-folk.

In urban centres, on the contrary, where the rulers and lineage chiefs had their establishments, the administration appears to have been watchful against transgression of customary norms by subordinate officials and merchant capital. It was able to enforce its interpretation of a 'legitimate conduct' more closely in Jodhpur and other core areas of the state. Higher levels of monetization and market transactions, characteristics of business in cities, implied relatively lesser discretionary power residing with the elites. The greater concentration of ohdadars in urban settlements indeed caused harassment and, faced with it, the artisans did not remain quiescent or servile, but promptly reported their problems to the state. The latter, acting as the umpire, often punished its own officials to restore wajabi. The interests and actions of different state agents often contradicted one another, and in the process generated incoherence within the state. In most cases an appeal to superior authorities brought justice, however incomplete and unsatisfactory, and the rulers punished their functionaries in pursuance of wajabi.

Petitions asking for the 'wrongs' to be set 'right' appear to have been expeditiously addressed, and while resentment against the ruling class is more than palpable, the picture that comes across is not one of adversaries locked in perpetual opposition. Artisanal complaints of transgressions confirm Chakrabarty's assessment that the 'worker's idea of fairness was related to his idea of what was customary (or *riwaz*)'.[108] Their protests in defence of customary rights always took place within an acceptance of domination since notions of what was fair and just was always with reference to the past. The subordinate echoed their perceptions of wajabi and 'legitimate conduct' in their petitions, and the authorities were, in some measure, the prisoners of this discourse of 'legitimate practice'. The poor, noted E.P. Thompson, imposed upon the administration some of the duties and functions of paternalism just as much as deference was in turn imposed upon them.[109] Petition after petition from artisans asked for justice, 'give and take' became fundamental to their exchange, and this 'moral economy' widely impinged upon early modern governance.[110]

CONCLUDING REMARKS

The significance of ritual display, the symbolic value of a royal lifestyle, and of conspicuous consumption were of vital importance in providing legitimacy of rule, and indigenous patronal practices often promoted demand and investment of resources in the economy. Elite needs, as much as those of their dependents, encouraged artisanal settlements in urban centres. Though city artisans suffered exploitation as much as their rural counterparts, the degree of it and the agents that inflicted it varied, the state officials perpetrating oppression in the case of the former, and hereditary landed castes in that of the latter. In fact it was 'feudal' rather than mercantile control that trammelled Marwari artisans and their productive talent. The officialdom, from hakims and jagirdars to kotwals, musrafs, karkuns, potedars, etc., often did not hesitate to have work done gratis, and coercive labour, sometimes without remuneration, was not unheard of even in cities. This oppression was made possible because, as yet, the pavan jat had not matured into a 'working class', and lacked a consistent self-definition, a clear consciousness of belonging to one 'class', or even clarity of objectives.

Multiple identities and agenda were common, whether in the case of relatively affluent craftsmen behaving as creditors to their poorer brethren, or caste mehatars behaving as masters of their community. The boundaries between the elites and the subordinate were blurred to that extent, an individual simultaneously enacting both positions. All power was not located in any singular elite—the multilayered social structure ensuring that sometimes the same individual was subaltern in one context and dominant in another. The collaborative role of caste mehatars exemplifies this in an institutionalized form, and there were numerous instances of individual artisans' working informally in tandem with the state's interest. It therefore needs to be recognized that a simplistic polarization between the elites and the subordinates is a falsehood. A romantic idealization of resistance on the part of artisans, therefore, would be unhistorical, and it must be acknowledged that caste solidarity itself was fragmented, and the roles and behaviours of individuals in society remained context-specific and localized, rather than fixed, immutable, and caste-determined.

Even so, the constitution of crafts into jati organizations, with their attendant collectivities and fraternal solidarities, did impart to them a bargaining strength and a political presence that impinged upon high politics every now and then. As pressure groups of sorts, they engaged in routine negotiations in defence of 'traditional' obligations and expectations, demanded concessions in situations of low labour availability, asserted their right to receive wages, and sought redressal against contravention of wajabi by the intermediary levels of authority.

Multiple levels of social contestation saw a variety of agents push their distinctive agenda in a dynamic, contentious society. The relationship between the state and its people was not simply one of hierarchical ordering, with the lower formations passively suffering the authoritative pronouncements of the upper orders. It was a dialectical one in which each was exercised by attempts to further its interests to win for itself whatever resources, power, and privileges it could, by aligning itself into a cohesive bloc against excessive depredations of the state. As such, the state was not just a central source of a one-way exercise of authority, but open to pressures and representations. Conscious of its fragile hold over the community organs, it engaged in considerable tight rope-walking as a 'manager' between competing interest groups in a co-operative conflictive game, thereby maintaining its precarious hold over different social groups. Multiple histories of a single time and place may thus diverge and converge in differently situated experiences.

The early decades of Vijai Singh's rule saw the ruling elites temper their basic and natural proclivity for exploitation with a relative show of benevolence towards the people. Grossly unequal as their mutual relations always were, acts of dominance were peppered with liberality, calculated acts of appeasement, and measured extortion. The Rathor discourse of legitimation ensured a paternalist approach towards its subjects, and the picture of unremitting subjection and oppression painted largely by European travellers finds only partial corroboration in local sources.

Artisanal responses to elite transgressions were constrained within the parameters of elite hegemony, yet watchful for points to exert pressure and seize advantage. The facade of deference, part of the 'counter theatre' of the poor, was maintained, but undercurrents of tension were just as surely present beneath the cover of patronage. From the third quarter of the eighteenth century, conditions began to alter, and pressures on the Rathor government gradually increased such that the patrimonial veneer began to wear off. Maratha demands multiplied, internal feuds proliferated, and the state got trapped in its own discourse. Did these changes lead to an alternate reading, a reinterpretation of wajabi? The following chapter focusses on this qualitatively transformed context in the last two decades of the eighteenth century, and examines how these changes and artisanal responses impacted on one another.

NOTES

1. This Nagaur ghazal, written by Yati Shri Manrup in AD1805, describes the convergence of a range of artisans to the city of Nagaur. See Vikram Singh Rathor (ed.) *Rajasthani Ghazal Sangrah, Parampara*, pp. 48–9. Other noteworthy ghazals in this collection includes those on the cities of Jodhpur, Maroth, Bikaner, Udaipur, etc. This genre of ghazal-writing as a distinct literary activity has already been discussed in Chapter 1, in the section on sources.

2. See Norman P. Ziegler, 'Action, Power, and Service in Rajasthani Culture: A Social History of the Rajputs of Middle Period Rajasthan', PhD dissertation, University of Chicago, 1973; and Edward S. Haynes, 'A Corinthian Capital on a Column of Ellora: The Transfer of the Concept of Feudalism to the Rajput States of North India', *Journal of Indian History*, vol. 57,1979, pp. 152–87. Also, his 'The Political System of Alwar: Patrimonialism and the Jagir System', paper presented at the 13th Wisconsin Conference on South Asia, cited in his article 'Patronage for the Arts and the Rise of the Alwar State' in Karine Schomer *et al.* (eds), *The Idea of Rajasthan*, vol. II, pp. 265–89.

3. The bhai-bandh-chakar had again given way to bhai-bandh, and to increased tensions in the relationship between the rulers and their nobility; see G.D. Sharma, *Rajput Polity: A Study of Politics and Administration of the State of Marwar, 1638–1749* (Delhi, 1977); also R.P. Vyas, *Role of Nobility in Marwar, 1800–1873* (New Delhi, 1969).

4. See Frances H. Taft, 'Rajas and Thakurs in Rajputana: The Case of Bikaner', in N.K. Singhi and Rajendra Joshi (eds), *Folk, Faith and Feudalism* (Jaipur, 1995), pp. 241–56, especially p. 241.

5. See Jagdish Singh Gahlot, *Marwar Rajya ka Itihas* (Jodhpur, 1991), p. 2. Some lands were granted to scholars and religious leaders for charitable purposes as well.

6. Chris Bayly, *Rulers, Townsmen and Bazaars*, p. 59.

7. For an elaboration of this view see Edward S. Haynes, 'Patronage for the Arts and the Rise of the Alwar State', in Karine Schomer *et al.* (eds), *The Idea of Rajasthan*, vol. II, pp. 265–89. Here he examines the changing patterns of patronage vis-à-vis arts in accordance with the requirements of the state and its ruling lineage during the reign of Pratap Singh Naruka.

8. Dirk H.A. Kolff, in N*aukar, Rajput and Sepoy: The Ethnohistory of the Military Labour Market in Hindustan, 1450–1850* (Cambridge, 1990), shows how values considered traditionally rajput were in fact recent acquisitions after they established close links with the Mughals.

9. R.P. Kangle trans. *The Kautilya Arthashastra*, vol. II, (Bombay, 1960) pp. 27–8; and *The Tuzuk-i-Jahangiri;* or *Memoirs of Jahangir*, translated by A. Rogers, H. Beveridge (ed.) , 2nd edn (Delhi, 1968) vol. I, pp. 7–8.

10. Gopal Narayan Bahura, *Literary Heritage of the Rulers of Amber and Jaipur* (Jaipur, 1976), pp. 77–8.

11. Sumit Guha has noticed similar interests of landed Maratha potentates in the Deccan region; see his essay 'Potentates, Traders and Peasants: Western India, c.1700–1870', in Burton Stein and Sanjay Subrahmanyam (eds), *Institutions and Economic Change in South Asia* (Delhi, 1996), pp. 71–84.

12. Richard G. Fox, 'Urban Settlements and Rajput Clans in Northern India', in R. Fox (ed.), *Urban India: Society, Space and Image* (Duke University, Durham, 1970), pp. 176–8.

13. See Frances H. Taft, 'Rajas and Thakurs in Rajputana', in Singhi and Joshi (eds), *Folk, Faith and Feudalism*, p. 241.

14. Emphasizing that pre-industrial urban centres were predominantly administrative capitals and provincial way stations, Gideon Sjoberg argues that nowhere did cities, even commercial ones, flourish without the direct or indirect support of a state system; see G. Sjoberg, *The Preindustrial City* (New York 1960), pp. 68 and 76. Richard G. Fox's views, as described in his article cited above, corroborate Sjoberg's conclusions for the cities in the Marwar region.

15. John Brush, in 'The Morphology of Indian Cities', in Roy Turner (ed.), *India's Urban Future* (Berkeley, 1960), p. 65, writes 'Many local rulers also fortified their towns. Soldiers and retainers, merchants and craftsmen crowded inside their walls for military protection and safety from robber bands. The palace, being the seat of power and wealth, became the focal point around which the people of highest status gathered for royal patronage as well as proximity to trade with all who came into and went out of the city'. When the boundary wall of the Sojhat fort was constructed, Nilgar Nura's house and shop, located close-by, came under it. He was therefore compensated by the Durbar, and given an alternate piece of land; see *JSPB* 34, 1834/1777, f. 164B.

16. Hamida Khatoon Naqvi too, in *Urban Centres and Industries in Upper India, 1556–1803* (Bombay, 1928), lists separate residential quarters such as the Loha Gali (blacksmiths' lane), Cheeni Tola (sugar-makers' ward), the Kinari Bazaar, Sabun Katra, and Nil Para at Agra. At Lahore she mentions Teli Wara, and Mochi Gate, and at Delhi the cobblers' quarters, Nil Katra, Kinari Bazaar, etc.

17. Caste-wise settlement was true for other regions as well; for instance, see J.S. Grewal's *In the By-Lanes of History* (Simla, 1975), pp. 3–32, for a similar demographic distribution in the town of Batala in eighteenth-century Punjab.

18. *JSPB* 14, 1831/1774, f. 41B, *JSPB* 1, 1821/1764, f. 36A, *JSPB*,18, 1834/ 1777, f. 26B. Similarly in Didwana one finds mention of the Pinjara muhalla, in

Merta a teli muhalla and a muhalla of Sirimali brahmins in Sojhat; see *JSPB* 14, 1831/1774, f. 139A, *JSPB* 21, 1835/1778, f. 87B, *JSPB* 22, 1836/1779, f. 121B respectively.

19. After confirming that Rangrez Bahadar of Merta intended to sell his land, the chauntara promptly ordered for its purchase by the state since it had a temple beside it. The sanad explicitly stated that the possession of land by a Muslim close to a temple seemed improper. Hence it instructed that Bhagat Girdhari Das may build the temple kitchen on it; *JSPB* 38, 1845/1788, f. 101A and *JSPB* 39, 1845/1788, f. 173B. In another document we have Mochi Sawantiye mention that he had a house in the Muslim muhalla of Sojhat which his brother sold off; *JSPB* 20, 1845/1778, f. 168A.Muslims generally preferred to settle near mosques and Hindus near temples; Mochi Ali tried to buy land near a mosque in Nagaur; *JSPB* 24, 1837/1780, f. 41B.

20. In Nagaur the darzi and the luhar colonies were separated by a platform between them. The khalisa land nearby had two vacant shops; hence one each was given to the luhar and the darzi communities after taking money to make pattas for them; see *JSPB* 53, 1836/1799, f. 42A.

21. *JSPB* 42, 1847/1790, f. 43B. In another case sunars Motiya and Navala of Merta had a dispute with their community over their share in the pool of taxes payable by the sunar community of the city; *JSPB* 54, 1857/1800, f. 260B.

22. For example, there were problems when fakirs built houses next to the julaha muhalla in Nagaur, and the administration was unable to distinguish between the two communities while making an assessment for house-tax. The julahas complained that they had been over-charged since the houses of fakirs had been enumerated along with their own; *JSPB* 16, 1833/1776, f. 43A.

23. *JSPB* 51, 1834/1797, f. 29A.

24. *JSPB* 22, 1836/1779, f. 166B. The instance of *khatiks* (butchers) of Sojhat, who threw stones on the Holi procession of the mochis of the city, also indicates the necessity of such separation; see *JSPB* 28, 1839/1782, f. 199A.

25. When the original house of Darzi Basta of Bilarha came under fort expansion, he was relocated in the julaha muhalla. Darzi Basta immediately expressed reservations about living in the colony of weavers, and requested an alternate location amongst his caste-fellows; see *JSPB* 9, 1826/1769, f. 164B.

26. The annoyance of the Sirimali brahmins of Sojhat to Pinjara Baghuda having his house constructed in their vicinity can be understood in this context. Despite the fact that the pinjara built his residence at the rear and not in front of the Sirimali colony, the brahmins were agitated and petitioned against his presence. The Sojhat kachedi directed its officers to survey the area properly and ascertain whether the location of the pinjara's house actually violated the norm. See *JSPB* 22, 1836/1779, f. 121B. In another case a pinjara from the pinjara muhalla of Didwana took umbrage when Kunjarha Chand, belonging to the caste of beggars, tried to build a hut in front of his house. The Didwana kachedi took Rs 40 from the pinjara and prepared documents ordering the Kunjara out of the colony for ever; see also *JSPB* 14, 1831/1774, f. 139A.

27. See David Hardiman's *Peasant Nationalists of Gujarat: Kheda District, 1917–34*, (Delhi, 1981) for an elaboration of how social and cultural solidarities of caste, more often treated as a divisive force in Indian society, in fact facilitated the mobilization of patidars in Gujarat and enabled them to conduct sustained agitiations against the colonial authorities.

28. Records show that chhipas and julahas of Nagaur often went together to the Tarkanji mosque, while the wives of julahas of Nagaur made pilgrimages to Balle Pir's fair together. Similarly the sunars of Jodhpur went together for holy dips at Sri Pokarji, while their women prayed together at Devi Ma Sati's shrine near Nadolai; see *JSPB* 49,1854/1797, f. 51B, *JSPB* 20, 1835/1778, f. 43A and *JSPB* 21, 1835/1778, f. 56B, respectively. Also see *JSPB* 5, 1823/1766, f. 26B and *JSPB* 34, 1843/1786, f. 233A.The objections raised by mahajans to the sunar women offering *chunri* at ma's idol could be effectively silenced due to the sunars acting in unison.

29. Chhipa Sultan of Pali preferred to get his dyeing tank made at Panchelai pond since all the other chhipas of the city had theirs at the same location; see *JSPB* 36, 1844/1787, f. 256A.

30. Chhipa Dole of Harsor stood guarantee on a loan Chhipa Bharundawar took from the mahajan for his son's engagement. In crucial times members of the brotherhood generally rendered help to their castefellows; *JSPB* 15, 1832/1775, f. 535.

31. Sunars Fata and Rupa of qasba Pali had a conflict over a platform between their houses; Rupa got the patta made in his favour though both had equal rights over it; *JSPB* 36, 1844/1787, f. 264A. Julaha Jume illegally occupied the house of Julaha Jalu of Bhorunda while the latter had gone *pardes*, and refused to return it even after the latter came back; *JSPB* 14, 1831/1774, f. 57A, *JSPB*, 5, 1823/1766, f. 149A. Sunar Motiram of Nagaur had a dispute with Sunar Chanda over the ownership of a shop behind their houses; *JSPB* 13, 1830/1773, f. 73A. Also see *JSPB* 20, 1835/1778, f. 39A. Luhars Nanag and Jivarhn of Merta had a property dispute even though there were five–six shops between theirs; *JSPB* 16, 1833/1776, f. 67A. Even in a family, Rangrez Hasan of Nagaur and his brother Ismail ended up having a conflict when the latter refused to partition their ancestral house; *JSPB* 20, 1835/1778, f. 40A. *JSPB* 26,1838/1781, f.146A. Also, *JSPB* 26, 1838/1781, f. 26B, and *JSPB* 54, 1857/1800, f. 262B, which records a conflict between a darzi and his nephew over a door in the darzi's house.

32. Hence there was tension when Julaha Pisu of Nagaur, armed with a patta that permitted him to build a door to his house on the western side, insisted on going ahead with the construction. His neighbours raised objections because a door implied a separate access to the dwelling, which would encroach on communal spaces; see *JSPB* 36, 1844/1787, f. 239B. Several documents indicate conflicts over the issue of building separate doors to individual houses.

33. *JSPB* 20, 1835/1778, f. 170A. In the absence of a patta, it became difficult to ascertain whether the claims of Luhar Hasan of Nagaur over his maternal grandfather's shop were valid or not; *JSPB* 14, 1831/1774, f. 8A.

34. *JSPB* 12, 1830/1773, f. 186A. In another case Mochi Ramle's shop in Merta was usurped by a *kandoi* (sweetmeat grocer) when the mochi was away for 25 years. The patta had expired, and there were problems in determining ownership; *JSPB* 22, 1836/1779, f. 82A.

35. When without conducting an enquiry they reprimanded him, he took his petition to the Jaitaran kachedi which ordered that the matter may be resolved by enquiring from the entire neighbourhood how the coloured water the chhipas' had used for dyeing had been disposed earlier; *JSPB* 20, 1835/1778, f. 189A.

36. For instance, Pali had a large population of dyers and printers; hence its dyers objected when Rangrez Badhukamal of Nagaur migrated there. They refused to allow him to dye with kasumba (an expensive dye) and then insisted that he must leave since there was no shop recorded in his name in the city. See *JSPB* 15, 1832/1775, f. 250A. The state, however, was inclined to encourage the settlement of craftsmen within their environs, and considerations such as those of excessive competition were of no consequence to them.

37. The concept is extremely flexible, and has been attributed a variety of meanings; I am using it in the context of the interpretation that Pierre Bourdieu gave it; see his 'Forms of Capital' J.C. Richards (ed.) *Handbook of the Theory and Research for the Sociology of Education* (New York, 1983).

38. Stephen P. Blake, *Shahajahanabad*, p. 105.

39. This was particularly true for well-to-do sunars: Sunar Ruple petitioned for permission to build a second storey to his house when his neighbour Sunar Fatiya constructed a house in front of Ruple's dwelling. See *JSPB* 36, 1844/1787, f. 258B.

40. For a detailed discussion on the distinctions between these two categories see Gervase Rosser, 'Crafts, Guilds and the Negotiation of work in the Medieval Town', in *Past and Present*, no. 154, pp. 3–31.

41. See Francois Bernier, *Travels in the Mogul Empire*, trans. on the basis of Irving Brock's version and annotated by Archibald Constable, 2nd edn revised by Vincent A. Smith, (Delhi, first published 1934, reprinted 1989), p. 256.

42. Ibid., p. 254.

43. Luhar Ajmeri of village Rohal was specially solicited for the Nagaur state wood-workshop and the khatis of village Panchale were summoned to Khinwasar since they were supposed to be experts at making camel seats (*palarhn*). Twenty skilled khatis of Bilarha were also specially sent for work at the kilikhana, with the promise of a higher-than-usual wage of Rs 4 each. See *JSPB* 23, 1836/1779, f. 35B, *JSPB* 41, 1846/1789, f. 441B, *JSPB* 43, 1848/1791, f. 41A, *JSPB* 23, 1836/1779, f. 201B, and *JSPB* 23, 1836/1779, f. 184B, respectively.

44. Jadunath Sarkar wrote way back in the 1920s that the Europeans followed the 'universal medieval system of giving dadani or advances to individual workers and looking after them in their cottages and securing deliveries of the goods at the proper time by means of an army of agents'; see Sarkar's 'Industries of

Mughal India: Seventeenth Century', *Modern Review*, (June 1922): 676. Alexander I. Tchitcherov then fleshed this argument out into a classic model in his work *India: Changing Economic Structure in the Sixteenth-Eighteenth Centuries: Outline History of Crafts and Trade*, 3rd rev. edn (New Delhi, 1998), pp. 173–76. Tchicherov asserted that buying-up was combined with money advances directly to the producers, rendering artisans in complete subjection to merchants; see pp. 167–79. Tapan Raychaudhuri, though attempting to present a relatively moderate picture, still wrote that the producer was under mercantile control even if the process of production remained considerably independent; see Raychaudhuri and Irfan Habib (eds), *Cambridge Economic History of India*, vol. I, pp. 281–2. Also see T. Raychaudhuri, *Jan Company in Coromandel*, 1605–1690: *A Study in the Interrelations of European Commerce and Traditional Economics*, (Gravenhage, 1962), p. 147; Om Prakash, *The Dutch East India Company and the Economy of Bengal, 1630–1720*, (Princeton, 1985); Joseph Brennig, 'Textile Producers and Production in Late Seventeenth Century Coromandel', *IESHR*, vol. 23, no. 4, (1986), pp. 333–56. Also see S. Arasaratnam, 'Weavers, Merchants, and the Company: The Handloom Industry in South-eastern India, 1750–1790', *IESHR*, vol. 17, no. 3, 1980, pp. 257–78, and the recently published study by Prasannan Parthsarathi titled *The Transition to a Colonial Economy: Weavers, Merchants and Kings in South India, 1720–1800* (Cambridge, 2001).

45. Rangrez Misari of Jaitaran reported that since part of his family resided in Arhandpur, he had transported expensive dyes like kasumbo and guli between Jaitaran and Arhandpur for years without having to pay transit tax (*rahdari*); see *JSPB* 36, 1843/1787, f. 199B.

46. This was true of Julaha Musa of Nagaur, (*JSPB* 9, 1826/1769, f. 58B), Julaha Nura of Merta, (*JSPB* 24, 1837/1780, f. 80B and *JSPB* 26, 1838/1781, f. 61B), Chhipa Bharundawar of Merta (*JSPB* 15, 1832/1775, f. 535), and many others are documented to have borrowed money to fund their own or their children's weddings.

47. For the manner in which Bengal artisans were sought to be attached to the English East India Company by its merchants, see N.K. Sinha, *Economic History of Bengal: From Plassey to the Permanent Settlement* (Calcutta, 1961–3), vol. 2, pp. 186–7. For a more general picture on this issue see Alexander I. Tchitcherov, *India: Changing Changing Economic Structure in the Sixteenth-Eighteenth Centuries: Outline History of Crafts and Trade*, 3rd rev. edn (New Delhi, 1998), p. 175.

48. *JSPB* 48, 1853/1796, f. 7A.

49. Dadani or the 'putting-out system' and subjugation of artisans to merchant capital was noticed by practically all historians writing on artisan-merchant relations. In making these generalizations, however, modern historiography failed to notice that all these are regions which saw a sudden rise in demand due to the arrival of European traders in a big way. The same developments would obviously not hold true for areas which did not have a parallel experience.

50. English merchant Peter Mundy's description of Bihar of early seventeenth century, Streynsham Master's observations on Bengal, Ch. Fawcett's on

Golkunda, and T. Raychaudhuri's on the Coromandel Coast, have all found evidence of dadani and mercantile control over artisans. See *The Travels of Peter Mundy in Europe and Asia, 1608–67,* vol. 2 (London, 1914), p.145; S. Master, *The Diaries of Streynsham Master, 1675–80,* and *Other Contemporary Papers Relating Thereto* (London, 1912), vol. 1, p. 400, vol. 2, pp. 14–15; Ch. Fawcett,*The English Factories in India,* New series (Oxford, 1936–54) vol. 2, pp. 160–1.

51. W. Foster (ed.) *The English Factories in India: A Calendar of Documents in the India Office,* British Museum and Public Record Office, (1618–69), (Oxford,1906–27), vols 1–13, see specially vol. I, AD 1618–21, pp. 194–5, vol. II, AD 1622–3, p. 98, and vol. III, AD1624–9, pp. 92 and 207.

52. *JSPB* 15, 1832/1775, f. 251B.

53. For instance, Rangrez Araf and sultan of Pali plied their trade entirely independently, and even arranged for expensive dyes like opium-based kasumba on their own. Nor does the case of Chhipa Bhikha, who contributed towards the purchase of a dyeing tank on the assumption that five printers would use it jointly, mention any mercantile interference. Bhikha was prevented from dyeing his fabrics at the jointly owned tank by Raju, one of the co-sharers of the tank. Rangrez Fazal mortgaged his indigo to borrow money from his caste-fellow Sirichand instead of approaching a merchant for help. See *JSPB* 38, 1845/1788, f. 208B; *JSPB* 36, 1844/1787, f. 39B; and *JSPB* 36, 1844/1787, f. 181A. respectively.

54. The last chapter on rural artisans had developed this point at length. Forms of extra-economic mercantile oppression found in villages were true for the urban areas as well.

55. Mahajans of Sojhat, for instance, objected to grooms of the dyer community riding horses during marriage processions, while those of Pali created obstacles on similar grounds during marriages among the sunar community; see *JSPB* 5, 1823/1766, f. 162A, and *JSPB* 3, 1822/1765, f. 396 respectively.

56. Mahajan Tilo of Sojhat borrowed Chhipa Dole's large *karhaw (*vessel for dyeing fabrics) and refused to return it when the former wanted it back; see *JSBP* 22, 1836/1779, f. 116A.

57. The details regarding the structure of Marwari markets have already been discussed in Chapter 2; hence I have not repeated them here.

58. *JSPB* 5, 1823/1766, f. 81B.

59. *JSPB* 18, 1834/1777, f. 25B.

60. *JSPB* 24, 1837/1780, f. 208B.

61. Ibid.Also see Ishwar Prakash, 'Organisation of Industrial Production in Urban Centres in India During the Seventeenth Century with Special Reference to Textiles', in B.N. Ganguly (ed.), *Reading in Economic History* (New Delhi, 1964), p. 48.

62. See Stephen P. Blake, *Shahjahanabad: The Sovereign City in Mughal India, 1639–1739* (Cambridge, 1991), p. 105.

63. Skilled khatis, paid wages at the rate of Rs 4 per month, were summoned to work at the kilikhana; see *JSPB* 23,1836/1779, f. 130A and ibid., 184B. Similarly, a

darzi, working as a 'Gajdhar' in the khema karkhana (tent workshop) was ordered to be given monthly instead of daily wages; see *JSPB* 25, 1838/178, f. 38.

64. *Jodhpur Bahiyat, Kala Basta,* no. 19, 1832/1775 mentions the *Kaparha ka Kothar*
of Nagaur. The evidence does not suggest that weaving, dyeing or printing operations were carried out in the same. In all likelihood, quality textiles were
procured by the Rathor rulers through a variety of arrangements.

65. The sources mention their presence at Nagaur, Pali, Sojhat, and Bilarha:
see *JSPB* 23,1836/1779, f. 35B mentions the Nagaur kilikhana. Also see *JSPB*
5, 1823/1766, f. 34B; *JSPB*,30, 1841/1784, f. 19B; *JSPB*, f. 224B, *JSPB*,41, 1846/
1789, f. 441B; *JSPB*, 23, 1836/1779, f. 184B.

66. For example, in AD 1766 the julahas and banawats of Nagaur were instructed
to weave for the Durbar alone and a concession of Rs 300 from the peshkash
tax was offered to the community to obtain their compliance. See *JSPB* 5, 1823/
1766, f. 81B.

67. Khati Reham Ali and some luhars were summoned to build a staircase, and
were allowed the freedom to use their own tools or those of the state for the
purpose; see *JSPB* 1, 1821/1764, f. 17B.

68. Luhars were also similarly commissioned, a document recording that a
raika (camel-messenger) was sent from Nagaur to bring a skilled luhar to make
wires; see *JSPB* 9, 1826/1769, f. 267B.

69. The appointing authority for mehatars is not clear in Marwari documents
but Stephen P. Blake mentions that in Shahjahanabad the city magistrate or
kotwal was expected to carry out this function; see Blake, *Shahjahanabad*, p.
113. Persian sources offer interesting details on the appointment procedure, the
duties and obligations, and the relationship of *bashis* with the court; proficiency
and skill in the trade, piety and good morals, and administrative acumen are
mentioned as the criteria for the selection to the position of bashi. See Mehdi
Keyvani, *Artisans and Guild Life in the Later Safavid Period: Contributions to the
Social-economic History of Persia,* (Berlin, 1982), pp. 79–80.

70. G.S.L. Devra, 'The Internal Expansion of Society and Formation of Medieval Polity', Presidential Address, Medieval India Section, 59th Session, *Proceedings of
Indian History Congress,* Patiala, 1998, pp. 17–18. Also, *JSPB* 49, 1854/1797, f.
74A

71. *JSPB*, 19, 1834/1777, f. 54A.

72. Blake, *Shahjahanabad*, p. 113.

73. *JSPB* 34, 1843/1786, f. 31A; and *JSPB* 23, 1836/1779, f. 35B, respectively.

74. *JSPB* 23, 1836/1779, f. 35B.

75. *JSPB* 6, 1824/1767, f. 46B.

76. *JSPB* 23, 1836/1779, f. 130A.

77. *JSPB* 43, 1848/1791, f. 41A; *JSPB* 45, 1850/1793, f. 85B; *JSPB* 34, 1843/
1786, f. 31A.

78. *JSPB* 19, 1834/1777, f. 163A.

79. See Gyan Prakash, *Bonded Histories: Genealogies of Labour Servitude in Colonial India* (Cambridge, 1990), pp. 1–12, 218–25 for a discussion on the subject.

80. *JSPB* 20, 1778, f. 183A; *JSPB* 23, 1836/1779, f. 35B; *JSPB* 54, 1800, f. 268B.

81. Ravi Ahuja, 'Labour Relations in an Early Colonial Context: Madras, c.1750–1800', *Modern Asian Studies*, vol. 36, no. 4, 2002, p. 806.

82. *JSPB* 32, 1842/1785, f. 165B; *JSPB* 23, 1836/1779, f. 184B; *JSPB* 41,1846/1789, f. 441B. But the truly talented one could even command upto Rs 7 per month, and that too from the Jodhpur state; see *JSPB* 54, 1857/1800, f. 7B.

83. State records refer to some artisans as karigar luhar or karigar silawat who were commissioned for special tasks; see *JSPB* 9, 1826/1769, f. 267B; *JSPB* 13, 1830/1773, f. 75A.

84. *JSPB* 23, 1836/1779, f. 104B; *JSPB* 44, 1849/1792, f. 19A.

85. Darzi Mane of Nagaur was unable to afford a funeral feast for his mother; harassed by his community for the same, he petitioned to the administration. The authorities granted him permission to organize the funeral feast as soon as he could muster Rs 5 This concession was made on grounds of his being indigent; *JSPB* 18, 1834/1777, f. 28B.

86. Julaha Musa of Nagaur suffered a similar fate, constantly threatened by his mahajan that he either repay the loan money immediately or hand over possession of his house to the mahajan; *JSPB* 9, 1826/1769, f. 58B. The state came to the rescue of Darzi Jetha of Jalor when Darzi Amichand put a lock on Jetha's house to force him to repay the loan his forefathers had taken. On the orders of the authorities, the lock was removed and Jetha asked to pay as per his resources; *JSPB* 5, 1823/1766, f. 142A; *JSPB* 11, 1829/1772, f. 175A.

87. *JSPB* 31,1841/1784, f. 25 B. Sunar Udayaram of Sojhat also found himself in a position to lend money to Nihalchand. In fact moneylending was one of the areas, apart from dealing in precious metals, that sunars handled along with the mahajans; see *JSPB* 31, 1841/1784, f. 72A.

88. *JSPB*, 22, 1836/1779, f. 166B.

89. Pandit Arhandidas of Sojhat was reduced to mortgaging his house with a darzi for a loan of forty-one rupees; *JSPB* 16, 1833/1776, f. 97B.

90. That concerns of statecraft commonly deployed the rhetoric of 'good governance' in other countries and periods as well is evident, for instance, from Steve Hindall's essay 'Dearth, Fasting and Alms: The Campaign for General Hospitality in Late Elizabethan England', *Past and Present*, no. 172, (Aug. 2001) pp. 44–86. Hindall notices that a second consecutive year of harvest failure saw Queen Elizabeth's 'great and princely care' take initiatives in public relations for the 'good and welfare' of her subjects. Ringing with the rhetoric of social justice, her orders eloquently articulate the 'prerogative paternalism' of the Elizabethan state.

91. *JSPB* 19, 1834/1777, f. 82A.

92. Khati Dale's complaint when he did not receive full payment for the two chariots he had crafted for Shri Huzur; *JSPB* 15, 1832/1775, f. 706.

93. *JSPB* 17, 1833/1776, f. 52A. Other silawats of Sojhat who made a well for Shri Paswan were also paid without delay by the administration; *JSPB* 17, 1776, f. 140B.

94. *JSPB* 5, 1823/1766, f. 34B.

95. On related issues, see Gloria Goodwin Raheja, *The Poison in the Gift: Religious Prestation and the Dominant Caste in a North Indian Village* (Chicago, 1988).

96. *JSPB* 8, 1825/1768, f. 58A. Kamal's petition also demonstrates that underlying the placid plea he made, he was conscious of the impropriety, and thought it judicious to draw the state's attention. His petition is an expression of a knowledge not dominated by power.

97. See Velcheru Narayana Rao, David Shulman, and Sanjay Subrahmanyam, *Symbols of Substance: Court and State in Nayaka Period Tamil Nadu* (Delhi, 1992), especially pp. 57–73.

98. *JSPB* 9, 1826/1769, f. 82A.

99. *JSPB* 13, 1830/1773, f. 64B; ibid., f. 1A.

100. *JSPB* 11, 1828/1771, f. 14B. The administration arranged for a temporary house and a karhaw when the wedding of a churigar's daughter was due; see *JSPB* 14, 1831/1774, f. 227A.

101. *JSPB* 9, 1826/1769, f. 70A.

102. *JSPB* 6, 1824/1767, f. 88B.

103. *JSPB* 14, 1831/1774, f. 135.

104. *JSPB* folio dated *Posh Sudi 13*, (number is not clear).

105. The khatis and luhars of the city were appeased with land grants for building temples specifically for their use; *JSPB* 1, 1821/1764, f. 36A; ibid., 1821/1764, f. 25B.

106. *JSPB* 14, 1831/1774, f. 114B.

107. Fifteen khatis to serve at the Sojhat kilikhana, for a luhar to serve at the Nagaur kilikhana, and numerous orders issued to silawats to report for work. See *JSPB* 12, 1829/1772, f. 57A; *JSPB* 13, 1830/1773, ff.12B, 75A.

108. See Chakrabarty, *Rethinking Working Class History*, p. 179.

109. See E.P. Thompson's *Customs in Common* (London, 1991) p. 71 for an elaboration of this mutuality. Also see Rudrangshu Mukherjee's *Awadh in Revolt,1857–58: A Study of Popular Resistance* (Delhi, 1984).

110. Concessions conceded in the past were seized upon by the lower orders as a 'right' which they fought to protect. The Jodhpur Durbar, for instance, sent an order (*parwana*) to the officers of the Jalor customs' treasury (*Sayar*) not to collect the chothai tax from the churigars on their insistence that the previous administration had exempted them from this payment; see *JSPB* 14, 1831/1774, f. 135. Rangrez Misari had not been asked to pay rahdari while transporting his dye materials (kasumba, gul, and nil) from village Arhandpur to Jaitaran earlier. On his complaint about the sayar's new demands, the latter was told to follow past practice and not charge indiscriminately; see *JSPB* 52, 1855/1798, ff. 52B.

6

Escalation in Stresses and Artisanal Responses

Though the Rathor state claimed and consumed a large share of the craft and agrarian produce, Vijai Singh was vigilant about ensuring subsistence security to his people, and this helped him gain legitimacy in popular perception. Tensions in their quotidian interactions were normal, but the early decades of Vijai Singh's administration saw the system work relatively smoothly as a consequence of a liberal interpretation of wajabi. Readings of 'legitimate' conduct that were favourable to the subjects, generous in the 'give' as much as the 'take', withstood stresses in their mutual exchanges. The last two decades of the eighteenth century, however, saw a gradual transformation in the political context, the state increasingly riven by internal tensions and contradictions. Was the Rathor regime still able to adhere to its old standards of moral order that had been part of the Rathor discourse in the previous three decades? Did the regime remoralize relations of control and consent, and was it compelled to redefine its principles of wajabi? Subordinate responses in retaliation to new pressures are integral to this exploration. Did the artisans, in view of enhanced stresses and a sense of injustice, evolve alternate strategies and take to confrontationist outbursts for tackling the new pressures? This chapter tries to assess why artisans still continued to accept the key values of the social order in which they lived, and why rebellion did not become the characteristic expression of artisanal politics.

ENHANCED STRESSES IN CHANGING TIMES

Military encounters with the Marathas had been a persistent feature of Rathor history throughout the eighteenth century. The reduction of Jodhpur as a tributary vassal of the Marathas in mid-eighteenth century began to cause a prolonged drain on the resources of Jodhpur, especially from 1756. Maratha demands for regular tribute instalments stressed the Rathor treasury, and their use of *pindaris*—units of unpaid Afghan cavalry—who fought in battle, looted, and generally lived off the spoils of war, adversely affected cultivation and revenue collections.[1] As seen in Chapters 4 and 5, these pressures had sometimes led to the imposition of new taxes by Vijai Singh's administration. The ruler's need for legitimacy and acceptance had, however, constrained him from getting too extractive or oppressive. In due course, Rathor occupation of Godwad, an immensely fertile province in 1770, and thereafter Sambhar, a highly coveted region that generated huge revenues from its salt lakes, brought relative relief to Vijai Singh's treasury and, gradually, he was able to stabilize and consolidate his position.

In the early 1770s the tribute instalments remained unpaid, and Mahad ji Scindia threatened devastation of Jodhpur's territories. He also demanded a share in the revenues of Godwad. Vijai Singh complied, and ensured a regular payment of tribute from 1772 to 1782.[2] Yet, to deter the maharaja from repeating non-compliance and delayed payments of tribute, Scindia's agent, Ambaji Ingle, encroached and devastated Rathor lands, ravaged the crops, and destroyed food and fodder in November 1776. The outflow in the form of tributes and pillage was a tremendous drain on the Rathor resources in the 1780s, and prompted Vijai Singh to launch, on the one hand, a grand plan to form an anti-Maratha confederacy with the Kachhwahas—the ruling clan of Jaipur—and on the other, enhance revenue demands from the subjects to meet the resource crunch.

The Rathor plan to throw the Marathas out of Rajputana necessitated improved military strength and, for this, Vijai Singh created a standing army enlisting mercenaries from Sind, Rohilkhand, and Umarkot. In the battle at Tunga in July 1787, he was successful in rendering a blow to the Scindias, but despite his best efforts, Mahad ji Scindia was able to regroup his forces and defeat the Rathors at Patan in 1790. The Marathas then went on to occupy Sambhar, Parbatsar, and Rupnagar. In the battle of Merta that soon followed in September 1790, the Rathors were again routed.[3] The news of their defeat demoralized the people of Jodhpur who, fearing a Maratha advance into Jodhpur, began to flee the city. Vijai Singh was compelled to negotiate a humiliating peace that included the payment of sixty lacs of rupees as war indemnity and tribute and the handing over of Sambhar, in addition to the usual tribute.[4]

The Rathor defeat and rout in the battles of Patan and Merta caused an irreparable damage to their prestige, political influence, military strength, and economic position. It resulted in a tremendous drain of men and money, and intensified instability by causing the sharpening of factional politics, civil strife, and revolts from the nobility. The closing years of Vijai Singh's reign from 1791–3 saw increased court intrigues and political murders over the issue of succession. Eventually, the kingdom got divided between two branches of the Rathor family, with Bhim Singh's occupation of the gaddi at Jodhpur and Man Singh's escape to Jalor, where he declared himself king. The kingdom thus remained fragmented for a decade till 1803, when Man Singh captured Jodhpur and reunited the chieftaincy into a single state.

During these years, the military technology and organization of the Rathors, as also most other patrimonial regimes, had undergone considerable transformation by moving towards the inclusion of firearms and artillery formations in their defence structures. Kinsmen and subordinate local chiefs/prebends could not be allowed access to such expensive and powerful arms. As a result, Vijai Singh recruited a standing army and invested in heavy artillery, especially during the 1780s.[5] The manufacture and import of firearms, the import of large numbers of war-horses, and the cash salary payable to the soldiery adept in the use of new weapons, were strategic requirements that entailed a critical dependence on a considerably larger supply of cash. Financial stresses in the Rathor patrimonial regime thus sharpened, with funds diverted toward tribute payment precisely when they were required for investments towards consolidating armed strength.

Simultaneously, increased economic impoverishment of the chieftaincy is visible both due to factionalism at the court, and because rival contenders for power often engaged in economic warfare to erode the financial base of an opponent.[6] The maharaja tried to meet the financial crisis by levying new taxes and raising the rates of existing ones; but in a situation of Maratha depredations, revolts of recalcitrant jagirdars, political turbulence, and economic dislocation, the people of Marwar resented the maharaja's attempts at tightening the purse strings. Widespread unrest and internal disaffection persisted under Maharaja Man Singh, and eventually invited, in 1818, British intervention in the internal affairs of Marwar.[7] The long-cherished autonomy of this powerful rajput state thus suffered another onslaught, and first having been subordinate to the Mughals and then the Marathas, Jodhpur finally came under British disciplining from the early nineteenth century.

Clearly, during the last quarter of the eighteenth century, the stability of Marwar had suffered a major setback. It is significant that in the early phase, prior to 1776; there are a negligible number of records that plead for tax exemptions or complaint against new impositions. Petitions from artisans address a range of issues including those pleading for relief from begar, but few complained against tax burdens. This was because the state administration, in its efforts to gain legitimacy, had ensured that their taxes remain within the bounds of wajib, and the subjects did not find reason for resentment. More often then not, past traditions were followed in this respect, and non-transgression of customary demands had helped Vijai Singh consolidate his position in the early decades of his rule.

Maratha demands of tribute and the Rathors' military needs led the rulers to pass down their burdens after the mid-1770s by not only raising the levels of taxation, but even levying new impositions in the latter decades. The state got increasingly preoccupied with marshalling adequate resources while at the same time remaining keen to control the realm. Unilateral shifts in its reading of wajabi, unacceptable to the artisan communities, become apparent. Customs and excise collections were intensified, and every conceivable commodity and activity was taxed to enhance resources, generating stresses that caused widespread distress. From here ensued repeated and recurrent conflicts and confrontations between the rulers and the ruled. In a document of 1797, the darzis of Didwana lamented their plight due to the levy of new taxes, and in no uncertain terms, identified the Marathas—Dakhaniyas, that is, those from the *dakhin* (south) in local parlance, as the source of all their misery. They remembered fondly the 'good old' days when the tax burden was smaller and prompt payment of wages marked Rathor rule. They complained that since the Maratha forays, they were continuously pressurized with new levies and often did not receive their wages when they worked for the Durbar. They asked the state how the poor were expected to manage with heavy taxes and irregular wages. *Irhn tare garib log majuri kirhn tare nibhe?*[8] A sense of injustice naturally invited resistance, and as had been the traditional practice, artisans petitioned the state against enhanced taxation and other transgressions in customary usage. As I discuss below, the change in the relationship was qualitative rather than transformational. Is then the picture painted by Bernier, Pelsaert, and Manucci, and reinforced by subsequent Orientalist writings that alleged the Indian polity as miserably unjust towards the downtrodden, accurate at least for the latter decades of the century?[9]

SHIFTING READINGS OF WAJABI AND INCREASED RANKLINGS BETWEEN THE RAJA AND RUNK

The cumulative impact of drain due to huge tribute instalments, and pillaging every time these were evaded or delayed, worsened the Jodhpur state's financial condition, and led the Rathors to squeeze the people harder. More confident after consolidating his hold over territories of Jodhpur, Vijai Singh now enhanced rates of the old taxes, imposed additional cesses, and sometimes even forced exactions.[10] In the Nagaur pargana for instance, villagers were ordered to contribute to the Deorhi dastoor, a nazrana submitted by village chaudharis to supplement the salaries of the hakim, mutsaddis, potedar, piyad bakshi, navisanda, chopdar, and pharas posted at the palace (*deorhi*) of the maharaja.[11] *Habub* was another new tax imposed for royal maintenance.[12] So was *rekh bab*, while the incidence of hukumnanma, an old tax, was doubled. Pressed for resources, the administrative authorities in different parganas, qasbas, and urban centres tried to raise revenues by taxing local communities residing there. The julahas of Parbatsar had been granted exemption from paying *sal bab* in 1731. After forty-eight years, in 1779, this tax was again demanded, prompting the local weavers to protest through petitions.[13]

The year 1789 seems to have been particularly difficult for the administration, forcing it to throw caution to the winds in making all round fresh demands, time and again. Pinjar bab, for instance, had never been imposed on the cotton-carders of the villages of Gorwad in Desuri, but was demanded in 1789.[14] The dyers of Pali had traditionally been dyeing with kasumba, an expensive dyeing material, without paying any special tax for it. In 1788 khatris and chhipas got permission to use kasumba after depositing a tax, and the state now decided to use this opportunity to earn extra revenue by taxing the rangrez community's consumption of kasumba as well. A sanad of 1789 therefore ordered that all the dyers residing in Pali must deposit a rupee with the Durbar on using a man of kasumba.[15] In the same year, a *ghar ginti* or house tax was imposed on the kumhars of village Dhakarhi in Sojhat, while those of qasba Maroth too complained that a sanad of vs 1822 had exempted them from paying *dand kholarhi* tax but this was again being demanded of them in 1789.[16] Yet again, we have the printers, basket-makers, goldsmiths, cobblers, and other leather-workers from Pali complain that *chaudhar bab* (a maintenance tax for the village headman) had earlier been levied at the rate of rupees three per household from those living in old Pali alone, but now in 1789, craftsmen residing in the market area of the new city had also been asked to deposit the same.[17] As is obvious from the cases cited above, there is no dearth of evidence that bears testimony to enhanced exaction of revenues and popular resentment against it. Towards the end of the century the additive impact of raised taxes had tormented people such that those with meagre resources were left completely indigent. Julahas Imambagas and Isakh of Nagaur, for instance, cited their reduction to complete impoverishment (*nandari*) as the cause for their petition for tax concessions.[18]

As problems in revenue collection mounted, the parganas were ordered in 1793 to raise seventy thousand rupees in the form of nazrana to the ruler to buy off the Maratha freebooters. The burden of additional levies borne both by the common people and the jagirdars thus increased further.[19] The administration now took desperate measures to raise quick money. These included farming away its revenues in a big way, known in contemporary literature as *muqata* or ijara. Land revenue of specific areas, the production of salt at the *namak ke daribe*, and the earnings from sayar or customs collections at important urban centres were often given away in ijara.[20] In 1792

Vijai Singh had already farmed out the revenues of parganas Merta, Didwana, and Nawa to the Marathas to fulfil their financial demands and then, again in 1808, some villages had to be given in ijara to the Marathas.[21] Such revenue farming practices sometimes added to the miseries of the already hard-pressed subject population.

The impact of the resource crunch percolated down and the officialdom too was gradually afflicted by it. They, in turn, tried to cut their losses by demanding labour in begar in excess of the 'legitimate' amounts. Artisans willingly accepted their 'normal' obligations for begar but in situations of extra burden that transgressed the limits sanctioned by custom, they questioned the 'excessive' extortions and protested.[22] The kumhars of Sojhat were traditionally obliged to supply roof-tiles (khaprali) to the Sojhat chauntara. After they had fulfilled their traditional obligation in the first instance, another demand for additional 6,000 roof-tiles was made. The kumhars refused to supply these since compliance would make them prone to continual pressures from the administration.[23] For transporting their goods, state officials sometimes seized in begar the cattle owned by subordinate castes. Karkun Nimba, for instance took away the bullocks of Kumhar Rodo of Desuri to go to Devali to offer prayers. Accompanying the official were four brahmins, and the entire party travelled without a break. During the return journey, they loaded iron on the kumhar's bullock cart, and this excessive strain on the bullocks cost the kumhar the death of one of them.[24]

Foucault argued that, in feudal times control over body and thereby labour, was more useful than control over property due to ill-defined property rights.[25] Perhaps, therefore, even though traditionally artisans had been entitled to take exemption from performing begar services once in a position to pay taxes and preferring to do so forced begar extortions now became common even if they paid their full share of taxes. This is evident from the petition of Kumhar Sukhe of Merta that, despite having resumed tax payment, sacks of clay continued to be taken away from him in begar by the local administration.[26] Another petition by Khati Jayaram of Jalor records that he was recruited in the army to craft goods for them, but, instead of receiving wages, he was ordered to work in begar despite his insistence that he was willing to pay his complete share of taxes.[27]

Elite confiscation of the belongings of the subordinate also became more common. For instance, a mochi complained when even after two months, functionaries of the Nagaur chauntara had not returned the twelve cots they had taken away in begar from him.[28] Khatis at Phalodi were also forced to perform begar by the local ohdadars[29] and the general atmosphere was vitiated by such frequent attempts to maximize extractions. Such recurrent incidents were aggravating the conflictual relationship between the state and the subordinate, and ranklings between the rulers and the ruled were now the rule of the day.

State officials and local administrative personnel suffered the burden of raised revenues just as much as the people. Constantly depleting resources saw them grab every opportunity to exploit those below them. The village authorities of Jalpedara in Phalodi, for instance, confiscated rupees twenty-one from the shed of Khati Kesara residing in their village, claiming that they suspected the khati of having procured the money through dishonest means. Kesara was able to recover his money only after he established that he had inherited the money from his father.[30] Chhipa Hafiz reported in 1779 that though in the past he had procured raw materials for printing from Nagaur without being taxed, the customs official (sayar daroga) was now demanding taxes. On Hafiz's refusal to pay the same, the daroga took away his yarns to punish him.[31]

Earlier the state had, on its own, provided support to the handicapped. This was evident in the case of Darzi Rupo, cited earlier.[32] But by the later decades, conditions had worsened, and a document of 1791 from the Merta kachedi informs that:

A petition is recorded here that the blind, lame, insane, childless men and sup-portless/abandoned women in the pargana used to receive grains (subsistence) earlier. Since the *danga* (disruption of law and order due to Maratha raids) (they) have not been receiving this aid. There are only about thirty-forty persons in need of such support, and if each could be given *dhai pav* (three-quarters of a kilo) of grains, they would be able to manage. The Durbar has ordered grains for rupees one each to be given per person. [33]

Innumerable instances exhibit attempts at non-payment or reduced quantum of wages being paid until the aggrieved artisan complained to higher authorities. In one instance Kotwal Isa of Desuri got a skilled khati to work on the boundary wall of the fortress. But when the khati complained that it was already two days and he had not been paid any daily allowances, let alone wages, the kotwal arrested him for his impudence.[34] The exploitative attitude of the officials also comes across from the case of the ohdadars who did not pay Rangrez Dansa of Bilarha for the dyeing work he had done for them till he pleaded at the kotwali.[35] And again, it is more than apparent in the petition of the khatis working at the Pali kilikhana. They lamented that the hakim's servant Sirimali Abhayram bullied them into doing his personal work at half the official rate of wages. The khatis finally complained at the kachedi when they found to their dismay that Abhayram was not forthcoming with paying the wages even at the reduced rate.[36]

The list of artisans' woes in this period did not end here—also common were disturbing trends like long salary dues outstanding against the state. Like its lesser officials, the state too repeatedly prevaricated payments till pressurized to honour its obligations. Khati Lala's father died without receiving his due wages, and on petitioning, Lala was able to secure no more than a year's arrears to enable him to perform his father's last rites.[37] The remaining amount presumably lapsed. Another record cites the petition of Khati Mohammad Ali, pleading for the wage arrears of his father. He, too, was able to get his father's salary dues for two years to perform the latter's funerary rituals.[38] Nagaur kilikhana bought iron tools from luhars Alabagas and Ahmad, but failed to pay them Rs 67 for the job. Only when Alabagas petitioned that in view of his daughter's wedding he desperately needed the money did the state pay him the due amount. Ahmad also received his wages only when he pressed upon the state the urgency of his requirement.[39] Interesting in these documents is that the petitioners, rather than assert their right over wages, chose to cite compelling needs when pleading for wage arrears. This servile approach calculated to appeal to the paternalistic postures of the maharaja was as effective as that which chose to challenge state power. In a period of financial stress, it successfully manipulated the unusually miserly mood of the rulers. With wages falling into default for extremely long periods, sometimes stretching over several years, it is hard to imagine how these poor men and their families survived in the intervening periods!

Due to the delays and default in payment of wages, artisans began to adopt dilatory tactics and evade state summons for labour till the state pleaded and, failing that, coerced artisans to obey their calls. Lapses on the part of the state made artisans reluctant to work for them and the state had to repeatedly pressurize them. In 1777, all construction workers (silawats, miners, beldars, and chejaras) of Merta, Bilarha, Sojhat, Didwana, Parbatsar, and Makrana, that is, north-eastern Marwar, were summoned for kamthana (building) work through repeated summons and reassurances about wage payment. In the face of their continuing reluctance to report for work, the artisans were finally threatened.[40] Record after record emphasized the date by when khatis, silawats, luhars, etc., had to report for duty.[41] Assurances that they would receive their wages without delay were also given to induce them to come.[42] If resistance on the part of artisans persisted, the state used coercive ploys to impress them into service by over-awing them. Towards the close of the century, documents report an incident where the state administration, in its desperation, had sent messengers on horse-back to scare the silawats of Makrana into immediately reporting for work. Disinclined to obey but fearful about the consequences of defiance, the stone-workers flew from their village with their families. The resultant chaos saw one of them lose an infant and another's wife had a miscarriage.[43] The fact that they chose to defy and desert their homesteads even when flight was not prudent at this juncture when their families were not in a position to travel, indicates the level of oppression they apprehended and wished to avoid even at great personal cost. The impressments of these workers, technically 'free wage workers' but in fact subjected to coercion in large measure, appears close to conditions faced by contemporary European soldiers and sailors who had often not chosen their employer (the state) freely though they were compensated with wages. Akin to conscription, these militarized labour recruitments were, a rare occurrence in pre-colonial times but appear to have become pervasive during British rule.[44]

Evasion of state work resulted in the administration getting unnecessarily suspicious of the artisans. Minimal delay on the part of artisans in reporting for work was now misconstrued as deliberate defiance, and the Durbar took serious note of it. There is evidence, though limited, of the infliction of atrocities and physical abuse also during the latter decades. The kotwal of Merta beat Sunar Simbhu with wooden rods for paying one taka less while lifting mud dug out of the Pudasar tank.[45] A guard (*sipai*) of the Pali kachedi went to summon Darzi Paima. On finding that the darzi was unable to leave immediately, the sipai fought with Paima and broke his instruments.[46] In another case, the son of the hakim of Pali beat a churigar and imprisoned him on the pretext of a complaint against the latter pending in the kachedi.[47]

In such circumstances, craftsmen often preferred self-employment and independence to remain out of the clutches of the state and its officials. 'Volunteering' for work on royal projects, once perceived as a matter of honour and recognition of their expertise at their craft, seems to have given way to procrastination in the last quarter of the eighteenth century. Higher levels of tax demands, failure of the state to pay regular and adequate wages, their demand of begar in excess of custom, and relatively intense forms of artisanal abuse intensified the friction and disharmony in the relationship between the artisans and the state. Clearly, difficult material realities faced by the Rathor rulers during the latter decades of the century translated into intensified pressures and oppression of those below.

Equally stark and important to note, however, is that while the state did enjoy a degree of freedom to act in response to its material environment, its character appears to have been critically dependent on historically constructed ideological and political traditions. Despite increased exploitation, numerous examples of patronage stand out in the records even in the context of the latter decades. A clear pattern fails to emerge, and these confounding shades of evidence demand a closer look. Contrary to the simplistic image conjured by Bernier and other European travellers regarding the completely suppressed state of labour in India, documents in fact suggest that even during the last years of the eighteenth century when the state was confronted with a politico-economic crisis of a considerably larger magnitude, exploitation and patronage remained the two ends of the continuum of exchanges between the two. Artisans continued to petition against different forms of oppression, claimed their right over wages, felt entitled to demand the same in case of delay and, most importantly, the state invariably accommodated their legitimate demands. The following record suggests the persistence of wajabi and the state's efforts to follow the legitimate course:

Luhar Nathu had a house in Luharpura on the outskirts of the Nagaur city. All houses broke down during the Maratha riots (*Dakhaniya dange*). His house too perished. Though others received compensation, he has not. Shri Huzur has ordered that a plot of six by five *gaz* be measured from the khalisa land for Nathu, and a patta made in his favour for the same.[48]

Rangrez Isakh of Balotra had enjoyed exemption from *bhachh birad* tax. He therefore resisted its appropriation and threatened relocation. His petition found a favourable response with the authorities ordering that the convention in this matter should continue to be honoured.[49] The julahas of Parbatsar informed the kachedi that they had not paid sal bab since vs 1731, when a sanad of that year had exempted them from this levy. They complained that this tax was again being demanded of them. The state did not insist on its demand and ordered in their favour.[50]

Artisans continued to not only extract favourable judgements in pursuance of tradition and past practice; in fact they even demanded and accomplished relief and concessions from taxation on claims of indigence and deprivation. In bad years, for instance, the collection of taxes fell substantially and, even if reluctantly, remissions were granted for whole parganas hit by drought, famine, floods, or pests. Rioting in the wake of Maratha raids, and internal feuds that got a spurt, affected production adversely and became an occasion for demanding concessions. Lakhara Sade Khan of Merta had to pay rekh or tribute to the state for the two villages he held; but since they were low-yielding and had produced a particularly poor harvest in 1785, he sought and was granted exemption.[51] Similarly, the julahas claimed they were impoverished due to riots caused by Lodha Sahmal and petitioned for tax concessions; the state ruled in their favour and reduced the revenue demand.[52]

Also interesting is that in these same years of financial distress when the state was pursuing a policy of extracting increased revenues from its population, it also tried to provide collective public good. Arrangement for loans for the purchase of seeds were made by the Durbar, and it ordered the local village authorities to reduce or withdraw their revenue pressures to endurable levels.[53] The remission depended either on the will of the ruler or in proportion to the loss suffered. Traders were prohibited from exporting foodgrains during famines so that the local people's requirements could be adequately met.[54] The hakims were ordered by the state to distribute cooked food everyday, especially amongst people unable to work—the blind, insane, handicapped, and orphans.[55]

The rulers continued to be anxious that the numbers of the producing groups residing in their kingdom should not dwindle. They therefore tried to restrain oppressive officials and local authorities whose exactions threatened to cause emigration. Though deteriorating central control was not always successful in curbing the exploitative proclivities of lower state functionaries, they certainly appear to be struggling to prevent *gair-wajib* conduct on the part of their ohdadars. A record cites that the hakim, karkun, potdar, and other mutsaddis of Desuri demanded beth begar unduly from Khati Dipe Lale. Since the latter had never been asked to perform begar services earlier, he complained at the kachedi. The officials were brought to book when the Durbar ordered that it did not encourage any new extraction of begar unless sanctioned by tradition. As a punitive measure, the officials were directed to pay double the labour charges for harassing the khatis.[56] Julahas and luhars of Nagaur had complained against the levy of new taxes on them by the local authorities. The state ordered that they must continue to enjoy the tax exemptions that previous sanads had granted them.[57] Rangrez Misari had not been asked to pay rahdari for transporting his dye materials (kasumba, gul, and nil) from village Arhandpur to Jaitaran earlier. On his complaint about the sayar's new demands, the latter received a reprimand for its indiscreet move.[58]

In many instances, thus, propriety and a sense of obligation continued to characterize state interaction with employees, particularly those with whom there existed long-standing relationships with their ancestors who had been in state service. The practice of certain norms over generations had a certain hold over the psyche of the dominant, and could not be thrown to the winds very easily. Habituated to certain forms of generosity vis-à-vis old and trusted employees and clients, the state felt constrained in the observance of conventional standards of wajabi. The following record is a case in point:

Songar (leather-worker) Udayraj of Jaitaran petitioned that three years ago he had served with the Merta army, and before that in the forces of Sambhar. He was present in the battles of Tunga and Khirima and served well. His marriage is due, hence Shri Huzur has ordered that rupees twenty five be presented to him from the Jaitaran Kachedi.[59]

In the last two decades of the century, the major dilemma of Rathor statecraft seems to have been to raise enough revenue to maintain the court, but the quantum of enhancement should not be so much as to drive the labouring population out of Rathor territories. Pressures did stress the inherently tense relations between the dominant and the dependant in this period, but the Rathors ensured that there occurred minimal fissures or ruptures in their mutual relations. The value of artisans to their rulers remained, and the state's efforts to appease and pacify their skilled workforce and contain the growing hostilities continued. The state conceded to pressures from the lower ranks as a result of calculated self-interest. Since none but those from the same occupational group could perform a certain trade, every settlement needed providers of basic services, and the state remained anxious about these concerns. Even if an individual from another profession was prepared to perform the task, the caste system forbade him from working on anything other than what ritual laws had prescribed, and also ensured that he never got the opportunity to develop the requisite skills. Hence, when the houses of many luhars of Luharpura in Nagaur collapsed due to the Maratha raids, the state was keen to ensure that they did not abandon the city.[60] The Durbar therefore ordered for the luhars to be given substitute houses on the crownlands in the city.[61] Not only this, the local administration was specially directed to charge the same low rate of taxation from them that they were paying while living in Luharpura, a low-class colony located on the fringes of the city. Though the rates of taxation were higher in the heart of the city, these luhars were protected against higher revenues as a special favour. In addition, the state took care to ensure that they settled together in the same muhalla since they preferred to live close to their caste-fellows. As discussed in Chapter 5, contiguous residence in caste muhallas had ensured considerable solidarity among different craft communities. In view of collective pressures exerted by a caste, the Jodhpur state continued to accommodate and relent before subaltern pressures even in difficult times.

Studies on other regions reveal similar patterns; Demirci's study of the seventeenth-century Ottoman administration, for example, noticed parallel concerns determining state conduct.[62] He analyses that the central dilemma of the Ottoman central government was to ensure that its people are not harmed, while it also did not lose any revenue. And records from the province of Kayseri led Demirci to conclude that when wrongs were committed, people fought back with determination and fearlessness, no matter what social level, ethnic group, or faith they came from.

The early modern Indian social structure thus appears to be an amalgam of contradictory and contestatory processes, puzzling rather than one that displayed easily discernible patterns. What is clear, though, is that the relations between the state and the people continued to be implicated in a perception of wajabi, though the gap between the state's reading and subaltern interpretation had widened considerably towards the close of the century. The fiscal adversities faced by the state, the heightened tensions at the court, and the relatively slack central control of the Rathors over the officials in this phase caused, in one way or another, increased infliction of atrocities, and occasional physical abuse of the latter. How did the artisans respond to such elite subjections? It has been already observed that in the face of transgressions, they were neither voiceless nor quiescent. Greater stresses faced by the state in the last two decades of the century had manifested in frequent discordant notes in their exchanges. Did these stresses cause the subordinate groups to turn rebellious and start a chain of revolts? The next section seeks to examine some assumptions about the absence of revolutionary potential among the lower formations in early modern India through the response of Marwari artisans to increased elite exploitation.

RETHINKING REVOLUTIONARY RESPONSES OF THE SUBORDINATE

In the context of this entanglement between the subordinate and the superordinate, it appears that though artisans were neither passive and docile, nor compliant, they did not become a 'revolutionary' force either. In the face of hierarchical stratification and resultant oppression, they struggled to maintain control over their lives and labour, though their negotiations for space were by and large peaceful and non-confrontationist. Even when the 'moral economy' showed signs of increasing impairment, artisanal responses usually remained constrained within the cultural confines of elite hegemony, and continued to display a preference for modes of protest other than open rebellion. Whether bold and aggressive, as in the case of Nai Paimle of village Behad and Kumhar Kusaliye of Bilarha qasba, or servile, as exemplified by artisans who did not dare demand their long-standing wage dues and used the pretext of pressing need to get what was rightfully theirs, artisans displayed a high degree of ingenuity in fashioning their responses to elite subjections according to their individual abilities and specific contexts.[63] Overt conflicts were limited to the interstices of routine interaction, and only moments or conjunctures representing complete frustration and loss of hope saw artisanal solidarity manifest in occasional instances of open insubordination, collective defiance, and organized resistance.

Such resistance was prompted by a consciousness constituted neither by one body of thought, one single set of values that helped interpret social reality, or one corpus of internally consistent guidelines for behaviour. Since the culture of subordinate groups was a complex, hybrid, inchoate amalgam of contradictory strands, vacillating in its emphasis of different aspects in different contexts, the simplistic dichotomy between hegemony and autonomy does not seem adequately revelatory. The hegemony of the dominant culture influenced the lower castes enough to generate in them a belief in hierarchy, but cannot be seen as totalizing; it did not prevent the formulation of alternative values and strands of thought. As noted by Ruud, culture appeared 'as many-voiced, open to other alternative impulses, to the restructuring of symbolic elements that derive from praxis'[64]. Artisans' lowly status caused a subjugated mentality, but the fact that craftsmen were aware of the acute demand for their skills, and for the resultant criticality of their presence to the region of Jodhpur, equally generated within them the impulse to resist exploitation. They leveraged upon this in their dealings with the state and the elites. Their non-substitutable skills lent them a degree of confidence far in excess of their low-caste status, and they appear to have demonstrated a minimum of hesitation in reporting matters to the authorities. The blending of crafts with agriculture, the enhancement of their indispensability through the establishment of monopolies, the forging of patron-client bonds, and in certain contexts, acceptance of landlords as masters or the state as employers, represent a range of survival strategies artisans continually invented and reinvented to bolster their position. Petitions, acts of evasion, or change of patrons through migration in the face of transgressions of traditionally sanctioned norms represent defensive rather than subversive acts, at least as far as artisanal objectives are concerned. If these defensive efforts to protect their interests failed, evidence indicates that more defiant and offensive forms of confrontation superseded deferential efforts on the part of supposedly 'weak, vulnerable, and timid' craftsmen. The latter, as I discuss later, sits uncomfortably with Chakrabarty's essentialization of indigenous culture as one that allowed little agency to the subaltern for resistance, the lower castes totally committed and unquestioning towards its dictates.[65] Given the potential for contestation within the concept of hegemony, the totalizing nature of its grip needs to be nuanced.

Although couched in the most deferential language, and to that extent contributing towards the maintenance of the ideology of dominance, petitions at the same time represent resistance, for they articulated artisanal plight and applied relentless pressure upon the state to abide by its high moral claims to legitimate authority. This path of resistance may have been docile, conciliatory, and non-provocative, but the objective was most definitely one of self-preservation, if not promotion. Read as such, artisanal petitions symbolize 'contradictory consciousness' that recent re-readings of Gramsci have noticed in his writings.[66] Co-existing with hegemonic cultural values, they represent a reconciliation between the desire of the subordinate to conform without compromising their own interests. As already noticed, petitions constituted the most commonly used instrument that artisans employed to continually appeal to the paternalistic basis that their relationship with the state had traditionally rested on. This show of deferential submission was a consequence of the fact that, rather than trying to uproot the system altogether, most of them concentrated on 'work-ing it...to their minimum disadvantage'.[67] Both because of their relatively low position in the socio-political hierarchy, as also because they did not care to effect fundamental changes in an order that they accepted as defi-nitely legitimate if not divinely ordained, craft groups in most cases tried to salvage their position within, rather than without the system.

Admittedly, petitions hardly represent a concerted effort to radically transform the extant order. If we go by the narrow and limited juxtaposi-tion between resistance and non-resistance used by Christine White, Mullins or Genovese, then petitioners were certainly not leaders of any 'real resis-tance'.[68] Indeed, Marwari artisans in this period display no ambition or confidence to change the extant power equations. They merely struggled to retrieve, protect, and maintain a minimal standard of subsistence. Some craft communities such as mochis did negotiate with the state for an en-hancement in their social status, demanding closer access to temple deities in shrines where they worshipped.[69] In the hope of upward social mobility, ivory bangle-makers too are recorded to have given up the custom of nata since it was a marker and a significant symbol of low-caste culture. Artisanal negotiations in a majority of the cases, however, asserted entitlement norms that were invariably inspired from the past. I cannot avoid the conclusion that, rather than reaching out for something new, Marwari craftsmen were more often struggling to retrieve 'what was', to protect and maintain a stan-dard of subsistence and a level of livelihood that they accepted as appropriate in an earlier period. Even this, though, may be qualified, because while ostensibly past practice was perceived as wajib and honoured, there was no unitary past. Historical junctures invariably displayed multiple realities and behaviours, and what then becomes relevant is the particular precedent that the petitioner chose to highlight. It were these spaces around the notion of wajabi that the subordinate harnessed to formulate, negotiate, and renego-tiate 'legitimate conduct'.[70]

I would argue that the seemingly innocuous acts of routine protests, presumably without any political significance, were not, trivial; they in fact influenced the contours of the early modern Indian State. The pressures from artisanal groups circumscribed the options available to the state, lo-cating it within parameters of notional wajabi conduct. By mitigating claims made on them, artisanal efforts went a long way in preventing further im-poverishment of subordinate groups. Although the boundaries of wajabi were constantly tested, it is important to consider the cumulative effects of such resistance and its ability to thwart the plans of those with more power and status.[71] Especially in the case of Marwar, it is evident that in the latter decades of the eighteenth century, when the Rathor regime was faced with acute financial stress, its propensity to raise taxes from the artisanate (and other groups) would have seen no limits had constant claims to wajabi not undercut their extreme exercise of power. In view of the gains that their resistance often brought, James Scott's model, now accepted by Adas too, that identifies as resistance all those acts that the subordinate commit to press their claims vis-à-vis superordinate classes, makes far greater sense.[72]

Such non-confrontationist resistance helped subordinate groups like craft castes make their political presence felt and assert their rights of 'citizenship'. Though the degrees of political participation may have varied, artisans were thus a part of the political process, and thereby the power structure itself. They may not have had a blueprint for change, but that does not take away from the essentially political character of their activity; it merely defines the quality of that politics by specifying its limitations. Indeed, unlike the nobles and landed magnates, they could not elevate a leader to rulership, but their support could constitute that critical signifier of a righteous king. The absence of such popular approval and support heightened the fragility of a regime. The inability of the Jodhpur king to function as pater familias would legitimate flight, withholding of dues, outright rebellion, and eventually cause fiscal breakdown. The role of subordinate groups was therefore critical to state formation.

In any event, the state entertained their petitions despite their belonging to the lower strata, and artisans, thereby enjoyed considerable access to the authorities and were reasonably empowered through the dispute-resolution mechanism. The frequency of artisanal petitions, even against state functionaries, suggests that they hoped for a judicious response from the authorities, even if they often suffered disappointments. It was a matter of deliberate policy, a result of the state's keenness to provide to the people a legal channel of communication and protest, and take remedial action before it boiled over in the shape of revolts against the state. By entertaining petitions as instruments of people's protest, the Rathors were in fact trying to contain their struggle within the hegemonic superstructure. As discussed in Chapter 2, record-maintenance of the petitions was new and unique to the eighteenth century, and seemed to have been the result of a calculated move on the part of the state. The judicial system, devised by the state for the control and discipline of the subjects, was in a sense appropriated by the latter for its own purposes. At the same time, by providing for petitioning, the rulers had created a space that helped them tackle subaltern pressures effectively, shaping their resistance in accordance with principles of justice defined and espoused by them in the first instance. The dominant thus simultaneously enabled and disabled resistance, and the subalterns turned the Rathor courts into sites of contestation.

Also important to note is that the multi-centricity of power and competition for controlling labour saw different layers of authority struggling to check one another. Subordinate working castes found oppression from certain quarters countered by patronage or protection from another engaged in counterweighing the deviations of 'errant' officials. Abuse from provincial level officials such as hakims, or local level functionaries like jagirdars, bhomias, chaudharies, and karkuns was checked by central government authorities, and those of the city officials often stood rectified through the intervention of the Durbar. Developments in the latter decades of the eighteenth century therefore, on the one hand, aggravated the tensions and multiplied the sufferings of the impoverished, and on the other, made them more resolute to struggle against the odds lined up against them. They constantly assessed their strengths as against their weaknesses, and protested elite endeavours towards further oppressing them.

Apart from petitions, a range of other strategies continued to be employed for self-defence. Emigrations had always been common, but seem to have increased during the last two decades of the century. Harassed by undue taxes, artisans often relocated to other more conducive locales. Shifting residence in accordance with availability of patronage was, as noticed earlier, the favoured strategy of artisanal resistance during this period. Khati Hire of village Angota, for instance, had migrated due to jat harassment in his village. The chaudhari of the village persuaded him to return, with the promise that he would give the khati land to cultivate, and the assurance that he would not be forced to do woodwork for the jats. Instead, three other khatis were induced by the chaudhari to settle in the village to carry out woodwork for the village-folk.[73] The services of Hire were clearly indispensable to the chaudhari, and he felt constrained to extend various concessions to the estranged khati, to monopolize control over Hire's skilled labour. Considerable spatial mobility and the constant flow of artisans between different settlements find frequent mention in the records. Their documentation appears to be the result of official anxiety about losing precious manpower resources, often amounting to an obsession that produced fairly abundant recordings of such artisanal relocations.[74] Such migrations or flight of artisans, sometimes even en masse, was a safe way of escaping the extractions of an exploitative local elite.[75] The kumhars of village Dhakarhi in Sojhat, for instance, migrated to other villages when *ghar ginti* or house tax was imposed on them. The administration had never collected it from them earlier, hence, despite the risks of dislocation, they preferred to protest rather than lie quiescent.[76]

While rural artisans thus played up their non-availability causing patrons tremendous difficulties in finding replacements, those residing in urban centres leveraged their numerical strength. Close interactions in caste muhallas, shared customary norms and the resultant sense of biradari consciousness helped artisans come together and make common cause with each other. Caste solidarity gradually emerged and fellow-members from the community often offered collective resistance against harassment and

repression. Tight caste organizations pursuing distinct trades saw them petition the state jointly for their fading paternalist favours for their wages,
and for protection from unjust demands of the ohdadars. Residing together
gave them opportunities to discuss their plight, exchange ideas whereby
they might collectively resist what they perceived as unjust, and work out
strategies for the amelioration of their condition. Collective forms of action were, therefore, the result of cohesion and fraternal loyalties. Issues of
concern to an entire artisanal community saw caste members get together
to proffer appeals as a single group. For instance, the kumhars of Desuri
got together and came to the kachedi to complain that a petty official had
misbehaved with the daughter-in-law of their caste-fellow, Kumhar Rupla.
They claimed that the official Ahmad Khan had insulted another woman
on an earlier occasion, and the hakim had desisted from taking Ahmad to
task. Despite the hakim's best efforts to save the official, the combined pressure exerted by the kumhar community ultimately led to the dismissal of
Ahmad Khan.[77] Through joint efforts, artisans continually attempted to mitigate shared anxieties and deprivations. The use of caste solidarity for
pressurising the authorities manifested in yet another form, as when a caste-
fellow approached his caste Mehatar for resolving his grievance.

Clearly, the perception that caste was the elemental factor that chained
or shackled Indian subordinate groups and made them fatalistic and com-
placent, needs rethinking.[78] In the context of disciplinary systems that
exploited the artisanate, it is somewhat paradoxical to imagine caste as a
politically enabling, empowering structure. But within a stratified society,
the disciplinary structures of the biradari among the urban artisanal caste
groups provided a coherence that enabled negotiation and resistance against
socially dominant political agencies. As much as the bedrock of social organization, caste in state-subordinate interactions emerges as the basis of
political organization, since it was caste consciousness, caste negotiations,
and eventually caste action that often won important victories for the subaltern. Mobilization along caste enabled social and political organization
against oppression.

In most cases, however, collective protest also remained non-confrontationist. It is sometimes contended that a docile, often deferential posture of
the subordinate while resisting breaches in state/elite conduct, was the result of their 'consciousness' of the social imbalance of power, and the
resultant calculation that confrontationist outbursts would be dangerous if
not suicidal. It was calculated to ensure self-preservation, and was the result of a fear of backlash and retribution.[79] In that sense, rather than the
hold of elite culture, it was calculated pragmatism that led the subordinate
to avoid defiance. It could be argued, rather, that in quotidian interactions,
people do not start by being confrontationist. It was in fact totally normal to
initiate a process of negotiation peacefully, rather than with aggression or

violence. If such an approach accomplished its objective of redressal, as deferential petitions often did, there was no further need to stage protests. If 'small voices' were conceded, exaggerated protest became redundant. They took aggressive overtones only when required, not when peaceful negotiations could resolve differences. Moreover, there was a clear realization that tangible advantages could be gained by soliciting the favour of the powerful. Hence, though struggling to break free from exploitation, artisans still maintained obsequious appearances in their negotiations for space.

Outbursts and violent encounters, in fact, occurred only when the threshold levels of endurance were crossed, when hopes of resolving tensions got frustrated, no meeting ground seemed in sight, and any accord between the opposite camps did not appear feasible. In the case of eighteenth-century Marwar, such hopeless, frustrating situations were more often the proverbial exception to the rule. Usually, the state felt constrained to operate within the limits of wajabi, though the fluidity of this concept provided spaces for variable interpretations, the dominant and the subordinate harnessing these to their own advantage. Tensions in their mutual relations, always present and common, intensified in the latter decades, but even then petitions and other traditionally sanctioned forms of protest ensured that ruptures did not become a pervasive reality.

On occasions when deferential protest failed to see the authorities respond favourably, artisans did take recourse to more defiant, even rebellious forms of protest. In terms of records, there were only fleeting expressions of outright collective defiance through riots and strikes, but the fact that these occasionally occurred is indisputable, casting doubt over Chakrabarty's argument that the cultural hegemony of the dominant completely encapsulated the value system of the lower formations. Julahas and charhawas for instance, had been obliged to deposit hasil at the sayar on selling their products. Earlier, when revenue demands were within 'legitimate' limits, they had deposited the same without reservations. In view of increased revenue burdens towards the end of the century, they ceased to do so.[80]

In an incident in 1788, khatis working at a royal construction site had failed to receive their salaries for over twelve months. Only a decade ago, such lapses had been tolerated and, on occasion, employees had died without receiving their wages.[81] But now, given the enhanced burden of taxes and pervasive distrust, the general mood of artisans seems to have been more belligerent. They began to insist on timely payment of wages, and struck work. The local authorities found themselves confronted by artisanal 'rioting everyday' (nit dango kare he) over non-payment of wages and non-provision of daily rations. Their action had the desired impact—local officials wrote with a sense of urgency to the higher authorities, and relief arrived immediately so that 'the rioting may stop' helo mit jaye.[82] Wajabi was thus restored through the self-exertions of the people, even the subordinate groups. Under pressure from collective articulation of protest, the state was compelled to accommodate artisanal self-assertion. It could not afford to be singularly predatory or parasitic, but rather, exercised power through strategies that combined coercion and repression with consent-building and concessions.

If petitioning and protest did not succeed, artisans did not stop at venting their anger directly. An instance of a major confrontation amounting to a proto-revolt comes to light for the year 1782 when the state's burden of taxes was perceived as unendurable, and craftsmen asserted their resentment by ceasing production to exert effective pressure on the authorities. The record states:

the khatis of Bilarha were ordered to pay *vachh virad* tax. Claiming that the Hakim's parwana (order) of CE1763 (VS 1820) had granted them exemption, they insisted that the state demand be withdrawn. The Durbar enquired from the local people, and learnt that in fact the khatis had paid this tax traditionally (sadamad); hence they refused to grant exemption.

The record further recounts that the rulers considered the prospect of allowing the khatis to perform begar in lieu of the tax, but when they realized that there was not enough work at the fort to have the khatis work in begar, they refused to relent. All the khatis then got together as one (*eko kar nei)* and struck work (*kam chhod baitha).* The state was alarmed and decided to appoint substitutes to replace the errant khatis. The administration further retaliated by banishing the defiant khatis, and also ordered that the rebels would be severely punished if they tried to influence the new recruits.[83] In its view, petitions were wajib, and so was a strike on non-payment of wages; but refusal to pay a tax that had traditional sanction and had only been withdrawn as a temporary concession, amounted to revolt and necessitated repression.[84] The khatis, on the other hand, contested this reading of the tax demand, convinced that a long-standing exemption had its own sanctity that could not be violated. Negotiations broke down and the rebels were banished. The outcome notwithstanding, what is of import is the momentary self-confidence and the resoluteness with which the khatis defended their customary rights. Nor should we lose sight of caution displayed by the state in first determining the validity of the complaints of the artisans. Between the two lay the spaces where the artisans could define the limits of wajabi demands.

Such determined resistance on the part of the khatis is a far cry from the docile acquiescence attributed to subordinate groups in pre-colonial India. Clearly, as notes Chakrabarty, 'custom', 'tradition', and 'legitimacy' were '…open to interpretation'.[85] It was the fluidity of the category of wajabi that left the khatis the space to define what was legitimate, to assert and to protest when denied their 'rights', and to defend and pursue their interest. It establishes that in situations of irreconcilable differences, the subordinate did not hesitate to engage in defiant aggression against those in power. Even at the cost of inviting state ire, the subordinate groups did not lie low to avoid confrontation, as deduced by James Scott.

This trend of open rebellion seems to have picked up momentum gradually. On 14 April 1814, the people from Jodhpur, Nagaur, Merta, Sojhat, and Jaitaran forced the ruler to reduce gharginti *lag* by rupees four, and hal lag by rupees four and a half.[86] Again, in 1817 the agriculturists of Balotra, Jalor, and Shiv stopped their ploughing, sowing and reaping operations when they were forced to pay ghar bab at the rate of rupees eight per house. The obstruction in agricultural operations was alarming for the rulers, and they immediately paid heed. [87] Collective action again manifested in 1835 when the confectionaries (*halwais*) of Jodhpur announced closure of all their shops to protest against the levy of a new tax, *kandoi-ri-lag*. When some of their community members failed to fall in line, their caste council ordered the heavy fine of rupees fifty-one each on the disobedient caste members.[88] Thus, one is repeatedly struck by instances of strikes, *dharna*, closure of shops, and refusal to work unless the conditions were within the scope of wajabi.

Rather than being disparate cases, these series of confrontations suggest a growing shift in the rulers' readings of wajabi. Equally, they represent a growing assertion from the subordinate of just and unjust, acceptable and unacceptable conduct, and thus signify fragments of proto-revolts. What seems apparent here is that consciousness is not merely a prior condition, but grows out of practice, protests graduating into a practice over time.[89] Since hegemony was unstable, constantly under pressure and challenge, counter-hegemonic ideologies crystallized to support recurrent assertions on the part of the subordinate.

Though the poor did not challenge the pattern of dominance, they incessantly questioned the interpretations and relative interests, roles, and obligations of their patrons and superiors. Also, such protests and resistance suggest that forms of organization and contact did exist within castes, capable of mobilization when necessary. In the last decades of the eighteenth century, there was a sharpening of conflict between the 'state' and the craftsmen, and the artisans refused to be consenting participants in their own abuse. Even if occasionally, the very fact that the artisans did sometimes confront their superiors is evidence of the existence of a subaltern consciousness that elite domination and hegemony had been unable to entirely supersede or suppress. Such protests are in contravention of the early reading of the Gramscian notion of 'false consciousness' attributed to the subordinate. Artisanal groups were able to sustain a culture consistent with their own needs and experiences rather than mirroring the worldview of the elites. Despite subordination and despite willingness to abide by wajabi, the latter remained a contested terrain and a site of unceasing negotiations.

The crafts' society also retained its distinctive cultural attributes in matters of social customs and rites that were finely attuned and reflected the imperatives of their own life worlds. The customs of bride price marriages, wives' ability to divorce their husbands and enter second marriages, sanction for widows' remarriage, and numerous others indicate the obvious sense of separateness among craft castes, and their unwillingness to embrace the standard 'Hindu' values due to the cultural hegemony of dominant castes. Even if occasionally somewhat embarrassed about their 'lowly' customs, and pushing them in directions that would help save face, the subordinate castes preserved enough autonomy not to abandon or get overwhelmed by elite norms. Though marginally influenced by their elite traditions,, artisanal customs in matters of marriage, property, and adoption, were not quite integrated into the domination or hegemony of the ruling classes.[90]

This resistance questions studies that reduced the Indian historical experience to the single dimension of hierarchy and its cultural hegemony. No doubt, protests occurred within the parameters of caste stratification, but the stereotyping and essentialization of 'Indian culture' as homeostatic, is problematic. Multiple, competing, and even contradictory strands comprised this culture, and these defy any easy or simplistic definition. Under pressure from these collective forms of resistance, essentially defensive in nature, the state was compelled to accommodate them. Its material need to retain artisans within its bounds, the paternalist discourse, and pressures 'from below' together ensured that it 'gives to get'. The Rathor state could neither afford to be singularly predatory nor parasitic; it rather had to exercise power through strategies that combined coercion and repression with concessions. Contradictory trends are therefore more than visible,' with exploitation and patronage unfolding hand-in-hand. Extractions and exemptions were recorded time and again, and oppressors and saviours were part of the same system.

CONCLUDING REMARKS

Clearly, the subalterns and the elites were locked in a constant and enduring relationship of tension and negotiation rather than insulated in autonomous worlds of their own. A mapping of their interaction reveals a ceaseless dialogue with the subaltern, ever keen to defend and retain, sometimes even push for space—manoeuvring and manipulating to evolve survival strategies, and forging resistance and avoidance protest vis-à-vis the state and its elites. The latter were equally seized with the need to maintain their dominant status by gauging and adjusting their mechanisms of power and instruments of appropriation in response to subaltern pressures. Rather than looking for dramatic confrontationist interludes in their otherwise 'peaceful co-existence', this study focussed on the 'everyday' struggles and the dynamics of routine politics that typified 'normal' relations between the two. Impressed by 'patient, silent struggles, stubbornly carried on by rural communities',[91] it drew attention to artisans as historical actors or agencies, the everyday forms of give and take, and their substantial role in social dynamics.[92] Since societal upheavals are not the only occasions when structures of power faced challenges from the subaltern, routine interactions between the two, beset with dialectical tensions, conflict and contestatory behaviour, are evident. Though less spectacular, these constituted the usual means by which the subalterns routinely defended their 'rights' and resisted demands on their resources. Far more enduring than confrontational outbursts, the basic endeavour to understand them was supported by the premise that cumulatively, routine resistance of this kind often had an appreciable impact on relations of subordination and domination and shaped the social order in profound ways.

This study therefore explored artisans negotiated with the administration and state authorities, tackled the local hierarchies, and dealt with their caste fellows. In doing so it located the issues of friction, the areas of conflict, and the pressure points that were at the root of the relationship. It highlighted the strategies adopted by the artisans and the state to minimize their respective disadvantages and maximize their opportunities. Artisan-elite interactions in early modern Marwar revealed that neither domination nor resistance was autonomous. Power and struggle appeared not as polar opposites, but as phenomena that co-existed and shaped one another.[93] Delving into their daily interactions, therefore, it highlighted 'the omnipresent tension and contradictions between hegemony and autonomy in consciousness, between submission and resistance in practice'[94], and focussed on the complex processes in which the two were constantly intermeshed. Resistance to domination inevitably tempered and altered its form, and the exercise of power, therefore, required the elite to constantly reassess the effectiveness of their 'weapons' and engage with those of the subalterns to construct still newer ones.

Such protests and resistance from artisans suggest that domination and hegemony, however strong, were never absolute. Clearly identifiable is a greater degree of autonomy and internal cohesion in pre-colonial artisanal politics than has generally been conceded. Artisans accepted the larger structures of power, caste hierarchy, and the state. But even while being almost synchronic in their acceptance of traditional authority, artisans expected it to conform to the minimum standards of justice and fair play. Through persistent protests, they forced the state to acknowledge the illegitimacy of many of its own actions, and those of its political agents. They demanded

the 'restoration' of an idealized paternal order, lost amidst Maratha invasions and resultant penury, and continually appealed to the paternalistic
basis that their mutual relationship was traditionally expected to rest on.
The simple historiographical construct of an exploitative state relentlessly
tyrannizing the artisan is therefore no more than a historical half-truth. The
situation was not one of grim, unquestioned repression, with power exercised from top down, but a far more complex situation of the two
'adversaries' assessing their relative strength, and leveraging upon it. Grossly
unequal as their mutual relations were, acts of dominance had still to be
peppered with benevolence, indulgence, and calculated acts of appeasement. Though the financial stress that the Marwar state was undergoing
during the latter decades of the eighteenth century shows the officials
exercizing their power over the low-born in more apparent ways, the artisans also do not come across as being content to submit to a condition of
abject dependency.

What is beyond dispute is that the political and social order were closely
intertwined, integral parts of a continuum, webbed together through intricate ties. Links between the raja and the praja inter-penetrated, and political
power was infact widely diffused rather than being uni-directional, with
authority flowing uni-lineally from state to society—the state insulated from
the influence of the latter. The relationship between the dominant groups
and the subordinate formations therefore needs to be understood not as a
stimulus-response dyad, but by situating it within a social field where the
state was fully implicated in popular struggles, continually shaped by, and
in turn modifying and reconfiguring the latter. All nuclei of power thus
jockeyed for political space to secure their interests.

Indeed, it was not unusual for contrary pulls to cause inconsistencies
and fuzzy policies, and the heterogeneity of agendas is more than evident.
Paradoxically, patronage at one level served as a corrective to the lopsided
distribution of scarce goods in pre-colonial India. It also accentuated inequality because the presence and the symbols of subordination enabled
patrons to demonstrate their superiority. Thus, though this study recognizes
the principle of wajabi or legitimacy as the anchor of the social space at the
intersection of state-subaltern relations, it does not see this cultural notion
as succesful in establishing any complacence, equilibrium, or homeostatis.
Though gaps in the readings of wajabi by the elite and the subordinate could
not preclude resentment, the ideology did, by and large, preclude affirma-
tive rebellion by containing exploitation within certain limits. These limits
of 'legitimate practice' were constantly contested, negotiated, transgressed,
and redefined. As Hasan notes, 'power both empowered and oppressed the
ordinary subjects. The normative system was both shared and contested!'[95]

Artisanal politics clearly complicate the reading of political formations,
for though they have been perceived as marginal in extant historiography,

they were in fact intrinsic to the stability and prosperity of eighteenth-century states. A history of the political culture of the early modern Indian state must take into cognisance the politics of subordinate groups, and how these impacted, and were in turn constrained, by the state. This study therefore argued for the expansion of the constitutive scope of state formation by including the lower strata and its engagements with the structures and processes of power and statecraft. Historians who have attributed the absence of revolutionary outbursts on the part of the Indian subordinate groups during the pre-colonial period to their inertia and complacence need perhaps to factor in the realities of wajabi before coming to any conclusions on the issue.

NOTES

1. See Stewart Gordon, *The New Cambridge History of India, II. 4: The Marathas, 1600–1818* (Cambridge, 1993), p. 193.

2. A letter from Mahad ji to Vijai Singh dated vs 1831, 30 April 1774.Pf.6, LN 29, Jd. records that the amount paid by the Rathors was rupees four lacs, eighty-nine thousand, four hundred and eighty-three, and seven annas. Another letter from Mahad ji to Vijai Singh dated vs 1832/14 July, 1775, Pf. 6, LN.30, Jd. records that rupees three lacs sixty thousand were paid by the maharaja for the years vs 1829–34/AD 1772–77 and another rupees four lacs thirty-nine thousand for the years vs 1835–39/AD 1778–82.

3. To meet the financial emergency, Gulab Rai, the favourite *pasban* (mistress) of the maharaja sold her ornaments worth rupees three lacs. Khichi Gordhan, a loyal noble, was also asked to arrange for another three lacs; see *Mundiyat Khyat* (Vijai Singh), pp. 226–7, no. 20.

4. See the letter from Vijai Singh to Mahad ji Scindia dated vs 1847/1791.ab no. 4, p. 45, Jd.

5. *Jodhpur Rajya ki Khyat*, part 3, Raghuvir Singh and Manohar Singh (eds) Ranawat, pp. 17 and 31.

6. Shiv Dutt Dan Barhat, *Jodhpur Rajya ka Itihas, 1753–1800* (Jaipur, 1982), pp. 137–47.

7. *Marwar Rajya ki Khyat*, vol. III, pp. 121–2; Shyamaldas, *Vir Vinod*, vol. II, p. 1574.

8. *JSPB* 49, 1854/1797, f. 112A.

9. See Bernier's quote and Tapan Raychaudhuri's corroboration of the view in Chapter one, p. 3 of this study.

10. *JSPB* 43, 1848/1791, f. 177A.

11. See *Jodhpur Haqiqat Bahi*, 1827/1770, f. 465, Jodhpur Records, RSAB.

12. The silawats of Makrana complained when *habub*, a new levy, was demanded from them; see *JSPB* 32, 1842/1785, f. 94B.

13. *JSPB* 22, 1836/1779, f. 103A.

14. *JSPB* 41, 1846/1789, f. 364B. The cotton-carders appealed against the demand.

15. *JSPB* 41, 1846/1789, f. 325A.

16. Ibid., f. 199B; ibid., f. 441B respectively.

17. *JSPB* 41, 1846/1789, f. 339B.

18. In view of their problem, they were allowed exemption from payment of sal bab; see *JSPB* 47, 1853/1796, f. 88B.

19. *JSPB* 40, 1850/1793, ff. 534, 544, and 555.

20. See *Haqiqat Bahi* no. 2, ff. 71, 73, and 75.

21. See the letter from Singhvi Inder Raj to Najar Moti Ram dated 18 Feb. 1808, *Arzi Bahi*-5, p. 245. In 1781 *kayali*—the post of the official weigher—in the main mandi of qasba Desuri was given on ijara to Kayal Amara for rupees eleven hundred and eleven; see *JSPB* 25, 1838/1781, f. 108, Jodhpur Records. Also see *Administrative Report of Marwar, 1884–85*, p. 11.

22. Khati Dipe Lale of Desuri refused to work without remuneration since earlier he had never worked unpaid for state officials; see *JSPB* 32, 1842/1785, f. 186A.

23. *JSPB* 50, 1854/1797, f. 38A.

24. Deeply pained, the kumhar complained and demanded compensation; see *JSPB* 49, 1854/1797, f. 182A.

25. Foucault, *Crime and Punishment*.

26. *JSPB* 34, 1843/1786, f. 183B.

27. *JSPB* 20, 1835/1778, f. 112A.

28. *JSPB* 23, 1836/1779, f. 50A.

29. *JSPB* 39, 1845/1788, f. 243B.

30. Ibid., f. 457B.

31. *JSPB* 23, 1836/1779, f. 47B.

32. *JSPB* 30, 1840/1783, f. 456B.

33. *JSPB* 43, 1848/1791, f. 105A.

34. *JSPB* 48, 1853/1796, f. 330A.

35. *JSPB* 19, 1854/1777, f. 168A.

36. *JSPB* 30, 1841/1784, f. 224B.

37. Ibid., f. 26.

38. *JSPB* 25, 1838/1781, document dated *Chait Bad 11, Budhwar*, (folio number is not clear); and *JSPB* 49, 1854/1797, f. 17B, respectively.

39. *JSPB* 43, 1848/1791, f. 41A and *JSPB* 45, 1850/1793, f. 85B. Khati Lalo Khwajbagas too was able to recover his wage dues only after impressing the authorities of his urgent needs; see *JSPB* 49, 1854/1797, f. 24A.

40. *JSPB* 19, 1835/1778, f. 308B.

41. *JSPB* 21,1835/1778, f. 300B; *JSPB* 23, 1836/1779), f. 130A and 184B; *JSPB* 25, 1838/1781, f. 90B; *JSPB* 41, f. 105B.

42. *JSPB* 25, f. 92B; *JSPB* 41, 1846/1789, f. 102A.

43. *JSPB* 54, 1857/1800, f. 268B.

44. For more on this, see Ravi Ahuja, 'Labour Relations in an Early Colonial Context: Madras, c.1750–1800', *Modern Asian Studies*, vol. 36, no, 4, 2002, p. 803.

45. *JSPB* 23, 1836/1779, f. 104B.

46. *JSPB* 20, 1835/1778, f. 191B. A kotwal of Merta beat Sunar Sambhu with wooden logs for paying one taka less for lifting mud dug out from pudasar tank; *JSPB* 23, 1836/1779, f. 104B. In another case, Rajavi Bine Singhal claimed that the land belonged to him, and refused to allow pinjaras Chodri, Arak, and Ujare to continue living in their houses located on the *ginarhin* (near the city's water channel) though their ancestors were buried in the mosque nearby, and they had been reading *namaz* there for long; *JSPB* 36, 1844/1787, f. 69A.

47. *JSPB* 37, 1844/1787, f. 239B. In another case the chauntara ohdadars of qasba Sojhat claimed that Ghanchi Likhama had supplied less oil then he had been paid for by the Durbar, and extracted Rs 9 from him even though he had delivered the full amount; *JSPB* 41, 1846/1789, f. 210B.

48. *JSPB* 48, 1853/1796, f. 9A.

49. *JSPB* 23, 1836/1779, f. 184B.

50. *JSPB* 22, 1836/1779, f. 103A.

51. *JSPB* 32, 1842/1785, f. 57A.

52. *JSPB* 47, 1853/1796, f. 88B.

53. *JSPB* 30, 1840/1783, f. 355A.

54. Ibid., f. 456B.

55. Ibid., f. 460A.

56. *JSPB* 32, 1842/1785, f. 186A.

57. *JSPB* 52, 1855/1798, ff. 55B and 59A.

58. *JSPB* 52, 1855/1798, f.52B.

59. *JSPB* 39, 1845/1788, f. 235B.

60. *JSPB* 42, 1847/1790, f. 28A.

61. Plots of 20 gaz by 12 gaz were ordered to be measured and given from khalisa territory in the city of Nagaur to luhars Alabagas, Yaru, Kayam, Bajid, Bahdar, and Jamal of Luharpura. The authorities ordered that pattas for the same be issued after taking Rs 20 each from every luhar; *JSPB* 43, 1848/1791, f. 84B,

JSPB 44, 1849/1792, f. 170A, *JSPB* 44, 1849/1792, f. 188A, *JSPB* 48, 1853/1796, f. 9A.

62. See Demirci, 'Complaints about *Avariz* Assessment and Payment in the *Avariz*-Tax System: An Aspect of the Relationship between Centre and Periphery. A Case Study of Kayseri, 1618–1700', *Journal of the Economic and Social History of the Orient*, vol. 46, no. 4, 2003, pp. 437–74.

63. *JSPB* 20, 1835/1778, f. 183A and *JSPB* 12, 1829/1772, f.172B respectively.

64. Arild Engelsen Ruud, 'The Indian Hierarchy: Culture, Ideology and Consciousness in Bengali Village Politics', *Modern Asian Studies*, vol. 33, no. 3, 1999, p. 720.

65. See Dipesh Chakrabarty, *Rethinking Working Class History: Bengal 1890–1940*.

66. See Joseph Femia, 'Hegemony and Consciousness in the Thought of Antonio Gramsci', *Political Studies*, vol. XXIII, (1), 1975, pp. 29–48; also T.J. Lears, 'The Concept of Cultural Hegemony: Problems and Possibilities', *The American Historical Review*, vol. 90, no. 3, 1985, pp. 567–93.

67. Eric Hobsbawm, in his article 'Peasants and Politics', *Journal of Peasant Studies*, vol. 1, no. 1, 1973, p. 13 explains the dynamics of peasant response to pressures from the dominant landed elite by acknowledging constrains that ring true for Marwari artisans too.

68. See White's article, 'Everyday Resistance, Socialist Revolution, and Rural Development'; also Gerald Mullin's *Flight and Rebellion*; and Eugene D. Genovese, *Roll, Jordan, Roll*.

69. *JSPB* 34, 1843/1786, f. 140B and *JSPB* 39, 1845/1788, f. 169B.

70. In the case of Nai Paimle, for instance, the petitioner contended that traditionally there was no sanction for his performance of begar at the jagirdar's mansion. Some others from his social strata may have earlier obliged, leading the jagirdar to assume compliance on the nai's part, see *JSPB* 20, 1835/1778, f. 183A. The full case has been cited earlier in Chapter 4.

71. For a useful study of the effects of such a 'cumulative effect' see B.J.T. Kerkvliet's *The Huk Rebellion*.

72. See Michael Adas' essay titled 'South Asian Resistance in Comparative Perspective', in Douglas Haynes and Gyan Prakash (eds), *Contesting Power: Resistance and Everyday Social Relations in South Asia* (Delhi, 1991) p. 296.

73. *JSPB* 24, 1837/1780, f. 174B.

74. Rangrez Badhukamal of Nagaur and Chhipa Isak of Siwana are recorded to have migrated to Pali, and Chhipa Ghulam Mahmad had migrated from Multan to settle in Nagaur; Nilgar Nuri had shifted from Sojhat to Malwa despite having a house and shop in Sojhat; Chhipa Deku of Pali also moved to Malwa to tide over a famine situation, while his brother who remained in Pali died; Chhipa Viram of Nagaur migrated to Kisangarh; see *JSPB* 15, 1832/1775, f. 250 and *JSPB* 36, 1844/1787, f. 289B respectively; also see *JSPB* 25, 1838/1781, f. 49A; *JSPB* 34, 1843/1786, f. 164B; *JSPB* 34, 1843/1786, f. 208B; *JSPB* 49, 1854/1797, f. 42B respectively.

75. It was this mobility of the artisans that led many patrons to prefer transforming them from free labour to servile bonded labour tied to their masters as halis and vasis; see *JSPB* 13, 1830/1773, f. 54A and 36B. Also see *JSPB* 15, 1832/1775, f. 228B; *JSPB* 18, 1834/1777, f. 33A; *JSPB* 26, 1841/1784, f. 149B.

76. *JSPB* 41, 1846/1789, f. 199B.

77. *JSPB* 53, 1856/1799, f. 162A.

78. Doubts on the role of caste as merely petrifying began to be cast in the 90s. Perceptions that saw caste as an enabling and empowering structure that helped the formation of coherent communities and brotherhoods that together pushed their demands and interests vis-à-vis others emerged by and by. See for instance, Ronald Inden's *Imagining India* (Oxford, 1990).

79. See James Scott, *Weapons of the Weak* for an elaboration of this view. In regions with a relatively different cultural milieu and coercive power of the state, his statement perhaps holds true and popular fears were valid. For instance, Charles Tilly's study of the Lustucru peasant rebellion against taxation in mid-seventeeth century France records that in the aftermath of the rebellion, the commander of the rebels was hanged, and more than 360 of the rebels sent off in chains to serve their lives as galley slaves; see Tilly's essay, 'Routine Conflicts and Peasant Rebellions in Seventeenth Century France', in R.P. Weller and S.E. Guggenheim (eds) *Power and Protest in the Countryside* (Durham, N.C., 1982,) p. 15 .

80. *JSPB* 48, 1853/1796, f. 7A.

81. The sons had claimed their father's dues, and that too on the pretext that they needed the money to fund their deceased father's funeral rites. See *JSPB* 25, 1838/1781, Document dated *Chait bad 11, Budhwar*, (the folio number is not clear on the document).

82. *JSPB* 39, 1835/1788, f. 40A.

83. *JSPB* 28, 1839/1782, f. 276A.

84. The churigars of Jalor, for instance, had petitioned that the previous administration had exempted them from payment of the chothai tax. Despite the resource crunch by the mid-1770s, the Jodhpur Durbar sent an order (parwana) to the officers of the Jalor customs' treasury (sayar) not to demand this tax from them; see *JSPB* 14, 1831/1774, f. 135. Confrontation, however, was gair-wajib, and needed to be summarily crushed.

85. Chakrabarty, *Rethinking Working Class History*, p. 180.

86. *Haqiqat Bahi*, Jodhpur, 1862–70/1805–13, no. 9, f. 483, Jodhpur Records, RSAB.

87. *Khabar* (undated) from Jalor by Bulakidas to Singhvi Fatehraj, Jodhpur Records, RSAB.

88. Conscious that solidarity vis-à-vis the 'state' would be critical to their bargaining strength, they strove to discipline erring caste-fellows; see *Khaifiyat*, 1892/1835, from kotwali Jodhpur, (reference cited by Padmaja Sharma, in *Maharaja Man Singh of Jodhpur and his Times*, p. 208).

89. For more on this, see Jean and John Comaroff, *Of Revelation and Revolution: Christianity, Colonialism, and Consciousness in South Africa* (Chicago, 1991), pp. 722–3.

90. Customs pertaining to the practice of widow remarriage, in particular, reveal artisanal anxieties to assuage elitist condemnation of this tradition. Arnold, in 'Gramsci and Peasant Subalternity in India', *Journal of Peasant Studies*, vol. 11, 1984, pp. 155–77 also argues that domination and hegemony, however strong, were never absolute, such as to totally preclude subaltern autonomy.

91. See Marc Bloch, *French Rural History*, trans. Janet Sondheimer (Berkeley, 1970), p. 170.

92. Till now they have largely appeared as anonymous contributors to statistics on taxes, labour migrations, and holdings etc.

93. A theoretical elaboration of this idea can be found in Michel Foucault, especially *The History of Sexuality*, vol. I, *An Introduction*, trans. Robert Hurley (New York, 1980), pp. 92–97.

94. Douglas Haynes and Gyan Prakash, in their Introductory essay titled 'Entanglement of Power and Resistance' make an excellent case for the need to see a continuum between the elites and subalterns, between structures of power and processes of resistance; see their co-edited volume *Contesting Power: Resistance and Everyday Social Relations in South Asia* (Delhi, 1991) pp. 1–20.

95. Farhat Hasan, *State and Locality in Mughal India*, p. 129.

Glossary

The definitions and meanings of the terms listed below reflect the sense in which they have been used in the original documents. The renderings are indeed approximate and incomplete, and should not be regarded as wholly accurate or definitive.

aais	this year
aarhn dirai	to say or do on oath
aath	wealth, property, *neg* given to artisans on auspicious occasions
adaren	to mortgage
adhela	lowest medium of exchange for small transactions
adhura nakh diyo	abortion
aidha	day of an important function
akas	jealousy, enmity
ambarath	construction, house, building
arat	oil-press
araz	petition
arhabi	objection
arhat mandh	extra cess on fields where irrigation was available
arzee	petition, an Arabic term incorporated into Marwari
asakhedho	quarrel, dispute
asaracho	quarrel
atkau	forcefully
aurang	a place where goods were manufactured
ausar mausar	funeral rites, most importantly, feast for community hosted by descendants of the dead
baderan	ancestors
bagar	cemented platform for storing hay, grains
bahar	troops
baharho	water channel functional during rains
bahla	shifting channels
bakhai	to provoke
bakshi	official

bal	tax for the maintenance of the army
balad	bullock cart
bandharas	tie-die workers
banias	merchants
balai	caste engaged in spinning and weaving, also in flaying dead animals
bandhej	tie-and-dye printing
baoris	water tanks
banjaras	carriers of foodgrains and salt over long distance
bapauti	ancestral, inherited from forefathers
bapidars	owners of ancestral land
baraje	objection
bararhna	door, opening
bas	colony, settlement
begar	unpaid service
beran	well
bhai-bandh	brotherhood, kinsmen
bharawas	those who caste bronze images
bhat	genealogist
bhata	stone
bhog	land revenue, akin to Mughal *mal*
bhoglawe	mortgaging house or an individual on taking a loan
bhomia	local term for zamindar
bhopi	people having spiritual powers, used by villagers to locate a culprit
birat	patron families
bohra	moneylender
buhar	mutual exchange of gifts social prestations
byav	first marriage
chakari	service
chamars	leather workers
chandani	self-immolation committed by charans to deter dacoits
charan	bards
charhawaa	Muslim caste of tie-and-dye printers
chaudhari	hereditary village headman
chaukas	enquire
chhatak	small demonation currency
chhintfine	cotton textiles
chhipas	textile printers
chitera	craftsmen who serrated depressions and engraved on an ornament
churigars	ivory bangle-makers
churi pahnai	remarried
dabgars	those who crafted musical instruments

*dakhaniya*s	local term for Marathas
*dalal*s	commercial brokers
darhsani hundi	ills of exchange payable on demand
dariba	the treasury where salt revenues were deposited
darshan	to view with respect
*dastur*s	schedules of land-revenue rates
desh	kingdom
dhak gayo	died
dhalai	casting of an ornament, a metalware or a statue
dhingala	lowest medium of exchange for small transactions
dhuan bhanchh	tax on every hearth/household
diwan	finance minister
dohali	revenue free land given in charity
dokh rakhane	due to enmity/jealousy
durastai	improvement, rectification
durbar	Rathor maharaja's court
faras	floor
farhgati karana	cancellation of claims, breaking of contract
fauj bakshi	minister in charge of military affairs
faujdar	official in charge of law and order at the provincial level
fauth	death
firohi	cess to guards for protection of crops
gaddi	throne
gahar	caste-wise processions during celebration of festivals
galat gayo	died childless
gali	a narrow lane
ganayat	relatives, bretheren
ganth bandhai	tying the knot, marriage ritual
garaj	self-interest
gehrain	to mortgage
ghar mein ghali	remarried
ghasmari	tax for grazing grass
ghazal	poetic compositions describing contemporary cities, penned by Jain saints
goli	slave
gor	group of cows
guli	*nil*, indigo
gumashta	manager and accountant of big businessmen
gunegari	penalty fines demanded by Rathor administration
haat	a shifting market, one held only on certain days of a week
habub	taxes imposed in the eighteenth century for royal maintenance
hakim	administrative head of a pargana

hali	a servile/bonded ploughman
hammals	porters at a market-place
hanti	tood prepared on weddings and other special occasions
harkanna rakhjo mati	without showing favour
hasil	land revenue
haveli	mansion
hundawan	commission of sahukars for discounting hundis
ijara	revenue farming
ijaredar	revenue former
inam	rewards in the form of cash, land or turban given by the maharaja to honour
izzat	honour
jaan	marriage procession
jagirdar	one entitled to the revenue of a land assignment in lieu of salary
jakharhiya	illicit relations
jariya	craftsmen who set precious stones on an ornament
jati panchayat	caste councils
jats	middle-level caste of land owners with considerable cattle wealth
jimarhn	community feast
jingars	makers of saddlery products
jogi	religious mendicant
juhari	offerings made to a deity
julaha	caste of weavers
jwar	cheap cereal grains popular among the poor of Marwar
kabarha	timber logs
kabeela	tribesmen, clansmen
kachedi	judicial office headed by a hakim at pargana headquarters
kadim	old
kamin	artisans and other lowly castes
kansa	platter of food customarily distributed on special occasions
kanwara	bachelor
karkhana	unit of centralized manufacturing-cum-ware house
kasab	occupation, profession, trade
kasid	messenger, letter carrier
kasumba	an expensive dye
katar	row of camels
kayals	weighers at a market-place
kehtab	dispute, conflict, argument

khalisa	crownlands
khamp	clan
khaprali	roof tiles
kharach-bhog	tax to pay those who assisted in the collection of bhog
khati	carpentar
khawwas	performers
khedo	enmity
khema karkhana	workshop for making and storing royal tents
khola	adoption
khons lini	snatched away
kootana	to beat, thrash
korhi	a bundle of twenty items
kori	rough cotton cloth
kosita	well
kothiwal	big businessmen, whole traders with an inter-provincial reach
kotri	mansion belonging to a bhomia, jagirdar or senior state functionary
kumhar	potter
kotwal	city superintendent
kunta	approximate revenue assessment
kuttiya	stone-cutters who handled rough cutting of semi-precious stones
kutumb	family unit
lada	a camel load
lag-bag	miscellaneous cesses and impositions
lagwar	illicit relations
lakh	hundred thousand
lakharhn	child from the first marriage brought along to second husband's house
lakharas	lacquer bangle-makers
lakhayacha	pillow, mattress
lapasi	sweet porridge prepared on auspicious occasions
lata	precise revenue assessment as per measurement
lerhon huve	contraction of a loan
lohiyas	iron traders, merchants engaged in selling ironware
loi	woollen blankets
luhars	blacksmiths
madan	forcefully
mahajans	merchants, moneylenders
mahimahi	internal
mahindar chakar	servant paid on a monthly basis
mairhn	wax

makool	appropriate, proper, approved, acceptable, as per intellect
malba	a pool of taxes to meet expenditures on communal welfare of village
mandi	a wholesale market, often for a single commodity
mansabdar	office holder
manti	husband
mapa	sales tax
mehatar	caste head who mediated between state and caste fellows
milano	present or nazar to hakim
minasaz	craftsmen who enamelled ornaments
mochis	cobblers
modo	door
mohars	gold coins
mokalo	permission
mool	original capital
muchalaka	a bond
moth	cheap lentil local to this region
muddati hundi	ills of exchange payable on the expiry of a stipulated period
muhalla	colony, settlement generally occupied by a single caste
mukata	revenue farming
mutasaddi	middle-level state officials
mutsaddis	new class of senior officers that emerged in the eighteenth century
na-aulad	childless
nadar	insolvent, bankrupt
nadiya	pond, tank
nai	barber
naido	close relative, kinsman
nakutiro	incapable, incompetent
nallahs	natural water channels
nata	remarriage
nat jana	to go back on one's words
nauni-pauni	'incomplete' inferior men
nayik	mine-diggers
nazrana	money and gifts presented respectfully
nekal	tax on export of commodities
nidan	weeding of fields
nidhe	survey
nilgar	caste of indigo-dyers
nisan	evidence
nithh	with difficulty, somehow

nyat	community
nyota	tax paid on occasions of marriage in the ruling family
ogarhn	bad character
ohdadars	officialdom
omrah	senior nobles (plural of amir)
pagh	turban
pagi	those who identified footprints to catch thieves
paisa	lowest medium of exchange for small transactions
pakhati	near-by or neighbouring
palakikhana	workshop where sedan-chairs were made
palarhn	camel seats
palit	ghosts
palledars	porters at a market-place
palle lagai	remarriage
pancharai	tax for grazing on leaves
paranai	married
parhawa	long wooden house
pari gayi	ran away
pasaiti	holders of ancestral land
patta	a document or contract given to a revenue payer indicating his rights and obligations
pattiwals	pavement sellers engaged in retail trade
pattus	shawl woven on a field of white
paur	last year
pavan jat (pun jat)	36 lowly occupational castes
pesar	tax on import of commodities
pesdasat	clerks of revenue collectors
petiya	allowance
phadiyas	low-denomination coins
pheriwals	pedlars who carried pack-loads for sale
pyad Bakshi	pay-master for non-army officials
qasba	semi-urban settlement
rahadari	transit tax
rail	floods
ramekarha	toys, clay play things
ramsaran	death
rand	widow
randol	wandering woman of doubtful character
rasaw	donkeys
rebari	camel owning nomads
regars	tanners of cattle hides
rela	floods
rui	natural springs
rith ke paise	tax on remarriage of women
saga	affinal relatives

sahukars	moneylenders
sair	custom's treasury
sakh	a witness's testimony
sand	female camel
sanjha mein	in partnership
santaro karayo	to get clean and renovated
sardars	hereditary chiefs, heads of clans
sarg	section
sarha	house
sarkar	administrative unit like a district
sarrafs	moneychangers
sathan	sugarcane
saya	witness, evidence, testimony
seer	unit of weight, equal to 16 chhataks
silawat	caste of stone-cutters
siropao	robes of honour presented by the maharajas
siyalu	monsoonal crop—kharif
suba	province
sunar	caste of goldsmiths
ta paur	year before last
tafawat	different, far apart, widely separated, distant, interval, distinction, dissimilarity
taftish	examine, scrutinize, investigate, search, study
tahkhana	basement
tahqiq	enquire, ascertain, verify the truth, investigate
taka	lowest medium of exchange for small transactions
taksir	to break, shatter, divide to produce a fraction
talab	summons calling or sending for somebody
talai	water tank
tarrash	stone grinders
telis	caste of oil-pressers
thappa	wooden dies for printing textiles
thikanedars	feudal magnates with substantial establishments
til	sesame seeds
togharhi	calf,
unalu	spring crop—rabi
uvarasi	inheritor
uwajabi	appropriate, proper
vasidar	agricultural labourers residing on the settlement of a bhomia/jagirdar
wasarhn	utensils, generaly made of clay
watan	hereditary patrimony of a chief
watan jagir	hereditary domain of a chieftain who served as a Mughal mansabdar
yati	Jain saints
yudhh kand	name of a chapter in Valmiki's Ramayana

Select Bibliography

The sources for Marwar's history are varied and rich, though they differ in volume and in chronological coverage. A general survey of these can be had from *A Guide to the Records in the Rajasthan State Archives* (Government Press, Bikaner, 1991), and from Rajasthan Oriental Research Institute, Jodhpur: Catalogue of Publications (Government of Rajasthan Publication, 1991). I have used the following categories of sources to study eighteenth-century Marwar.

Unpublished Archival Sources

Marwari Language/Local Vernaculars

The following bahis are preserved in the Jodhpur, Bikaner, and Jaipur sections at the Rajasthan State Archives, Bikaner (RSAB).

1. *Jodhpur Sanad Parwana Bahis* nos 1–54, that cover the period 1764–1800/ 1821–57. The series continues into the twentieth century, spread over about 156 bahis. These bahis are of varying thickness, with folios tied together in a cloth-covered bind. They are chronologically arranged year-wise, one to two bahis for each year. A majority of them follow a similar format, recorded as petitions from people and the state response to them. These judicial records cover a very wide range of issues, from petitions against taxes and elite exactions to disputes over the flouting of normative behavioural patterns of different communities. It also includes news reports that kasids brought to the diwan's office, along with the state orders in this regard.
2. Khas Rukka Parwana Series number 10 bahis, of which no. 1, that covered the period 1822–1774/1765 – 831, was relevant for my study. This bahi comprises letters written by the rulers of Jodhpur to important traders in and around Marwar.
3. *Jodhpur Arzi Bahis* are collections of state responses to petitions from different social groups, especially Gosain brahmins. Bahi no. 6 has arzees from miscellaneous castes, including artisans.

4. *Jodhpur Byav ri Bahis* contain detailed accounts of the expenditure incurred on royal marriages. I have used Bahi no. 1 that covered the period 1776 – 1808/1719 – 51 and no. 2 from 1809–1908/1752 – 1851.

5. *Jodhpur Patta Bahis* nos 1 – 7 cover the eighteenth-century period. They detail the grant of land assignments by the state to the subjects.

6. *Jodhpur Bahiyat: Kala Basta*, cover the period 1810 – 50/1753 – 93. I have used Bahi no. 3, 1821/1764, which describes construction and repair work undertaken by the state in that year; Bahi no. 9, 1823/1766 contains accounts of the *Khema Karkhana*; no. 17, 1832/1775 is titled *Hazri Karigaran wa Mazdooran*; no. 18, *Bahi Talke Kamtha Tatha Hazari*, and no. 19, 1832/1775 called *Nagaur ke Kothar ki Bahi*. Bahis no. 20, 1832/1775; no. 27, 1835/1778; no. 39, 1836/1779; and no. 44, 1837/1780 pertain to state kamthanana or construction work on forts, palaces, royal gardens, etc. Bahi no. 52, 1840/1783 is on *Daru wa Shor* (*Barood* gun powder) production.

7. *Jodhpur Bahiyat: Safed Basta*, covers 1831–1900/1774 –1843. Bahi no. 5, 1836/1779 is *Baroodkhane ke Roznamache ki Bahi*; no. 6, 1836/1779 *Kamtha Talke Jama-Kharach*; no. 40, 1886/1829 *Bahi Pali ke Shorkhana*; no. 41, 1886 – 88/1829 – 31 *Jodhpur Garh ki Tankshala*; and no. 51, 1883/1826, *Zanani Dyorhi, Kaprha ka Kothar wa Haziron*.

8. *Jodhpur Ohada Bahiyan* record the recruitment of different officials to different posts in state workshops at the kilikhana, farrashkhana, and *kaparha ka kothar*, etc. with the dates of their appointment.

9. The *Jodhpur Bahiyat* collection contains bahis from different parganas, beginning from 1886/1829.

10. *Jodhpur Hath Bahi*, starting from 1771/1828, are like personal pocket diaries of the rulers.

11. *Jodhpur Haqiqat Bahi*, 1820 –30/1763 –73, contains newsletters from different parts of the kingdom.

12. *Bikaner Kagad Bahis*, nos 1–11, covering the period 1811–1857/54 –1800 provided information on different aspects of state-subject interaction in the neighbouring kingdom of Bikaner, ruled by a collateral branch of the Rathors.

13. *Bikaner Kamthana Bahis*, no. 135, 1759 – 61/1702 – 4; no. 2, 1808 – 14/1751–1757; no. 204, 1812/1755 contain details on the recruitment of construction workers, their wages, and the expenses on different raw materials.

14. *Bikaner Sawa Bahis* have information on commercial taxes imposed on different communities in different qasbas. I have used *Sawa Bahi Anupgarh* no. 2, 1818 – 21/1761 – 64, and *Sawa Bahi Mandi Sadar* no. 10, 1821 – 2/1764 – 5.

15. *Zakat Bahis* in the Bikaner Section provide information on inter-provincial and inter-regional trade. Bahi nos 81 and 84 mention trade routes, commercial taxes, and individuals from different communities engaged in trade.

16. *Bahi Parwana Sardaran, Bikaner*, no. 2/2, 1800 – 1900/1743 –1843 throws light on the interaction of the maharaja with the subordinate hereditary chiefs.

17. *Daftar Diwan Huzuri* in the Jaipur Section contains chitthis despatched by the office of the Jaipur Diwan to its officials, especially amils, in response to complaints from the subject population. His instructions in 48 chitthis pertain to extortions and oppression suffered by artisans and peasants in eighteenth-century Jaipur state.

18. *Dastur Komwar Records* in the Jaipur Section of RSAB document land, titles, and other honours awarded by the maharajas of Jaipur to individuals of different castes from amongst their subjects. The entries are arranged caste-wise in alphabetical order and contain dastur or usage observed in respect of persons of different castes and communities. Of the 32 volumes, no. 23 is particularly relevant for understanding the artisans' position in the Jaipur state.

19. *Arhsatta Karkhanejat* in the Jaipur Section of RSAB contain *tozi* records (on separate sheets) on the different state workshop-cum-warehouses, the commodities manufactured and the wages given to the workers there. For example, there are records on the chhapakhana, rangkhana, khushbukhana, khemakhana, farrashkhana, etc.

The following bahis at the Jodhpur District Archives, Jodhpur (JDAJ) have proved useful in collating information on different aspects of the economy of the state.

(a) *Kotwali Chabutara Jamabandi Bahi*, pargana Jalor, nos 753 and 754 helped understand the land revenue structure of the kingdom.

(b) *Jama-Kharach Bahi*, pargana Jalor, 1836/1779 is a good source for understanding the income and expenditure flows of the state.

(c) *Dastari Records* (Kharita and Chitthis), File Nos 32 – 115 were useful in comprehending the political and diplomatic context of eighteenth-century Marwar.

English Language

Foreign and Political Department Consultations, National Archives of India (NAI).

Home Political Proceedings, NAI

Rajputana Agency Files, (1800 – 1845), NAI

INSCRIPTIONS

Jaina Inscriptions, Parts I–III, Puran Chand Nahar (ed.), Calcutta, 1918 – 29.

CHRONICLES
Marwari Chronicles

Muhnot Nainsi, *Marwar-ra-Pargana-ri-Vigat*, Narain Singh Bhati (ed.), vols I–III, Jodhpur, 1968 – 9.

Marwar ri Khyat, (MS no. 199), Anup Sanskrit Library, Bikaner.
Vijay Vilas: Maharaja Vijay Singh ji ka Yudhh Varnana, (Incomplete Manuscript no. 45) at Rajasthani Shodh Sansthan, Chaupasani, Jodhpur.

Persian Chronicles

Abul Fazl, *Akbarnama*, Bibliothica Indica Series, vol. II and III, Calcutta, 1873 – 87, English trans. by H. Beveridge, vols I–III, (London, 1897 – 1910).
————, *Ain-i-Akbari*, Nawal Kishore Edition, 1882, Eng. trans. by Blochman, vol. I, (1873), and Jarett, vol. II and III; revised, Sarkar, vols II–III, (Calcutta, 1949).
Saqi Mustaid Khan (1710 – 11), *Maasir-i-Alamgiri*, Agha Ahmad Ali (ed.), Bibliothica Indica, Calcutta, 1870 – 3; trans. J. Sarkar, Calcutta, 1947.

EUROPEAN TRAVELLERS' ACCOUNTS

Col. James Tod, *Annals and Antiquities of Rajasthan, or the Central and Western Rajput States of India*, William Crook (ed.), 3 vols, rpr. Delhi: 1990.
Francisco Pelsaert, *Jahangir's India: The Remonstrnatie of Francisco Pelsaert* (Cambridge, 1925), translated by W.H. Moreland and P. Geyl.
Francois Bernier, *Travels in the Mogul Empire, AD 1656–1668*, trans., on the basis of Irving Brock's version and annotated by Archibald Constable, Second Edition revised by Vincent A. Smith, Delhi: first published 1934, rpr. 1989.
John Malcolm, *A Memoir of Central India*, 2 vols, London: 1824.
Joseph Salbancke, Journal in *Purchas His Pilgrims*, vol. III, 'Voyage', 1609, Mac Lehose.
Lieutenant A.H.E. Boileau, *Personal Narrative of a Tour Through the Western States of Rajwara, in 1835, comprising Beekaner, Jesulmer, and Jodhpoor* Calcutta, 1837.
Peter Mundy, *The Travels of Peter Mundy in Europe and Asia, 1608–67*, 2 vols, London: 1914.
Rev. Reginald Heber, *Narrative of a Journey Through the Upper Provinces of India: From Calcutta to Bombay, 1824 – 25*, 2 vols, London: John Murray, 1828.

NEAR CONTEMPORARY OFFICIAL WORKS

Political Agent, Marwar, Major C.K.M. Walter's *Gazetteers of Marwar, Mallani, and Jeysulmere*, Calcutta: 1877.
Rajputana Gazetteer, vols 1, 2, and 3A, Erskine, Scottish Mission Industries, Ajmer: 1908 and The Pioneer Press, Allahabad: 1909.
Mardum Shumari Raj Marwar, 1891, 2 vols, Jodhpur.
Phiroz R. Kothawalla, *The Census of Marwar*, 1911.

Lt. Colonel Archibald Adams, *The Western Rajputana States: A Medico-Topographical and General Account of Marwar, Sirohi, and Jaisalmer,* London: 1900.

Jodhpur Administration Report, 1883–4, Jodhpur.

Hardayal Singh, *Report Majmui-Halat-wa-Intizam Marwar,* Jodhpur, 1885.

Sojhat-re-Mandal-ri-bat, Narain Singh Bhati (ed.), published in *Parampara,* vol. 11, Jodhpur.

Report on the Relief Operations undertaken in the Native States of Marwar, Jaisalmer, Bikaner and Kishangarh in Rajputana during the Scarcity of 1891–92.

SECONDARY SOURCES

Abu-Lughod, Laila, 'The Romance of Resistance: Tracing Transformations of Power through Bedouin Women', *American Anthropologist,* 17(1), pp. 41 – 55.

Adas, Michael, 'From Avoidance to Confrontation: Peasant Protest in Pre-Colonial and Colonial Southeast Asia', *Comparative Studies in Society and History,* 23 (2), pp. 217 – 47.

Ahuja, Ravi, *The Crisis of Empire in Mughal North India: Awadh and the Punjab, 1707–1748,* New Delhi: Oxford University Press, 1986(a).

———, 'Aspects of Agrarian Uprisings in North India in the Early Eighteenth Century', Sabyasachi Bhattacharya and Romila Thapar (eds), *Situating Indian History for Sarvepalli Gopal,* New Delhi: Oxford University Press, 1986(b). pp. 146 – 66.

———, 'The Origins of Colonial Labour Policy in Late Eighteenth Century Madras', *International Review of Social History,* vol. 44, 1999, pp. 159 – 95.

———, 'Labour Relations in an Early Colonial Context: Madras, c.1750 – 1800', *Modern Asian Studies,* 36 (4), 2002, pp. 793 – 826

Alam, Muzaffar and Sanjay Subrahmanyam (eds), *The Mughal State: 1526 – 1750,* New Delhi: Oxford University Press, 1998.

Alam, Muzaffar, 'Eastern India in the Early Eighteenth Century "Crisis": Some Evidence from Bihar', *Indian Economic and Social History Review* (*IESHR*), 28 (1), 1991, pp. 43 – 71.

Ali, Mohammad Athar, *Mughal Nobility under Aurangzeb,* Bombay: Asia Publishing House, 1966.

Anderson, Michael R. and Sumit Guha (eds), *Changing Concepts of Rights and Justice in South Asia,* Oxford: School of Oriental and African Studies, 1998.

Appadurai, Arjun, 'Number in the Colonial Imagination', Carol Breckenridge and Peter van der Veer (eds), *Orientalism and the Postcolonial Predicament: Perspectives on South Asia,* Philadelphia: University of Pennsylvania Press, 1993, pp. 329 – 430.

Arasaratnam, S., 'Weavers, Merchants, and the Company: The Handloom Industry in South-eastern India, 1750 – 1790', *IESHR*, 17 (3), 1980, pp. 257 – 88.

Arora, Shashi, 'The Practice of Sale of Girls and their Position in Rajasthan, 1700 – 1800 AD', *Proceedings of Rajasthan History Congress*, Bikaner Session, 1984, pp. 33 – 45.

Aryan, Subhashini, *Folk Bronzes of Rajasthan*, New Delhi: Lalit Kala Akademi, 1994.

Asopa, Ram Karan, *Marwar ka Sankshipt Itihas*, Jodhpur: Hindi Sahitya Mandir, 1934.

Aziz, Abdul, *Mansabdari System and the Mughal Army*, Delhi: Idarah-i-Adabiyat -i-Dehli, 1972.

Bahura, Gopal Narayan, *Literary Heritage of the Rulers of Amber and Jaipur*, Jaipur: Maharaja Sawai Man Singh II Museum, 1976.

Bajekal, Madhavi, 'The State and the Rural Grain Market in Eighteenth Century Eastern Rajasthan', *IESHR*, 25 (4), 1988, pp. 443 – 73.

Banerjee, Anil Chandra, *Aspects of Rajput State and Society*, New Delhi: Rajesh Publications, 1983.

Barhat, Shiv Dutt Dan, *Jodhpur Rajya ka Itihas, 1753 – 1800*, Jaipur: Rajasthan Hindi Granth Academy, 1991.

Barnett, Richard B., *North India Between Empires: Awadh, the Mughals and the British, 1720 – 1801*, Berkeley: University of California Press, 1980.

Bayly, Christopher A., *Rulers, Townsmen and Bazaars: North Indian Society in the Age of British Expansion, 1770 – 1870*, South Asian Studies, Cambridge: Cambridge University Press, 1983.

———, *The New Cambridge History of India: Indian Society and the Making of the British Empire, II.I*, Cambridge: Cambridge University Press, 1987.

———, *Empire and Information: Intelligence Gathering and Social Communication in India, 1780 – 1870*, Cambridge Studies in Indian History and Society, Cambridge: Cambridge University Press, 1996.

Bayly, Susan, *The New Cambridge History of India: Caste, Society and Politics in India from the Eighteenth Century to the Modern Age, IV.3*, Cambridge: Cambridge University Press, 1999.

Bhadani, Bhanwar Lal, 'Population of Marwar in the Middle of the Seventeenth Century', *IESHR*, 16 (4), 1979, pp. 415 – 42.

———, 'The Pastoral Sector in the Economy of Seventeenth Century Marwar', paper presented at the Second International Seminar on Rajasthan, Udaipur, 17 – 21 December, 1991 (mimeographed paper at RSAB.

———, 'Land Tax and Trade in Agricultural Produce in Seventeenth Century Western Rajasthan', *IESHR*, 29 (2), 1992, pp. 215–26.

————, 'Role of Merchants and Markets in Agrarian Trade in Seventeenth Century Western Rajasthan', paper presented at the Seminar on Trade and Commerce in Rajasthan, Institute of Rajasthan Studies, Rajasthan Vidyapeeth, Udaipur (mimeographed copy at RSAB, n.d.).

————, *Peasants, Artisans and Entrepreneurs: Economy of Marwar in the Seventeenth Century*, Jaipur: Rawat Publications, 1999.

Bhadra, Gautam, 'The Mentality of Subalternity: Kantanama or Rajadharma' in Ranajit Guha (ed.), *Subaltern Studies VI: Writings on South Asian History and Society*, pp. 54 – 91, New Delhi: Oxford University Press, 1989.

Bhargava, V.S., *Marwar and the Mughal Emperors, 1526–1748*, Delhi: Munshiram Manoharlal, 1966.

Bhargava, Meena, *State, Society, and Ecology: Gorakhpur in Transition, 1750–1830*, New Delhi: Manohar, 1999.

Bharucha, Rustom, *Rajasthan: An Oral History, Conversations with Komal Kothari*, New Delhi: Penguin, 2003.

Bhatnagar, V.S., *Life and Times of Sawai Jai Singh, 1680 – 1743*, Delhi: Impex India, 1974.

Blake, Stephen P., *Shahjahanabad: The Sovereign City in Mughal India, 1639 – 1739*, Cambridge: Cambridge University Press, 1991.

Bloch, Marc, *French Rural History*, trans. Janet Sondheimer, Berkeley: University of California Press, 1970.

Bose, Sugata (ed.), *South Asia and World Capitalism*, New Delhi: Oxford University Press, 1990.

Braddick, Michael and John Walter (eds), *Negotiating Power in Early Modern Society: Order, Hierarchy and Subordination in Britain and Ireland*, Cambridge: Cambridge University Press, 2001.

Breman, Jan, *Patronage and Exploitation: Changing Agrarian Relations in South Gujarat*, Berkeley: University of California Press, 1974.

Brennig, Joseph, 'Textile Producers and Production in Late Seventeenth Century Coromandel', *IESHR*, 23 (4), 1986 pp. 333 – 56.

Brouwer, Jan, *Makers of the World: Caste, Crafts and Mind of South Indian Artisans*, New Delhi: Oxford University Press, 1995.

Chakrabarty, Dipesh, *Rethinking Working Class History: Bengal 1890 – 1940*, New Delhi: Oxford University Press, 1989.

Chakravarti, Anand, *Contradiction and Change: Emerging Patterns of Authority in a Rajasthan Village*, New Delhi: Oxford University Press, 1975.

Chakravarti, Uma, *Rewriting History: The Life and Times of Pandita Ramabai*, New Delhi: Kali for Women, in association with the Book Review Literary Trust, 1998.

Chandavarkar, Rajnarayan, *The Origins of Industrial Capitalism in India: Business Strategies and Working Classes in Bombay, 1900 – 1940*, Cambridge: Cambridge University Press, 1994.

Chandra, Satish, *Parties and Politics at the Mughal Court, 1707–1740*, Aligarh: People's Publishing House, 1959.

——, *Medieval India: Society, Jagirdari Crisis, and the Village*, Delhi: Macmillan, 1982.

Chatterjee, Indrani, *Gender, Slavery and Law in Colonial India*, New Delhi: Oxford University Press, 1999.

Chattopadhyaya, Brajadulal, *The Making of Early Mediaval India*, New Delhi: Oxford University Press, 1994.

Chaudhuri, K.N., 'The Structure of Indian Textile Industry in the Seventeenth and Eighteenth Centuries', *IESHR,* 11(2), 1974, pp. 127–82.

Chauhan, Brij Raj, *A Rajasthan Village*, New Delhi: Vir Publishing House, 1967.

Cohn, Bernard S., 'The Changing Status of a Depressed Caste' in McKim Marriott (ed.), *Village India*, Chicago: University of Chicago Press, 1955 pp. 53–77.

——, *Colonialism and its Forms of Knowledge: The British in India*, New Delhi: Oxford University Press, 1997.

Commander, Simon, 'The Jajmani System in North India: An Examination of its Logic and Status across Two Centuries', *Modern Asian Studies,* 17 (2), 1983, pp. 283–311.

Crill, Rosemary, *Marwar Paintings: A History of the Jodhpur Style,* Jodhpur: India Book House Ltd., in association with Mehrangarh Publishers, 2000

Davis, Natalie Zemon, *Fiction in the Archives: Pardon Tales and their Tellers in Sixteenth Century France,* California: Stanford University Press, 1987.

Demirci, Suleyman, 'Complaints about Avariz Assessment and Payment in the Avariz-Tax System: An Aspect of the Relationship between Centre and Periphery, A Case Study of Kayseri, 1618–1700', *Journal of the Economic and Social History of the Orient,* 46 (4), 2003, pp. 437–74.

Detha, Vijay Dan, *Batan ri Phulwari: Rajasthan ri Kadimi Lok Kathawan* (ed.) Komal Kothari, 14 vols, Borunda: Rupayan Sansthan, 1962.

Detha, Vijay Dan, and Bhagirath Kanorhiya, *Rajasthani Hindi Kahavat Kosh*, Borunda: Rupam Prakashan, 1977.

Devra, G.S.L., 'Bikaner Niwasi aur Deshantar Gaman Pravarti: Satrahavin avam Atharvin Shatabdi mein', *Proceedings of Rajasthan History Congress,* (1974), pp. 25–33.

——, 'Rural Indebtedness in the Bikaner State, AD 1700–1800', paper presented at a seminar at Baroda University, Baroda, 1979.

—— (ed.), *Maharaja Ganga Singhji Centenary Volume*, Bikaner: Junagarh Fort, 1980.

—— (ed.), *Some Aspects of Socio-Economic History of Rajasthan: Jagdish Singh Gehlot Commemoration Volume*, Jodhpur: Rajasthan Sahitya Mand, 1980.

——, *Rajasthan ki Prashasnik Vyavastha*, Bikaner: Bharti Prakashan, 1991.

———, 'The Internal Expansion of Society and Formation of Medieval Polity', Presidential Address, Medieval India Section, 59th Session, *Proceedings of the Indian History Congress*, Patiala Session, 1998.

Dirks, Nicholas B., *The Hollow Crown: Ethnohistory of an Indian Kingdom*, Cambridge: Cambridge University Press, 1987.

Dube, Saurabh, *Untouchable Pasts: Religion, Identity and Power among a Central Indian Community*, Albany: State University of New York Press, 1998.

Dumont, Louis, *Homo Hierarchicus: The Caste System and its Implications*, 2nd edition, trans. from French by Mark Sainsbury, Chicago: Chicago University Press, 1980.

Evans, P., D. Rueschemeyer, and T. Skocpol (eds), *Bringing the State Back In*, Cambridge: Cambridge University Press, 1985.

Foster, W. (ed.), *The English Factories in India: A Calendar of Documents in the India Office*, British Museum and Public Record Office, (1618 – 69), Oxford,1906 – 27.

Foucault, Michel, *The History of Sexuality,* New York Pheon, 1978.

———, *Discipline and Punish: The Birth of the Prison*, trans. by Alan Sheridan, London: Penguin Books, 1991.

Fox, Richard G. (ed.), *Urban India: Society,Space and Image*, Durhem: Duke University, 1970.

———, *Kin, Clan, Raja and Rule: State-Hinterland Relations in Pre-Industrial India,* Berkeley: University of California Press, 1971.

Fukazawa, Hiroshi, *The Medieval Deccan: Peasants, Social Systems and States, Sixteenth to Eighteenth Centuries*, New Delhi: Oxford University Press, 1991, Rpr. 1998.

Fuller, C.J., 'Misconceiving the Grain Heap: A Critique of the Concept of the Indian Jajmani System', in J. Parry and M. Bloch (eds) *Money and the Morality of Exchange,* Cambridge: Cambridge University Press, 1989, pp. 33 – 63.

Gehlot, Jagdish Singh, *Marwar Rajya ka Itihas*, Jodhpur: Maharaja Man Singh Pustak Prakash Mehrangarh Museum Trust, 2nd edn, 1991.

Genovese, Eugene, *Roll, Jordan, Roll: The World the Slaves Made,* New York: Vintage, 1972.

Ghurye, G.S., *Caste, Class and Occupation in India*, Bombay: Popular Book Depot, 1957.

Ginzburg, Carlo, *The Cheese and the Worms: The Cosmos of a Sixteenth Century Miller,* trans. by John and Anne Tedeschi, London: Routledge & Kegan Paul, 1980.

Gold, Ann Grodzins and Bhoju Ram Gujar, *In the Time of Trees and Sorrows: Nature, Power, and Memory in Rajasthan*, Durham: Duke University Press, 2002.

Gooptu, Nandini, *The Politics of the Urban Poor in Early Twentieth Century India*, Cambridge: Cambridge University Press, 2001.

Grewal, J .S., *In the By-Lanes of History*, Simla: Indian Institute of Advanced Study, 1975.

Grover, B.R., 'An Integrated Pattern of Commercial Life in the Rural Society of North India during the Seventeenth and Eighteenth Centuries', *Proceedings: Indian Historical Records Commission*, 37, 1966, pp. 125 – 30.

Guha, Sumit, 'An Indian Penal Regime: Maharashtra in the Eighteenth Century', *Past and Present*, 147, 1995, pp. 101– 26.

Guha, Ranajit and Gayatri Chakravary Spivak (eds), *Selected Subaltern Studies*, New York: Oxford University Press, 1988.

Guha, Ranajit (ed.), *Subaltern Studies: Writings on South Asian History and Society*, vols I –VI, New Delhi: Oxford University Press, 1982 – 9.

———, *Elementary Aspects of Peasant Insurgency in Colonial India*, New Delhi: Oxford University Press, 1983.

———, 'The Small Voice of History,' Public Lecture delivered in Hyderabad on 11th Jan. 1993.

Guha, Sumit, ' The Handloom Industry of Central India: 1825 – 1950', *IESHR*, 26 (3), 1989, pp. 297–318.

———, 'Potentates, Traders and Peasants: Western India, c.1700 – 1870' in Burton Stein and Sanjay Subrahmanyam (eds), *Institutions and Economic Change in South Asia*, New Delhi: Oxford University Press: 1996, pp. 71–84.

———, 'The Politics of Identity and Enumeration in India c.1600–1990', *Comparative Study of Society and History*, 2003, pp. 148–67.

Gupta B.L., *Trade and Commerce in Rajasthan During the Eighteenth Century*, Jaipur: Jaipur Publishing House,1987.

Gupta, Ashin Das, *Malabar in Asian Trade, 1740–1800*, Cambridge: Cambridge University Press, 1967.

Gupta, S.P., 'Village of Medieval Rajasthan: An Economic Profile,' Paper presented at the Second International Seminar on Rajasthan, Udaipur, 17–21December, 1991, (mimeographed copy at RSAB).

Habermas, J., *Legitimation Crisis*, tr. Thomas McCarthy, London: Heinemann, 1976.

Habib, Irfan, *The Agrarian System of Mughal India, 1556–1707*, Bombay: Bombay Publishing House, 1963.

———, *Essays in Indian History: Towards a Marxist Perception*, New Delhi: Tulika, 1995.

Hand-Printed Textiles in Rajasthan: A Study. Documentation and Survey, National Craft Institute for Hand-Printed Textiles, Dondlod House, Hawa Sarak, Jaipur, 1986.

Hardiman, David, *Feeding the Baniya: Peasants and Userers in Western India*, New Delhi: Oxford University Press, 1996.

Hasan, Farhat, *State and Locality in Mughal India: Power Relations in Western India, c. 1572 – 1730*, Cambridge: Cambridge University Press, 2004.

Hasan, S. Bashir, 'Textile Production in Mughal Malwa', *Proceedings in Indian History Congress*, Mysore, 1993, pp. 29 – 39.

Haynes, Edward S., 'A Corinthian Capital on a Column of Ellora: The Transfer of the Concept of Feudalism to the Rajput States of North India', *Journal of Indian History*, vol. 57, pp. 152 – 87.

————, 'The Political System of Alwar: Patrimonialism and the Jagir System', paper presented at the 31th annual meeting of the association for Asian Studies, 1979.

Heesterman, J.C., *The Inner Conflict of Tradition: Essays in Indian Ritual, Kingship and Society*, Chicago: Chicago University Press, 1985.

Hegel, G.W.F., *The Philosophy of History*, trans. J. Sibree, New York: Dover, 1st published in 1899.

Hindall, Steve, 'Dearth, Fasting and Alms: The Campaign for General Hospitality in Late Elizabethan England', *Past and Present*, no. 172, (Aug. 2001), pp. 44 – 86.

Hobsbawm, Eric, 'Peasants and Politics', *Journal of Peasant Studies*, 1 (1), 1973, pp. 3 – 22.

Hutton, J.H., *Caste in India: Its Nature, Function and Origins*, Cambridge: Cambridge University Press, 4th edn, 1963.

Inden, Ronald, *Imagining India*, Oxford: Basil Blackwell, 1990.

Jain, K.C., *Ancient Cities and Towns of Rajasthan: A Study of Culture and Civilisation*, Delhi: Motilal Banarsidass, 1972.

Jain, V.K., *Trade and Traders in Western India, AD 1000–1300*, New Delhi: Munshiram Manoharlal, 1990.

Joshi, Chitra, *Lost Worlds: Indian Labour and Its Forgotten Histories*, Delhi: Permanent Black, 2003.

Kangle, R.P. (trans.), *The Kautilya Arthashastra*, vol. II, Bombay: 2nd edn, Delhi: Motilal Banarsidass, 1969.

Kanorhiya, Bhagirath and Govind Aggarwal, *Rajasthani Kahavat Kosh*, Jaipur: Panchsheel Prakashan, 1995.

Karashima, Noboru (ed.), *Kingship in Indian History: Japanese Studies in South Asia*, no. 2, New Delhi: Manohar, 1999.

Keyvani, Mehdi, *Artisans and Guild Life in the Later Safavid Period: Contributions to the Social Economic History of Persia*, Berlin: Klaus Schwarz Verlag, 1982.

Khan, Ahasan Raza, *Chieftains in the Mughal Empire during the Reign of Akbar*, Simla: Indian Institute of Advanced Studies, 1977.

Kolff, Dirk H.A., *Naukar, Rajput, and Sepoy: The Ethnohistory of the Military Labour Market in Hindustan, 1450 – 1850*, Cambridge: Cambridge University Press, 1990.

Kotani H. (ed.), *Caste System, Untouchability and the Depressed*, New Delhi: Manohar, 1997.

————, *Western India in Historical Transition: Seventeenth to Early Twentieth Century*, New Delhi: Manohar, 2002.

Kothari, Sushila, 'The Urban Population of 17th Century Marwar', *Shodhak*, 23 (2), 1994 pp. 64 – 7.

———, 'Estimated Rural Population of 17th Century Marwar', *Shodhak*, 24 (2), 1995, Manohar, pp. 80 – 3.

Kumar, Nita, 'Urban Culture in Modern India: World of the Lower Classes' in Indu Banga (ed.) *The City in Indian History*, New Delhi: Manohar, 1995, pp. 191– 205.

Kumar, Sunil, 'Assertions of Authority: A Study of the Discursive Statements of Two Sultans of Delhi' in Marc Gabonier, Francois 'Nalini' Delvoye and Muzaffar Alam (eds) *Making of Indo-Persian Culture*, New Delhi: Manohar, 1999, pp. 37 – 65.

———, *The Present in Delhi's Pasts*, Delhi: Three Essays Press, 2002.

Lalas, Sitaram (ed.), *Rajasthani Sabad Kos*, Jodhpur: Rajasthani Shodh Sansthan, Chaupasani, 1988.

Magier, David, '*Topics in the Grammar of Marwari'*, PhD Thesis, 1983.

Mayaram, Shail, *Against History, Against State: Counterperspectives from the Margins*, Delhi: Permanent Black, 2003.

———, *Resisting Regimes: Myth, Memory and the Shaping of a Muslim Identity*, Delhi: Oxford University Press, 1997.

Mayer, Adrian C., *Caste and Kinship in Central India: A Village and its Region*, Berkeley: University of California Press, 1966.

McLane, John R., *Land and Local Kingship in Eighteenth Century Bengal*, Cambridge: Cambridge University Press, 1993.

Menariya, Motilal, *Rajasthani Bhasa aur Sahitya*, Prayaga: Hindi Sahitya Sammelan, 1960.

Misra, S.C., 'Social Mobility in Pre-Mughal India', *Indian Historical Review*, 1 (1), 1974, pp. 36 – 43.

Misra, V.N. and S.N. Rajaguru, 'Palaeoenvironment and Prehistory of the Thar Desert, Rajasthan, India', *South Asian Archaeology*, 1985, Karen Frifelt and Per Sorensten (eds), London: Curzon Press, Reprint, 1989, pp. 296–320.

Mitr, Meera, *Maharaja Ajit Singh avam Unka Yug*, Jaipur: Rajasthan Hindi Granth Academy, 1973.

Moore, Barrington Jr., *Social Origins of Dictatorship and Democracy: Lord and Peasant in the Making of the Modern World*, Boston: Beacon Press, 1966.

Moreland, W.H., *From Akbar to Aurangzeb: A Study in Indian Economic History*, New Delhi: Oriental Books Reprint Corporation, 1923.

———, *India at the Death of Akbar: Delhi: An Economic Study*, Delhi: Reprints and Trans. Publications, 1974.

Morris, Morris D., 'Values as an Obstacle to Economic Growth in South Asia: An Historical Survey', *Journal of Economic History*, XXVII (4), 1967.

Mukerjee, Rudrangshu, *Awadh in Revolt, 1857 – 58: A Study of Popular Rebellion*, New Delhi: Oxford University Press, 1984.

Mukherjee, Mridula, 'Peasant Resistance and Peasant Consciousness in Colo-
    nial India: 'Subalterns and Beyond', Part 1 and 2, *Economic and Political
    Weekly*, 8 Oct. and 15 Oct., 1988, pp. 2109 – 20 and 2174 – 86, respectively.
Mukhia, Harbans, 'Illegal Extortions from Peasants, Artisans, and Menials
    in Eighteenth Century Eastern Rajasthan', *IESHR*, XIV (2), 1977, pp.
    231 – 46.
Munro, William A., *The Moral Economy of the State: Conservaton, Community
    Development, and State Making in Zimbabwe*, Athens: Ohio University Press,
    1998.
Myrdal, Gunnar, *Asian Drama: An Inquiry into the Poverty of Nations*, 3 vols,
    New York, 1968.
Naqvi, Hamida Khatoon, *Urban Centres and Industries in Upper India, 1556 –
    1803*, Bombay: Asia Publishing House, 1968.
Nath, Aman and Wacziarg, Francis (eds), *Arts and Crafts of Rajasthan*,
    Ahmedabad: Living Traditions of India Series, Mapin Publications,
    1987, rpr. 1994.
Ojha, Pandit G.S.H., *Jodhpur Rajya ka Itihas*, Ajmer: Vedic Mantralaya, 1941.
Ortner, Sherry, 'Resistance and the Problem of Ethnographic Refusal' in
    Comparative Studies in Society and History, 37 (1), 1995, pp. 173 – 93.
Pal, H. Bhisham, *Handicrafts of Rajasthan*, Publications Division, Ministry
    of Information and Broadcasting, Government of India.
Palriwala, Rajni, 'Transitory Residents, Invisible Workers: Rethinking Lo-
    cality and Incorporation in a Rajasthan Village,' in Kumkum Sangari
    and Uma Chakravarti (eds) *From Myths to Markets: Essays on Gender*, New
    Delhi: Manohar, 1999, pp. 237 – 73.
Parihar, G.R., *Marwar and the Marathas, 1724 – 1843*, Jodhpur: Hindi Sahitya
    Mandir, 1968.
Parthasarathi, P., *The Transition to a Colonial Economy: Weavers, Merchants and
    Kings in South India, 1720 – 1800*, New York: Cambridge University
    Press, 2002.
Peabody, Norbert, 'Cents, Sense, Census: Human Inventories in Late
    Precolonial and Early Colonial India' in *Comparative Studies in Society
    and History*, 43(4), 2001, pp. 819 – 50.
————, *Hindu Kingship and Polity in Precolonial India*, Cambridge: Cambridge
    University Press, 2003.
Pearson, M.N., *Merchants and Rulers in Gujarat: The Response to the Portuguese
    during the Sixteenth Century*, Berkeley: University of California Press, 1976.
Perlin, Frank, 'Of White Whale and Countrymen in the Eighteenth Cen-
    tury Maratha Deccan: Extended Class Relations, Rights, and the
    Problem of Rural Autonomy under the Old Regime', *Journal of Peasant
    Studies*, 5(2), 1978, pp. 172 – 237.
————, 'Proto-Industrialisation and Pre-Colonial South Asia', *Past and
    Present*, 98, 1983, pp. 30 – 95.

————, 'Changes in the Production and Circulation of Money in Seventeenth and Eighteenth Century India : An Essay on Monetisation Before Colonial Occupation' in Sanjay Subramanyam (ed.) *Money and the Market in India 1100 – 1700*. Delhi: 1994, pp. 276 – 3070.

————, 'Money Use in Late Pre-olonial India and the International trade in Currency Media,' in J.F. Richards (ed.) *Imperial Monetary System of Mugal India*, New Delhi: Oxford University Press, 1987, pp. 232 – 373.

Prakash, Gyan, *Bonded Histories: Genealogies of Labour Servitude in Colonial India, South Asian Studies*, Cambridge: Cambridge University Press, 1990.

Prakash, Ishwar, 'Organisation of Industrial Production in Urban Centres in India During the Seventeenth Century with Special Reference to Textiles' in B.N. Ganguly (ed.) *Readings in Indian Economic History*, New Delhi: 1964, pp. 44 – 52.

Prasad, Beni, *History of Jahangir*, London: Oxford University Press, 1922.

Price, Pamela G., *Kingship and Political Practice in Colonial India*, Cambridge: Cambridge University Press, 1996.

Raheja, Gloria Goodwin, *The Poison in the Gift: Religious Prestation and the Dominant Caste in a North Indian Village,* Chicago: Chicago University Press, 1988.

Rai, Mridu, *Hindu Kings, Muslim Subjects: Islam, Rights, and the History of Kashmir*, Delhi: Permanent Black, 2004.

Ramaswamy, Vijaya, 'Weaver Folk Traditions as a Source of History', *IESHR*, 19(1), 1982, pp. 47–62.

————, 'Artisans in Vijaynagar Society', *IESHR*, 22(4), 1985 pp. 417–44.

————, *Textiles and Weavers in Medieval South India*, New Delhi: Oxford University Press, 1985.

Rana, R.P., 'Agrarian Revolts in Northern India During the Late 17th and Early 18th Centuries', *IESHR*, 17(3 – 4), 1981, pp. 287–326.

Rao, Velcheru Narayan, David Shulman and Sanjay Subrahmanyam, *Symbols of Substance: Court and State in Nayaka Period Tamil Nadu*, New Delhi: Oxford University Press, 1992.

Rathor, Vikram Singh, *Marwar ka Sanskrit Itihas*, Jodhpur: Rajasthani Granthagar, 1996.

Raychaudhuri, Tapan and Irfan Habib (eds), *Cambridge Economic History of India*, vol. I, Cambridge: Cambridge University Press, 1982.

Rhys Davids, T.W. and S.W. Bushell (eds), *On Yuan Chwang's Travels in India, (AD 629 – 45)*, 2 vols, (London, 1904 – 5; photo-offset edn, Delhi, 1961). Abridged trans. and commentary by T. Watters titled Buddhist Records of the Western World, 2 vols, (London, 1869, photo-offset reprint, Delhi, 1969).

Richards, John F. (ed.), *Kingship and Authority in South Asia*, Madison: University of Wisconsin, 1978.

Robb, Peter (ed.), *Dalit Movements and the Meanings of Labour in India*, New Delhi: Oxford University Press, 1993.

——— (ed.), *The Imperial Monetary System of Mughal India*, New Delhi: Oxford University Press, 1987.

——— (ed.), *Rural South Asia: Linkages, Change, and Development*, London: Curzon Press, 1983.

Roy., Tirthankar, *Traditional Industry in the Economy of Colonial India.*, Cambridge: Cambridge University Press, 1999.

Rudd, Arild Engelsen, 'The Indian Hierarchy: Culture, Ideology, and Consciousness in Bengali Village Politics', *Modern Asian Studies*, 33 (3), 1999, pp. 689 – 732.

Ruhela, Satya Pal, *The Gaduliya Lohars of Rajasthan: A Study in the Sociology of Nomadism*, New Delhi: Impex India, 1968.

Sahai, Nandita Prasad, 'Artisans in a Mughal Province: A Study of Eighteenth Century Marwar', PhD Thesis, Dept. of History, University of Delhi, 2001.

———, 'Collaboration and Conflict: Artisanal Jati Panchayats and the Eighteenth Century Jodhpur State', *The Medieval History Journal*, vol. 5 (1), (2002), pp. 77 – 102.

———, 'Artisans, the State and the Politics of Wajabi in Eighteenth Century Jodhpur', *IESHR*, 41 (1), 2005, pp. 41 – 68.

———, 'Crafts in Eighteenth Century Jodhpur: Questions of Class, Caste, and Community Identities', *Journal of the Economic and Social History of the Orient*, 48(4), 2005, pp. 524 – 51.

———, 'Crafts and Statecraft in Eighteenth Century Jodhpur', *Modern Asian Studies*, 40, 2006, forthcoming.

Said, Edward, *Orientalism*, New York: 1979.

Saksena, B.P., *History of Shah Jahan of Dihli*, 1st published in 1932, Allahabad: Central Book Depot, 1962.

Salim, Prince, 'Some Aspects of the Sair Ijara in Marwar During the Eighteenth Century', *Proceedings of Rajasthan History Congress*, Bikaner, 1984.

Saran, Richard, D., 'Conquest and Colonization: Rajputs and Vasis in Medieval Period Marwar', PhD Thesis, Dept. of History, University of Michigan, 1978.

Sarkar, Jadunath, *History of Aurangzeb: Mainly based on Persian Sources*, 1st published in 1912 – 24, Bombay: Orient Longman, 1972 – 4.

Sarkar, Sumit, 'The Kalki-Avatar of Bikrampur: A Village Scandal in Early Twentieth Century Bengal' in R. Guha (ed.) *Subaltern Studies VI*, New Delhi: Oxford University Press, 1989, pp. 1 – 53.

Schomer, Karine, Joan L. Erdman, Deryck O. Lodrick, and Lloyd I. Rudolph (eds), *The Idea of Rajasthan, Explorations in Regional Identity*, 2 vols, New Delhi: Manohar, 1994.

Scott, James C., *Domination and the Arts of Resistance: Hidden Transcipts*, New Haven: Yale University Press, 1990.

————, *Moral Economy of the Peasant: Rebellion and Subsistence in Southeast Asia*, New Haven: Yale University Press, 1976.

————, *Weapons of the Weak: Everyday Forms of Peasant Resistance*, New Haven: Yale University Press, 1985.

Shah, A.M., 'The Rural-Urban Networks in India', *South Asia*, II, 1988, pp. 1 – 27.

Shah, Paras Raj, 'Famines in Western Rajasthan Through the Ages', *Proceedings of Rajasthan History Congress*, 1970, pp. 88 – 93.

Sharma, Dashrath (ed.), *Rajasthan Through the Ages*, 2 vols, Bikaner :Rajastan State Archives, 1966.

Sharma, G.D., 'Some Agricultural Taxes in Marwar', *Proceedings of Rajasthan History Congress*, Beawar Session, 1973.

————, 'State Land Revenue Demand in Marwar During the Seventeenth Century', *Proceedings of Rajasthan History Congress*, Pali Session, 1974 , pp. 69 – 73.

————, *Rajput Polity: A Study of Politics and Administration of the State of Marwar, 1638 – 1749*, New Delhi: Manohar, 1977.

————, 'Vyaparis and Mahajans in Western Rajasthan During the Eighteenth Century', *Proceedings of Indian History Congress*, 41st Session, Bombay, 1980, pp. 377 – 85.

Sharma, Padmaja, *Maharaja Man Singh of Jodhpur and His Times,1803–1843*, Agra: Shiv Lal Agarwala, 1972.

Sharma, Sanjay, *Famine, Philanthropy and the Colonial State: North India in the Early Nineteenth Century*, New Delhi: Oxford University Press, 2001.

Singer, Milton and Bernard S. Cohn. (eds), *Structure and Change In Indian Society*, Chicago: Aldine Publishing Company, 1968.

Singh, Chetan, *Region and Empire: Punjab in the Seventeenth Century*, New Delhi: Oxford University Press, 1991.

Singh, Dilbagh, 'Rural Indebtedness in Eastern Rajasthan during the Eighteenth Century', *Proceedings of Indian History Congress*, Pali, 1974.

————, 'The Role of the Mahajans in the Rural Economy in Eastern Rajasthan During the Eighteenth Century', *Social Scientist*, 1974, pp. 20 – 31.

————, *The State, Landlords, and Peasants: Rajasthan in the 18th Century*, New Delhi: Manohar, 1990.

Singh, Hira, 'Classifying Non-European, Pre-Colonial Social Formations: More than Quarrel Over a Name', *The Journal of Peasant Studies*, 20 (2), Jan. 1993, pp. 317 – 47.

Singha, Radhika, *A Despotism of Law: Crime and Justice in Early Colonial India*, New Delhi: Oxford University Press, 1998.

Singhi, N.K., and Rajendra Joshi (eds), *Folk, Faith, and Feudalism*, Jaipur: Rawat Publications, 1995.

Sinha N.K., *Economic History of Bengal: From Plassey to the Permanent Settlement*, Calcutta, 1961 – 3.

Sinha, Nandini, *State Formation in Rajasthan: Mewar. Seventh to Fifteenth Centuries*, New Delhi: Manohar, 2002.

Sivakumar, Chitra and S.S. Sivakumar, 'The Meaning of Social Order in the Tamil Country' in Peter Robb (ed.), *Meanings of Agriculture: Essays in South Asian History and Economics,* New Delhi: Oxford University Press, 1996, pp. 332 – 89.

Sjoberg, Gideon, *The Preindustrial City*, New York: Free Press, 1974.

Skaria, Ajay, *Hybrid Histories: Forests, Frontiers and Wildness in Western India*, New Delhi: Oxford University Press, 1999.

Skocpol, T., *States and Social Revolutions: A Comparative Analysis of France, Russia, and China*, Cambridge: Cambridge University Press, 1979.

Spivak, Gayatri Chakravarty, *A Critique of Postcolonial Reason: Toward A History of Vanishing Present*, Cambridge: Harvard University Press, Massachusetts, 1999.

———, 'Can the Subaltern Speak?' in C. Nelson and L. Grossberg (eds) *Marxism and the Interpretation of Cultures*, Urbana, 1988, pp. 271 – 316.

Stein, Burton and Sanjay Subrahmanyam (eds), *Institutions and Economic Change in South Asia*, SOAS Studies on South Asia Understandings and Perspectives Series, New Delhi: Oxford University Press, 1996.

———, 'World Economies and South Asia, 1600 – 1750: A Sceptical Note', *Review* (Fernand Braudel Center), XII (1), 1989, pp. 141 – 48.

———, 'Rural Industry and Commercial Agriculture in Late Seventeenth Century South-Eastern India', *Past and Present*, 126, 1990, pp. 76 – 114.

———, (ed.), *Merchants, Markets and the State in Early Modern India*, New Delhi: Oxford University Press, 1990.

Subrahmanyam, Sanjay (ed.), *Money and the Market in India, 1100 – 1700*, New Delhi: Oxford University Press, 1994.

———, *Penumbral Visions,* Michigan: University Michigan Press, 2001.

———, *Explorations in Connected History: From the Tagus to the Ganges*, New Delhi: Oxford University Press, 2005.

Sunder, Nandini. *Subalterns and Sovereigns: An Anthropological History of Bustar 1854 – 1996*, New Delhi: Oxford University Press, 1997.

Swarnalatha, Potukuchi, 'Revolt, Testimony, Petition: Artisanal Protests in Colonial Andhra', *International Review of Social History*, vol. 46, 2001, Supplement, pp. 107 – 29.

Tambiah, Stanley, 'The Galactic Polity in Southeast Asia' in *Culture, Thought and Social Action: An Anthropological Perspective* Cambridge: Harvard University Press, 1985, pp. 252 – 86.

Tchitcherov, Alexander I., *India: Changing Changing Economic Structure in the Sixteenth-Eighteenth Centuries: Outline History of Crafts and Trade*, 1st edn, 1965, 3rd edn, New Delhi: Manohar,1998.

Teltscher, Kate, *India Inscribed*, New Delhi: Oxford University Press, 1995.

Tessitori, L.P., 'Notes on the Grammar of the Old Western Rajasthani with Special Reference to Apabhramsa and to Gujarati and Marwari', *The Indian Antiquary*, Jan.-Feb., 1914.

———, 'Progress Report from the Work done during the Year 1916 in Connection with the Bardic and Historical Survey of Rajputana', *Journal of Asiatic Society of Bengal*, N.S.13, 1917.

Thakur, Laxman S., 'Artisans in Himachal Pradesh, circa AD 700 – 1440: A Study Based on Epigraphs', *IESHR*, 23 (3), 1986, pp. 303 – 12.

Thompson, E.P., 'Eighteenth Century English Society: Class Struggle without Class' *Social History*, 3 (2), 1978, pp. 133 – 66.

———, *Customs in Common*, London: Penguin Books, 1993.

Turner, Roy (ed.), *India's Urban Future*, Berkeley: University of California Press, 1960.

Vanina, Euginia, *Ideas and Society in India: From the Sixteenth to the Eighteenth Centuries*, New Delhi: Oxford University Press, 1996.

Vashistha, R. K., *Arts and Artists of Rajasthan*, Delhi: Abhinav, 1995.

Verma, Tripta, *Karkhanas Under the Mughals: From Akbar to Aurangzeb: A Study in Economic Development*, Delhi: Pragati Publications, 1994.

Vyas, R.P., *Role of Nobility in Marwar, 1800 – 1873*, New Delhi: Jain Brothers, 1969.

Weber, Max, 'Politics as a Vocation' in *From Max Weber: Essays in Sociology*, tr.and ed. H.H. Gerth and C. Wright Mills, New York: Oxford University Press, 1946.

———, *The Hindu Social System*, ed. and trans. H.H. Gerth and D. Martindale, Minneapolis, 1950.

Weller, R.P. and S.E. Guggenheim (eds), *Power and Protest in the Countryside*, Durham, N.C., 1982.

Wink, Andre, *Land and Sovereignty in India: Agrarian Society and Politics under the Eighteenth Century Maratha Svarajya*, Cambridge: Cambridge University Press, 1986.

Wiser, William Henricks, *The Hindu Jajmani System: A Socio-Economic System Interrelating Members of a Hindu Village Community in Services*, Lucknow: Lucknow Publishing House, 1st edn, 1936.

Ziegler, Norman P., 'Action, Power, and Service in Rajasthani Culture: A Social History of the Rajputs of Middle Period Rajasthan', PhD dissertation, University of Chicago, 1973.

———, 'Some Notes on Rajput Loyalties During the Mughal Period' in J.F. Richards (ed.), *Kingship and Authority in South Asia*, 2nd edition, Madison: South Asian Studies, University of Wisconsin, 1981, pp. 215 – 51.

Index